The 'Magnificent Castle' of
CULZEAN
AND THE KENNEDY
FAMILY

AVISE · LA · FIN ·

The 'Magnificent Castle' of CULZEAN
AND THE KENNEDY FAMILY

MICHAEL MOSS

Twixt Wigtoun and the toun o' Ayr
Portpatrick and the Cruives o' Cree
Noe man need think for to byde there
Unless he rides wi' Kennedy

EDINBURGH UNIVERSITY PRESS

Maps showing the principal places in south-west Scotland referred to in the text and plan of the policies showing the principal places and features can be found on the endpapers or inside cover.

OPPOSITE
TITLE PAGE

The coat of arms of the Marquess of Ailsa. The motto can be translated as 'consider the end'.

© Michael Moss 2002
Edinburgh University Press
22 George Square
Edinburgh EH8 9LF

Set in Minion
Designed by Mark Blackadder

Printed in Italy by Graphicom srl

A CIP record for this book is available
from the British Library

ISBN 0 7486 1722 1 (hardback)
ISBN 0 7486 1723 X (paperback)

Contents

For Mary,
Marchioness of Ailsa
and her family

Cassillis
Maybole
Ayrshire

It gives me great pleasure to write this forward to a book about the Kennedy family, who became the Marquesses of Ailsa in 1831. Their home was originally here at Cassillis and then later at Culzean Castle on its rocky prominence above the sea on the Ayrshire Coast.

My late husband's uncle, Charles the 5th Marquess, gave Culzean and its contents to the National Trust for Scotland. Until recently the Trust portrayed Culzean as a masterpiece of design by that famous Scottish architect Robert Adam, which it is.

My husband felt passionately that the efforts and sacrifices that his family had made over successive generations to preserve and embellish the estate had received scant recognition. Last year the Trust remedied this omission by opening a permanent exhibition about the family in the castle.

This book finally sets the record straight and makes the castle a much more fascinating place, even for me. Michael Moss has found out things I did not know or reminded me of things, which I did know but long forgotten.

I am proud of being a Kennedy and am delighted that this book makes it possible for me to share their remarkable history and that of one of Scotland's greatest country houses with you.

I hope you will enjoy reading it as much as I have enjoyed being part of its conception.

Mary Ailsa

Preface

Culzean Castle and Country Park, on the Ayrshire coast, sums up in one place all that The National Trust for Scotland stands for with its unique combination of historic buildings, gardens, woodland and coastline providing enjoyment and education for thousands of visitors each year. Yet with so much on offer for visitors today, it can be easy to forget that this was built as a private residence, which came into the Trust's care in 1945 thanks to the generosity of the 5th Marquess of Ailsa and the Kennedy family. The link with the Kennedys, of course, stretches far back and this well-researched and beautifully illustrated book sets on record their story. I congratulate Michael Moss on this superb book and commend it, and the ongoing work of The National Trust for Scotland, to you.

ROGER WHEATER,
CHAIRMAN OF COUNCIL,
THE NATIONAL TRUST
FOR SCOTLAND,
2002

Acknowledgements

This book could not have been written without the support and encouragement of a large number of people, but above all the Marchioness of Ailsa and her sons the Marquess of Ailsa and Lord David Kennedy and her daughter, Lady Elizabeth Drummond. The Marchioness generously allowed access to the family papers in her possession, while the Trustees of the Ailsa estates (chaired by John Blair of Anderson Strathern) gave me permission to use the extensive collection of papers in the Cassillis and Culzean estate office held in Maybole Castle and to consult the family's banking records held by Coutts. The factor, David Gray, and his staff at the estate office have been unfailingly helpful, even though at times they have thought me quite mad to spend hours amongst very dirty old books and papers. In understanding and exploring the castle, I have been fortunate to be able to draw on the support of Jonathan Cardale and Gordon Riddle at Culzean and their staff, at what has been a difficult time. The tour guides have been especially helpful in drawing my attention to details, which they have observed after countless hours on duty. I owe a special debt of gratitude to Debbie Jackson, who was formerly the educational officer at the castle, for allowing me access to her pioneering research into the history of Culzean, particularly for giving me copies of her extended essay 'Robert Adam: the building of Culzean Castle' for her graduate diploma in museum/gallery studies at the University of St Andrews and her unpublished 'The History of the Kennedys of Cassillis and Culzean', a copy of which is available in the Carnegie Library at Ayr. The staff of the National Trust for Scotland West Regional Office led by Michael Hunter and at the head office have taken a lively interest in the project and sent me copies of numerous reports and papers. Ian Gow, the curator, has been inspirational and has gently but firmly inducted me into the arcane practices of architectural history and the even more obscure world of country house history which takes you to rarely visited parts of libraries. He also introduced me to that sagacious architectural historian, Eileen Harris, whose masterly book on Robert Adam's interiors has recently been published. Carolynn Bain, the Trust's archivist, has helped me find my way about piles of boxes all confusingly labelled 'Culzean'. Allen Paterson, the chairman of the NTS's Gardens' committee and a stern critic, has put me right about the names of plants and the history of gardening. Lady Cindy Shaw-Stewart, until recently chairman of the NTS Curatorial committee, has been both a pillar of good sense and a source of information about her native Yorkshire where strangely the Kennedys have had contacts. There is no one who knows more about the history of Ayrshire families than Jamie Hunter Blair of Blairquhan and his cheery voice and sense of humour have been immensely reassuring. He has also kindly allowed me to consult his family papers and his delightful library. Sir Charles

Fergusson of Kilkerran, whose father and mother were much involved in the early days of Culzean in the hands of the NTS, has been equally helpful, giving me access to the impressive family archive and recalling his early memories of visits to the castle.

I owe many other debts of gratitude to: De Witt Bailey; the staff of the rare books and manuscripts reading room of the British Library, for going out of their way to make life easy for me; Tom Barclay; John Breslin, House of Lords Record Office; Mandy Briant-Evans; Lawrence Brockliss; Duncan Bruce of the St Andrew's Society of New York; David Burrell for allowing me access to his notes on the Culzean shipyard; Patrick Cadell; Brigadier Duncan Cameron, formerly deputy director of the NTS, for reading and commenting on the text; Roy Campbell whose encyclopaedic knowledge of west of Scotland agricultural history is unrivalled and who with his usual critical eye has read and commented on the text; Brian Carpenter and Jan Wood of the Devon Record Office; Castle Milk & Corrie Estates; Dorothy Champion; Pamela Clark of the Royal Archives; Bill Connor, Leeds District Archives; Robert Cooper, grand secretary of the Grand Lodge of Scotland; Rosemary Crill of the India & South-East Asia Department at the V. & A.; Professor Valerie Cromwell formerly director of the History of Parliament Trust; Joseph Ditta of the New York Historical Society; Professor Simon Dixon; R.A. Gordon Duff; Colonel David Eliot of the Somerset Light Infantry; Iain Flett; Anders Forsgren; John Gallimore formerly of Weatherbys; Jim and Joan Goldie; Lucinda Green of the Wiltshire & Swindon Record Office; Eleanor Gawne of the Royal Institute of British Architects; Dr Eric Graham; Trevor Graham; Katarina Grant of the V. & A.; David Hamilton who has helped with golfing history; Major D.L.J. Harrap of the Duke of Wellington's Regiment; Mrs Diana Harding, archivist to the Royal Yacht Squadron; the Earl of Harrowby and his archivist, Michael Bosson; Ann Heneage; Claire Hill of the Lutyens Trust; Captain J.M. Holtby of the Queen's Royal Lancers Regimental Museum; John Hume; Dr Joanna Innes of Somerville College Oxford; Sten-Åke Jonsson; Dr Colin Kidd of the Department of Scottish History, University of Glasgow; David Killicote; Sir Ludovic Kennedy; Sir Bryce and James Knox; Edward Knoblauch of the Institute for New York State Studies; Sheree J. Leeds, the museum curator and archivist of CGNU; Lieutenant Commander C.B. Lutyens for sending me details from his family papers; Dr James Macaulay; Sally McInnes of the National Library of Wales; Andrew McLean, archivist to the Mount Stuart Trust; Lynda McLeod of Christies; Martin Mitchell of Tattersalls; Mr Monnickendam; Angela Morrison and Fiona McDougall of the British Golf Museum at St Andrews; Philippa Moss; Dr Thomas Munck; Dr Peter Nockles; Cynthia O'Connor of the Royal Irish Academy; Dr John Orbell of ING Barings; Mrs Orr Ewing; Commander Roger Parkes; Justine Pearson of Surrey History Centre; Nicholas Phillipson; Professor Peter Radford; Dr Kate Retford; Dr Dick Repp of St Cross College Oxford; Gudrun Richardson of the Royal Society; Lady Jane Roberts of the Royal Collections; David Rollo of the Royal Artillery Institute; the Earl of Scarborough; Stephen Schechter; Dr John Shaw of the National Archives of Scotland; Roger M.C. Sims, librarian archivist of Manx National Heritage; David Simpson; Dr Davod Starkey; Dr John Stevenson; David Ross Stewart; Professor Hew Strachan of All Souls of Oxford; Marianne Strandin, Jämtlands läns museum; George and Eva Swapp; Dr Deborah Turnhall; Alison Turton; Professor David Walker for answering innumerable questions; Fiona Walker of Newark Castle; Helen Watson of the Scottish National Portrait Gallery; Kevin Wilbraham and his staff of the Ayrshire Archives Centre; Frances Wilkins for sharing her extensive knowledge of smuggling in the Isle of Man and the North Channel; Guy Wilson of the Royal Armouries, Leeds; Miss E.P. Wood of the Priory Museum Reigate; Helen Wood of the London Metropolitan Archive; Lucy Wright and Philip Winterbottom of the Royal Bank of Scotland

Archives; and Charles Wyvill of Constable Burton Hall, Leyburn, for information about his forebear Sir Marmaduke Wyvill. The quotations from the letters in the Royal Archives and from the correspondence of King William IV and his officials are reproduced by the generous permission of Her Majesty Queen Elizabeth II.

Lastly this book could never been completed if Sir Graeme Davies, the Principal of the University of Glasgow, had not encouraged me to become a research professor within the Faculty of Arts. I owe him a special debt of gratitude.

I could never have brought the whole concept of this book to fruition without the encouragement of Vivian Bone and her colleagues at Edinburgh University Press.

MICHAEL MOSS,
UNIVERSITY OF GLASGOW,
2002

Through the ruined arch

I first passed through the ruined arch to visit Culzean some forty years ago while on holiday in Ayr, staying in the home of Mrs Brand, with whose late husband Dr Brand my mother had been in general practice in the early days of the war. Although my mother had roots in the west of Scotland, she did not remember how to pronounce the name of the castle to the amusement of her Ayrshire friends. The holiday is engraved on my memory for two reasons: my father left his hat behind (always a cause of exceptional drama) in a curious hostelry in Maybole; and I caught a most vicious stomach bug after swimming in the sea at Ayr. Nevertheless Culzean left a vivid impression to the extent that when I returned some ten years later it was like visiting an old friend. The view from the mortar battery in the castle forecourt is spectacular and the cliff top walk is for me one of the great walks in the United Kingdom, to be numbered with Housteads in Northumberland, the Suffolk coast path from Dunwich to Southwold, and a few others. Everything about the castle and its policies is so unexpected and varied that it never ceases to charm and intrigue. An encounter with any part of it raises hosts of questions – how did it come to be, who were and are the Kennedys, how could anyone have put a red carpet on the stairs and so on and so on.

Five years ago my family and I moved to rural

The ruined arch at the entrance to the causeway to Culzean. The arch is symbolic of the branch of Freemasonry of which the family was members.

Ayrshire and I became fascinated by the history of the county and its people. Sometime later I was elected a member of the executive committee of the National Trust for Scotland and I thought it would be useful to embark on a project where the bulk of the sources were in Edinburgh. I hit on Culzean as reputedly the family and estate papers were deposited in the National Archives of Scotland. My original intention was to make a leisurely study, filling in the gaps and extending some features. It came as a surprise that the collection of records in Edinburgh was incomplete and contained very little from the nineteenth century and almost nothing from the twentieth. At first I thought gaps in the nineteenth century could be filled by using the large number of letters of the 1st Marquess of Ailsa amongst the Peel and Grenville manuscripts in the British Library, but I soon became aware through the generosity of the Marchioness of Ailsa and the trustees of the estate that there are as many, if not more papers, still in the hands of the family and in the estate office. In fact so complete is the archive that many books could be written about different facets of what until the late 1950s was an enormous estate – by far the largest in Ayrshire, even if much of the ground was of poor quality.

These discoveries placed a completely new complexion on my enterprise and made it possible to write an almost unbroken history of the estate and the family from the late seventeenth century. This was a challenging undertaking, not least because, apart from the pioneering work of John Ward, Roy Campbell and David Hancock, there was little frame of reference for the study of landowners in the west of Scotland.[1] Ian Anstruther's study of the Earls of Eglinton and the Eglinton tournament (an event so notorious in the nineteenth century that it is surprising there is only one book about it) touches on the family's persistent financial difficulties, which were exacerbated by this extravagance but not caused by it.[2] Likewise the fortunes of the Loudoun estates in east Ayrshire are not central to Henry Blyth's treatment of the 'wicked Marquess of Hastings' (1842–68) who gambled everything away in pursuit of Lady Florence Paget.[3] Although there has been research into the Butes, who were the second largest landowners in Ayrshire,[4] aside from Monsignor Sir David Hunter Blair's now dated biography of the 3rd Marquess very little has been written about the later Marquesses.[5]

For Scotland as a whole, apart from Keith Brown's recent book on the early modern nobility,[6] there has been virtually no research into the great landed families such as the Hamiltons and the Buccleuchs despite the fact that their extensive archives were amongst the first to attract the attention of the National Register of Archives (Scotland).[7] The exception is the work of Eric Richards on the Dukes of Sutherland whose wealth really derived from their English estates.[8] Although David Cannadine's work purports to be about the whole of the United Kingdom, in practice Scotland is largely overlooked for the simple reason that there is a lack of secondary literature for him to draw on.[9] Aside from political or notorious figures, such as the Marquess of Montrose,[10] Anne Duchess of Hamilton,[11] Henry Dundas,[12] Old Q – the 4th Duke of Queensberry,[13] and the Elgins,[14] there are few biographies of members of the aristocracy. Equally remarkable is the scarcity in Scotland of the nostalgic musings of the owners of country houses about the properties they owned, mostly written after the

First World War when their way of life seemed doomed for ever.[15] This may be explained by the dominance of the monumental and tedious works of Sir William Fraser, who made a tidy living out of calendaring and publishing the papers of noble and sometimes not so noble families.[16] All this is in stark contrast to England, Wales and Ireland where there is a plethora of literature which makes its absence in Scotland all the more puzzling.

The lodestars for any study of the aristocracy in England are the works of Lawrence Stone,[17] J.V. Beckett[18] and John Habakkuk, whose penetrating Ford Lectures at the University of Oxford provide the context for any case study, albeit the legal framework in Scotland was different from England.[19] Alongside the work of these scholars whose preoccupation, like Cannadine's, is largely with the aristocracy lie the studies of David Spring,[20] George Mingay,[21] and F.M.L. Thomson,[22] who represent a long tradition of enquiry into English agricultural history. The whole of this corpus of work is helpful to students of the great estates in Scotland but does not define it, for, as in so much else, Scotland was and is different. The genre of writing about country houses and their families is represented quintessentially by Elizabeth Bowen in her wonderful paean for her demolished family seat in County Cork – 'It was a clean end. Bowen's court never lived to be a ruin.'[23] Equally poignant is Vita Sackville West's *Knole and the Sackvilles* published in 1923.[24] So popular was this work that it was reprinted twice the following year, again in 1926 and in 1930 and 1931, confirming the interest of the English in their great country houses. Visiting such houses had been popular since the eighteenth century and many owners would happily allow their peers to view their homes. My own ancestor, the Reverend Claude Beaufort Moss, would instruct his chauffeur to turn off the road and drive through private parkland so that he could inspect some interesting house glimpsed through the trees. The threat to such houses led in the 1930s to moves to save them through the formation of the Country Houses

Committee by the National Trust, so wittily described in the writings of James Lees Milne.[25] The working of the committee and acquisitions by both the National Trust and later the National Trust for Scotland, awaits critical study. The passing of country houses into the care of both the government and the National Trust stimulated scholarly research and publication, as did the more formal opening of houses to the public by families themselves.[26] This tradition has continued.[27] In Scotland it is best represented by Ian Lindsay in his magisterial study of Inverary,[28] Charles McKean,[29] James Macaulay[30] and Ian Gow, who is now the curator of the National Trust for Scotland.[31]

The work of all these scholars contain echoes of my intention in embarking on a study of Culzean and many common threads, but none matched my objectives which are best characterised by David Cannadine:

> From the standpoint of the historian, the particular difficulty with the country-house cult, in both its sentimentalised and its institutionalised forms, is that the people who had once built, owned and occupied such houses rarely receive the notice they deserve, and all too often possess no substantial historical identity whatsoever. At best they are represented by the (often indifferent) family portraits on the wall, and by a genealogical table coyly printed near the back of the guide book … But what is invariably missing is any sense of these people as three-dimensional figures, as members of the national elite of wealth, status and power, who collectively made British history from the time of the Tudors to the late nineteenth century.[32]

I must confess that I had not read his words when I made just such a criticism of the guidebooks of the National Trust for Scotland at a property managers' conference some three years ago. Although the genealogical table is at the front of the Culzean guidebook,[33] his strictures apply. The portraits are by no means indifferent including works by Mosman, Batoni, Mather Brown and Lutyens, but there is no indication as to what the Earls and Marquesses did, if anything, and what their political views might have been. From their titles they were self-evidently not senior figures in the armed services – albeit the 11th Earl is described intriguingly as 'Captain Archibald Kennedy, Royal Navy of New York'. In the nineteenth and twentieth centuries they were not, unlike other Ayrshire noble families, pro-consuls nor did they hold any great offices of state. In the guidebook Sir David Kennedy, the 10th Earl, who commissioned Adam to convert the house into its classical form, remains a shadowy figure. Indeed there is no explanation as to why as a bachelor with a perfectly good house of his own, he should have wanted to embark on such an immense undertaking, particularly as the heir to the title (if not necessarily to the estate) was a remote American cousin. Having been rude about such guidebooks, here was a challenge to put my money where my mouth was.

ÆTATIS 58
1623

CHAPTER 1

Bloody feuds:

TO 1710

Unlike the Cassillis branch of the family, the Kennedys of Culzean may never have achieved great offices of state or served the Empire as pro-consuls, but that is not to say they did not hanker after office at least at the period when building work was going on at Culzean. The buildings today are rich in symbolism. The ruined arch and the broken-down battlements of the causeway speak of the end of a ferocious and bloody past. This imagery reaches a peak in the castle on the site of the old family fortress now converted to peaceful purposes. Until the beginning of the eighteenth century Ayrshire was a violent place with bitter feuds between the principal families: the Kennedys, Dalrymples, Montgomeries, and Boyds. The new castle metaphorically draws a line between the old ways of settling scores by beating up the neighbours and the new ways of post-Union Scotland, recourse to the law and the politics of Westminster. The last two were inseparable – the judicature were political appointments and redress could easily depend on who was 'in' and who was 'out'. The Union in 1707 left Scotland with fewer parliamentary seats than in the Edinburgh parliament but with the same narrow franchise. Ayrshire was unusual in having a relatively large number of voters – a hundred in 1741. Moreover, unlike some counties, these votes were well distributed amongst the county families and many were uncommitted, providing the opportunity for the internecine warfare of the previous generation to be carried on by new, but no less destructive, means.[1]

Culzean was originally known as Cove, taking its name from the three coves beneath the cliffs. Culzean, or Collean as it was more commonly spelled until the late nineteenth century,[2] was the name of the original family home down the coast at Turnberry. The Kennedy family of Culzean traces its origins to Sir Thomas, the younger son of Gilbert, 3rd Earl of Cassillis, a cultivated man and a pupil of the celebrated reformer and classical scholar George Buchanan, who thought so highly of him that they travelled abroad together. The family for generations had lived at Cassillis House near Dalrymple, at Maybole Castle and at Castle Kennedy on Loch Inch outside Stranraer. Returning to Scotland in May 1537, the 3rd Earl was appointed Lord of his Secret Council by King James V. Taken prisoner at the Battle of Solway in 1542, he was converted to Protestantism by Archbishop Cranmer while in London. He helped to negotiate the marriage of the infant Mary, Queen of Scots to the Dauphin in 1554. Remaining in France for four years, he firmly rejected the French demand that the Queen's husband, now Francis II of France, should also become King of Scotland. He was poisoned at Dieppe in November 1558 on his way home. His successor Gilbert, the 4th Earl, was appointed a councillor to Queen Mary and was at her side when she was defeated at

> *Gilbert, 4th Earl of Cassillis.*

Langside to the south of Glasgow in 1568. His brother Thomas was taken prisoner and rewarded for his loyalty with a knighthood on the coronation of James VI. He was granted a charter by his brother the Earl in 1569 over the lands of Culzean (a huge tract of land extending from Ayr to Girvan) and presumably began building or enlarging the castle. The coastal strip of land contained some of the best land in the west of Scotland, on which 'a wide range of crops may be grown with little difficulty'.[3] Nine years later their sister Jean, the wife of the 1st Earl of Orkney, was to tie the scarf round the queen's eyes before her execution at Fotheringay. The Cassillis family still has her crucifix and other tokens of her affection given to Lady Jean that fateful morning.

The 4th Earl of Cassillis, a supporter of the Reformation, infamously toasted Allen Steuart, the

LEFT
Sir Thomas Kennedy of Culzean

RIGHT
The silver crucifix presented to Lady Jean Kennedy by Mary Queen of Scots on the morning of her execution in 1587.

commendator of Crossraguel Abbey to the south of Maybole on a spit in the 'black vout' of the castle at Dunure in an effort to gain possession of the Abbey's lands. Kennedy of Bargany in the Girvan valley, learning of this affront, attacked Dunure with a large force and rescued the singed commendator, who complained to the Privy Council. The Earl was consequently imprisoned in Dumbarton Castle until he agreed not to molest the commendator again. Nevertheless he was eventually successful in gaining control of much of the Crossraguel lands. He was outwitted in a similar attempt to win much of the lands of Glenluce Abbey in Wigtownshire by the Gordons of Lochinvar, who persuaded the Dean, Michael Leirmonth, to forge a charter in their favour.[4] No less bloodthirsty than his brother, Sir Thomas, now known as Master of Culzean, played a game of golf

on the links at Ayr against a monk from Crossraguel, which, if the monk lost, he was to forfeit his nose.[5] There is no record of the outcome of this encounter.

The 4th Earl died in 1576 and was succeeded by his eldest son John, who was only nine years old. Instead of appointing his only surviving brother Sir Thomas, Master of Culzean, as tutor or trustee of his son's affairs during his minority, the earl nominated his brother-in-law John 8th Lord Glamis, Chancellor of Scotland and a supporter of the Regent Morton. As a result:

> thair fallis gritt ewill-wil betuix the
> Chanssellar and the Master, for the
> Tutory. The Chansellar sendis in
> Carrick, for to mak prowisione for his
> cuming in the cuntry; bot not lang
> befoir his cumming, the Maister

The ruins of Crossraguel Abbey to the south of Maybole, which are now cared for by Historic Scotland.

> destroyitt all the prowisione, bayth in
> Carrick and Galloway.

Confrontation continued for almost two years until March 1578 when the Regent Morton summoned a convention of nobility at Stirling. While there Lord Glamis was accidentally shot by the Earl of Crawford. Following his death the Master of Culzean succeeded to the tutorship.[6]

There ensued a bitter feud between Sir Thomas and Kennedy of Bargany over the lands of Bronistoune (Brunston) which both sides claimed as heirs to Black Bessie Kennedy, a mutual cousin. In his early teens the Earl became secretly engaged to a daughter of the Earl of Glencairn, the senior member of the Cunninghame clan. When this became known he was advised to flee to France. On his way he passed through Edinburgh and while

there, to the annoyance of Sir Thomas, he appointed Mure of Auchindrane to be his baillie at Blairquhan (another Kennedy strong-hold) until his return. When he came back in about 1585, Sir Thomas per-suaded the Earl to dismiss Auchindrane, who was outraged. Shortly afterwards the Earl fell out with his uncle over a mis-understanding. Sir Thomas accused the Earl's younger brother, Hew, Master of Cassillis, of trying to get hold of the keys to the tower house in Maybole 'to lett in sum men to cut his thrutt!' The Master protested his innocence but Sir Thomas persisted. Swords were drawn and Sir Thomas locked up the Master in Dunure to cool his heels. Meanwhile the Earl was contemplating 'to blow up the hous [of Bargany] in the air', using powder he had brought back with him from a visit to Italy. Sir Thomas counselled against such a hot-headed plan as 'the died wold be thocht werry crewall to put so many innocent saullis to death'. Instead he pro-posed killing young Gilbert Kennedy of Bargany while he was out hunting. Old Bargany, getting

The ruins of Dunure castle where the Abbott of Crossraguel was roasted.

wind of this plan, accused Sir Thomas Kennedy, who claimed he had only made the suggestion to convince his nephew of the folly of his original more destructive scheme.

On the death of Old Bargany in November 1596, Sir Thomas Kennedy of Culzean at once commenced legal pro-ceedings against his son in an effort to recover the adjoining estate of Newark (between Culzean and Ayr) which he believed was lawfully his. Indignant Gilbert Kennedy conspired with the Master of Cassillis, Auchindrane and Dunduff to murder Sir Thomas. On New Year's Day 1598, they waylaid him in Maybole on his way home from dinner. Sir Thomas made his escape, baffling his pursuers 'by the mirkness of the nycht'. He at once secured redress and Auchindrane and his confeder-ates were put 'to the horn' and their property con-fiscated. At the same time the Earl of Cassillis also took action against Bargany to recover unpaid debts. King James VI intervened and ordered the two factions to settle their grievances amicably. There was a temporary truce during which a

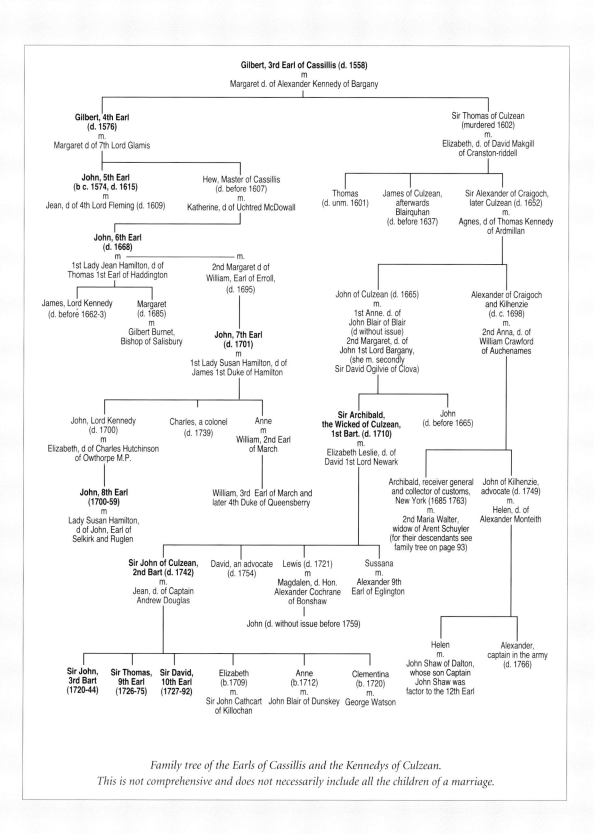

Family tree of the Earls of Cassillis and the Kennedys of Culzean.
This is not comprehensive and does not necessarily include all the children of a marriage.

violent quarrel broke out between the Earl and his tenants in Galloway.

After securing an interdict against them, the Earl hurried to Castle Kennedy, his home at Inch. He gave notice of his intention of holding a court at Glenluce to dispossess his tenants. On learning the news, they besieged him in his house by surrounding Loch Inch and preventing any access. However the minister of Colmonell, who was with the Earl, managed to get permission to leave the castle on the feeble pretence of going to church. He hurried to Bargany with a message from the Earl 'giff he vald cum and mak his relieff he (the Earl) wald mend all his misbehawiour that he had done to him, and think of him by all his kin to his lyffis end!' Bargany, seizing his opportunity finally to settle the feud, gathered his forces and rode south. On arriving at Inch he succeeded in negotiating an amicable settlement. When

The old tower house in Maybole, the town house of the Earls of Cassillis, photographed in the late nineteenth century. For almost two hundred years it served as the factor's house and estate office. The bay on the right was added by the Edinburgh architect David Cousin in the mid-1850s.

he tried, however, to hold the Earl to his word, the Earl conveniently forgot his offer. Shortly afterwards the Earl also fell out with Blairquhan, who invited him to stay with the intention 'to cum the neist nicht to slay me Lard in his awin bed'. Warned, the Earl left by the 'back zett, and without nay gud-nicht'. Although Blairquhan made a formal alliance with Bargany against Cassillis, the truce was temporarily patched up. With the marriage of James Mure of Auchindrane's younger son and Helen Kennedy, daughter of Sir Thomas of Culzean, a permanent peace seemed possible –'all bygones to be past among them'. Mure of Auchindrane's lands were restored. Perhaps the misunderstanding between the Master of Cassillis and his brother, the Earl, was laid to rest because the Earl threatened to leave his estates to their stepbrother?

The feud between Cassillis and Bargany, however, continued sucking in other families with long-standing vendettas against each other. As in all such feuds, motives were confused and the reason for quarrels often forgotten. Their disagreement now centred on the teinds (tithes) of the tenpound lands of Girvanmains, which were rented by the laird of Girvanmains from Bargany, who in turn held them from the Earl of Cassillis. Annoyed that Bargany had not paid his teinds, the Earl resolved to take what he was due by force. On learning the news, Bargany and Girvanmains with their supporters turned the farm yard into an armed camp. The Earl retaliated by ordering his servants to cut some of the standing corn. Their task completed, they were intercepted by Bargany, who captured their horses and carts. Furious, Cassillis spent the following day, the Sabbath, mustering his forces to cut the rest of the corn. Not to be outwitted Bargany did likewise. He was on the ground early on the Monday morning with six hundred horsemen and 'tua hunder hagbutteris'.* He was joined by Lord Ochiltree with one hundred horse, giving him a total of nine hundred men by the time Cassillis appeared with a similar force but not so well-equipped with firearms. At this juncture Lord Cathcart appeared on the field and negotiated a 'trauellit' – a truce – between the two parties whereby Bargany could cut the corn and give his security for the payment of the teinds.

Castle Kennedy at Inch, near Stranraer in Wigtownshire, which was sold by the 7th Earl of Cassillis to Sir John Dalrymple, 1st Viscount Stair, in 1677 to pay off some of his debts.

Although bloodshed was avoided, the feud became more intense and complex as Cassillis was infuriated by the size and strength of Bargany's forces. With growing impatience, he called for the house at Girvanmains to be burned down. Exasperated, Bargany began again to plot Cassillis's murder. Both the Master of Cassillis and Sir Thomas Kennedy of Culzean were implicated. On the day it was intended to set upon the Earl on his way to Castle Kennedy, Sir Thomas was riding with the party and Mure of Auchindrane stayed his hand. The following day Auchindrane went boldly to Castle Kennedy to remonstrate with Sir Thomas, who inveigled him onto the island with a view to kidnapping him. Cassillis then accused them of conspiracy to murder. Sensing the danger he was in, Auchindrane made good his escape in an abandoned boat and rode straight to Bargany at Ballantrae. Bargany tried to bluff it out by sending emissaries to Cassillis to ask who had put the idea of conspiracy to murder into his head. Cassillis denied ever having made such a suggestion. Staggered by such effrontery, Auchindrane threatened to denounce him at every market cross, whereupon the Earl admitted he might have made some such remark. Concluding that Sir Thomas had informed on them, the conspirators decided to be rid of them both. Almost immediately Auchindrane got cold feet and warned Sir Thomas not to ride into the trap set for him by Bargany's brother. Sir Thomas went post haste to Edinburgh to complain to the king, who summoned Bargany to explain himself.

*A hagbutt was a primitive form of musket and a huggbutteris those who carried them.

11

Again an uneasy truce was concluded but it did not last long and the two families were soon quarrelling again. Eventually, returning with a few followers from Ayr in a blizzard on 11 December 1601, Gilbert Kennedy of Bargany was set on by the Earl with a party of two hundred horsemen who had been lying in wait. Despite the overwhelming odds, Bargany put up a stiff resistance but was soon dismounted and seriously wounded. He was taken to Ayr where he was tended in his final hours by the surgeon Peter Lowe. This vicious attack was universally despised and Bargany was praised for his courage – he 'was the bravest manne that was be gotten in ony land, of hiche statour, and weill maid, his hair blak, bott of ane cumlie face, the brauest horsmanne and the elbest of mony at all pastymis'.

The Earl of Cassillis as soon as possible sought a royal pardon for his crime which was granted early in 1602 on the intercession of Sir Thomas Kennedy of Culzean, to the annoyance of Lady Kennedy of Bargany. Getting wind of Sir Thomas's intention of riding to Edinburgh on 12 May 1602, Auchindrane and his friends ambushed him at Saint Leonard's chapel in the south-west corner of what became the old Ayr racecourse at Seafield. They slew him 'maist cruellie with schottis and straikis' and robbed him of his valuables along with a thousand gold merks. Incensed by this outrage, the Earl of Cassillis and his brother vowed revenge on the Mures of Auchindrane. For the next five years there were repeated acts of violence between the two. The feud finally came to a tragic end on the shore at Girvan when Thomas Dalrymple was brutally murdered by the Mures. After a protracted enquiry, father and son were executed in Edinburgh in 1611. The Kennedys of Bargany died out in 1630 and the estate was sold to the Hamiltons (later Dalrymple-Hamilton), who still own the property but not the mansion house.[7]

Sir Thomas Kennedy's heir, his brother James, sold the Culzean estate in 1622 to a third brother, Alexander Kennedy of Craigoch, so as to be able to buy the more productive Blairquhan estate in Straiton with its imposing and well-appointed castle.* Craigoch is between Maybole and Dailly on the Water of Girvan (NS295045). Alexander, who was knighted in 1632, had seven children and it was from the second son, Alexander of Craigoch and later Kilhenzie that the present Marquesses of Ailsa are descended. Kilhenzie Castle, which now does duty as a farmhouse, is just outside Maybole on the road to Dailly. The Englishman, Sir William Brereton, visited Culzean in 1634. His arrival was unwelcome as Sir Alexander did not relish the prospect of a stranger taking too much interest in what went on inside. Arrangements were hurriedly made for a reception. He was greeted by one of the sons of the family. He showed him cursorily round the house where Sir William later recorded he 'found there no hall, only a dining-room or hall, a fair room and almost as large as the whole pile, but very slatternly kept, unswept, dishes, trenchers, and wooden cups thrown up and down and the room very nasty and unsavoury'.[8] He was no doubt put out by his reception as Sir Alexander intended:

> Here we were not entertained with a cup of beer or ale; only one of his [Sir Alexander's] sons, servants, and others took a candle, and conducted us to the cave, where there is either a notable imposture, or most strange and much to be admired footsteps and impressions which are here to be seen, children, dogs, coneys and divers other creatures.

He went on to recount that these impressions in the sand could be smoothed out, only to reappear during the night. He observed – 'The cave hath many numerous passages and doors, galleries also, and a closet and divers rooms hewed with mighty labour out of a hard limestone rock.' This was a time-honoured trick to put the curious off explor-

---

*The old castle was demolished in the 1820s to make way for the present house. Some details of the old house survive in the kitchen court. In 1623 James Kennedy relinquished Blairquhan to the Whitefoordes, from whom it passed to the Hunter Blairs in 1786 (J.T. Jackson, *Blairquhan*, 2000, pp. 3-10)

View of WHITEFOORD CASTLE from y.ᵉ S.W.

ing. Hungry and thirsty Brereton left Culzean in search of sustenance. He had to travel several miles away from the estate before finding anyone willing to give him supper.[9]

As an Episcopalian, Sir Alexander Kennedy played little part in the Civil War. He supported the Parliamentary cause at the outset but later switched to the Royalists. He died in 1652 and was succeeded by his eldest son, John, who with his brother Thomas matriculated at Glasgow University in 1632.[10] John was in the Scottish parliament as a commissioner for Ayrshire in 1656, 1659 and again after the restoration of the monarchy in 1661. He was appointed a justice of the peace for Ayrshire in October 1663. With the coming of more settled times, it was probably John who considered it safe to breach the barmekin (battlement) wall and construct three terraces as hanging gardens. Judging

The old castle at Blairquhan as it was in 1787.

from a later drawing, these were elaborate, with walls extending out on either side of the castle to provide shelter for the upper terrace and a central stairway to the second terrace. At the same time John filled up the moat to the north-east to make a more convenient approach to the castle and to provide shelter for his garden. Hanging gardens or terraces were popular at the time. The most spectacular example to survive in the west of Scotland is at Barncluith near Hamilton which dates from the early sixteenth century. Across from the terraces at Culzean, John Kennedy laid out a walled deer park and was probably responsible for enclosing the fifty acre Cow Park,[11] also a reflection of more settled times. He died in 1665 and was followed by his eldest son Archibald.

Although he had a Presbyterian tutor, Archibald later recalled:

I always frequented the church with my family as some of the Episcopalian Clergie yet alive will bear witness, nor did I ever goe so much as to a Conventicle tho' the most of all the neighbourhood did resort to them, some for curiosity, others because it was their principall.

The picture room or long drawing room at Culzean, which was originally the great hall of the Castle.

Still a minor when he inherited the estate and title, the youthful Archibald also attended the University of Glasgow in 1672 before continuing his studies in France where he learnt to play the bass viol.[12] While there he attended a reception at Versailles with the Duc de Chartres, the heir to the Duc d'Orleans and nephew of Louis XIV:

Chartres & his sister Mademoiselle were both their the Duke went round one his foot & his sister in a coadch of eight horses, it is not to be imagined/wonderful to watch the vast number of people that came their, it being a holy day, & so the peasants idle & the burgers, unspeakable numbers of people came from Paris besides those that are in masque a great many others very well clothed & of good fashion doe dance, and their generally all the common people; but above all the thing that is most admirable is to see the vast number of violers that come there, and most of them very bad.[13]

14

The Duc's father much admired the playing of the viol.[14]

Sir Archibald returned from France in time to fight at the Battle of Bothwell Brig in 1679 when the covenanters were soundly defeated:

> Tho' our shire was not called to attend
> the King's host yet I went from my own
> house thoro a part of the Rebels' camp
> to the great hazard of my life attended
> only by my own servants – there being
> none of our gentrie would goe at that
> tyme & joyned the King's armie at
> Moorhead.

On going home to Ayrshire he described it 'as a county where the most bigott ffanaticks did abound'. His loyalty and, no doubt, an exchange of cash earned him a baronetcy in 1682. Two years later he was appointed captain of militia,[15] which he boasted 'putt me to a considerable expense in providing ane equipadge, the best in the Kingdom'. He took his duties seriously and went to great:

> pains … to pursue and extirpate out of
> these pairts those rebellious ffanaticks
> who owed it lawfull to kill the King and
> all his adherents. I fell in blood with
> them, wherein two was killed upon the
> spott and four taken prisoner, which
> occasioned me for some time to keep a
> guard about the house.[16]

He was chosen as a member of the Scottish parliament in 1684, but did not take his seat because fresh elections were called on the death of Charles II early the following year. On this occasion he lost to Sir William Wallace. In any event he was ordered home by the Earl of Perth 'where your interest lyes & there convocat such of your friends & others will joine wth you, & act for His Majestie's service against all revolt as occasion offers to you'.[17] On 9 June the Duke of Queensberry wrote to him 'we are well pleased with your defence & care in the King's

service … pray continue to keep down the rogues; all is quiet in England, the Marquis of Atholl is very near to Argyll & we expect hourly to hear of action.'[18]

In recognition of his new found responsibilities, he was elected a commissioner of supply for the county. The commissioners were responsible for local government and were chosen at this time from amongst the gentry who were not members of the nobility. In July Sir Archibald and the laird of Ballantrae captured Gilbert McAdam, a Covenanter, while at prayer. When he tried to escape Sir Archibald shot him. He is buried in the graveyard at Kirkmichael with the following eloquent epitaph 'shot by the Laird of Colzean for his adherance to the Word of God & Scotland's Covenanted Work of Reformation'.[19] Frightened by the possible reaction, Sir Archibald prudently fled to France with a letter of introduction from the Earl of Dumbarton, the commander-in-chief in Scotland and a relative, to Sir William Trumbull, James VII's envoy to the court of Louis XIV.[20] He returned as soon as the coast was clear.

On learning of the news of the Prince of Orange's landing at Torbay, symbolically on the anniversary of the Gun Powder plot, 5 November 1688, Sir Archibald's first inclination was to hurry south, but he was delayed by instructions to march to Glasgow with the rest of the Ayrshire gentry under the command of his cousin the Earl of Cassillis. On being released from service in December he rushed to London, but King James had already fled to Rochester on his way to France. He remained in the capital for some time becoming associated with the Jacobite circle of the Earl of Balcarres and John Graham of Claverhouse, Viscount Dundee. He was offered command of a company in the guards by Lieutenant General Douglas which he refused as he considered it beneath him.

Disappointed, Sir Archibald went home where he learned of James II & VII landing at Kinsale in Ireland early in 1689. He offered to go as Balcarres's emissary to Ireland to try to persuade James II to

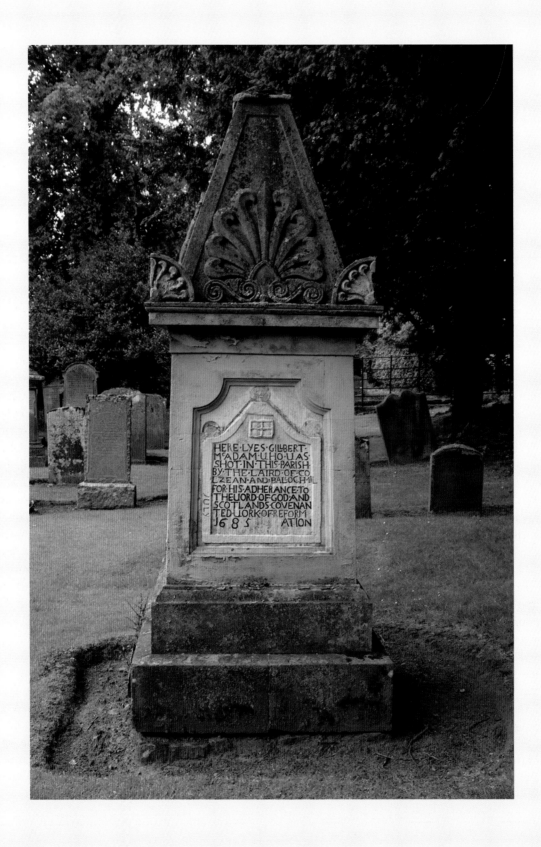

come to Scotland and join Dundee's forces. Balcarres immediately accepted his offer. He later claimed he 'left my wife & eight children to the furie of the rable who were then everywhere in arms'. He travelled south from Culzean to Portpatrick where he was taken prisoner 'by the Irish mob that had cumm from their own country upon Lieutenant General Hamilton's approval'. He claimed that he had murdered a man and was fleeing for his life. Duped, the Irish Protestants let him go and he made for Dublin, arriving there at the end of March 1689. Towards the end of his life he proudly noted 'I have the honour to be the first gentleman of all Scotland that left his all & went to serve his master, for I was so luckie to come to Dublin the very day after the King.'

Although King James was keen to go to Scotland, his advisers were cautious, suggesting the first move must be to take Londonderry. According to Sir Archibald, who accompanied him, 'he was made to beliefe the town would surrender upon his approach, but it fell out for other ways, for they returned their answer out of the mouth of their cannon.' On James's return to Dublin, Sir Archibald, spoiling for a fight, went north to Belfast to serve under General Buchan and was present at the rout of the Protestants at Killeleach (Killylea) where he was nearly 'killed in the head'. After the victory he returned to Dublin where, according to his own account, the king praised his loyalty and courage and sent him back to Derry. On 8 April he received the coveted commission as Lieutenant Colonel of a regiment of horse.[21] The following month the Williamite government issued a warrant for his arrest on suspicion of treason.

In late July Archibald went north with Colonel Carron and a party of reinforcements for Viscount Dundee's Highland army. They took boats from Cushendall on the Antrim coast to Mull 'wherein

we landed next day after having mitt with a violent storm at sea so that we were almost drowned'. After two days they arrived at Lochmaben where they learned of Dundee's death at the Battle of Killiecrankie on 27 July. They were joined by the Earl of Dunfermline, who had been with Dundee when he died and expected to succeed him as commander-in-chief in Scotland. He was understandably annoyed when the less experienced Carron was preferred. The dismal party remained in Mull for three months and their spirits were even more depressed, as in Sir Archibald's words, 'we had nothing stronger to drink but the water of Lochie, nor any bread but Barley bread ground in their quorns, noe salt nor had we so much as a bed to lye upon but lay the whole tyme in our own clothes.' With winter closing in, he set off across Scotland making for the home of his stepfather Sir David Ogilvie, the brother of the Earl of Airlie, in Angus. Here he met his younger brother Thomas and they spent the whole winter in Glen Clova 'in a pitifull Highland cottage he [the Earl] having noe other house in any repair'. Learning of the plot to restore King James hatched by Sir James Montgomerie of Skelmorlie on the north Ayrshire coast, they left Glen Clova but were arrested on 12 May 1690. They were taken to Montrose and then to Edinburgh where they were confined in 'close prison' for eight months and their estates sequestrated. During 1691 the Earl of Cassillis, Sir Archibald's cousin, intervened and obtained his kinsman's release 'till I should be convict of the crime laid against me'. The sequestration of his properties was also suspended. Towards the end of the year his wife fell ill and he was allowed to go home to Culzean with two dragoons as guards. At the end of his parole, he was taken back to Edinburgh where he was finally released on bail of £1,000 and the sequestration finally lifted.

The gravestone of Gilbert McAdam in Kirkmichael graveyard with the inscription: HERE LYES GILBERT MCADAM ỤHOỤAS SHOT IN THIS PARISH BY THE LAIRD OF COLZEAN AND BALOCHIL FOR HIS ADHERANCE TO THEỤORD OF GOD AND SCOTLANDS CONVENANTED ỤORK OF REFORMATION 1685.

It was restored by those sympathetic to the covenanting cause in 1829.

Hearing of the possibility of a fresh invasion, Sir Archibald 'provided myself in two hundred pounds sterling worth of house airms', but following the defeat of the French fleet at La Hogue on 19 May he was summoned to Edinburgh to swear allegiance. This he pigheadedly refused to do and was committed to the Canongate Tolbooth. Languishing in prison, he learned that the Lord Advocate knew all about his adventures in Ireland and Mull and was preparing to bring charges of treason – 'Upon which I found beall [bail] and came out'. He was fined a year's rent for his part in supporting the Jacobite cause and because he still refused to swear allegiance was forbidden to own arms or horses. At least he was allowed to live at home. His close friend Lord Kennedy, the heir to the Earl of Cassillis and unlike his father a Jacobite, was forced to live abroad. On quitting the country in July 1695 Kennedy wrote emotionally 'I cannot express the sorrow and regrait I have for the want of your good company. I am just now going on board a ship that sailes strait for Hamburg and honest Will Seaton is with me.'[22]

The wild countryside in the Forest of Buchan which is amongst the most beautiful in Scotland.

Sir Archibald's troubles were not over. On learning of the plan of the Duke of Berwick to invade England in 1696, he foolishly purchased 'very nice horses'. However when the plot to assassinate King William was uncovered, a warrant for his rearrest was issued. Warned in advance he sent his horses to Bargany for safe-keeping and hid himself in the caves beneath Culzean. Although he was not discovered when the castle was searched, the soldiers left at once for Bargany where all his horses were seized.[23] He remained in fear of further imprisonment for the remainder of his life, despite being reappointed a commissioner of supply for the county in 1704. When the supporters of the Protestant succession, known as Whigs, gained power in England in 1705, they began to negotiate the union of the two parliaments of Scotland and England. Spies were employed to report on the likely allegiance of the Scottish gentry. Sir Archibald was considered still to

be a Jacobite sympathiser.[24] In 1708 at the time of the Pretender's abortive invasion of England, he wrote to the Earl of Airlie 'I have been waiting … a call from the government to re-enter prison', but he hoped that the quiet life he lived at Culzean would save him.[25]

Chastened by his experience of living rough and in prison, Sir Archibald spent his time at Culzean hunting, hawking, farming and gardening. Hunting was in the Kennedy blood since 1500, when James IV had granted his mistress Janet Kennedy, the half-sister of the 1st Earl of Cassillis, a lease of the hunting in the Forest of Buchan, the wild country between Straiton and Newton Stewart. She seems to have appointed her half-brother hereditary ranger of the Forest of Buchan, a title some of his descendants delighted in. During the seventeenth century the Earl built a lodge at Hunt Ha' deep in the forest to the east of the Dungeon.* Sir Archibald asked the Earl

*Although it is still marked on 1:25 ordnance sheet at N480859, no trace survives amongst the trees.

> *Ailsa Craig, the rocky island in the Firth of Clyde, owned by the Kennedys of Culzean, from which the Marquesses of Ailsa take their title.*

Marischal to supply him with hawks in 1695, but the Earl was unable to send him any until the following year. Three years later Lord Mont-gomerie, the son of the Earl of Eglinton, sent him a setter for hunting. He shot 'solan geese' (gannets) from Ailsa Craig and sent them to his Jacobite friends, who included the Duke of Gordon, the Earl of Dunluce, the Earl of Antrim and the Earl of Perth.[26] The Duke thanked him, stating they were not known in the north-east, but 'loock werry weill'.[27] The Earl of Perth was surprised that the geese 'have come very much fresher than could have been expected at so vast a distance' and added 'I confess it is hard to live in the Countrie such as yours is & therefore the Country cannot be too great in your conversations.'[28] At about this time Sir Archibald innovatively began to enclose the 460-acre Turnberry Park (what is now Turnberry golf course) to create permanent pasture for rearing and fattening black Galloway cattle.[29] This was one of the earliest examples of enclosure in south-west

Scotland.[30] In 1701 the Duke of Hamilton sought his advice about cattle:

> I am now turned drover and am going to make an essay how the Arran stots [cattle] will doe in Lankesheir. If you can furnish the bearrer with ten young cows that have had calves I shall pay in their prices when appoint.[31]

William Abercrummie (Abercrombie), who described himself as the minister of Minnibole (he was in fact the Episcopalian minister of Maybole from 1680 to 1687) noted of Culzean during these years:

> standing upon a rock above the Sea, flanked upon the South with very pretty gardens and orchards, adorned with excellent tarases [terraces], and the walls loaden with peaches, apricotes, cherries, and other fruits; and these gardens are so well sheltered from the north and east winds, and ly so open to the south that

the fruit and herbage are more early than at any other place in Carrick.[32]

The Collegiate church in Maybole, the traditional burying place of the Kennedy family with their monument at the back. On the death of the 2nd Marquess in 1870 the burying ground was moved to the cemetery field at Culzean.

OPPOSITE
The 7th Earl of Cassillis whose support for the covenanting cause led to his virtual ruin.

According to Walter MacFarlane of that Ilk, who collected Abercrummie's work, he reserved such flattering descriptions for those, such as Sir Archibald, who had adhered to the Episcopalian faith and repressed the Covenanters. In 1705 Sir Archibald embellished his terraces by ordering from his mason John Anderson of Ayr stone ornamental flower-pots displaying eight different coats of arms representing the family's pedigree. These were so expensive that John Anderson, no doubt well aware of Sir Archibald's financial problems and political sympathies, insisted that Sir Archibald's heirs would honour the debt.[33] With trade improving, Sir Archibald constructed saltpans on the shore at Maidens, in which sea water was evaporated over coal fires to leave salt crystals. These were leased out in 1709 to Hugh Hamilton, an Ayr merchant, who was also the tenant of the newly enclosed Turnberry Park.[34]

Sir Archibald died in 1710 and stories quickly

began to circulate amongst Presbyterians about the terrible nature of his final illness and the diabolical events at his funeral, which make Tam O'Shanter's dream seem relatively innocuous. The Devil attacked the cortege on its way from Culzean to Maybole for interment in the collegiate church, and carried off Sir Archibald's soul to Mount Etna, 'one of the craters of the nether fires'. As luck would have it, crossing the Mediterranean (not the most direct way from Culzean to southern Italy):

> an Ayr vessel beheld a woeful spectacle … ; and in the evening what should they see but a fiery chariot come towards them careering along the surface of the deep! Round it were many deils, but he that drove was none other than the muckle Deil himself. And as the ship met the chariot, the skipper put his speaking trumpet to his lips and cried out: 'From whence to where?' And the driver made answer: 'From Culzean to Hell.' Such an answer might have daunted almost anyone else except the skipper, but as skippers never lie nor swear, nor do anything that is wrong, this one's courage did not slack off in the very slightest. 'What cargo?' he shouted. 'The soul of Sir Archibald, the Wicked,' was the blood-curling reply.[35]

At the time of his descent into Hell, Sir Archibald was heavily in debt, owing some £80,000 Scots (about £10,000 sterling). His principal creditors were his children for whom he had made provision of £14,000 Scots, presumably in case he should again find himself on the wrong side of law. He also owed money to his mason, John Anderson, who had prudently made sure his heirs would pay for the flower-pots, and to another Ayr mason, Thomas Campbell.[36] John Anderson's widow still had not received the final payment for the flower-pots by 1721.[37] The description of Sir Archibald's funeral scarcely does justice to this complex man who remained fiercely loyal to his Episcopalian faith. A keen sportsman, he was well-educated, had travelled widely, presumably spoke French, and played the bass viol. His commitment to the Jacobite cause cost him dearly.

Sir Archibald's cousin, the 7th Earl of Cassillis, who had rescued him from prison and bankruptcy, had died in 1701, a year after his eldest son the Jacobite Lord Kennedy. He also left substantial debts incurred largely because of his support for the covenanting cause during the reigns of Charles II and James II.[38] Much of the furniture in Cassillis House had to be sold and it took six years to sort out his tangled affairs.[39] The heir to the earldom, his grandson John, was only a year old. His second son Charles was an army officer and was to die without issue in 1739. His daughter Anne was married to the Earl of Selkirk and Ruglen and this was to be significant when his grandson John, the 8th Earl, also, died without children in 1759.

CHAPTER 2

Prudent smugglers:
1710−44

Sir Archibald was succeeded by his son, Sir John, a prudent supporter of the Glorious Revolution, who nevertheless seems to have retained his Jacobite sympathies. He was married to Jean, the daughter of Captain Andrew Douglas, reputedly of the Douglas of Mains family whose seat was in Milngavie to the north of Glasgow. As part of her dowry, Jean Douglas brought with her Scipio, a slave whom her father had purchased in the West Indies and who originated from Guinea. Sir John had two brothers, one of whom, David, had attended the University of Glasgow with him in 1694.[1] Sir Archibald then sent John to continue his studies at Utrecht in the Netherlands where he lodged with the Earl of Balcarres, who had fled the country in 1690 after the Montgomerie plot. Writing in about 1697 to Sir Archibald, Balcarres explained:

> I assure you he [John] has been very
> diligent and frugal beyond many of his
> countrymen – but tho' he has studied
> very weal it will be another year in my
> opinion to perfite him in what you
> intend him for and since one year more
> either in France or in this place will
> make him fitt to do for himself so he
> will be the less burdensome to you.[2]

John spent the autumn of 1697 visiting the towns in the Low Countries, leaving Leith on 15 September and arriving at Brile ten days later. At the end of the year he went on to Paris.[3] David became a successful advocate and died a wealthy man in 1754.[4] Lewis, the third brother, became the collector of customs in Irvine and died in 1748,[5] and his only son John, a lieutenant in the navy, was to die childless. Sir John also had two sisters, the younger of whom, Susanna, was considered a great beauty and was the third wife of the 9th Earl of Eglinton, a privy councillor to William III.

Sir John remains an enigma but there is much to suggest that his father had in mind a mercantile career trading in a variety of goods, particularly wine and spirits, both legitimate and contraband. The Firth of Clyde was a notorious centre for smuggling of both foreign wines and spirits, and the caves beneath Culzean were ideal for hiding such stock from the enquiring eyes of the Revenue officers. Since they formed part of the castle, they were well defended on the shore, with a stout door and gun ports. In 1726 a boat, which Sir John owned jointly with David Kennedy of Drumellan, sank in the Firth of Clyde with a cargo of bear – a type of barley well-suited to the wet conditions of the west coast of Scotland and extensively used for making *aquavitae*.[6] In another incident one of their boats was seized running (smuggling) goods from the Isle of Man with a total loss of £334.[7] Relanding goods from the Isle of Man was common practice up and down the west coast as rates of duty on the island were much lower than on the mainland because it was con-

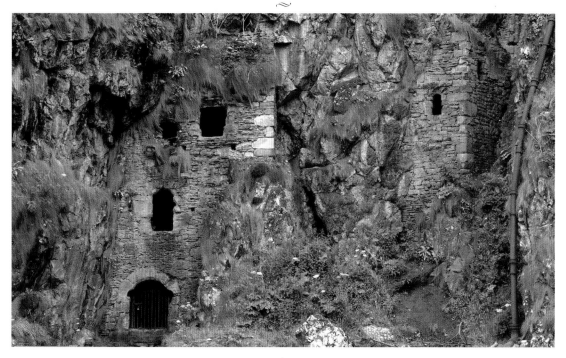

trolled, not by the government, but by the proprietor, the Duke of Atholl.[8] Apart from David Kennedy, Hugh Hamilton and John Vance, merchants in Ayr, and Alexander Anderson a merchant in Kilmarnock were partners with Sir John in these activities.[9] Anderson seems to have smuggled large quantities of soap, then a dutiable product, from Londonderry.[10]

Until his father's death Sir John was resident at the family's town house in Maybole, but after 1710 he seems to have lived quietly at Culzean, taking little interest in local politics. He employed as his factor on the estate John McIlvane Younger of Grimmet, who lived in Thomaston Castle just to the north of the Culzean, which still stands. McIlvane, who described himself as a merchant, became a close friend and a confidant in Sir John's trading activities.[11] From March to December 1733 he sold Sir John thirty pints of claret, eight pints of genever, three dozen bottles of claret and white

OPPOSITE
Susanna Kennedy, daughter of Sir Archibald Kennedy and third wife of the Earl of Eglinton, who was considered to be one of the greatest beauties of the day. Reputedly, she preserved her good looks well into her seventies.

ABOVE
The fortified entrance to the caves beneath Culzean, which were used to house smuggled goods.

wine, and seven pints of brandy. In September 1735 alone he supplied Sir John with two dozen bottles of white wine, six dozen claret and a half pound of both green and Bohea (black) tea.[12] McIlvane seems to have had quite a large business. For instance, in 1742 he delivered to a Hugh Clerk ten dozen magnums of claret, four dozen of Burgundy, and four dozen 'Pruniack' white wine. The crews of the wherries were tipped with tobacco and whisky. Occasionally McIlvane enjoyed some of his own stock, as at Halloween 1739 when his household consumed four bottles of claret. Apart from their wine and spirit business, McIlvane and Sir John also acted as agents for the Edinburgh merchants, Dundas & Angus, previously Dundas Whiteford & Co., in buying and selling cloth.[13]

Sir John also fostered linen manufacture on his estate, possibly to provide export cargoes. In 1718 he formed a partnership with John Vance, a merchant in Ayr, and

Nicholas Dunbar, the son of the salt officer in Turnberry, to build a linen works at Culzean 'Mainnes' on a site known as Jamestoun just inland from the Maidens. The cost of the works, which Dunbar was to manage, was some £200 and it contained three looms. Shortly afterwards a second weaving shop was erected at Turnberry. In 1720 the partners came to an agreement to sell all their production to William Ewart, a bleacher.[14] During these years Scipio, Lady Jean's slave, not only was taught to read and write but also learned something of textile manufacture. In 1725 then aged about thirty, he penned a remarkable document binding himself to serve Sir John for a further nineteen years:

> Bee it known to all these present Mr Sipio Kennedy from Guinea,[15] servant to Sir John Kennedy of Cullean, for as much as in my infancy I was brought and redeemed by Captain Andrew Douglas, father-in-law to the said Sir John, and was in a certaine way of being in perpet-

Thomaston castle on the road between Culzean and the Maidens, which was the home of the McIlvane family.

ual servitude in the West Indies Ilinnes had it not been my happiness to fall into his hands purchased by his money with whom I remained for three years or thereabouts. At which time I was present to ye said Sir John and his Lady who ever since I have continually recd clothing, maintenance and education with more than ordinary kindness and ye instruction and example of his family.[16]

Scipio married a local girl, Margaret Gray, in October 1728, who was already carrying his child. He took the surname Kennedy, a common practice amongst black slaves.[17] Seven more children followed, including a son Douglas (born 26 March 1732), who was to become body servant to Sir John's son, Thomas. Scipio continued to be employed at the castle as a sort of butler, but he and his wife were soon engaged in weaving cotton and linen goods. In 1735 John McIlvane paid him for a pair of dark 'wistet stocken given to Mr Kennedy jr. summer last'.[18] In 1742 he supplied McIlvane with

Wine bottles excavated in the caves beneath Culzean and a seal from a bottle dated 1741 found at Cassillis.

cotton yarn and linen napkins.[19]

With his extensive commercial interests, Sir John refused to be moved by an impassioned plea from his sister, the newly widowed Countess of Eglinton, in 1734 to stand for parliament for Ayrshire in the forthcoming election – 'Did I not believe that it was for the interest of your ffamilie (as it is undoubtilly for the honnour of it) I would not dar to propose it. The long minority of my son makes me greatly affrayed of losing the interest of his ffamilie in this shire.'[20] He did however take sides against the Eglinton interest in the election of 1741 when he supported the anti-Walpole Whig candidate, Patrick Crauford, against the sitting MP, the Honourable James Campbell. Campbell was the second son of the Earl of Loudoun, who was married to Lady Margaret, the daughter of the Earl of Eglinton. Sir John Kennedy's action elicited a stinging rebuke from his sister:

> It is with astonishment and concern that I am told by all the members of the opposition to my Sons interest that you tell them you'l support them all that's in your power. I don't know what my family has done to deserve this at your hands, nor can I perceive the honour or interest your self can obtain from it, if measures are such in your opinion that you can't joyen them; I think the relation you stand in to my Family should impose Silence at least. As my Lord Eglintoun had no Fortune from your House, I except that good office was to be my dower but to my great disappointment I find that my own relatives are the People I have to thank for the Foulest Favours ...[21]

Like his father Sir John was a keen gardener. William Boutcher, one of the most skilled nurserymen in Scotland at the time, supplied him in 1730 with three nectarine trees, three peaches, and three apricots.[22] He was certainly growing vegetables in 1733 when he planted peas, onions, kidney beans,

carrots, parsnips, turnips, radishes, and broad beans.[23] These were grown in the walled garden he had constructed at the foot of the terraces in what had been a defensive dry moat.[24] He was again planting fruit trees in 1741 which suggests he may also have been responsible for constructing other terraces to the south-west of the castle to accommodate an additional orchard.[25] These are now obscured by trees and undergrowth.[26] It was probably he who built the three ornamental dovecotes at Hopeton Hill, Thomaston, and Turnberry Park. These were elaborate affairs encircled by woodland and may have also served as navigation marks from which lights could be shown to smugglers on the frequent misty nights in the North Channel.[27]

In the early 1730s Sir John seems to have moved into Ayr during the winter rather than into his town house in Maybole, but he continued to use Culzean in the summer and, perhaps more importantly, for his smuggling activities. After the Union of the Parliaments in 1707 with the growth of the Atlantic trades, Ayr, like Glasgow and the other

LEFT
The ornamental dovecotes illustrated on the estate map of 1755.

RIGHT
Lady Cathcart's lodgings in Ayr which were rented by Sir John Kennedy of Culzean and used for his wine and spirit business.

Clyde ports, prospered. Most of the local aristocracy and gentry owned or rented homes in Ayr or nearby in Alloway, including the Earls of Loudoun, Dumfries and Eglinton.[28] In 1725 The Honourable Colonel Charles Cathcart, later the 8th Baron Cathcart, and Captain (later Colonel) Lawrence Nugent of Newfield, near Dundonald in Ayrshire, rented what was known as the 'pasturage of the hills' – in fact the links – with the intention of improving them. Their tack or lease specified that they should bear:

the charges of levelling the sandy hills and rising grounds of the said lands, and covering the most sandy parts thereof with wreck [wrack – seaweed] or rubbish of the town, and to improve the most barren and sandy parts thereof by digging or plowing up the same, and sowing thereon clover or other grass seeds, for procuring a green sward on the ground; or to improve some other way which shall be judged effectual.[29]

As a serving army officer Cathcart was infrequently in Ayr and very seldom after he inherited his father's estate and title in 1732. He died in 1740 on the voyage to America to take up his appointment as commander-in-chief of the British forces there. His lodgings in Ayr were rented by Sir John as his family home in the winter months and as business premises.[30] At the same time Colonel Nugent loaned Sir John £500 sterling.

By his wife Jean Douglas, Sir John had twenty children, only six of whom survived into adult life. These were three sons, John (the 12th born and second son so christened on 5 January 1720), Thomas (the 17th born 12 February 1726) and David (the 18th born 25 June 1727), and three daughters, Elizabeth (the 3rd born 3 November 1709), Anne (6th born 30 November 1712) and Clementina (13th born 26 December 1720). Elizabeth was to marry (in 1729) Sir John Cathcart, 2nd Baronet of Carleton who lived at Killochan on the Girvan Water. This alliance was no doubt intended to heal the breach between the two families as the Cathcarts had always taken the

LEFT

Killochan Castle by the Girvan Water in Ayrshire, photographed in the 1880s.

RIGHT

Kilhenzie castle, pronounced Kilhinny, which was the home of John Kennedy, the forebear of the present family of the Marquesses of Ailsa.

side of their neighbours, the Kennedys of Bargany, against the Kennedys of Culzean. If this was the intention, it was to turn out, after the death of the 10th Earl in 1794, a total failure. Anne married John Blair of Dunskey near Portpatrick in Wigtownshire in 1738 and Clementina, the youngest, married George Watson of Bilton Park, outside Harrogate in Yorkshire (date of marriage unknown). John Kennedy, the eldest son, was sent to school in Irvine to board with William Cunningham who provided him with a thorough grounding in the classics.[31] John and David both attended the University of Glasgow. John matriculated in 1735. His classmates included Andrew Fletcher of Saltoun, who was the son of Lord Milton, the Lord Justice Clerk, and was himself to become auditor of exchequer in Scotland.[32] The Kennedy family soon became close friends of the Fletchers.[33]

When he had completed his studies John seems to have joined his father in business in Ayr. His father, Sir John, died on 28 June 1742, leaving his estates to his eldest son, whom failing his next son Thomas, whom failing his third son David, whom failing the male issue of the marriage of his eldest daughter Elizabeth to Sir John Cathcart of Carleton. Of little importance at the time, this clause was to become very significant.[34] Sir John was buried with his forebears in the collegiate church at Maybole. His hearse was decorated with two large lozenge-shaped hatchments bearing his arms and surrounded by sixteen quarterings showing noble descent over four generations, painted by Roderick Chalmers, the Ross Herald. The guests were entertained with plain almond biscuits, common biscuits, two large seed cakes and no doubt a 'sufficiency' from the cellars.[35] His eldest son, the second Sir John, began at once to repair and alter the castle, ordering six hundred Easdale slates from John Nisbett, wright in Glasgow.[36] Easdale is an island south of Oban, which was noted for the quality of its roofing slates.

His mother, however, was allowed by agreement with her son, John (and later Thomas), to continue to occupy the castle for the remainder of her life.[37] Under the terms of her marriage settlement she already had the use of the furniture. This was listed in an inventory of 1743. She was given the green bed, feather bed and closet box along with the window curtains in the Green room; the washing bed, the feather bed, the pair of half chest of drawers, and foot stool in the fore room; with the curtains and the carpet, and the feather bed in the Lady's closet with their bolsters and pillows; the trunk in the mid-room; the second best table in the little dining room; and the timbers of a tent bed. These were supplemented by the:

> blanquets upon the Green room, the
> fore room, and closet beds with as many
> more of a middling kind as will make
> up twenty pairs. The twilt on the Green
> room bed and the two looking glasses in
> the Green room and fore room, one of
> the Chuff beds in the nursery, the chim-
> neys in the Green and fore rooms with

tongs, fire shovels, pockers and clad per-
taining thereto.

She was also left six chairs in the Yellow room, six chairs and an easy chair in the Green room and one dozen drinking glasses with a water jug. The Green and Yellow rooms were so called because of the colour of the bed hangings. The position of these rooms in the castle becomes clearer from later evidence. Lady Kennedy had a variety of kitchen utensils including a hogshead for working ale and a cooling tub.[38] It was stipulated in her marriage settlement that, although she was to have the use of the plate in the castle, if she chose to move out it remained the property of the family and she would be entitled only to one-third of its value. She was allowed at her own request to rent for the remainder of her life Turnberry Park and the Mains of Culzean or home farm and the adjoining Cowpark of about six hundred acres altogether which were towards the west of the castle.[39]

Under the terms of her husband's will, Lady Kennedy's second son Thomas, who was only sixteen and possibly already at the University of Glasgow, was left £1,000 for 'buying me a post or place or putting me into some business or employment'. Since he was a minor his father instructed that his mother, Sir James Fergusson Lord Kilkerran, a judge in the Court of Session, John Kennedy of Kilhenzie, an advocate, and Archibald Craufurd of Ardmillan should be appointed curators to look after his affairs.[40] In choosing them he struck a careful balance between the supporters of the Protestant succession (the Whigs) and the Jacobites (the Tories). They had little to do at first except to ensure that Thomas received the money left him.

For his part Thomas had already decided on a career. Shortly after his father's death he went to Major General Sir John Whitefoord of Blairquhan 'and acquainted him with my Inclination to serve in the Army this campaign' in the war of the Austrian succession.[41] Whitefoord suggested he purchase an ensigncy in Colonel John Johnson's 33rd regiment of footguards, which had recently served with distinction at Dettingen in June 1743. Taking this advice he was commissioned as an ensign into the regiment on 4 October 1744 and embarked for Flanders.[42] Lacking funds he was forced to hire his mounts.[43] He joined the regiment at Aix-la-Chapelle the following month and spent the winter in quarters at Maestricht. There was little activity during 1744 and for much of the year he simply moved around the country.[44] In these months of military inactivity, he became friendly with other serving officers of aristocratic descent, James Caulfield, Viscount (later 1st Earl) Charlemont; Henry Douglas, Earl Drumlanrig and son of the Duke of Queensberry; Lord Middleton; and the Honourable John Ward, later Viscount Dudley.[45]

The second Sir John signed a procuratory of resignation in April confirming the terms of his father's will that in the event of his death the estates should pass to his brothers, Thomas and David, and then through the female line. He died at the age of twenty-four on 10 April 1744, and the deed for some reason was not registered until 1747.[46] The inventory of his estate, which excluded all the property already held by his mother, provides some further clues as to the arrangement of the rooms in the castle. On the ground floor there were three rooms – a little dining room, a mid-room, and a north room. The dining room contained a clock and case, a Ferguson rotulo table, possibly the best table, and two brass branches, presumably to hold the candles to light the room. There appear to have been no chairs, suggesting that neither Sir John nor his mother were in the habit of eating there. The mid-room had a chest of drawers and cushions and the north room a tortoiseshell case and comb and a glass stand for sweetmeats, along with a card table in a cupboard. On the stairs up to the next floor were a glass cupboard and 'glass lorrys'. In the great hall or dining room there were portraits of Sir Archibald and his wife, Captain Douglas and his wife, and General Lesley (Leslie), Lord Newark, together with a 'deck for a sumpture horse'. It is possible from other evidence to conjecture that on

the second floor were the Green and Yellow rooms, Lady Kennedy's quarters. On the third floor was the Crimson room, the best furnished room in the castle which was obviously Sir John's living room and bedroom. It contained the Crimson bed with its flower covering along with mattresses and pillows, a tapestry wall hanging, a 'Japan' table, a green Windsor chair, an easy chair, six chairs, two footstools, chimney brasses, a large looking glass, two chamber pots and portraits of Sir Thomas, Sir John and his wife, and Lord Bargany. In the adjoining jamb room was a writing desk, screen and 'floor cloth' (carpet). On the fourth floor in the garret was an 'ark' (box) for feathers, a big wheel (presumably a Scots 'muckle' spinning wheel) and two family portraits. At the very top of the house in what was termed the 'high garret' were family letters and a small library of sixty-three books.

Outside the castle were the pantry, with a cellar beneath containing amongst other things a barrel of ale and a 'gelly' (jelly) pot. Alongside was a nursery and a secure closet and press containing the charter chest, the best pair of pistols, a silver handled sword, a barometer and a thermometer. There was a kitchen, a brewhouse, a bakehouse, a milkhouse which was also used for making cheese, the stable which housed the chaise, a little milkhouse used by the gardener to store tools and a barn which served as a stable.[47] Later evidence states there was also a high school and a 'laigh' school. Apart from his clothes, Sir John's principal assets in Cathcart's lodgings, his house in Ayr, were a dozen silver knives, forks, and spoons, a salver, candlesticks, a silver teapot, six china tea cups and saucers and five 'caffie [coffee] muggs', a variety of glassware and a very well-stocked cellar including champagne, Madeira, canary, mountain and white Lisbon, presumably his stock in trade as a wine and spirit merchant.[48] By the time of Sir John's death in 1744 the overall debt on the estate had been reduced from £80,000 Scots in 1710 to £33,000 Scots, of which the greatest proportion was a loan from the Earl of Cassillis, presumably advanced initially when Sir Archibald was in difficulty after 1690.

CHAPTER 3

The well-travelled man:

1744–75

With Sir John dead, it was left to the curators of his younger brother Sir Thomas, as he now was, to administer the Culzean estates. As it turned out this was a major undertaking as the property had been much neglected by the elder Sir John. The curators' first task was to appoint a reliable factor, whom they could trust. Although at pains to make it clear that he was prepared to leave the choice to his curators, Sir Thomas wrote from Holland proposing his father's factor John McIlvane. His mother, Lady Kennedy, supported this choice 'as it was amongst the last words his poor Brother spoak, desiring before us all who were present that John McIlvain [of Grimmet] might continue to act for his Brother as he had done for him'.[1] Her fellow curators disagreed most strongly and Lord Kilkerran replied tactfully:

Daldluff, the home of William Blane, now an excellent farm shop.

> There was all the Inclination in the World to gratify you in that matter all of them [the curators] being fully persuaded of his entire honesty and of his sincere good will to the family. But as the management of your affairs requires more skill than he can be supposed to have, It is the opinion of your curators that William Blane should be the Man.[2]

Blane owned a small estate at Dalduff on the road from Maybole to Crosshill and was the factor on Lord Kilkerran's own nearby estates. Blane knew all about the smuggling as did the curators, but they were prepared to turn a blind eye to it providing they got their share of Lisbon (port), claret and rum. Although Sir Thomas was happy with his curators' decision, he was not the least bit happy about the factor's terms of reference and wanted them (wisely as things turned out) extended to include the supervision of all the moveables in the castle. The curators were not keen, believing they would have troubles enough in managing the estate without having to become involved in family disputes about the furniture.[3] Lady Kennedy remained suspicious and insisted that Blane should be offered a salary of only £20 a year and invited McIlvane to become her partner in managing Turnberry Park and the Mains and Cow Park at Culzean.[4]

The delay in arranging for factoring the estates caused further deterioration. Lady Kennedy reported to Lord Kilkerran in June: 'I understand Everything is going to ruiny about Cullean, the servants being all gone off Except two having nothing to subsist on nor is ane of the sheep clipped either at Turnberry or Cullean Park with the grass become a common good.'[5] Directly the factoring was arranged William Blane set about putting the estate in order. He reported that the tenants were considerably in arrears and had difficulty in paying their rents as

'The Grain is generally bad in the County a great many people have Oats of which the horses will not eat and several People have Meall that when made in Pottage they vomit presently.' Consequently the curators had little money to discharge their obligations. One of their first actions, however, was to build a house for Scipio Kennedy, Sir John's freed 'slave', and his family inland from the castle where he could carry on his weaving trade. Scipio was by this time a trusted family servant, responsible for much of the cooking in the castle and this was reflected in the cost of his house, some £90 sterling.[6] Known as Scipio's Land, this was situated at about where the Camellia House now stands.[7] It quickly became a useful rendezvous for the smugglers.

Short of cash after his brother's death Sir Thomas borrowed from Thomas Dundas of Fingask, a prominent Edinburgh merchant with whom his father had done business, to cover his expenses while in Flanders. Between May and early October 1744, he had borrowed just over £213. By November Dundas wanted his money back as he had bills to pay in London and he applied to the curators for payment. Although Lord Kilkerran was of the opinion that 'Sir Thomas has called for money pretty liberally', he proposed that curators should find the necessary cash.[8] Not surprisingly William Blane shared this opinion:

The magnificent portrait of the young Captain Sir Thomas Kennedy painted by William Mosman, which hangs in the saloon at Culzean.

> Sir Thomas has no money and I under-
> stand expects to be pretty liberally sup-
> plied And really Company comes now
> and then to see him and he must go out
> to Visit his friends I believe your
> Lordship [Kilkerran] and the other
> curators will be of opinion he must have
> some allowance on that account As also
> for buying Horses (for he has none but
> Hirelings) and clearing some small
> accounts.[9]

Unable to raise the money from the rental of the estate, they negotiated a loan from the Royal Bank of Scotland.

At the same time Lady Kennedy and her third son David were 'in great want of money', as the curators had been unable to pay them their annuities with the affairs of the estate in such confusion.[10] David, just fifteen, had matriculated at Glasgow in 1742 with the intention of becoming an advocate like his uncle. He had in his class Sir Walter Maxwell of Pollok and his brother George, and John Moore, who was to become a leading surgeon and a distinguished literary figure in Glasgow. On his eldest brother's death in 1744, the £1,000 left by his father to Thomas to assist him in a career was to be passed by the trustees to him. After completing his studies at Glasgow in May 1744, David Kennedy planned to go to Edinburgh to train in law.

Before leaving Ayrshire, he holi-dayed for a fortnight on Arran 'to try how he agreed with the Goat milk or whey'. He was advised by his uncle David 'not to meddle' with the executory, even though he had an interest in his father's estate.[11] It was not until June 1745 that William Blane was able to find £50 to meet his and his mother's needs. David qualified as an advocate in 1752 'with very great applause'.[12] He was obviously an able scholar as he was quickly appointed an examiner by the Faculty of Advocates.[13] Later evidence suggests he was of a jovial disposition. His financial troubles and those of his mother were exacerbated when John McIlvane died in penury on 18 September 1745, leaving his aged father and an orphaned illegitimate daughter. Sir Thomas wrote emotionally to the family friend Lord Melton, beginning 'As we are not made for our-selves alone' and ending with a plea that the daughter be allowed to inherit her grandfather's Thomaston estate.[14]

Sir Thomas seems to have returned briefly to Culzean in February 1745. While there he wrote to the Earl of Loudoun seeking permission to dispose of his commission as an ensign and purchase a cap-

taincy, which was granted.[15] He was back in Flanders in time to take part in the battle of Fontenoy at the end of April in which the 33rd were in the thick of most of the fighting. For three hours they withstood the continual fire of three batteries. Sir Thomas was lucky to escape unscathed. Lt Colonel Clements was killed.[16] In early September his regiment was recalled home to meet the threat of the Jacobite rising. These journeys to the continent took him through London where he stayed with his cousin the Earl of Cassillis in his house in Albemarle Street where the dowager Lady Cassillis and her friend Lady Mordington kept an illegal gaming house.[17] In the late autumn Sir Thomas hurried to Culzean to attend to his affairs and help raise additional recruits. He was on his way to Newcastle by the end of October to join General Wade's forces, which were supposed to block the Jacobite army's route south; and he was a member of two companies which held Fort William for the Crown in the spring of 1746.

Back in Edinburgh Sir Thomas commissioned a full-length portrait of himself from the artist, William Mosman, which has been described as his 'most successful large-scale work'.[18] Mosman depicted Sir Thomas in nonchalant pose, interestingly holding Vauban's famous book *De l'attaque et de la défense des places* open at plate xiv showing plans for undermining fortifications.[19] Framed in the classical architrave in the background appears to be a scene from the campaign in Flanders. Vauban was fashionable reading amongst the military as along the border between Flanders and France his fortifications were everywhere to be seen. The imagery suggests that at this stage Sir Thomas had ambitions to continue his military career. If this were the case he changed his mind within a year, perhaps deterred by the vicious repression of the Jacobites in the wake of Culloden. He was back in Flanders in October but seems to have returned to Ayrshire in the spring of 1747. At home he became a non-operative member of the Masonic Lodge St John No. 11 in Maybole, to which his father and brothers also belonged. No records

of the lodge survive from before 1770. Although there were ninety-six members in 1776, the lodge did not meet frequently but always commemorated the feast of St John with a band playing and banners flying.[20]

On coming of age in 1747 Sir Thomas invited William Blane to continue as factor but he had to find a replacement for John McIlvane to manage his farms and those rented by his mother. He asked his friend and fellow mason, Archibald Kennedy, who was a wine and general merchant in Maybole, to be his overseer at a salary of £25 a year.[21] Realising this would be an onerous responsibility, he was at pains to ensure that, before accepting, Archibald consulted his family and friends, particularly his father, Hugh, who was the gardener at Culzean.[22] Archibald knew all about John McIlvane, as he had bought dried fruit, sago and cocoa from him as early as 1739.[23]

Having made up his mind, Archibald Kennedy moved into Culzean, occupying a bedroom in the garret and running his wine merchanting business and the smuggling activities from the castle. He already had a large wholesale and retail trade in rum, Lisbon, claret, spirits (presumably whisky), and Congo tea, most of which he ran from the Isle of Man, employing John Allan of Ballantrae as his intermediary.[24] Allan, who used Scipio's house as a meeting place with his customers at Culzean, acted as an agent for George Moore, a well-known Manx smuggler.[25] Not surprisingly Archibald Kennedy immediately ran up against Lady Kennedy, who resented this intrusion and did her best to undermine him. Nevertheless she regularly purchased contraband claret and Lisbon from him, as did Lord Kilkerran despite his legal office.[26] Under pressure Lady Kennedy did undertake to enclose the Mains at her own expense. William Blane reported in August 1748, 'There is nothing yet done to the Park of the Mains but if the Lady continues the same way disposed it will be fallen about in winter which is the best time for quarry stone.'[27] One of Archibald Kennedy's first duties was to fit up a billiard room alongside the 'little old stable'

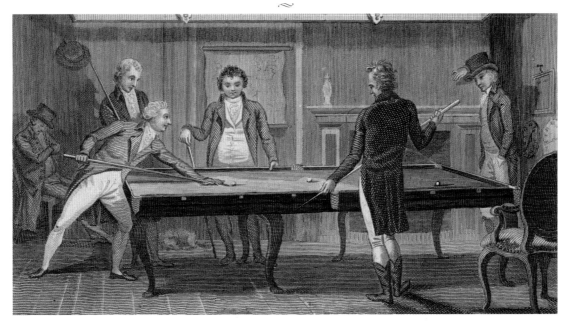

presumably the 'barn' in the 1744 inventory.[28] At the time billiards was played on a small square table with a cue shaped like a hockey stick held over the shoulder. It was then often played for large odds. There were different rules depending on the number of players and the number of balls, such as bricole, one game, four game, hazard (the most popular), and carambole – a French variant.[29]

Gentlemen playing billiards.

Sir Thomas, for his part, went away, but not before telling Archibald that he could call on the support of his uncle David, the advocate, and his aunt, the Countess of Eglinton, notwithstanding her disagreement with his father. During the summer of 1747 he stayed with his sister at Bilton Park in Yorkshire and then went to London before returning to Ayrshire. So as to avoid sharing the castle with his mother, he took the tack (lease) of the Holehouse, a large farm just at the gate of the castle. He warned Archibald Kennedy, 'I beg also as you are a brother Mason you will not let my intentions in this affair be in the least known to any person.'[30] By this time he had resolved to follow his father's example and complete his education abroad. He was particularly anxious to learn to play the bass viol, like his grandfather. He chose to attend l'Académie d'Équitation at Caen in Normandy.[31] There were several such academies in France at the time, which taught riding, fencing, music and languages.[32] They were popular with the British aristocracy as preparation for the grand tour to view the legacy of classical antiquity. Sir Thomas was in Edinburgh for Christmas and New Year 1747. With an eye to the future as the direct male heir to the earldom of Cassillis, Sir Thomas cautioned Archibald before leaving:

> I have one thing to recommend to you which is that you will take particular notice in looking through my papers if any there concern my Relation to the family of Cassillis and put them by themselves so as you can put your hand on them when you want them.[33]

He almost certainly had expectations as the 8th Earl of Cassillis, who had no children, had 'a high esteem' of him.[34] In the knowledge that the Cassillis title, if it descended through the male line, would pass from him to his brother David and then to the heirs of John Kennedy of Kilhenzie, Sir

Thomas in January 1748 signed a procuratory of resignation confirming that the Culzean estates should pass in like manner. This ran counter to his brother John's procuratory which had specified that after Sir Thomas and David the estate should pass through the female line.[35]

Sir Thomas sailed for Caen in August 1748. In Caen he appointed a man called Bulstrode as his tutor. Bulstrode was suspected of having strong Jacobite tendencies. He had been tutor to the Catholic George Talbot, 4th Earl of Shrewsbury, when he was in Italy from 1739 to 1741. Horace Walpole, the essayist, was suspicious of Bulstrode as 'not the most faithful', believing he might be trying to recruit his charge to Jacobitism. By the end of April 1740 Shrewsbury and Bulstrode were definitely moving in Jacobite circles. After Shrewsbury returned home, Bulstrode remained in France at Boulogne to act as tutor to Shrewsbury's younger brothers, both of whom were to become Catholic priests.[36] It is unlikely that he would have dared to come to Britain after the 1745 rising. Presumably he remained in France on the look out for possible impressionable charges. Caen, as a Channel port, was strategically placed. He seems not to have mastered a great deal of the language, as his letters recommending Sir Thomas Kennedy were written in appalling 'English schoolboy French'. Grandly calling himself De Bulstrode and describing the academy as 'L'Académie Royalle a Caen', he penned a letter to the chamberlain of King Louis XV, Marquis d'Albergaty, in March 1750:

> recommender Le Chevalier Kennedy qui vous sere charmer de connitre et come il est de mes amis j'ay croit que il ae pouvoir mieux m'ademer qu'avons qui est portée d'inclination a obliger les votre. C'est un amateur de musique et La bonne compagnie et come cela se trouve dans notre ville et que personne n'en fait mieux les honneurs vous m'obligera beaucoup de Le produire partout.

In an accompanying open letter he wrote:

> Je suis persuader que mon amy sera goutée par ces attentions et pollitesses pour Le beau Saxes. Il l'a l'agrement de savoir La Musique et de jouer de La Basse de Violle cela lui donner un autre plus Libres dans Les compagnies qui en sont amateurs.[37]

There is no record of whether these introductions had any effect, but Sir Thomas was in Paris from March to April 1750 and does seem to have become an accomplished viol player.

While in France, Sir Thomas fretted about his estate, his brother David, and his cellar, which he hoped would be well stocked with rum. Archibald Kennedy was unable to provide comfort about David's affairs – 'I have a fresh demand from your brother who is no small expense at present.'[38] However he reassured him – 'And your cellar shall be well stocked with the Best of Rum according to desire'.[39] In August 1748 William Blane wrote gleefully that the smugglers had suffered a setback:

> Some of [them] have had a misfortune by their Isle of Man Trade within this two weeks. Wm. McClure as I am informed has lost between £40 and £50, Wm. Arthur in Cullean Mill about £30, Robert Graham about £8 or £10, David Leermont about £15 and Archibald Kennedy about £20 and all by the Irish cruisers. I wish it could have the effect to make them quit the Trade in which case this misfortune might prove a benefit to them.

He added – 'Some quantities of grasshoppers have been seen in England', but he hoped that 'our climate will not agree with them'.[40] This letter confirms that there was a whole network of smugglers resident on the estate. William McClure of Drumbeg (just below Turnberry) and his sons

Archibald, John and Thomas were notorious smugglers. John had a wine and spirit business in Alloway, similar to that of Archibald Kennedy. Robert Graham was involved in other ventures. The reference to the Irish cruisers is to excise cutters recently deployed in the Irish seas for just this purpose. Archibald Kennedy's customers included Sir Thomas's brother-in-law Sir John Cathcart of Killochan, the Reverend James Laurie of Kirkoswald, who confined his purchases to claret, and Dr Bannerman of Maybole.[41]

Sir Thomas wrote regularly to Archibald Kennedy telling him 'to preserve the Gaim and fishing on my grounds' and to punish 'all offenders without fear or favour'.[42] In his absence Archibald annually paid seven pence apiece for the harvesting

Culzean by moonlight painted by Alexander Nasmyth in the early nineteenth century, depicting smugglers landing contraband from a wherry at Seggenwell.

of solan geese (gannets) which he sold through his business.[43] Sir Thomas asked his brother-in-law, Sir John Cathcart, to look out for a good pointer or setter for him in return for which he would obtain 'the best fowling piece that can be bought at Paris or London'. He reminded Archibald Kennedy to lay in casks of 'the best rum'.[44]

His main concern was to find ways of increasing the income of the estate either through agricultural improvement or by exploiting any minerals. With the growth in demand for dairy products from Glasgow and its surrounding towns and for beef cattle from England since the Union, estate improvements were fashionable, particularly the enclosure of fields, the planting of shelter-belts, the abolition of strip cultivation and the application of lime, marl and organic fertilisers.[45] Strip cultivation, which evolved throughout Europe in the middle ages, was known in Scotland as 'runrig'. In this method of farming the arable land or 'infield' was divided up into rigs or strips separated by furrows which sometimes but not always acted as primitive drainage ditches. The crops grown on each rig were rotated every year to prevent over-cultivation. So as to ensure that all tenants shared the best land rigs were also rotated between them. This handicapped improvement as, unless all the tenants agreed, there was a real danger of conflict. On the higher ground, which made up a good proportion of the estate, most of the farms were in permanent pasture. Sir Thomas and Archibald Kennedy amalgamated farms into larger units, encouraged where possible the application of lime and the rotation of crops, and supported the production of black cattle for which Carrick had an enviable reputation.[46] The bullocks, fattened on lowland pasture in other parts of the estate, were driven to England to be sold when they were four years old.

They could not develop the Mains or Home Farm, immediately adjacent to the castle, as it was in the hands of Lady Kennedy. The hill land around Thomaston immediately inland from Culzean was Sir Thomas's and it was here he concentrated his attention at first. The ground was enclosed with new stone dykes.[47] Again his mother interfered, summoning Jim Scott, an engineer working at Kilkerran, to explore for coal late in 1750. In January of the following year Archibald Kennedy reported that he had found 'as good Lymestone as in Scotland and is assured of marls', which were used as a fertiliser. Archibald Kennedy cautioned that no pits should be dug until Sir Thomas returned.[48] Later in that year he was happy to announce that 'the salt pans [at Dougalston in the Maidens] have gone on all summer and we have plenty of fine salt'.[49]

Since he had decided to make his main home at Culzean rather than Ayr, Sir Thomas was also concerned about the garden and policies. He had already decided to provide a pleasing prospect from the house by planting the deer park opposite the terraces with trees and shrubs, as it was 'for no other use'.

> On my return I suppose there will be a greater demand for a well-plenished garding than there has been for these several years past from which reason I would have him [Archibald Kennedy's father] begin to furnish it as soon as possible with the things that can be raised in a year or two such as Fruit Trees, Sparagrass [asparagus] and many other things that must be in the ground some years before reaping the advantage of them.[50]

With this in mind the walled garden was repaired and enlarged and the long brick wall at the foot of the terraces lengthened.[51] Within the walled garden a 'garden chamber',[52] presumably a summer house, was built and walks laid out – the gravel walk and Dovecot walk which terminated at a new dovecote to supplement the one at Thomaston.[53] This seems to have been situated at what is now Piper's Brae. A nursery garden for growing on trees and shrubs was also created.[54] David Limont supplied the new garden with bee hives.[55]

Sir Thomas was displeased when his mother countermanded or altered these instructions and went so far as to suggest Archibald was drinking to excess. He was even more annoyed when Archibald Kennedy did not reply promptly to his letters: 'It is now eight months since I had the pleasure of hearing from you which does not little astonish me, as I was exact in answering your last'.[56] Despite the provocation he advised his factor that he was not keen to confront his mother: 'to write to my lady about it I am persuaded would rather do hurt than good'.[57] By October 1749 when he had been away for sixteen months, he was irritated that his mother had never bothered to communicate despite his writing to her 'several times'.[58] Matters began to

resolve themselves the following year with the death of William Blane, whose affairs were found to be in chaos.[59] Sir Thomas appointed Archibald Kennedy his factor with 'power to uplift the rents of my estate and to count with my Tennents for the same but also to turn out such tennents as are not able to pay'.[60] The power to evict unsuitable tenants suggests that improvement was very much uppermost in his mind. Archibald at once set about sorting out the estate papers which were in confusion. He got his own back on Lady Kennedy by firing a cannon repeatedly on Sir Thomas's birthday on 12 February 'three glasses of good strong punch intervening between each fire', no doubt confirming her suspicion that he was a dangerous alcoholic. Three days later he reported:

Lord Kilkerran, one of the trustees of Sir Thomas Kennedy, later the 9th Earl.

As to Mr Blane's circumstances they appear more and more gloomy every day … I believe the effects will not answer a third of the principal sums. This was strange a thing as has happened in our days for the week before he died The Great Lord Kilkerran would have lent him £500 upon a simple bill* if he had required it and from these you may judge what others would have done.[61]

By January 1750 Sir Thomas was also planning major building works, beginning with the demolition of 'Japie's' house on the cliff to the north-west

*Bills of Exchange were the principal negotiable financial instruments of the time.

of the castle: 'I desire your good order as much as will be necessary for the casting of Japie's house as I shall ocation for it the next spring for to build stables with'.[62] These new stables can be clearly seen in the drawing of Culzean by John Clerk of Eldin.[63] The entrance to the castle was across the causeway and then round and under a new tower in the centre of the stable block. (This tower gate survives, modified by Robert Adam and his brothers.) So as to facilitate access the old plane tree that stood in the courtyard was felled.[64] Sir Thomas also decided to convert the ground floor of the tower house into two dining rooms, a large one for entertaining and a smaller one for day-to-day use.[65] This involved demolishing the partition wall between the little dining room and the mid-room to make a space equivalent in size to the great hall on the floor above. The old North room was converted into a little dining room. He seems to have returned home briefly in April 1750 and appointed 'Mr Clyton' as his 'undertaker' for the project. This was probably Thomas Clayton, who had worked on several houses designed by the Adam brothers, such as Dumfries House near Cumnock. Archibald Kennedy did not believe he made much out of the contract as 'after about two months work the whole roof came down about their ears'. Convinced that the ceiling 'may stand to forturity as it is better fixed', he reported that the large dining room was finished before Christmas and 'my Lord Eglintoun being here at the time was rightly well pleased and much taken with the Execution of the work'.[66] He added as a footnote:

> There are grand Golf Matches at Girvan
> every fortnight. The parties generally are
> Bargandy [Bargany], Ardmillan,
> Penmore [Pinmore], Mr Cathcart, the
> Minister, and Doctor Bannerman, which
> occasions harmony and friendship and
> Sir John is judge of fair play at that and
> the drinking, there are after complaints
> ffor the most part of the next day of
> sore heads and great druiths [thirst].

He also reported that: 'Robberies and breaking of houses in this country were never as frequent and if doors and windows are impregnable they venture down the chimney vents'.[67] Little is known about the interior design of the large dining room, except that it had two big windows looking out across the terraces and 'big' doors.[68] Since Sir Thomas was in Italy, nothing was done to furnish these rooms.

So as to be able to prepare the food for the many guests expected in the new dining room on Sir Thomas's return, the kitchens were remodelled and enlarged and repairs carried out to the 'Crimson' and 'Green' rooms.[69] The work on the kitchen involved the construction of a completely new oven which required no fewer than 2,000 bricks.[70] The old upstairs dining room became a drawing room where Sir Thomas could hang his growing collection of pictures. At the same time he instructed Archibald Kennedy to tell his father to 'transplant all the barren and bad kind of fruit trees and put new ones in their place'.[71] Taking him at his word Archibald Kennedy's father stocked the new garden with fruit trees purchased from the gardener at Dalquharran in the Girvan valley.[72] The terraces were planted with herbaceous and annual plants such as chrysanthemums, double poppies, yellow lupins, pheasant eye pinks, sweet peas, gillyflowers (stocks), marigolds, candytuft, sunflowers, larkspur, and Sweet Williams.[73] To help pay for these improvements, Sir Thomas called in his debts which included an advance of £700 to his aunt, the Countess of Eglinton. Unable to pay in cash she gave him the Citadel in Ayr, the old Fort of St John.[74] By 1790 it had 'a large kiln and brewery in it'.[75]

Sir Thomas also encouraged Archibald Kennedy to push ahead with estate improvements. During the winter of 1751–2 Ayrshire had experienced 'a terrible dearth the victuals being so scarce in the County that your Tenants were obliged to buy all their meal from the seed time until the harvest last … This occasioned a scarcity of money among them.' For those who lived near the coast matters were made worse by the failure of the

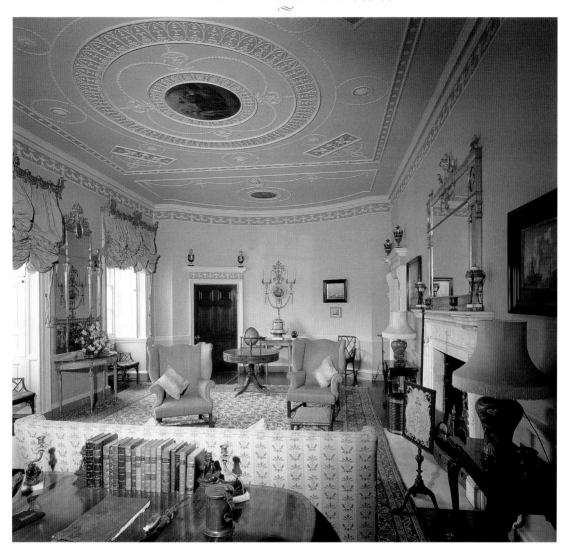

herring fishings on which they depended to supplement their income.[76] Archibald Kennedy's response was to break the tacks [leases] on some of the more fertile ground and begin the difficult process of improvement, which required the goodwill of the tenantry to be successful.

After he left Paris in May 1750, Sir Thomas travelled to Italy to see the sights and join his friends from his time in the army. He was in Turin for most of the summer before journeying on to Milan. For the first six months of the following

The old eating room at Culzean. This room was created in 1750 by Sir Thomas Kennedy as his new dining room with spectacular views to the south over the terraces. It was simply redecorated by Robert Adam in fashionable style.

year he was in Rome,[77] probably resident at least for part of the time with his fellow Scot, Abbé Peter Grant. The Abbé has been described as 'an amiable busybody ever anxious to attend the more distinguished British travellers' and was long suspected of Jacobite sympathies.[78,79] In 1773 Isaac Jamieson, the British consul in Naples, dubbed him 'a damned rascal' and 'a Scotch Rebel' for introducing British visitors to the Young Pretender.[80] Sir Thomas's fellow house guest was Viscount Stormont, the son of the Earl

of Mansfield.[81] Sir Thomas certainly flirted with Catholicism, obtaining a plenary indulgence from Pope Benedict XIV (1740–58) for himself and fifty relatives. This did not preclude him from worldly pursuits. He laid a bet in April 1751 about the possibility of shipping contraband wine from Scotland. Archibald Kennedy hurriedly arranged for Captain Clerk to dispatch the necessary consignment 'which I hope shall come safely, if it does you will certainly clear your wager'. To reassure Sir Thomas that he was not the only one enjoying all the excitement, Archibald Kennedy added 'Mr Hamilton of Bargany was here about two nights, with your brother about ten days agoe and very merry when good Dr Bannerman was fairly laid aside.'[82]

A view of Ayr by Slezer showing the Citadel.

In May 1751 Sir Thomas, Lord Middleton, and the Honourable John Ward were visiting palaces in Rome under the tutelage of their friend Lord Charlemont. According to another member of their circle, John Phelps, they also 'made our musical Academy twice every week to be adorn'd by the English Students in Sculpture & paintings who were invited to send in their best Works. Our Room was soon fill'd greatly to the Credit of the several Artists, some of whom I think cannot failt to do honour to their Country in both these Arts.'[83] While there Sir Thomas purchased 'Pyranesi's' [Piranesi's] *Views of Rome*, Raphael's *Gallery of Psyche*, *Musea Capitoloni*, the *Book of Statues*, *Archi Trionfabi*, *Agro Romani*, and prints of the sculptures in the Palazzo Verospi.[84] More mundanely he bought feather ribbons, white shoes and a Swiss ball. He and his friends decided they should participate in the Whitsuntide carnival 'when Masquing in the streets is carried on by Nobility here to a great degree of Magnificence. It was resolv'd that we ought to briller [dazzle] for the honour of our Country, & a Triumph of British Liberty was agreed upon for the subject.' The tableau was to be staged on a 'Triumphal Car' drawn by four horses, with Lord Bruce taking the leading part of Liberty. Sir Thomas portrayed Virtue wearing a helmet and a close-fitting taffeta vest with John Ward on his left as Truth in a transparent robe with 'her Haird flowing negligently over her shoulders'.[85]

During the year Joshua Reynolds included Sir Thomas in his well-known *Parody of the School of Athens*. Here he is depicted in the Pythagorean

group on the left playing a treble viol along with Charlemont and Phelps in what seems to be a direct reference to the musical academy.[86] Later in a caricature based on the *Parody*, Reynolds depicted him as a violist with his friend John Ward, who was not in the original painting. This time Reynolds poked fun at their origins, by painting Charlemont, an Irish peer, with bunch of shamrock in his hat, Ward with a rose, Kennedy with the badge of St Andrew and Phelps, a Welshman, with a huge leek.[87] P.L. Ghezzi also painted Sir Thomas as a violist with his friend John Ward and Pancrazi dedicated a plate in his *Architita Siciliane* to 'Sigre Tommasso Kennedy Baroneto Scozzese'. A love of music was to remain with him for the rest of his life. On returning to Scotland he joined the exclusive Edinburgh musical society after it had enlarged its membership in 1752.[88] He subscribed ten guineas towards the cost of constructing the Society's St Cecilia's Hall in the 1760s.[89]

The plenary indulgence obtained by Sir Thomas.

Sir Thomas left Rome in July 1751 and went to Viterbo, travelling on to Siena and Livorno (Leghorn) in October and arriving in Florence in December. He was in Venice in January 1752, returning to Rome in April when he laid a wager:

Lord Charlemont and Sir Thomas Kennedy are to produce each of them horse mare or gelding to be brought at any price not exceeding forty pounds to run a match in the Isle of Man for one hundred pounds on the first Tuesday in July 1755 one heat, four miles, weight ten stone; play or pay.[90]

This is a reference to the Isle of Man Derby, a precursor of the modern Derby, which was run near Castletown from the late seventeenth century.[91] There is no record of whether Charlemont or Kennedy entered a horse in the race in that year.

During that year the factor did, however, enter one of Sir Thomas's horses in a race for a saddle at Kirkoswald.[92]

In May 1752 Sir Thomas went to Tivoli and then to Naples. He was back in Rome in October when James Russell depicted him in his painting of *British Connoisseurs* standing in front of the Colosseum. Sir Thomas appears on the left talking to Charlemont, along with Charles Turner, Sir William Lowther, Thomas Steavens, and Lord Bruce. He left Rome in November for a repeat visit to Leghorn and Florence where he purchased prints, copies of old masters and 'ten cases of statuary', presumably to decorate his new rooms.[93] These did not arrive at Culzean until 1756. Altogether he acquired ten paintings depicting Venus, town dancing, Sansouvine's Bacchus, a group of wrestlers, Venus bathing her feet, an idol

Parody of the School of Athens by Joshua Reynolds, which was painted in 1751 as a skit on Raphael's School of Athens and depicts Sir Thomas Kennedy playing the viol in the group on the left.

of bronze, Mercury, a listening slave or grinder, Ganymede, and group of Cupid and Puck.[94] He visited Vienna in January 1753 and by June he was on his way to Capri. John Ward commented to Charlemont about this trip:

As Sir Thomas loves the sea and shooting, I fear he'll stay there so long that he'll forget his English likewise. In that case the Abbé du Bois* must look out for another corrector of the Press for the English part of his works.[95]

*Abbé du Bois is a shadowy figure, who seems to have acted as tutor in Italian to Charlemont's circle of friends. He was also included by Reynolds in the *Parody of Athens* where he is depicted engaged in some literary enterprise (see O'Connor, *The Pleasing Hours*, p. 128).

This suggests that he had no intention of going home for the present. It is not known if Bulstrode accompanied him during these Italian excursions, but he was in Italy in 1753 as he was painted out hunting with other Jacobites.[96]

Relations between Sir Thomas and his mother remained strained. In her will drawn up in 1751, which she indiscreetly let Archibald Kennedy see, she left Sir Thomas only £40 to pay for the enclosure of the Mains which she had failed to do, and the rest of her property, including all her livestock, she bequeathed with some small exceptions to her only other surviving son David.[97] In the summer of 1753 Lady Kennedy vacated the castle in high dudgeon and went to live at Barnton outside Edinburgh with her daughter Anne who was married to John Blair of Dunskey.[98] She took with her 'no less than seven feather beds, seven bolsters, and about 20 pillows'.[99]

British connoisseurs in Rome, showing Lord Charlemont on the far left talking to Sir Thomas Kennedy.

Many of these furnishings she was entitled to under the terms of her marriage settlement, but her husband and sons could never have imagined that she would remove them. She contravened the agreement with her sons by taking all the family plate when she had agreed to accept a payment of one-third the value as compensation in the event of her leaving the castle. Archibald Kennedy noted bitterly:

What devastation this removing has made upon the house is Intolerable, she has indeed left some things of no great avail … You have not a chair in the whole house you can sett down upon and for feather beds, bolsters, pillows, blankets, sheets and table Linnen I need speak of nothing but poverty and it will be some time before these defects can be

supplied. I have the whole house to white wash in the roofs, the pannellings are to be cleaned, the staircase to be plaistered & whitened & Gods knows what.[100]

Sir Thomas was clearly not willing to incur too much expenditure, as Archibald wrote again on 21 June:

the house of Cullean is not very commodious for lodging many Company. I would propose out of the old broken furniture at Cullean to make up as many chairs, tables and Tent beds as will furnish it and this I think I may do with little expense and have it readie for you against your return.[101]

Cleaning the castle during the summer uncovered far more serious problems than Archibald had anticipated:

Some of the artefacts purchased by Sir Thomas, photographed by the 3rd Marquess in the 1880s.

OPPOSITE
Lady Anne Blair, sister of Sir Thomas Kennedy, with whom his mother went to live.

But God only knows what will be done with your office house, your Bake House won't stand until you return, the Brewhouse I have thatched it this summer but it is very Crazy. The high school where the men sleep is rather worse, the Laigh school was blown down long agoe and altogether exhibited but a very melancholy view but of all of these I will mention nothing further if you may think on them qu [when] you come home. As you will have a great deal to doe about the house and a good deal of timber will be needed and that of necessity you must have ffor whole roof of the big house must goe off as the Sarking is all gone and I wish yt [that] it may stand till your arrival and that it will take at least 2,000 to 3,000 dales [deals] besides fir planks and as you will have a good deal of building to do I would propose that in the spring when the Norway and

Denmark ships goe about for Timber if I can find any one or two of the countrey that want here Timber to Join them for you and bring home such a quantity as I'll be advised you'll want yourself.[102]

Sir Thomas was not to be hurried and began to investigate other ways of improving the house and surrounding buildings which were still standing. His first proposals were to convert 'the nursery into a dining room for servants and the high school for the women' and to build for his own use 'a little house betwixt the old one and the windows look to the sea'. On exploring these ideas Archibald Kennedy supported the first two but the construction of the little house he found 'impossible to be done ffor from the inside of the wall towards the precipice is scarce two foot from the precipice'. He suggested instead that the existing office house should be demolished and replaced with a much larger building.[103] The condition of the building can not have been helped by 'terrible storms of wind, hail, rain, lightening, and thunder this winter (1753–4) the like almost never heard of in this season'.[104]

With his mother intent on leaving Culzean, Sir Thomas could now think about returning to Ayrshire. In March 1753 Archibald Kennedy let him know he had prepared his bolthole: 'I have set up three beds in the three upper rooms of the Holehouse which are so contrived you may move them where you will at pleasure.'[105] He also fitted up sixteen stables probably for race horses.[106] His market for wine and spirits now extended over a good deal of southern Ayrshire and in addition to established customers included numerous hostelries.[107] During the year Sir Thomas instructed Archibald to buy clandestinely a wherry in the Isle of Man, presumably so that they would be less dependent on John Allan. Unfortunately Archibald was forced to reveal the identity of the purchaser;

As to the wherry you mention I was obliged of necessity to reveal the secret of

buying one for your use to persons who I am sure will keep it and who are part owners in one I am thinking may answer your purpose. She is 24 tons burden, built last year for the Isle of Man trade but stout and well rigged, goes well and has a long boat.

Her prime cost was £166 and Archibald thought she could be got for £200. At present she was employed in the fisheries off the North Cape. There is no record as to whether the transaction went ahead but the evidence of the scale of their smuggling activities would suggest they probably had their own boat.[108] Temptingly Archibald Kennedy reported to Sir Thomas that 'we have gott plenty of oysters at the Maidenhead a thing never heard of before in our country'.[109] In the event Sir Thomas set out for home in the autumn when he had received definite news of his mother's departure, going by way of Rome, Geneva, Dresden and Paris. He was in London by mid-March 1754 where he remained for the rest of the year.

While there he purchased all manner of goods for his empty house. Archibald had already told him to buy table and bed linen in London, as there was a greater choice than in Scotland, but he also sent a list of things considered necessary for the large dining room. In March he had proposed buying in Edinburgh for the dining room 'glasses and sconces' and 'two looking glasses one for the Jamb and another for the mid room'.[110] In the event and on the instructions of Sir Thomas's uncle David, he only purchased the looking glasses for the large dining room and a dozen chairs for the little dining room, leaving Sir Thomas to buy in London the glassware and to 'gett a sett of china dishes and saucers for Breakfast and afternoon Tea, a sett of coffee and chocolate cups and saucers with slop bowls …'[111] In May he had already sent north two tent beds and a box of silver knives.[112] All the copper kitchen utensils were nevertheless bought locally.[113] With the prospect of his imminent return Archibald Kennedy wrote reassuringly:

I have white washed all your house and stair case from top to bottom and have cleaned all your bed heads and curtains and washed all the panellings with hot water and soap and made all as clean as possible.[114]

He used 'Irish lyme' to paint the outside of the castle.[115] He also hired two kitchen maids (Elizabeth Johnstone and Janet McClymont) at thirty shillings a year and two gardeners who had to sleep in the billiard room and lived partly on potatoes and gleanings from the garden.[116] Fully laden Sir Thomas arrived home early in 1755 after an absence of almost eight years.[117]

On his return, Sir Thomas began in earnest to exploit such minerals as there were on his properties and to make improvements to the estate, including the enclosure of open 'outfield' ground and the construction of new farmhouses.[118] Directly Lady Kennedy moved out, Archibald Kennedy contracted experts to resume the search for minerals, including the Earl of Eglinton's coal grieve, who 'I hear has good skill'.[119] The only workable deposits were found at Dalziellily or Dalzellowie on the Craigoch estate. There was some dispute about the ownership of the deposits, as the Kilhenzie estate had been purchased in 1749 by Lord Kilkerran, although an exception had been made of the coal and coal-heughs on the forty-shilling land of Craigoch. Since the seams broke through the surface of the ground, they were easily set alight and shortly after the sale, the herd of the tenant of Craigoch accidentally started a fire which continued for more than thirty years and led locals to call the place 'Burning Hills'.[120] Despite the danger of fire and doubts about ownership, the coal workings were leased to a David Cuming to exploit at a rental of £50 a year together with the supply of coal to Culzean.[121]

In 1754 William Graham of Douglaston, tacksman of the saltpans at the Maidens, died. The inventory of his estate included 'a sufficient well-going Pann with a sufficient Bukkie Pott, a whirle barrow and a pan bucket with three iron hoops'.[122] Sir Thomas took the works into his own hands. John Innes, late tidesman and (salt) officer at Turnberry, was appointed manager and his father and brother-in-law 'makers of salt'. Innes was certainly implicated in the smuggling at the castle, but had been dismissed from the excise service because of his Jacobite leanings. The collector of customs at Ayr had reported to the Board of Excise in 1752:

> I have since had occasion to speak with Mr Hugh Hamilton, minister of Girvan, … he told me that he did not choose to write in so ticklish an affair but that … James Innes (salt officer at Turnberry) is strongly suspected of disaffection and has been known several times to drink the health of the young Pretender, by the name of Charlie Jamieson, and that he is a person of very infamous and immoral character.

The collector of customs could find no tangible evidence of these allegations, but reported that Innes was a 'very good friend of the smugglers with whom he is remarkable intimate …' It was probably for this reason rather than his Jacobite sympathies that he was dismissed.[123]

The following year Archibald Kennedy and the McClures suffered a further blow to their trade when in April John McClure, the Alloway wine and spirit merchant, unsuccessfully attempted to reland a large consignment of wine and spirits for customers at Culzean, Drumbeg, Ayr and Loans, near Irvine. On leaving the Isle of Man the boat had been driven towards the Irish coast, where it had been intercepted by smugglers from Donaghadee who captured it. Kennedy lost two hogsheads of wine* which George Moore had promised him:[124]

*Hogsheads were unusually large casks for the smuggling trade. Most smugglers preferred to ship in 'ankers', small barrels which a man could carry.

I've been speaking to Archibald McClure who is now here about your two hogsheads of wine which he relanded and telling him that an opportunity offered whereby to forward them he advised as best not to miss it I have therefore delivered said two hogsheads this day filled up into the care of John McClure of Alloway who gives me assurance of his diligence etc.[125]

Kennedy along with the other customers refused to pay for goods they had not received and which, as far as they were concerned, had been lost by John McClure's negligence. Eventually Moore was forced to relent and offered Kennedy a dozen bottles of his best Lisbon or claret on settlement of his account of £36.[126]

Much of the Culzean estate was hill ground stretching south-east down to the borders of Wigtownshire and Lanarkshire and only suitable for summer grazing. The next of Sir Thomas's estate improvements seems to have been concentrated on the lower, more fertile lands along the coast and up the valleys where black beef cattle could be pastured. Reputedly their condition was poor, and such husbandry as there was both unproductive and inefficient with little crop rotation and no enclosures. Since Archibald Kennedy was not a farmer, John Foulis was recruited as farm overseer

Part of the plan of the Culzean estate drawn for Sir Thomas Kennedy by John Foulis in 1755. The walled garden beneath the castle can be seen clearly. The Cow Park became the site of the Swan Pond.

OPPOSITE

The cottages in the main street at Straiton, which were built as part of his improvements by the 9th Earl of Cassillis in the 1760s.

for the property around Culzean.[127] He lived near Elintone and his father, also John, was the factor to the Earl of Eglinton. He conducted a survey of all the fields, reporting on their condition and their soil. This information was marked on an elaborate estate map drawn up by Foulis in 1755. Two years later, Foulis's father was commissioned to report on the condition of the Greenan estate, which Sir Thomas had recently acquired. His lengthy response was as much a commentary on the whole improvement movement as on the property:

When a gentleman proposes to grant a lease of his Estate or any considerable part thereof for all his life – Three things are to be maturely weighed – The Abilities of his Tenant to be contracted with – The Probable value of the lands to be set and the condition the Lands are to be left in at the Expiry of the leases.

The most eligible method of attaining these great aims of a larger Rent; and Land put in good order seems to be, That Both Master & Tenant contribute thereto in their several spheres.

He continued by describing the lands of Greenan as in very poor condition, 'lying open' to the winds,

'fences decayed', over-cropped and consequently 'hardly worth the present rent'. He recommended 'inclosure and division' 'into proper parks' of between a hundred and a hundred and sixty acres and regular liming. Since much of the pasture was infested with perennial weeds such as 'sorrel, docks, rag weed, couch grass, clownswort (butterwort), knotgrass, pimpernel and thistles', he proposed close cropping with sheep. He favoured stone dykes to hedges, which take several years to mature and 'considerable expense in the upholding and cleaning for the first six or seven years. In concluding his rhetoric ran away with him:

The elevation of a design for a 'Casine' designed for Sir Thomas Kennedy by William Chambers in 1759. This was never built.

> Here is a Bible to the covetous; for
> where can even the greedy get so much
> without exerting his foot or losing an
> hours Rest for it – But still here is much
> higher encouragement to the Benevolent
> heart and the Man of Taste, to whom
> this Memorial is addressed, who at the
> same time he advances his own Interest
> considerably; ornaments and enriches

> his County, gives bread to the poor and
> hungry – and secures or rather by his
> Generosity Creates, an estate to his
> Posterity …
>
> The generality of Landlords,
> who have attempted raising great
> Rents from their Estates only by
> their mighty Fiat; have only met
> with payments as slight as their
> improvements were: Their paper
> and ink improvement was paid in
> paper and ink rents.[128]

The minister of Kirkoswald recalled in the early 1790s that John Foulis junior put his father's advice to good effect:

> About twenty years ago, the husbandry
> of this parish underwent a total and
> happy revolution. The farms were
> straightened, and they began to be
> enclosed and subdivided with ditch and
> hedge. Almost, in the course of ten
> years, the farms in the whole parish,
> were thus inclosed and divided. The

sheep were entirely banished; and instead of five or six mean looking horses, every farmer got four horses, each of them equal in strength to two of the former ones, with a cart horse to each.[129]

Liming was encouraged and strict crop rotation introduced. The minister's memory was not quite accurate as these events had occurred at least thirty years before. Despite his claims, Foulis was not entirely successful in extinguishing the runrig system of strip cultivation on the arable lands near the coast, but he did plant shelter belts which improved yields. There was marked but isolated resistance to improvements in the south-west, with bands of so-called 'levellers' pulling down the dykes which enclosed the new fields. Landowners had, therefore, to proceed with caution to avoid protest, which in the long run might be counter-productive. Sir Thomas also improved his properties in the Girvan valley around the village of Straiton which itself was completely rebuilt.[130]

In 1755 Sir Thomas purchased land alongside

The house with the pillars was Sir Thomas Kennedy's town house in Maybole. The dining room at the rear has spectacular views across to the Carrick Hills. It was later owned by Robert Burns's friend William Niven and now serves as a branch of the Bank of Scotland.

the back vennel in Maybole to build a modern Palladian villa presumably as a winter retreat. Sir Thomas commissioned a design from James Adam but it is not known if his drawings were used in the final building, which still stands and is now the Bank of Scotland in the town. At the rear it has a half octagon drawing room with magnificent views across a walled garden to the Galloway hills. Later, in 1759, Sir Thomas was persuaded by his friend and mentor, Lord Charlemont, to invite Sir William Chambers to design a detached banqueting house which was half the size of Adam's house. Chambers also supplied drawings of a simple 'casine' 'commanding four fine views' unimpeded by porticoes.[131] Although the dimensions of this less expensive building coincide with those of Sir Thomas's later extension to Culzean, it is not known if it was intended for Culzean itself. It is conceivable that it was built on the top of Craiglure Hill* overlooking Loch Lure (now incorporated

*This lodge was abandoned by the 1st Marquess of Ailsa in favour of a more convenient site nearer to the road. The site is still visible on the top of Craiglure Hill.

within Loch Bradan) in the hills above Straiton. It appears in pencil outline on the plan of the southern part of the barony of Straiton drawn up in 1765 and the ruins can still be seen in the trees above the Loch Bradan car park and picnic site.[132] There is no doubt that in all his many building operations Sir Thomas was obsessed by vistas.

The planting of the new garden at Culzean started in December 1755 but was disrupted by 'violent storms' which persisted into the New Year. The first task was to plant a shelter belt from Little Hogstoun on the south-east of the castle to Scipio's land. No sooner had the work been completed than 'some malicious persons pulled up several of them and also cutt some Oaks in the Deer Park'. Furious that the 'levellers' were at work in the parish, Archibald Kennedy 'made advertisement at the Kirk and proposed half a guinea to any information as to the transgressors'. He began sowing vegetables in January and February 1756 'some sallad seeds in the Garden, turnip, savoys, kaill, planted shallotts & Garlic, pull up hotbeds & sowen Melon and Colyflower'.[133] The hotbeds were made up of rotting horse manure and more delicate plants grown in frames. In 1755 William Miller, the well-known Quaker proprietor of the nursery at Holyrood in Edinburgh, had written to Sir Thomas providing advice on the construction of hotbeds which ran counter to contemporary practice:

> The melon seed I've sent is not new and believe there is not better kind to be had anywhere. I do not approve of Tanner Bark being put in the Hotbed, being Ready to send up to the top of the bed, Great Quantities of filth, Like Humane Dung, which poisons the roots of any plant and never turns to any good account of it if it is at all to be used; it is in the Bottom of ye Bed and a Great thickness of Dung laid on top of it, to prevent if possible that stuff coming up but if Dung in Plenty can be had, I would not advise to use any of it for that

purpose the Great use of Bark is for plunging Pots with plants into where the Roots are confined in the pot.[134]

With the weather improving in March 1756, a further shelter belt of oak, ash, elms and plane trees was planted from Thomaston Glen inland from the castle and Scipio's land. Peaches, apricots and nectarines were planted along the length of the brick wall and other fruit trees on either side of the Gravel and Dovecote walks. This was followed in April 1756 by tulip trees, walnuts, hickory, spindle, black cherries and flowering shrubs. As everyone who gardens on the west coast knows to their cost, healthy spring growth can often be set back by bad weather in early May and 1756 was no exception with 'high winds, haill, rain and strong frost the first five days'. Undeterred, planting continued with yellow and blue lupins against the brick wall, and in the policies fifty-six walnut trees, twelve elms and twelve oaks and a miscellany of specie trees including a Judas tree, a spicewood tree, an ash leafed maple, a cornus, and an Angelica tree.[135] As the entries in the diary of planting ceased in May, there is no record of how all these trees fared. In 1760 Sir Thomas planted five hundred English elms in the Culzean policies (some of which still stand) and made further extension to the walled garden which was now used for growing fruit and vegetables on a large scale. Peach, plum, cherry, apricot and pear trees were planted against the walls in 1760 and 1761 and more in 1765 by which time James Barclay was the gardener.[136, 137]

Sir Thomas also seems to have built a new library in about 1760 to replace the book room at the top of the tower house, which was stocked in part by Gavin Hamilton, who was commissioned by Sir Thomas to paint a portrait of his aunt, Susanna, Countess of Eglinton.[138] Books purchased included Angelou's letters, Du Halde's *History of China*,[139] *History of the Air*,[140] *Natural History of Bees*,[141] *The Art of Metals*,[142] *The Architecture of Palladio*,[143] Gay's *fables*,[144] Gay's *Wine, a poem*,[145] and Clarke's history of Gustavus Ericson.[146] Sir Thomas may have contacted Hamilton while he was in Florence in 1760, visiting the Marquis Frescobaldi, a member of one of the great Florentine families.[147] To complete his wide interests he kept a pack of forty-three slow hounds for the Ayrshire and Dumfriesshire hunt.[148]

Sir Thomas and Archibald Kennedy continued their smuggling activities at least until 1758, as in that year George Moore complained about the late payment of bills.[149] By now the activities of the revenue cutters in the Irish Sea were making smuggling more hazardous and with the outbreak of the Seven Years' War in 1756, there was a real danger that those caught smuggling would be 'pressed' into the navy. Nevertheless, as a petition to the customs from Turnberry in 1760 suggests, smuggling was still rife: 'That the petitioner is surrounded by smugglers and frequently disturbed by them is certainly true and it is as true that no officers on his station can hinder them from carrying on their trade.'[150] Sir Thomas had a stroke of luck during 1757 when the four hundred-ton privateer *Dorset* was wrecked on the shore at Drumbeg below Turnberry on 20 November. After the outbreak of war the government issued 'letters of marque' to private shipowners giving them permission to attack and capture enemy ships. Captain Francis Pinney, Matthew Grove and Bryant Reynolds had registered the *Dorset* of Poole in April of that year.[151] She had a complement of two hundred men and carried twenty-five carriage and twelve swivel guns. With the vessel engulfed by the waves, two of Sir Thomas's men, Matthew Ross and James Underwood, succeeded in getting a line aboard, neverthelss only six men and one boy survived and were taken care of by James Stewart at Culzean Mill. Using a capstan, normally used for beaching boats, the vessel was winched towards the shore where her goods were removed before she foundered. Salvaged, the *Dorset* was sold by the well-known Glasgow merchant and banker Colin Dunlop, who acted as banker for Sir Thomas and Archibald Kennedy's smuggling transactions with George Moore.[152]

There was still smuggling on the coast in February 1765, when the customs commissioners in London were informed that preparations were in hand to land a very large quantity of spirits at various points on the Carrick coast including Turnberry, Culzean Bay and the Heads of Ayr. A previous enquiry in the Isle of Man suggested that the trade now included silks, 'all kinds of grocery goods', and tobacco as well as wines and spirits. The smugglers were also exporting coal and woollens by way of the Isle of Man.[153] It seems likely that Sir Thomas was party to these transactions in collaboration with Robert Kennedy, a Liverpool merchant who was married to Elizabeth, the daughter of John Maderell of Ballycorckish in the Isle of Man.

The 8th Earl of Cassillis died childless in 1759 at his London home in Albemarle Street. Before his death he had entailed the whole of the Cassillis estate to Sir Thomas whom failing his brother David, 'whom failing, to any person or persons he should nominate or appoint to succeed to his estates …'[154] Entails effectively made a Scottish estate inalienable and ensured it passed from one generation to another. They had received statutory protection in 1685 and were not without their critics, particularly because it was impossible for the 'heir in possession' to raise funds for improvement or commercial development on the security of the estate. To avoid this problem in practice only a portion of most estates was ever entailed, but this in itself could cause difficulty if the heir at law was different from the heir at entail as was to happen at Culzean.[155] Because of these restrictions many Scottish landed families were reluctant to entail their estates at all unless as with the Cassillis estates there was an ulterior motive. By the middle of the eighteenth century only a fifth of Scotland was entailed compared to half of England where entails involved no statutory protection and could be broken by consent in each generation.[156]

Sir Thomas claimed the title of Earl of Cassillis as the direct male heir. He was challenged through the female line by William Earl of March and Ruglen, who was to become 4th Duke of Queens-

berry in 1778 and was later better known as 'Old Q' – a notorious rake.[157] He perhaps hoped to succeed, as his maternal grandfather, the Earl of Ruglen, had gone to some trouble to relieve the Earl of Cassillis's debts in 1715.[158] The case hinged on whether there had been any descent through the female line in the Cassillis family. This was not unknown in Scotland as some titles and estates descended in this way. The Court of Session by a narrow majority found in favour of Sir Thomas and this was confirmed on appeal to the House of Lords in February 1762.[159] The widowed Lady Cassillis was Old Q's aunt and was understandably not best pleased by her husband's decision to leave his property to Sir Thomas Kennedy. Her friend Isa Douglas

The Earl of March and Ruglen, later the notorious 4th Duke of Queensberry, who unsuccessfully challenged Sir Thomas Kennedy for the Earldom of Cassillis.

sympathised with her, particularly at the loss of what she regarded as her own possessions at Cassillis including her crystal tumblers:

If there was any hopes of getting them backe even tho yr Laps [your Ladyship] ner be bay them might watte [wait] some time to see what Can be don both for them & the littel bowl I hope you'll get Back all your china & a great many other things you left at Cassillis which they can pretend no right to particularly Lord March's picttar [picture] and they have got too much already to let them keep any thing belonging to yr Laps.[160]

In seeking the title Sir Thomas was after not only the property, considerable as it was, but the political influence it would bring. Since the Cassillis and Culzean estates had at one time been one, they fitted well together comprising a wedge of land from Cassillis across almost to Dalmellington and including Cassillis House and Maybole Castle. Since the Cassillis estates had been neglected, Sir Thomas, now 9th Earl of Cassillis, began a similar process of improvement as had already taken place on his Culzean property. Writing in the 1790s the minister of Kirkmichael, which contained much of the Cassillis land, commented:

Cassillis House painted by Alexander Nasmyth for the 1st Marquess. This was inherited by Sir Thomas Kennedy of Culzean when he became 9th Earl of Cassilis.

About 30 years ago the country was for the most not closed: low ill paid rents, poor farmers, starved cart horses, no carts, and scarcely a tolerable instrument for husbandry, prevailed everywhere. Now the reverse condition is the case. The farms, two or three excepted, are inclosed, and subdivided; the hedges in many places excellent strong fences; the work of ditching and hedging understood and generally well executed.[161]

As in Kirkoswald sheep rearing, which had been unproductive, was banned except for domestic use, and the breeding of black cattle and the growing of oats were encouraged. In 1762 the 9th Earl purchased Newark Castle, towards Ayr, along with its thousand-acre estate as a home for his brother David, with whom he was now on better terms. Reputedly this was paid for by cutting down and selling the Dalrymple wood on the Cassillis estate which fetched the princely sum of £1,037.[162] Although Newark had once been part of the Cassillis estate, the Earl's aunt, the Countess of Eglinton, could not understand what he saw in it: 'It has neither wood nor coall and only a little old

shell of a house.'[163] David disagreed and, embellished, it became his much-loved home. Newark had been converted to more peaceful purposes in the 1680s when the grounds had been enclosed to form a park and an orchard planted.[164] Directly he took possession, David appointed his brother's factor Archibald Kennedy to look after his property.[165] Not long after buying Newark for his brother, Sir Thomas improved communications between his properties and Ayr by building a new bridge across the River Doon within a quarter mile of its mouth. At the same time Sir Thomas was negotiating with his mother, who was living with his sister at Barnton House at Cramond, near Edinburgh, for the return of the furniture and plate she had purloined from Culzean, in return for a settlement of £4,565. She proved so obdurate that he had to threaten legal proceedings before she would agree terms.[166]

The 9th Earl was back in Italy again in 1764 when he spent two months taking

LEFT

Newark Castle near Ayr, which the 9th Earl purchased as a home for his brother David, who later became 10th Earl and commissioned Robert Adam to remodel Culzean.

RIGHT

The portrait by Pompeo Batoni of Sir Thomas Kennedy, 9th Earl of Cassillis, which was commissioned during his second trip to Italy in the mid-1760s. For a long time it was thought to be of his brother David, the 10th Earl.

the waters at Viterbo, followed by a month in Rome with the Abbé Grant.[167] While in Rome Sir Thomas sat for Pompeo Batoni, a fashionable portrait painter, probably on the Abbé's recommendation.[168] His portrait was not completed until May 1768 when Grant informed him that it had been dispatched by way of Leghorn and added somewhat gratuitously 'with regard to a wife your dearest Lordship has no time to lose and this I think it should be now your first and principal thought'.[169] Coutts, the Earl's London bankers, were surprised to receive a demand for the payment of the outstanding fifteen guineas from the Abbé. The Earl had to apologise 'as the portrait should have been sent over long before this, I omitted mentioning to you when last at London.'[170] He spent September 1764 in Madeira and was in Paris by Christmas. He went south to Marseilles and Montpellier in the spring and returned home by way of Geneva.[171] While in Marseilles he commissioned a local

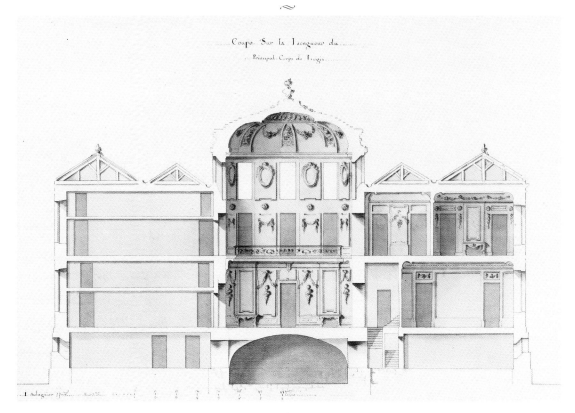

architect, I. Artagnier, to produce a set of drawings of a country house with a large oval salon on the *piano nobile*.[172] After his return he was frequently in Bath for the sake of his health.

Illness did not prevent him from sharing with Old Q a passion for blood-stock, for in 1765 he imported five Arab stallions from Smyrna for the colossal sum of £4,352, presumably to improve the quality of his racing stable.[173] These were vastly more expensive than the original estimate of £600 provided by Andrew Turnbull.[174] On arrival in England they were taken to Constable Burton Hall near Leyburn in North Yorkshire, the home of Sir Marmaduke Wyvill, a noted breeder and trainer of racehorses. Here they were cared for by his head groom George Theakston.[175] After their delivery, Turnbull wrote to the Earl from Bath: 'I hope your Lordship will have the finest horses in Great Britain.' He added that he understood there was

A section of the proposed house for Sir Thomas Kennedy by the French architect I Artagnier.

'much gout in your disorder' and advised that at Bath 'I am of the opinion that the air and company would be of more service than the waters.'[176] The Earl's interest in horse breeding seems to have been relatively short-lived, as by the time the *Sporting Calendar* began to be printed in 1770, he is not listed as an owner of either race horses or stallions.[177] He was, however, at Newmarket for the racing in 1772.[178]

Owning racehorses went hand in hand with drinking and gambling. In June 1763 the Earl penned a note to his factor, Archibald Kennedy, when clearly the worse for drink and the loser in a wager:

I had ocation to Borrow from Ardmillan [James Craufurd] about seventy pounds and as he wants it before he goes home I have sent my servant Hugh Wilson to you to get from you any money you

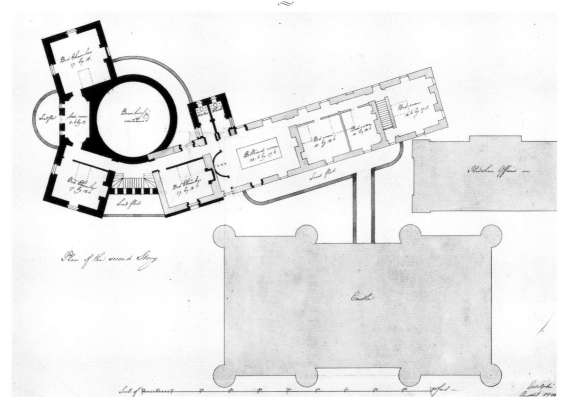

Plan of the second Story

A ground plan of the new wing which included the office houses.

have; whatever you have send to him and take his receipt for it until I see you.[179]

The 9th Earl's mind returned again to building at Culzean in the mid-1760s and to the project to reroof the house which Archibald Hamilton had first mooted a decade earlier. All the roofs and turrets of the old castle were stripped and the walls heightened. This involved casing the whole building in scaffolding and ten thousand new slates being shipped from Easdale in Argyll plus quantities of Bath stone.[180, 181] It was a massive undertaking involving many masons and carpenters under the direction of George Smith:

The Roof and Turret of Cullean were stripped about the middle of June 1766. The masons began to build and Repair it the 22 of June and finished the mason work there on 15 September thereafter in the forenoon.

September 10 part of the masons and the 15th the rest of them went to clearing the rock for laying the foundation of the Office houses in the East and to hew stone for the building.[182]

The Earl spent part of the time while the roof was off the castle in St Andrews playing golf,[183] otherwise he lived in his brother's house at Newark.

Internally the whole top floor of the tower house was remodelled. The ceiling of the Crimson room was lowered so as to allow the roof to be made flat, a new bedroom was built on the attic floor above, and the book room in the garret was removed. The bedroom of the factor, Archibald Kennedy, was refurbished, a window fitted and a fireplace installed. When the new roof had been completed, the foundation stone of a new block, known as the 'office houses of Culzean' was laid on 17 September at 8.00 in the morning, no doubt

with full masonic ceremonies.[184] This eight-bayed two-storey plain functional block took two years to complete and was built to the north-west of the tower house on the cliff top facing out to sea.[185] The plaster work in the building was carried out by John McClure of Ayr, who was later to work at Culzean for Robert Adam. Apart from offices, the building also included a replacement billiard room. By now the table had become oblong and modern cues had been introduced. New balls for the table were ordered in 1772, along with a large cage for a parrot.[186]

At the same time a summer house and hunting lodge with bedrooms for the Earl and his brother was built at Starr (later known as Fore Starr) on a spectacular hilltop location a mile beyond the south end of Loch Doon. James McBain, who regularly visited the then substantial ruins in the 1920s, conjectured that much of the

The ruins of the 9th Earl's hunting lodge at Fore Starr, high in the hills above Loch Doon, which was built in about 1765.

building material had been pillaged from Castle Doon.[187] The remains can still be found by those intrepid enough to scramble up above the Gala Lane at the head of Loch Doon. Here in what was a substantial house the 9th Earl could indulge his passion for shooting, following in the footsteps of his forebears further south at Hunt Ha'. At the same time a smaller fishing lodge was built at Craigmalloch beside Loch Doon, which was equipped with a new fishing boat.[188] Fore Starr was (and still is) a remarkably remote spot only accessible by horseback, but was rich in blackcock, and the rivers and lochs full of the rare Atlantic char. The site he chose above the River Gala (Gallow) Lane commanded awe-inspiring views on every side. After heavy rain the Gala Lane often 'overflowed its banks, and destroyed the meadows'. In the late 1780s, to prevent this from happening, the Earl of Cassillis and McAdam of Craigengillan cut the rock at the north end of Loch

Doon 'over which the loch discharged itself' into the River Doon.[189] Between 1771 and 1774 Sir Thomas totally refurbished Maybole Castle, the Cassillis tower house in the town, at a total cost of £441. As at Culzean the roof had to be largely replaced and McClure was again used to replaster the house from top to bottom.[190] The family burying ground in the ruined collegiate church was also put in good order. It is difficult to know why he should have wished to abandon his modern Palladian villa further up the street in favour of this ancient Cassillis stronghold unless it was another facet of his romantic attachment to the family past.

In addition new offices for the estate were built at Kirkoswald with an adjoining house for the factor. These were required for a further thrust in estate improvement, particularly the final extinction of the runrig. The factor, Archibald Kennedy, resigned in 1766 and was succeeded by John Kennedy of Ballony, who died suddenly four years later. He was followed in turn by Captain Robert Kennedy of Daljarrock, who managed the estate from Kirkoswald and his home near Pinwherry.* Since 1760 he had been in debt to the Earl.[191] He was elected a bailie of Maybole in 1772.[192]

An experienced farm manager, or 'land steward' as he was titled, John Bulley was recruited from Essex in the south-east of England to replace John Foulis who had died. His specific task was to improve the Mains adjacent to the castle, which the Earl's mother had occupied until her death in 1767. Bulley arrived in December 1773 and found most of the land on the six-hundred-acre farm was 'in the hands of several small tenants, except about thirty acres which had been limed, but quite worn out and in the worst condition'. The tacks were broken and Bulley immediately set about levelling the ridges and liming and manuring the ground to grow barley or bear for cattle feed.[193] The new tacks throughout the estate laid down very specific conditions for improving the ground, such as that for Halloun, Robinson and Yonderton in Kirkmichael in 1783:

*Daljarrock House survives as a caravan park.

It is Furder Expressly agreed that whatever Lands the said William and James Logans shall Improve with Lime or Marle They shall only be at liberty to take three succeeding crops and thereafter to Rest the lands Four years Before breaking up again Unless they shall Dress the same land a Second time with Dung or compost in which case they shall be at liberty to take three more crop before laying it Down to whatever land the said William and James Logans shall plough contrary to this agreement they hereby become bound to pay the said Lord Earl Three pounds sterling per Aiker over and above their current Rent.[194]

John Bulley reputedly introduced turnips into the crop rotation for the first time in Carrick. His main complaint was 'I have not a proper farm-yard, nor a house or shed for feeding cattle, or for the conveniencty of raising near so much dung as might be made …' He was confident, however, that 'these things will come'.[195] At the same time the Earl decided to replant the oyster bed on the shore at the Maidens, bringing Norfolk oystermen to Culzean at considerable expense for the purpose.[196]

To pay for these further alterations and other new ventures the Earl began to borrow heavily from his friends, including the Duke of Atholl, the Marques of Annandale, the Earl of Hopetoun, Sir John Whitefoord and his Hunter Blair cousins. It is likely that they were willing to lend as they all had interests in American and West Indian plantations and the Earl in partnership with Robert Kennedy, his erstwhile smuggling associate, was now engaged in the slave trade. When the British government purchased the fiscal privileges over the Isle of Man from the Duke of Atholl in 1765 and raised duty in an effort to stamp out the illicit trade, the smugglers shifted their operations further afield and diversified into other activities.[197] The Revenue increased their vigilance on the shore at Culzean,

seizing a considerable quantity of spirits that January and intercepting a Manx wherry the following month.[198] Such incidents made it increasingly unsafe for a peer of the realm to be directly involved in smuggling. Robert Kennedy had begun shipping slaves to the Guinea coast in 1760, but only on a large scale after the closure of the Isle of Man.[199] Between 1767 and 1774 he owned four slave ships named *Lord Cassillis* and it would seem likely that the Earl not only gave his permission but was also an investor in the voyages.[200] It cannot be coincidental that Robert Kennedy retired in about 1778 to live at Greenan Castle as the Earl's tenant.[201] The

Greenan Castle, which was acquired by the 9th Earl and became home of the slave captain Robert Kennedy and then later the factor Richard Campbell.

Earl also purchased a sixteenth share in the *Bute*, an East Indiaman, which was managed by Andrew and James Moffat who were leading 'husbands' or shippers. They were also associated with Moffat, Davis & Bell, the Jamaican correspondents of Alexander Spiers, one of Glasgow's most prominent tobacco lords.[202] Its first voyage yielded a handsome clear profit of £138 for an investment of only £180.[203]

At the same time as his apparent involvement in the slave trade, the Earl drew on his funds for a mistimed speculation in Florida with the help of Dr William Stork, who wrote to the Earl in 1767 explaining his plans:

I propose to begin your settlement on a frugal plan, and to place at first five white Men servants, consisting of three carpenters, one cooper and an overseer, together with 10 Negroes upon your Estate. I have procured the servants, and on account of their Industry and Sobriety have preferred Scotch to English.[204]

Stork intended to produce rices, cotton, and indigo. General James Grant of Ballindalloch, who was governor of East Florida, contradicted this advice: 'no produce will answer the expense of white labour'.[205] To help further this investment, the Earl became a member of the East Florida dining club in London, whose members numbered the Duke of Buccleuch, the Earl of Thanet, Viscount Townshend, and Lord Grosvenor.[206]

John Bell, the Earl's Edinburgh lawyer, was concerned about these ventures. On learning in 1770 of a proposed loan of £10–£12,000 from Colonel William Fullarton of Fullarton in Ayrshire, John Bell cautioned the Earl: 'There is nothing so disagreeable, or so dangerous to a man's credit, as to be constantly in the market in the borrowing way.' While recognising the urgent need for cash, he suggested that in the future the Earl should keep £2,000 at call with his bankers to cover any emergencies.[207] In response the recently established Florida plantation along with a holding in Tobago inherited from the Earl of Cassillis were sold as the outlook in North America was not propitious. The Earl, however, retained his share in the *Bute*. As it turned out this was a wise choice; she earned him a profit of over £100 on every voyage until his death. In 1769 he invested directly in East India stock and speculated successfully in it in 1771.[208]

Any further easing of the Earl's financial position was handicapped by the collapse in the summer of 1772 with spectacular debts of the Ayr Bank of Douglas & Heron. The bank had been established in 1768 by a number of prominent landowners in south-west Scotland including the Dukes of Buccleuch and Queensberry.[209] Although neither a shareholder nor a large depositor, the Earl was affected by the crash as many of his tenants paid their rents in bills of exchange drawn on the bank.[210] On 3 August 1772 John Bell warned the Earl of the likely consequences: 'The Banks have gave over taking Douglas notes some days before the Bank stopt payment and have taken none since.' He went on to say that it was still possible to get rid of them through merchants and advised:

I think you had better send them in to be disposed of in that way in order to prepare a fund for payment of your interest due at Martns [Martinmas – 11 November]. Without doing something of this kind I do not see how you can possibly pay your interest at Martns as I dare say the bulk of your rents will be paid in that case [i.e. in Douglas & Heron paper].

In short the Bank has wrought an infinite mischief upon themselves and the country, which nobody yet seems to know where it will end. Your Ayr Branch in particular is cried out against loudly for still continuing to issue their paper after they stops payment.[211]

Bell's advice came too late as the family papers to this day contain a sorry bundle of unpaid drafts on the bank from tenants.[212]

Some of the Earl's borrowings were undoubtedly used to advance his political ambitions. In 1767 his brother David declared his intention of standing for parliament for the County of Ayr at the next election against the Eglinton interest and secured the support of the Earl of Loudoun. After complicated and almost certainly expensive manoeuvring David Kennedy won the backing of the Earl of Dumfries; the Earl of Glencairn; Lord Auchinleck, the father of James Boswell (the biographer of Samuel Johnson); and Sir Adam Fergusson of Kilkerran on the understanding Cassillis would support their candidate in the following contest. At the general election in 1768 Kennedy won the seat by forty-five votes to Archibald Montgomerie's twenty-seven.[213] On his arrival in London his brother, the Earl of Cassillis, gave him £1,000.[214] Although David Kennedy never spoke in the House, he had ambitions for office, believing incorrectly in 1771 that he was to be appointed a baron of the Scottish Exchequer at the princely annual salary of £5,000.[215] The year before, George Dempster wrote to Sir Adam Fergusson suggesting that Kennedy might succeed Lord Gardenstone* as a judge of the Court of Session: 'I hope before long David Kennedy may be laughing and shaking in Gardenstane's easy chair.'[216] Early in 1773 David formed an alliance of the 'three earls', his brother Cassillis, Eglinton and Loudoun, against his supporters in the 1768 election. His brother at once explored ways of 'creating' votes on his estates by making fictitious freeholds.[217] This was a common, if unscrupulous, practice at the time. Auchinleck was furious, telling Kennedy that it would mean 'the annihilation of the gentlemen's interest' and put his weight behind Sir Adam Fergusson.[218] It is likely that it was this rift which prompted James Boswell's much quoted remark in his journal of April of that year:

> I called on Mr David Kennedy and found him the same joker as formerly and nothing more. It struck me a little that the gentlemen of Ayrshire should be represented in Parliament by a good honest merry fellow indeed, but one so totally incapable of the business of the legislation and so devoid of the talents which distinguish a man in public life. I threw myself into the humorous rattling style and plagued him with a new-invented dialogue between his brother, Lord Cassillis, when setting out for London [to attend parliament]. "My Lord, provisions are growing dearer, you

must allow a little more." "Davy, you have very well already." "But, my Lord, I have learnt to drink porter in London." "Well, Davy, you shall have another £100."[219]

In the event at the 1774 election Sir Adam Fergusson won with sixty votes against Kennedy's forty-seven.

Much to his surprise the 9th Earl was, however, elected as a representative peer for Scotland in November. It is not clear what made him want to stand fifteen years after inheriting the title during which time he had largely buried himself and his opinions on his property. Under the terms of the Treaty of Union only sixteen Scottish peers, elected from amongst their number, were allowed to sit in the House of Lords. Elections were usually 'fixed' by the government but on this occasion it was disputed as the peers were fed up with being dictated to. Lieutenant General Sir James Oughton, the commander-in-chief for North Britain, reported to the Earl of Dartmouth that the Earl of Haddington objected to 'ministerial lists' and that the Earl of Selkirk asserted the independence of the peerage system inaugurated by the Duke of Grafton in 1766, and warned that the lists 'unless checked might end in dragooning them into obedience and the ministers' dictates'.[220] According to a letter from the Earl of Cassillis to the Earl of Loudoun, he was invited at this juncture by none other than the Prime Minister Lord North and the Earl of Suffolk to allow his name to go forward, possibly because of his Whig sympathies.[221] He carried the day by thirteen votes, and he was so taken aback that he had to ask the Earl of Suffolk if he could be excused attendance at Parliament until 'well after the Christmas Holly days'.[222]

He did not live long enough to enjoy the fruits of his success, becoming ill the following summer and dying in Edinburgh on 30 November 1775, leaving debts of over £30,000.[223] His funeral at Kirkoswald and subsequent interment in the collegiate church at Maybole was a sumptuous affair

*Francis Garden, Lord Gardenstone, Senator of the College of Justice, 1764–70, died 1793.

with a hearse and five mourning coaches travelling from Edinburgh to Culzean – a journey of six days in each direction at a cost of £226.[224] The Reverend James Wright, a fellow mason whom he had appointed minister of Maybole, later wrote a most sycophantic obituary:

> He was cut off in the prime of which the world had expected would be but about the midst of his days; and at the very time when his great abilities of mind and his eminent talent for business were just about to be made known to the supreme court of the kingdom.
>
> Although he was never prodigal, yet no man could be more liberal in his expenses, where there was need of assisting his friends, or of promoting the good of society.
>
> He resided mostly at home that from a sense of duty he might watch over the interests of the district of the country wherein he lived and that he might cause the profits of his large estate to circulate among those by whose industry they were raised.[225]

Sir Thomas left the whole of his estate to his brother David with only one large legacy of £1,000 to his nephew Captain Andrew Cathcart of the 15th Regiment of Foot. He made several small bequests: £20 to Matthew Biggar – his friend and the minister at Kirkoswald for whom he had recently built a new manse – to bury him and for mourning; a year's wages to each of his servants, Douglas Kennedy (Scipio's eldest son), Hugh Main and Joseph Baird; a life rent of £30 to Hugh Wilson, another servant; and a life rent of £60 to Elizabeth and Barbara Morson, who looked after him in London.[226]

Earl Thomas was a remarkable man. Like his grandfather Sir Archibald; he was full of contradictory passions, an aesthete and a musician who was devoted to blood sports, a student of classical antiquity who spent a fortune on restoring ancient tower houses, a soldier in the Protestant cause who flirted with Jacobitism and Rome, a linguist who preferred the isolation of rural Ayrshire, and a man who on the whole eschewed the public stage and yet at the end of his life became a representative peer, necessitating long sojourns in London. His brother David, as 10th Earl, secured his seat as a representative peer in 1776 with the support of Lord Mount Stuart, the eldest son of the Earl of Bute.[227] The cost of attending the election at Holyrood and entertaining his supporters was £146.[228] He remained a representative peer until 1790, acting with the opposition to Pitt and voting against the Regency in 1789.[229]

CHAPTER 4

The jocular builder and American cousins:
1775–92

On succeeding to the title and the estates, David, the new Earl, at once set about rescheduling his brother's debts by negotiating a huge loan of £30,000 from the trustees of the wealthy heiress, Miss Henrietta Scott, eldest daughter and co-heir of General John Scott of Balcomie in Fife, who was later to become the 4th Duchess of Portland. She had estates in Ayrshire and perhaps the Earl had thoughts of an advantageous marriage.[1]

The other problem he had to resolve was the continuing fire in the Dalziellily coal seam which had already destroyed about five acres of new plantings at Tradunnock on the neighbouring Kilkerran estate and were reportedly threatening the workings there. Shortly before the 9th Earl's death, Sir Adam Fergusson of Kilkerran had protested that David Cuming, the tenant of the workings, had encouraged the fire to spread. Immediately the Earl had ordered the pits to close and appointed two respected coal-masters to review Cuming's working method. On being told that the works 'were going on properly; and there was no hazard of spreading the fire', he gave permission for them to be reopened. Sir Adam was furious and the day after his brother's funeral, the new Earl was served with a summons which claimed he 'had no right to work the coal'. Sir Adam also sought damages 'on account of having his lands covered with rubbish' and 'of the destruction

Domus conditor, the builder of the house, David 10th Earl of Cassillis, who commissioned Robert Adam to enlarge Culzean in 1776.

of his property by burning the surface and trees planted thereon'.[2] Having obtained an interdict against Cassillis, Sir Adam proceeded to have the workings stopped. In a judgement in January 1777, Lord Coventoun, however, declared that Sir Adam had no right to have the pits stopped and in any event was ill-advised to have planted trees so near the workings. Moreover he had no doubt that the mineral rights did belong to the Earl and that Sir Adam's actions were simply an attempt to appropriate all the deposits for himself.[3] Although the judgement was in his favour, the 10th Earl had already agreed to exchange the workings for other Kilkerran lands, leaving himself with no coal on his estate.[4]

Undeterred by the burden of debt on the estate and perhaps still relying on income from Robert Kennedy's slave trading, the 10th Earl was determined to build a new home worthy of his political ambitions and his brother's memory. At first he thought of moving the family seat to his home at Newark, but he had changed his mind by the time Robert Adam wrote to Sir Rowland Winn in August 1776 that he was 'under an engagement to go … to visit the Earl of Cassillis, who has an old Castle that he wished my advice about'.[5] This description hardly did justice to the 9th Earl's extensive building operations at Culzean and elsewhere on the estate. The 10th Earl was certainly as

interested in building as his brother and one of his first acts was to rebuild under his own direction the parish church at Kirkoswald. His own gallery included an open fire to warm him during long winter sermons. His successors would use the fire irons to good effect to bring to a close an unnecessarily long-winded discourse.[6] It has been suggested that during his visit to Culzean, Adam took a hand in the final design of the new building.[7]

Within less than a year Robert Adam was sketching the cliff top site and making proposals for alterations to the various buildings. The first project was to construct a large new kitchen and an east wing, adjoining his brother's two-storeyed cliff top block. This was an awkward site. Creating the cellars for storing food and wine and laying the foundations involved the removal of huge quantities of rock. Day after day the cliffs must have echoed to the sound of explosions used to dislodge the stone.[8] The unusual location of the kitchen in front of the castle was almost certainly to service the dining room on the other

Culzean sketched from the west by Robert Adam in 1776. The old castle is in the centre, with the turret stair at one end of the terrace gardens on the right. Between the turret and the castle can be seen the Palladian roof of the new tower gate and on the right of the picture is the so-called slant block.

side of the courtyard. The Earl paid Adam £150 for this phase of the work.[9] The next operation was to extend the house itself by filling in the 'L' shape of the old castle to form a rectangular house with turrets at each corner. The refashioned castle contained another drawing room opposite the Picture Gallery – the old great hall – and additional bedrooms. In 1779 Adam modified his design by replacing the old laundry tower to the south-west with an imaginative circular brewhouse with a conical roof. In May 1780 Adam was paid a further £250.[10]

At the same time the tower gate was to be heightened and crenellated. All the retaining walls and the terraces were to be embellished with battlements and mock fortifications. The walled garden was moved to its present site some distance from the house, in the Scots manner. Laid out in 1782 it included a pleasure garden and new glass houses, with grand entrance gates. These must have been among the first greenhouses in Scotland and appear to have been against the wall which today supports the

vinery. The wall behind would have been heated by means of flues to force early fruit.[11] Twenty years later the garden was described as 'well stocked with vines, peaches, and a good selection of shrubs, herbaceous plants and flowers'. The walls surrounding the old garden were reduced in height to create a fashionable sunken garden. The costs were formidable and the work prodigious. Between 1777 and 1780, the Earl had paid through Hugh Cairncross, his master of works, alone, almost £4,000 which would also have included work on farm buildings.[12] This first stage was completed in the summer of 1782 and was described by a visitor in 1787 as doing 'great credit to Adam, the architect, and will, when complete, stand unrivalled in its way'.[13] The final payments for this work was £200 in 1782 to the partnership of R. & J. Adam and £115 in 1783 followed by £125 in the next year to Robert Adam himself. William Cairncross, Hugh's brother, who was a London cabinetmaker, received £120.[14]

Some commentators have assumed that building work continued after 1782 and have argued that

Culzean from the east also drawn in 1776, with the tower gate in the foreground, on the right the slant block and on the left Holehouse farm. Armed smugglers are portrayed on the shore.

the records in the Ailsa muniments are missing.[15] Given that accounts seem to have survived for all the major alterations at Culzean since the construction of the dining room, this seems most unlikely and it is more probable that they never existed in the first place as no work was undertaken. When the 4th Marquess left the muniments to the nation in 1943, C.T. McInnes of Register House (now the National Archives of Scotland) reported:

Lady Ailsa had been most industrious and anxious in having all the papers gathered together for safe transfer to the Register House. I was assured that even the attics had been searched and cleared out; and that there were no papers at all in the stable lofts and outhouses; and none of historical importance in the factor's office.[16]

It is hardly likely that a family, which had come to venerate Adam so highly, would have overlooked such important accounts if they had existed. The

assumption that the accounts are missing has led to assertions that the construction of the great north tower and staircase were started much earlier than was the case.

With such an ostentatious new house it is hardly surprising that Earl David, now in his early fifties, was considered a good match. In 1782 James Boswell composed a scurrilous song about him:

The Coopers they came to Lord Cassillis
    at Colzean
With their hoops all tight and ready
From London they came down,
    baith the black and the brown
And they wanted to give him a lady

Your Lordship, we pray, may not say us nae
For it's now full time you was girded
Qoth the Earl, 'Faith my dears, so great are my fears
In conscience I'd rather be yearded*

* buried

LEFT
The interior of the new kitchen at Culzean restored by the National Trust for Scotland.

RIGHT
One of the original gates to the walled garden designed by Robert Adam and moved when the gardens were enlarged.

The reference appears to be to the Miss Coopers, the daughters of Sir Grey Cooper, a political friend of the Earl and supporter of the Whig ministry of the Marquis of Rockingham in 1765.[17] Cassillis was furious, but unlike James Stuart of Dunearn, who was similarly lampooned by Boswell's son Alexander, he did not resort to pistols with fatal consequences. Boswell apologised and they gradually returned to speaking terms. Cooper remained on good terms with the Earl, acting as go-between with the Duke of Portland. By this time he and Viscount Stormont, alone of the Scottish peers, were in 'permanent opposition' to William Pitt's administration.[18] In April 1789 Cooper sent Cassillis an eyewitness account of the celebrations for the recovery of King George III from his fit of madness:

I was at St Paul's & a most magnificent
exhibition it was; Two Psalms were sung

in the Dome, as the Royal family passed by in coming to & returning from the Choir, by 8,000 charity children piled in rows one above another. There was something very sublime & affecting in the united & according voices of so numerous a chorus of children ascending to Heaven: for we have the highest authority for saying that such is the Kingdom of Heaven – I had not seen the King since his Illness, my seat was at some distance from the canopy under which their majesties sat, but it seemed to me that his countenance was much altered & particularly about the eyes; he passed it is said through all the streets & all the acclamations of his people without once looking out of his carriage or bowing to any of them.[19]

A view from the south after the first phase of Adam's alterations were completed, showing clearly the central staircase from the front of the old eating room down to the first terrace. It also depicts the viaduct before it was improved with mock fortifications.

During the mid-1780s Earl David accelerated the enclosure of farms in distant upland parts of the estate and began widescale planting. In about 1787 his attention returned to the improvement of the Mains. He commissioned Adam to design 'an extensive and very commodious plan of offices' and a farm steading to replace his brother's office block. Constructed in about 1788 on the promontory half a mile to the north of the castle, this new model farm included everything that John Bulley could have wanted, including a house for the land steward, dairy and a dairyman's house, stables, calf rearing and poultry sheds and barns.[20] Bulley and the factor Captain Kennedy were advocates of dairying, which was to become the mainstay of the estate. The minister of Kirkoswald reported in the 1790s:

The dairy was in a most neglected state in this parish twenty years ago. Good butter and cheese were scarcely to be

found. Now the milk cows are changed to the better, put into parks sown down with white and yellow clover, when they live in the house by night or by day, are fed red cut clover. Every steading of farm houses has an apartment by itself for a milk house, and every conveniency furnished to it. Both butter and cheeses are now exported from the parish to the markets of Ayr and Paisley.[21]

The home farm at Culzean with the castle in the distance painted by Alexander Nasmyth.

These developments almost certainly reflected improvements in the Ayrshire roads in the 1770s. Bulley was still land steward in 1790 as the factor paid him £500,[22] but by 1793 he had taken the tenancy of Attiquin on the Blairquhan estate, which is to the south of Maybole on the road to Crosshill. He died there on 2 May 1803.[23] The results of the handiwork of Bulley and his predecessors

around Kirkoswald were recorded by Robert Heron on his journey though the western counties of Scotland in 1792: 'We saw around us a country highly cultivated and populous fields with well-built walls and often subdivided with thriving hedges.'[24]

It was not until the new home farm and offices were completed that Adam could persuade the 10th Earl to demolish his brother's office houses and build the saloon, great circular staircase and adjoining rooms. He had been considering such a bold initiative since at least November 1784 when Adam drew a design sketch for him. A rather ungainly set of plans was submitted the following summer but replaced two years later by a more considered scheme, which almost doubled the size of the castle.[25] A grand new entrance arch was to be erected on the south side of the castle courtyard leading down to a battlemented causeway with at its end a massive ruined arch, framing the castle. A wash house was to be

built behind the tower gate. The third terrace, along with the central stairway in front of the dining room was to be removed and the ground levelled. According to Adam's brother-in-law, John Clerk of Eldin, the Earl gave him a free hand: 'the whimsical but magnificent Castle of Colane … on which the Earl … encouraged him to indulge to the utmost his romantic genius'.[26]

The home farm now serves as the visitor centre.

These massive operations, which by any standard can only be construed as 'sheer extravagance',[27] rendered the castle uninhabitable. Work began in 1788. Over the next two years £5,000 was spent, mostly on demolishing the buildings and quarrying. When work began on the interior, all the bedroom furniture was put into store.[28] The well-known landscape gardener Thomas White of Retford, a pupil of Capability Brown, was engaged to lay out the policies.[29] White had an extensive Scottish practice and was at the time working on his grandest commission at Cullen House in Banffshire for the Duke of Gordon. He rejected the picturesque in favour of the classical and permanent landscape. He was criticised by his contemporaries for slavishly imitating Brown's designs and for his insensitivity to the past.[30] No drawing of his plan for Culzean survives but it is probable that it included the Swan Pond and the new approach through the Swinston or Cat Gates rather than the more direct route along the then public road down the hill from Glenside. Before this could be done the public road would have to be moved along a line from Glenside to Swinston.[31] The Earl paid White £30 17 shilling and 5 pence in 1790 which was probably for plans.[32] (In 1786 he had charged the Duke of Gordon £52 10 shillings for plans of a much larger scheme.[33])

Dendrological evidence suggests that White planted the avenue of silver firs on either side of the road from the castle to the walled garden. This would have screened the new lawns leading from

the old garden up the hill to the new walled garden, passing over what had been Scipio's house, which was presumably demolished.

Meanwhile the Earl, still a bachelor, continued to live at Newark when in Ayrshire,[34] adding to that estate adjoining properties including part of Greenan, which had passed out of the family by marriage, and other properties on the outskirts of Alloway.[35] He also began to refashion Cassillis House, presumably with the help of Hugh Cairncross who had ambitions to be an architect, but little is known about what was planned. At about the same time he built a paper works on the south side of the River Doon near its mouth at Doonfoot.[36]

By December 1789 the Earl was strapped for cash and he had to ask his bankers if they could meet the interest, if only in the short term, on the loan of £30,000 which had been taken over from Miss Scott by William Campbell, a wealthy Nabob, who purchased the Craigie estate on the outskirts of Ayr in 1783.[37] In February 1790 the Earl became seriously ill while in London. By now his debts were

Robert Adam's final design for the north front of Culzean with the imposing drum tower in the centre and the laundry tower to the right, 1787.

well over £60,000 and the income from the rental about £4,050.[38] With no direct heir the Earl had to consider how to dispose of his estates. Providing no other claimant came forward, the heir to the earldom was Archibald Kennedy, a wealthy naval captain who was born in New York. Originally the 10th Earl intended following the terms of his father's will to leave all his estates to his nephew Sir John Cathcart of Carleton, the son of his eldest sister Elizabeth. When Sir John died without issue in 1785, his brother Sir Andrew Cathcart assumed he would inherit Culzean as:

no alteration was made upon the natural and legal course of succession and as the same habits of friendship subsisted and many obligations by the Representative [Sir Andrew] upon his uncle were continued, the Representative continued without any suspicion that any alteration had taken place.[39]

In fact the Earl had changed his will (although not the deed of entail of the Cassillis estate) in 1783 to leave the residue of his property including Culzean, Cassillis and his London home, now in South Park Street, to his cousin Captain Archibald Kennedy RN, who had returned from New York to live in London two years earlier. He left £500 each to Sir John Cathcart of Killochan and his brother Andrew, a lieutenant colonel, and £500 each to his sisters Lady Anne Blair and Mrs Clementina Wilson, and to the widow of his lawyer John Bell WS. He left £200 to Thomas Kennedy, the only son of his factor Robert Kennedy of Daljarrock and £300 and his clothes to his principal servant, Gilbert McHaffie.[40]

In February 1790, the Earl entailed all his property (including the Cassillis estate which was already entailed) to Captain Kennedy with the exception of some, mostly more distant, properties – the Citadel in Ayr (now used as a distillery) and Culzean and Cassillis Castles and their policies. Scottish entail law had been reformed in 1770 by the Montgomery Act which allowed proprietors to obtain loans for improvement providing that in the event of their death the interest and repayments did not commit their successors to more than two-thirds of the income from four years' rent. Improvements were tightly defined and all qualifying expenditure had to be registered annually with the relevant sheriff court.[41] Under the terms of this arrangement and presumably with the consent of his creditors, on his death trustees were to manage the Culzean and Cassillis estates (apart from Culzean Castle and its policies) from which they were to meet the interest on his enormous debts and create a sinking fund gradually to pay them off along with any legacies. He nominated as trustees the Earl of Eglinton, the Earl of Cassillis (Captain Kennedy) and his son Lord Kennedy, the Lord President, the Lord Justice Clerk, the distinguished lawyer Mr Henry Erskine, Sir William Miller of Glenlee, David Cathcart of Greenfield, a fellow advocate (later a judge in the Court of Session with the title Lord Alloway), and his own Edinburgh lawyer John Hunter. The unentailed distant por-

tions of the estate (mostly in Wigtownshire and valued at some £9,000–£10,000) were to be sold to help defray the debt.[42] The trustees had no powers to sell any other part of the entailed property or 'to raise money or bestow the rents on the most necessary repairs'.[43] The estate and the affairs of the Earl were in effect in the hands of receivers and if there had been no entail everything would have been sold. The creditors, including the trustees of Henrietta Scott, must have agreed to these arrangements. The Earl added a codicil to his will in 1792 whereby the legacy to Sir Andrew Cathcart was increased to £1,000 since his brother was dead and that to Gilbert McHaffie was rescinded as he had been given the lease of a farm on generous terms.[44]

Captain Kennedy was the son of Archibald, receiver general and collector of customs of New York, and the grandson of the 10th Earl's uncle, Alexander Kennedy of Craigoch and Kilhenzie. Reputedly Archibald had gone to America in July 1710 in the entourage of Governor Robert Hunter, the governor of New York, whose family came from Hunterston near West Kilbride on the Ayrshire coast.[45] Not long after his arrival he was given the freedom of the city by the Common Council, suggesting that already he was considered to be someone of importance. Hunter commissioned him as a 'Lieutenant of Fuzileers' in the following year to take part in the invasion of Canada. In April 1712 he joined the regular army as a third lieutenant in an independent company of foot at New York and was appointed adjutant of all four companies of regular soldiers in the colony. He held this post both under Hunter and his successor Governor Burnet, rising to the rank of captain, a title he used for the remainder of his life.

He became increasingly frustrated by the failure of the British government to provide adequate protection for the American colonies. Burnet, whose mother was the daughter of the 5th Earl of Cassillis, sent him to London in 1721 to intercede for more sustained support for the military to defend the border with Canada and to support the Iroquois Indians with whom Britain had signed a treaty. As he later put it 'we have assisted them in their Wars and Wants, and they have assisted us in our Wars, and we have their Furs'.[46] It was anticipated that the Iroquois would secure the allegiance of the six Indian nations of the Great Lakes and the Ohio and Mississippi valleys. Trade with the Indians had traditionally been through Albany, far to the north on the Hudson River. By this time Albany was in the hands of Dutch merchants who preferred to buy pelts in bulk from the French in Montreal. In this they threatened the security of the colony by allowing the French to gain influence over the Indians through the purchase of pelts.[47] When the Board of Trade rejected this appeal, Kennedy with his eye to the main chance traded his commission for the appointment as receiver general of the province of New York and as collector of customs for the port.[48]

On his return empty-handed, Governor Burnet with the support of Kennedy and fellow Scots such as James Alexander, a lawyer and surveyor general of New Jersey, and Robert Livingstone, speaker of the Assembly, tried to cut off the trade between Albany and Montreal. A British trading post was established at Oswego on the shores of Lake Ontario. This policy of seeking to gain the confidence of the six nations was not maintained and in fact the prohibition on trade with Montreal was overturned by the British government in 1729. Nevertheless the policy continued to be of central importance to Kennedy and his friend and fellow Scot, Cadwallader Colden, who had succeeded Alexander as surveyor general of New Jersey. In their view the consequence of granting land in remote areas almost rent-free was that the borders areas remained unsettled and therefore undefended unless Indian protection could be guaranteed. The six nations resented the appropriation of land without settlers with whom they could trade. In an effort to redress this problem, on taking up his post as receiver general Kennedy set about compiling a list of all land grants and the rents due. This confirmed what they both suspected, extensive fraud and evasion. For the next

forty years Kennedy was untiring in his efforts to improve the revenue of the Crown. He was often handicapped by the attitude of both the colonial and British governments. When he took up his appointment, the customs house was a dilapidated store built by the Dutch West India Company, which was eventually demolished as a public nuisance.[49] In 1742 the New Jersey assembly approved a measure to enforce collection of taxes, only to be vetoed by the Privy Council.[50]

Between 1713 and 1739 Kennedy himself patented some twenty-five thousand acres of land and another twenty thousand which he owned jointly with others. Although a large extent, it was in fact a modest acreage in comparison with that acquired by other government servants. Annoyed that he had no decent official place of business, in 1745 he purchased from Peter Bayard two houses in Broadway 'near the Fort' – Number 2 to serve as a customs house and Number 3 as his town house. He later persuaded the Common Council to sell him the site of the demolished customs house, which he considered was in danger of becoming 'a Dunghill and a Nuisance'. When he made his first will in 1738, he referred to lands in upper New York, two farms at Pavonia, near Hoboken in New Jersey, Negro slaves, plate, books, furniture, a chaise and several boats and canoes, which he presumably used to carry out his duties. In a codicil dated March 1745 he left his two Broadway houses to his daughter Catherine.[51] His principal residence outside the city was at Pavonia. His most profitable deal was the purchase in 1746 for £100 of Bedlow's Island, where the Statue of Liberty now stands, and which he sold to the city for use as a pest house in 1758 for £1,000.

By his first wife, a Miss Massam whom he married shortly after his arrival in New York, he had four sons, James, Robert, Archibald, Thomas, and a daughter, Catherine. As they were growing up the family became close friends with that of Benjamin Franklin. James was to be killed in the Carthegina expedition and Robert died unmarried before 1749.[52] The receiver general married his second wife in 1736 – Maria Walter, the widow of Arent Schuyler. The Schuylers were a prominent New York family of Dutch extraction, who like him were committed to better relations with the native Indian population so as to improve the security of the colony.[53]

As a prominent citizen and government official, it is only to be expected that Archibald Kennedy became a close confidant of successive governors. He refused, however, to become ensnared in New York's factional politics, notably during Governor Crosby's period of office from 1732 to 1736. Under Governor Clinton (1743–53), with a group of fellow Scots including Cadwallader Colden, he became a member of the 'Governor's Club', which effectively ran the colony. Entirely consistent with his character and his perception of his duty as an officer of the Crown, he was not willing to take sides in the bitter feud between Clinton and Chief Justice James De Laney, leading Colden to complain of his 'Laconick Stile'.[54] He may have been pusillanimous in politics, but in the early 1750s he became an outspoken pamphleteer in warning time and again of the need for good relations with the Iroquois in the defence of the northern border against the:

> barbarous *Canadians*, who are esteemed
> never in France, a Race of Men lost to
> all Principles of Honour upon which
> that Nation prides themselves, take
> pleasure in wantonly burning cottages
> and the inhuman torturing and murder-
> ing of harmless old women and helpless
> infants.[55]

Altogether he penned six essays between 1750 and 1755, five of which were published during his lifetime and of three of which he acknowledged the authorship. These were 'Observations on the Importance of the Northern Colonies under Proper Regulation' (1750), 'The Importance of Gaining and Preserving the Friendship of the Indians to the British Interest, Considered' (1751), 'An Essay on the Government of the Colonies'

(1752), 'Serious Considerations on the Present State of the Affairs of the Northern Colonies' (1754), 'A Speech Said to Have Been Delivered Some Time before the Close of the Last Session, By a Member Dissenting from the Church' (1755), and 'Serious Advice to the Inhabitants of the Northern-Colonies on the Present Situation of Affairs' (1755).[56] In these successive pamphlets he was critical of the Albany Commissioners of Indian Affairs, who attempted to steer a neutral path in their dealings with the Mohawks in the difficult transition from fur trading to settled agriculture, and to keep their trade route open with Montreal.[57] Having witnessed Indian discontent with the Commissioners at first hand, he advocated with Colden a Crown-appointed Superintendent of Indian Affairs and an inter-colonial defence force. These were to be paid for out of local excise duty on furs and goods traded with the Indians. When he sent the draft of his 1751 manuscript to be printed by James Parker, he forwarded it for his comments to Benjamin Franklin, who willingly endorsed it and added his own commentary.[58] Kennedy had already proposed that the government at Westminster needed to be much better informed about the American colonies. Condemning the Navigation Acts as repressive and contrary to 'the Conceptions we have of *English Liberty*', he had recommended a policy which would encourage the expansion of colonial trade to the mutual benefit of the United Kingdom:[59]

> [I]t is infallibly true, that whatever
> Wealth the Plantations gain, by any
> Article of Trade of Great Britain, is so
> much Gain to Great Britain, since every
> such Acquisition is sure to centre there
> at last; and therefore it is the Interest of
> Great Britain to encourage and promote
> the Industry and Labour of the
> Plantations …[60]

In his 'Serious Considerations on the Present State of the Affairs of the Northern Colonies' of 1754, which was dedicated to Henry Pelham, the prime minister, who had appointed him receiver general, Kennedy echoed Franklin's own views by forecasting difficulties in Anglo-American relations: 'nor will any country continue under subjection to another only because their Great Grandmothers were acquainted'.[61] He was critical of the British government for allowing the French to encroach on the northern border and for its failure to realise that in any campaign the Iroquois Indians would be of far more use than regular troops.[62] During that year Franklin took his advice before penning his own essay 'Short Hints towards a Scheme for Uniting the Northern Colonies'.[63] Although his advice and admonitions largely fell on deaf ears, Kennedy was important in helping shape American opinion and British policy. After 1756 he ceased to print his views, nevertheless he remained politically active and continued a prominent member of the Scottish community. During that year he helped found the St Andrew's Society of New York.[64] He resigned from the Governor's Council in 1761 and died at the age of seventy-eight in June 1763 still in office. Benjamin Franklin attended his funeral. He was remembered as 'a Gentleman who always sustain'd a fair and amiable Character' and whose passing was 'universally lamented by all his Acquaintances'. By this time he was reputed to have been worth £600 a year and had ceased regularly to transmit his customs accounts to Britain.[65] He left his property to his eldest surviving son, also Archibald, by then a captain in the Royal Navy.

This Archibald, who as a young man with two elder brothers had no expectations of any inheritance, was 'early bred to the sea' and found favour with Captain (later Admiral) Peter Warren, who served on the American station from 1735 to 1741.[66] Given his father's loyalty to the Crown and commitment to trade, it is perhaps not surprising that he encouraged his younger son to become a naval officer. It is not known when young Archibald joined the Royal Navy, but he was promoted to be a lieutenant in 1744 while serving on HMS *Royal Oak*. In 1746 he was posted to the sloop HMS *Otter*

on which he served for the next five years. At first the *Otter* was stationed in the Channel, stopping and searching enemy shipping which entailed constant action and good seamanship. With the prospect of peace in 1748, the ship was sent to North America to police the Chesapeake tobacco trade. Although he must have been pleased to be back in America, this was tedious work with long spells in harbour. The only action was against pirates and, in August 1748 the *Otter* captured a Spanish privateer.[67] She sailed for Britain in 1751 when Archibald was transferred to HMS *Centaur*.[68] Almost immediately he was back in North America, but this time in his home town of New York. Much of the time was spent at anchor in the North River with occasional sorties out to sea. He served as captain of HMS *Centaur* in 1753, returning to Britain two years later.[69]

During 1754 a further conflict had erupted between the American colonists and the French along the Canadian border, which was to have wider ramifications. After the crushing defeat of General Braddock's expeditionary force in 1755 by a mixed force of French and Indians, confirming the warnings of Captain Kennedy's father, reinforcements were ordered to be sent out from England under the command of the Earl of Loudoun. Considerable confusion and delay ensued, particularly over the shipping of the stores and troops.[70] Captain Kennedy, who was appointed along with Joshua Loring, captain of brigantines on Lake Ontario, was given the unenviable task of commanding a flotilla of about a dozen transports to be assembled at Deptford, presumably because he was familiar with the upstream navigation of the Hudson River. He spent the spring of 1756 wearisomely assembling his charges, checking they were seaworthy (some were not), mustering sufficient crew many from the press-gang, loading stores and finally embarking troops.

Eventually he set sail in late May, but even then there were delays because of contrary winds in the Channel and some ships ran aground. This was dangerous as the cargoes included large consign-

ments of gunpowder.[71] Every time the flotilla anchored, there were desertions and more men had to be pressed. It was not until late August that he finally shepherded his charges into New York 'without the least uncommon accidents during the voyage'. He had been there only a short time before news came that Fort Oswego on the shores of Lake Ontario and the destination for his cargoes and his brigantines had fallen to the French with the capture of over 1,500 men. He was still in New York in mid-October 'in a sort of purgatory by his Lordship's orders'.[72] He wrote to the Earl of Loudoun begging to be relieved and reporting that his officers and men were deserting in their droves to enlist with privateers. Desperate to be back in Britain now that war had been declared with France, he wrote again in mid-November to report that only Captain Harris, himself and his surgeon

Looking along the viaduct towards the old Tower gate in the 1880s.

remained at their posts, but still there was no relief.[73] He put his enforced residence in New York to good use, marrying the wealthy heiress Catherine, the daughter of Colonel Peter Schuyler, who left him Petersborough across the River Passaic from Newark. He bought from Colonel Abraham De Peyster Number 1 Broadway, which was next to his father's New York property, and set about building one of the finest houses in the city.[74]

He was destined to remain in America for another eight months superintending transports, enjoying married life and overseeing the building of his new home. He left New York in late June 1757 in the company of his friend Benjamin Franklin, who at that time was employed as a contractor to the army. He had been much delayed, along with everything else, in settling his accounts. According to him Captain Ludwige of the packet in which they took passage had boasted 'before we sailed, of the swiftness of his ship; unfortunately, when we came to sea, she proved the dullest of ninety-six sail [in the convoy], to his no small mortification'. Troubled about the cause when a similar vessel began to gain on his ship, Ludwige ordered the forty passengers to stand as near the ensign staff at the stern as possible to lift the bow. This had the desired effect, 'the ship mended her pace, and soon left her neighbour far behind, which prov'd what our captain suspected, that she was loaded too much by the head'. After adjustments had been made to improve the trim, 'the ship recover'd her character, and proved the sailor in the fleet'. With his confidence restored, he boasted his ship had once made thirteen knots per hour. Kennedy:

> contended that it was impossible, and no ship ever sailed so fast, and that there must have been some error in the division of the log-line … A wager ensued between the two captains, to be decided when there should be sufficient wind … Accordingly, some days after, when the wind blew very fair and fresh, and the captain of the packet, Ludwige, said he believ'd she went at the rate of thirteen knots, Kennedy made the experiment, and own'd his wager lost.

Off the Scilly Isles, Ludwige decided to run up the Channel at night to avoid French privateers. A lookout was placed in the bow to watch for the light on the Bishop's Rock. He failed to see it until very late. With the captain fast asleep, Kennedy, hearing the alarm, rushed on deck, and seeing the danger ordered all hands to wear (jibe) the ship. This was a hazardous manoeuvre as the yards swinging round with great force could break a mast. Thanks to Kennedy's swift action the ship was saved and made Falmouth the next day.[75] On his arrival at the Admiralty he was promoted to the rank of post captain,[76] briefly commanding the fifth

rate man-of-war HMS *Vestal*, almost certainly to qualify him for this rank.

With the United Kingdom now at war with both France and Spain in what was to be known as the 'Seven Years' War', Captain Kennedy was given command in 1758 of HMS *Flamborough* which joined Commodore Howe's squadron to take part in the ill-fated attack on Cherbourg in late August and early September.[77] After a spell patrolling the Channel, he was ordered to the Portugal and Mediterranean station as the senior officer with the task of protecting British trade with Portugal.[78] This was a potentially lucrative posting for an ambitious young post captain. One of the attractions of a naval career at the time was the huge rewards, which could be gained in prize money by the capture of enemy tonnage during a conflict. The captain of a vessel was entitled to three eighths of the value of the ship and its cargo, and a capitation fee for the number of prisoners taken. If he was cruising alone rather than under the command of a flag officer, he was entitled to the whole share, otherwise he had to give one eighth to his superior officer.[79] There was a good deal of luck in winning prize money. Some stations were more lucrative than others and smaller faster ships, such as the *Flamborough*, were more successful than large heavily gunned men-of-war. It was not unknown for captains to offer bribes to their fellow officers not to serve in such vessels.[80] The Portuguese station was one of the most lucrative, since not only was it an independent command and prizes were to be had, but also there was a ready trade for a prudent naval commander in smuggling contraband gold from Lisbon. Although strictly illegal, it was connived at by the Portuguese authorities as there was a large imbalance of trade with Britain. By common agreement naval ships were not searched by the customs on leaving port. Officers going ashore in Lisbon simply had their pockets filled by English merchants and were well rewarded for their pains.[81] They were entitled to carry bullion, or 'treasure' as it was termed in His Majesty's vessels, and to charge 'freight money' for its transport. Unlike prize money, this was divided only between the flag officer (one third) and the captain (two thirds).[82]

Captain Archibald Kennedy was energetic and valiant, and hardly a day at sea passed without an exchange of shot and a pursuit. Sometimes his impetuosity led to trouble, when he fired on British vessels including warships, but he could excuse himself as his duty was to stop and search. He quickly struck lucky, capturing early in September the two hundred ton *St Bruno* or *St Jean Baptista*, a heavily laden French East Indiaman.[83] Within days the *Flamborough* was hit by a hurricane which carried away the mizzenmast and threatened the main mast. When he realised that without a main sail the ship would be in danger of being broached by the heavy sea, he belayed the order to cut down the rigging. He was convinced that his command was about to founder with all hands, but he survived and the *Flamborough* put into Lisbon to refit. Back in action in November, he pursued and captured a notorious French brig privateer, carrying sixteen carriage guns and six swivel guns.[84] Her commander Jean Joseph Gussen from Marseilles, reputedly one of the best sailors in Europe, had captured no fewer than thirty-two English vessels in the previous three years.[85]

In the spring of 1760 the French had fitted out two frigates, *la Malicieuse* and *l'Opale*, to attack the only lightly protected convoys between the United Kingdom and Portugal.[86] Early in March they fell in with a convoy near the Bayona Islands and captured and burnt HMS *Penguin*. Kennedy in HMS *Flamborough* sailed in company with HMS *Bideford* to intercept them. On 4 April he sighted:

> four sail of ships in the North East quarter … I stood for them, being to Leeward, and they not making any alteration in their course, soon came near within gunshot of the headmost, who brought to at five in the afternoon. I fired several shot to invite her to action, shewing my colours at the same time.

> About half an hour the sternmost brought to.

Captain Kennedy identified two of the vessels as the French frigates which were accompanying two merchantmen. These made for port as soon as the *Flamborough* approached. Kennedy quickly overtook the sternmost French frigate and exchanged broadsides. He left her to the *Bideford*, which was three miles to the leeward and at 6.30 p.m. engaged the leader. During the next two and half hours of close action, the *Flamborough*'s 'masts, rigging and sails' were 'very much shattered and most of the running rigging cut to pieces …' The damage was hurriedly repaired and the battle resumed until eleven when the Frenchman broke off. Kennedy gave chase but the *Flamborough* 'being much disabled and every course and topsail rendered useless, it was in vain to pursue the enemy any longer'. Despite the hail of fire, only five men were lost. The *Bideford* inflicted similar damage, but herself suffered serious damage with the loss of her captain and lieutenant. It later transpired that on arrival at Brest both French frigates were found to be too badly damaged for further service.[87]

On 30 June in recognition of his gallantry he was gazetted captain and promoted to HMS *Quebec*, a thirty-two gun frigate. Within a month he was back in command of HMS *Flamborough* and struck lucky almost at once by capturing off the coast of Portugal the snow (similar to a brig) *Comte de Guiche*, a French privateer of eighteen carriage guns and with a crew of fifty-four, which belonged to the port of Bayonne.[88] Kennedy finally left the *Flamborough* in October when the British 'factory' (in other words the merchant community) at Lisbon presented him with a silver plate engraved with a scene of his encounter with the Euro French frigates (valued at £200) 'for his bravery and the protection, he always afforded their trade'.[89] This plate was later to become one of the treasures of Culzean after the death of the 1st Marquess in 1846. The Earl of Kinnoull, the British minister in Lisbon, reported to the secretary of state, William Pitt:

The Flamborough, Captain Kennedy, sailed with the Trade for England on 1st – I should not do justice to that gallant and sensible officer, if I omitted to inform you that at the same time that his diligence and bravery at sea entitled him to the esteem of all British merchants residing here of which they gave him an honourable testimony at his departure, his discreet and proper behaviour in Port has acquired him the good opinion of the Court and the Minister in so much that His Most Faithful Majestie [the King of Portugal] has been pleased more than once to signify to me by his General of the Marine & his Secretary of State for that Department, how acceptable the conduct of Captain Kennedy had been to His Majestie ever since he came upon the situation.[90]

Broadway from the Bowling Green By William James Bennett, probably in 1826. The first house on the left was the home of Captain Archibald Kennedy, later the 11th Earl of Cassillis. The third house was the home of his father Archibald Kennedy, the receiver general.

Kennedy was then appointed to HMS *Blonde*, a thirty-two gun frigate captured from the French the year before, taking the crew of the *Flamborough* with him. He was again posted as senior officer on the Portugal and Mediterranean station. In February 1761 after a hotly contested action in which his main mast was shot through, he captured off Cape Finisterre a large French letter of marque privateer bound from Bordeaux to St Domingo, carrying eighteen carriage guns with a crew of seventy-five.[91] His luck held and the following month he took *La Grande Serpente*, a twelve gun French privateer with a chosen crew of one hundred and sixteen men. He rescued in April the Spanish settee *Pregrin*, which was in distress, and in June captured a French brig of twelve guns and with thirty-two men and retook the *Penelope*, previously taken by the French. In mid-January 1762 he engaged the *Bertin*, a French East Indiaman of five hundred tons, carrying twenty guns and one hundred and eighty-nine men, homeward bound from Mauritius laden with coffee, sugar and spices. At first the enemy got the better of the encounter and shot away the *Blonde*'s topmost yard-arm. She bore away and Kennedy, ordering the wreckage to be cut away, gave chase. He captured this rich prize, reportedly worth £150,000, and brought her to Lisbon. He remained in the *Blonde* until the Peace of Paris in 1763.[92] Altogether he probably netted some £200,000 in prize money during the war, which was mostly invested in British or Portuguese government bonds.[93]

His next command was HMS *Coventry*, a twenty-eight gun frigate, and he was ordered to North America, sailing by way of Madeira and Bermuda. He was given command of all the Royal Navy ships on the New York station and was the second most senior officer in North America after Rear Admiral Lord Alexander Colvill, who was stationed in Nova Scotia. With the backing of the British government, which his father had never had, his duty was to enforce customs regulations, the Navigation Acts and the hated Sugar Act of 1764, which imposed higher taxes on imports of foreign textiles, wines, coffee, indigo and sugar. It was anticipated that his local knowledge and connections would be helpful in pursuing smugglers. He was resolute in carrying out these duties, ordering HMS *Hawk* to sea early in 1765, despite the ice, to prevent smuggling and protesting vehemently to the Admiralty when the New York merchants tried to have his captains arrested for seizing contraband goods.[94] After his years of action off the Iberian coast, Kennedy can have had no doubt that this posting would be fraught with difficulty, even if it would allow him to live in comfort either in his town house or in the country at Petersborough. The presence of naval vessels in the North River was not only to police trade but also to serve as a threat in case of trouble. The *Coventry* remained at anchor for months on end. Between 16 October 1763 and 31 June 1765 she was only at sea for twenty-four days. It is not surprising the crew became rest-

less and Kennedy, normally a humane man, had to resort to flogging to maintain discipline. However, he refused to execute serious miscreants, preferring sentences of fifty lashes.[95]

The greatest test of his command and reputation came during the Stamp Act crisis in the autumn of 1765. This tax-raising measure required that official revenue stamps should be fixed to all printed matter, such as newspapers and broadsides; and legal documents, such as leases, insurance policies and ship clearances, as indeed they were in Britain. The Act, which was to come into force in November, immediately roused hostility in the colonies, even though its purpose was to contribute towards the cost of the defence of the colonies. Since Captain Kennedy's father had long argued for some form of taxation for this purpose, it was hardly likely that his son would raise objections. After riots in Boston resistance spread like wildfire. On 3 September his father's old friend, now acting governor, Cadwallader Colden summoned him to discuss his fear that there was a plot to destroy the stamps on their arrival. Kennedy at once blockaded the port, instructing the naval ships under his command to stop and search every vessel which approached. Any ship found to be carrying stamps was to be escorted to Fort St George where its cargo was to be discharged. It was another six weeks before any ships carrying stamps arrived. In the meantime Kennedy had to deal with the resistance in other colonies. The stamp officer from Maryland arrived in New York and requested the use of a naval vessel as a stamp office. Quite properly he referred the matter to his admiral, but as soon as possible he ordered HMS *Hawke* to Maryland to give support. Later, Governor Sir William Franklin of New Jersey asked if their stamps could be stored for safe-keeping on board a naval ship. Kennedy, with Colden's backing, declined on the grounds that there was no room, the stamps would get damp, the vessels could be ordered to sea at a moment's notice and that if they remained on station they would soon be laid up for the winter. Admiral Colvill endorsed this course of action.

The consignment of stamps for New York arrived on 23 October. The *Edward*, which was carrying them, was escorted to Fort St George where there was no wharf to unload her large and varied cargo beneath which the stamps were stowed. When no merchant sloop could be secured for this purpose, Kennedy in exasperation ordered the naval sloop *Gaspee* to take her cargo on board and the boats of HMS *Guardland* to deliver the stamps to the fort. Greatly relieved, Colden wrote to the secretary of state, Henry Conway 'the officers of the Navy and Army with the greatest alacrity give me every assistance I desire'. There was no disturbance until Halloween when an on-the-whole good-natured mob roamed the streets breaking the odd window. The situation turned ugly the following day. Colden's carriage was burned and the house of the garrison commander was sacked. Scared stiff, Colden asked Kennedy to take the stamps on board ship. Again he refused, citing the reasons he had given before to Governor Franklin, and arguing it was too risky to remove the stamps from the fort. With time to reflect Colden agreed that Kennedy was right. However, on 6 December he told quite a different story in a letter to the Board of Trade in which he claimed that the Sons of Liberty had insisted that Kennedy take the stamps on board HMS *Coventry*:

> This I did not oppose but Captain
> Kennedy absolutely refused to receive
> them, & with good reason, for he was
> aware of their design to force him to
> deliver them to the Mob, by Threatening
> to destroy the houses he was possest of
> in the City, of which he had in his own
> and his Wife's right more than perhaps
> any one Man in it.

This was a calumny.

Meanwhile on 4 November the mayor of New York had written to Kennedy begging him to take the stamps on board HMS *Coventry*. Quite properly the captain replied that he could only act on the instruction of the governor and the provincial council who had already endorsed his course of action. This did not prevent the city fathers recording in their minutes on 5 November that Kennedy 'Cannot and will not' accept the stamps. After this exchange the city fathers took the stamps into their custody. To cover themselves, the provincial council copied the city fathers' minute into their own minute book and went so far as to send a transcription back to Britain. Their clear intention was to lay the blame at the captain's door, but they were to get more than they bargained for. The captain, unlike his father, was a man of action.

The tactics of those opposed to the Act was to intimidate the stamp distributors, force their resignation and then carry on business as usual on the grounds that no stamps were to be had. On 5 December the New York customs house began to clear ships unstamped. Kennedy immediately sought advice from the newly arrived Governor Sir Henry Moore and the customs authorities. Their response was equivocal, but the captain knew his duty. He ordered HMS *Guardland* to intercept and seize all unstamped clearances and informed Admiral Colvill that he had closed the port. There was uproar amongst the city merchants, and on Christmas Eve an effigy of Colvill was burned by the mob. An attempt to set fire to Kennedy's mansion at No. 1 Broadway was thwarted by the mayor. Despite this threat to his property, the captain was not to be moved. On 28 December the merchants, now badly frightened and with large numbers of unemployed seamen roaming the streets, wrote to him demanding an explanation for his actions in view of the fact that every other port in America was open. His reply was masterly, no doubt reflecting his experience of dealing with the Lisbon merchants a decade before: 'I shall always cheerfully do every thing in my power consistent with my duty to favour the Trade of this place, to which I sincerely wish the greatest prosperity.'

There can have been no one in New York who did not know of the captain's resolution in the face of the enemy; after all, he had huge silver salver in his house to prove it. The merchants, fearful of their own property at the hands of the mob, had no alternative but to agree. On 2 January the ice forced the naval ships into harbour and the blockade ended. A month later a letter arrived from Admiral Colvill informing the captain that he had no authority to seize unstamped consignments as it was purely a matter for the customs, a legal nicety if ever there was one.

In Britain the misrepresentation of the captain's actions by the governor, the provincial council and the city fathers had serious repercussions. Captain John Corner was sent to New York with orders to relieve Kennedy of the command of HMS *Coventry* for 'lack of zeal for His Majesty's service'. This was a most serious charge, akin to cowardice in the face of the enemy. Kennedy, knowing only too well the danger of his position, at once sought the help of Cadwallader Colden, who readily agreed to write in his support. He spent a fortnight in scrupulous preparation of his defence before embarking for home. Back in London the Lords of the Admiralty were quickly persuaded that he was not guilty of any crime: 'Let him know that their Lordships are satisfied with his conduct for the reasons contained in his letter and the enclosed papers, and they will take early opportunity to employ him.' He returned in triumph to his command on 25 September 1766 and soon became commanding officer of the North American squadron until the appointment of Commodore Samuel Hood in July 1767.[96] Four months later Kennedy set sail for England. He arrived off the Lizard on 10 December and proceeded to Chatham early in 1768 where HMS *Coventry* was paid off on 15 February. Captain Kennedy requested leave to return to New York to look after his affairs and in 1774 requested an indefinite extension.[97] He was placed on half-pay and never sought another command. His first wife, Catherine Schuyler, died some time after the Stamp Act crisis and in April 1769 he married Anne, the daughter of John Watts, another New York merchant. By her he had at least four sons: Archibald, the eldest (born 1770),

Ludovic (born 1771), John (born 1771) and Robert (born 1773) and a daughter Anne (born 1774). Knowing trouble was brewing in America, he left his substantial pickings in prize money and fees for carrying contraband bullion invested in England.

On the declaration of the American War of Independence in 1774, Captain Kennedy professionally sided with the loyalists and was employed in the defence of New York, which the British held throughout the war.[98] One of his main responsibilities was the construction and manning of the fortifications. His house at No. 1 Broadway became the British headquarters. During the war he seems to have become friendly with his fellow Scot Lieutenant Colonel John Small who raised the 2nd Battalion of the Royal Highland Regiment in 1778.[99] During that year Kennedy was apprehended by the Council of Safety of New Jersey and ordered to move to his property in Sussex County. At his protest, they relented and he was allowed to go to his Petersborough estate. When Prince William (later to become King William IV) arrived in New York in 1781 as a midshipman on HMS *Prince George*, Captain Kennedy and his family befriended him. Young Archibald struck up a lifelong friendship with the Prince who was only five years his senior. Captain Kennedy decided to leave America towards the end of the year taking his young family to safety in Britain and making a home for himself in London.[100]

Shortly after he arrived he opened a bank account with Thomas Coutts,[101] who soon became a close friend, and drew up his first surviving will. He clearly hoped that his family would eventually be able to return to America. He still owned the Pavonia estate, which he left to his eldest son Archibald, and property in New York known as Barbados Nick, which he left to his next son Ludovic. He appointed as his executors in America his brothers-in-law, Robert and John Watts, and Dr Jonathan Mallett, inspector general of His Majesty's Hospital in New York, who was married to his sister Catherine. His British executors were his distant cousin, David Earl of Cassillis, Lady Jane

Riddell of Hampstead, and William Sheriff of Arlesford House, Hampshire.[102] Lady Jane Riddell was the daughter of James Buchanan, a successful Virginian merchant, who began his career in Glasgow and later moved to London. The Buchanans were well-connected in colonial American society and Kennedy had had business dealing with them there.[103] She was the widow of Sir John Riddell, a partner in Buchanans.

Captain Kennedy seems to have returned alone to New York late in 1782 just before the end of the war. On his arrival, he found his house at Pavonia had been burned and much of his property confiscated, including his town house at No. 1 Broadway which had been appropriated by none other than George Washington himself. This was later returned to him. Disappointed, he left his American property in the charge of his

HMS Flamborough *in action against two French frigates in 1760. She was commanded by Captain Archibald Kennedy, later the 11th Earl of Cassillis. His success in putting both enemy ships out of action earned him the respect of the British community in Lisbon who presented him with a silver salver with an engraving of the painting. This is still a treasured family possession.*

brothers-in-law and returned for good to London. Here he began to use his considerable wealth to build an even larger fortune.

He had no interest in landed property, which he could easily have afforded, preferring to live modestly but well in fashionable London. At first Captain Kennedy rented a house in Percy Street off Rathbone Place, and then in Mortimer Street, off Cavendish Square, where he and his wife became friendly with Sir Grey Cooper and his family, who were well known to the Earl of Cassillis.[104] He must have got to know his cousin as in 1783 the Earl secretly signed a deed of entail in his favour confirming that the Culzean estates as well as the Cassillis estates (already entailed to him) would pass to him and his male heirs.[105] Captain Kennedy later bought a house at No. 12 Charles Street in Mayfair, not far from his brother-in-law, Dr Jonathan Mallet in

Bryanstone Square, who by this time had also come home. Captain Kennedy was pensioned off by the navy in September 1787. Curiously, one of his first purchases on his formal retirement was a 'best sea chest with a box' and two locks for £1 11 shillings and 6 pence, perhaps because he expected to be making regular sea voyages to Scotland. It would seem he visited Culzean at least once during these years as he jokingly told the Earl that he could capture the place on any night with a dozen gamekeepers armed with nothing more than dog whips.[106]

During these years in London John, the captain's third son, completed his education; Ludovic, the second son, died; and in 1784 his eldest son, Archibald, was commissioned in the 16th Regiment of Foot.[107] He was gazetted as an ensign on 16th April 1784, aged just fourteen, joined his regiment in Ireland where he was to remain for the next six years, being promoted lieutenant in May 1788. He soon showed himself to be an outstanding and fearless horseman. Writing in 1794 Captain W.J. Erskine, a fellow officer, commented:

I have been out hunting regularly three times a week since I came here some-times on my charger and sometimes on a troop horse … My Charger is just such a horse as Lord Cassillis would give 200 guineas for, he is the best hunter I ever crossed & no leap you can shew him but he will clear …[108]

Apart from his naval pension of £93 a year,[109] Captain Kennedy had assets in the United Kingdom of at least £200,000 invested in government stock and mortgages, which would have given him an income of about £7,000 a year, more than many members of the aristocracy.[110] In 1786 he took a stake in the East Indiaman, the *General Elliot*, and the following year purchased a redeemable annuity worth £20,000.[111] Under the terms of such a loan the borrower, usually the owner of an entailed estate or the heir, agreed to pay the lender an annuity each year for the remain-der of their life and repay the principal on their death. Since, unlike a mortgage, there was an

element of chance in such arrangements, they were not subject to the usury laws, which limited interest payments to 5 per cent. Early repayment was entirely a matter for the lender and if the borrower turned out to be very long lived repayments could far exceed the capital. Captain Kennedy devoted some of his wealth to travelling on the continent with his friend Colonel John Small, who had also come home on half-pay.[112] During one expedition he drew a not altogether flattering caricature of his companion.[113] Directly his cousin the Earl of Cassillis signed the new deed of entail in 1790, Kennedy settled half his English fortune on his eldest son on the understanding he would have no further claim against his estate either there or in North America.[114]

It is difficult to be certain how much of the final phase of building at Culzean was completed by 1790. In March, a month after the new deed of entail, again secret, was signed, the Earl wrote to John Ballantyne, the cashier of the Royal Bank of Scotland in Ayr:

Prince William, later King William IV, serving as a midshipman on board HMS Prince George in 1781, engraved by Francesco Bartolozzi and Paul Sandby.

I have a letter by last post from Hugh Cairncross acquainting me that he will immediately want fifty pounds sterling more than his credit upon you now extends so I here desire that you will advance it and as the Work cannot now stop I must beg you will give him what money he may call for … till I return to Scotland at which period I hope my operations will be at an end for I am really wearied of Building and wish to be at rest.[115]

Ballantyne, who would have had a pretty good idea of how things stood at Culzean, must have known that this was little more than wishful thinking. On 23 April Adam wrote to Hugh Cairncross, now working at Dalquharran in the Girvan valley for Thomas Kennedy of Dunure, who was married to Adam's niece, stating:

I have not seen Lord Cassillis since his illness but hear he is a great deal better in his health – one day that he was with me before his illness he desired me to make out Designs for his Saloon and Staircase and particularly the ornamental stucco which his Lordship said he intended should be done by Mr Coney though he knew he was given to drinking, yet he did not like new people and was to employ him. This I suppose neither his Lordship nor Mr Coney has informed you of, and I shall be obliged to you for acquainting me when these resolutions are taken as it enables me to settle better with his L[ord]ship here – send me a list of what drawings you think will be necessary by return of post and I will get them put in hand directly as I can draw them as they may best answer the rooms for which they are intended.

I have never received from Lord Cassillis the drawing of the saloon chimney piece etc. which you sent him, but your ideas about them in the meantime will enable me to get forward with them.[116]

This suggests that contrary to the Earl's assertion, the saloon and staircase were not much beyond the design stage. Although reportedly recuperating, he was to remain a semi-invalid until his death two and half years later, for much of the time unable to venture out.[117] On 5 October 1790, the Earl wrote to Hunter & Co., bankers in Ayr to ask them to meet a bill of £320 from William Cairncross, Hugh's brother and a cabinet-maker in London, for 'chimney pieces he had been carving'. He explained he hoped to be able to find that money and also 'what else you may be in advance for me' by November.[118]

A drawing of the castle by S. Hooper published on 25 February 1791 shows the drum tower

roofless, with a considerable amount of work still to be done. Francis Grose, who included the drawing in his *Antiquities of Scotland* published in 1797, commented in something of an understatement: 'This edifice here represented was erected by the present Earl … when this view was taken it was not quite complete.'[119] Hugh Cairncross's account book includes no payments for work on the house after January 1792,[120] although some vouchers were retained by the Earl himself, possibly because Cairncross was under instruction from the creditors not to accept any more commitments.[121] Most of the work carried out during 1791 was in decorating and fitting out the library, the bedrooms and the octagonal ante-room to the saloon which was to be used

Captain Archibald Kennedy, who became 12th Earl of Cassillis and 1st Marquess of Ailsa, riding his racehorse Champion first winner of the Ayr Gold Cup, reputedly painted by Ben Marshall in 1800.

for billiards now that the old billiard room had been demolished.[122] The external works including the new coach house, the foundations of which do not even appear in the Hooper drawing, and ruined arch, also seem to have been left unfinished by the time of Robert Adam's sudden death in March. His final account, settled on 9 March, related to work undertaken in 1791, presumably the designs for the saloon and staircase.[123] Interestingly the original drawings for the staircase in the Soane museum show the simpler Ionic orders on the first floor and the more elaborate Corinthian capitals on the floor above.

It is likely that the creditors would not have allowed any more work to proceed other than to make the castle wind and watertight, and would

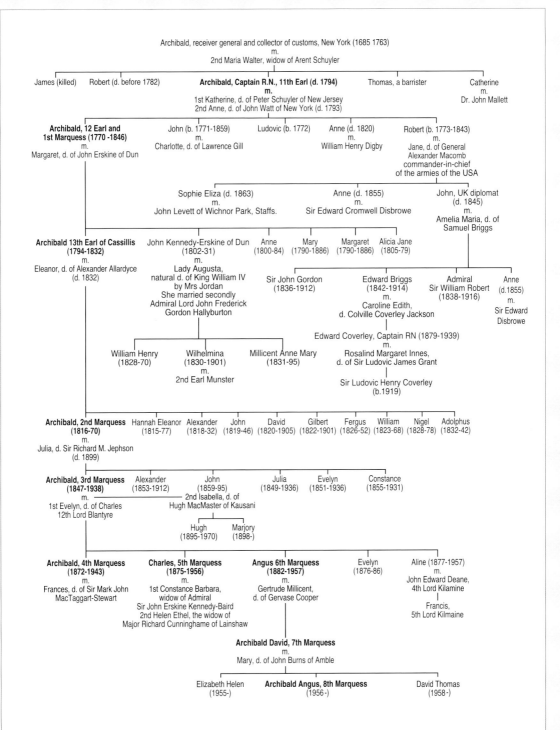

Archibald, receiver general and collector of customs, New York (1685 1763)
m.
2nd Maria Walter, widow of Arent Schuyler

James (killed)   Robert (d. before 1782)   **Archibald, Captain R.N., 11th Earl (d. 1794)**   Thomas, a barrister   Catherine
m.   m.
1st Katherine, d. of Peter Schuyler of New Jersey   Dr. John Mallett
2nd Anne, d. of John Watt of New York (d. 1793)

Archibald, 12 Earl and   John (b. 1771-1859)   Ludovic (b. 1772)   Anne (d. 1820)   Robert (b. 1773-1843)
1st Marquess (1770 -1846)   m.   m.   m.
m.   Charlotte, d. of Lawrence Gill   William Henry Digby   Jane, d. of General
Margaret, d. of John Erskine of Dun   Alexander Macomb
                                                                                               commander-in-chief
                                                                                               of the armies of the USA

                    Sophie Eliza (d. 1863)   Anne (d. 1855)   John, UK diplomat
                    m.   m.   (d. 1845)
                    John Levett of Wichnor Park, Staffs.   Sir Edward Cromwell Disbrowe   m.
                                                                                              Amelia Maria, d. of
                                                                                              Samuel Briggs

Archibald 13th Earl of Cassillis   John Kennedy-Erskine of Dun   Anne   Mary   Margaret   Alicia Jane
(1794-1832)   (1802-31)   (1800-84)   (1790-1886) (1790-1886)   (1805-79)
m.   m.
Eleanor, d. of Alexander Allardyce   Lady Augusta,
(d. 1832)   natural d. of King William IV   Sir John Gordon   Edward Briggs   Admiral   Anne
                                        by Mrs Jordan   (1836-1912)   (1842-1914)   Sir William Robert (d.1855)
                                        She married secondly   m.   (1838-1916)   m.
                                        Admiral Lord John Frederick   Caroline Edith,   Sir Edward
                                        Gordon Hallyburton   d. Colville Coverley Jackson   Disbrowe

                                                                              Edward Coverley, Captain RN (1879-1939)
                                                                              m.
            William Henry   Wilhelmina   Millicent Anne Mary   Rosalind Margaret Innes,
            (1828-70)   (1830-1901)   (1831-95)   d. of Sir Ludovic James Grant
                                 m.
                                 2nd Earl Munster   Sir Ludovic Henry Coverley
                                                                             (b.1919)

Archibald, 2nd Marquess   Hannah Eleanor   Alexander   John   David   Gilbert   Fergus   William   Nigel   Adolphus
(1816-70)   (1815-77)   (1818-32)   (1819-46)   (1820-1905) (1822-1901)   (1826-52)   (1823-68)   (1828-78)   (1832-42)
m.
Julia, d. Sir Richard M. Jephson
(d. 1899)

Archibald, 3rd Marquess   Alexander   John   Julia   Evelyn   Constance
(1847-1938)   (1853-1912)   (1859-95)   (1849-1936)   (1851-1936)   (1855-1931)
m.   ─ 2nd Isabella, d. of
1st Evelyn, d. of Charles   Hugh MacMaster of Kausani
12th Lord Blantyre
                                                Hugh   Marjory
                                                (1895-1970) (1898-)

Archibald, 4th Marquess   **Charles, 5th Marquess**   **Angus 6th Marquess**   Evelyn   Aline (1877-1957)
(1872-1943)   **(1875-1956)**   **(1882-1957)**   (1876-86)   m.
m.   m.   m.   John Edward Deane,
Frances, d. of Sir Mark John   1st Constance Barbara,   Gertrude Millicent,   4th Lord Kilamine
MacTaggart-Stewart   widow of Admiral   d. of Gervase Cooper
                               Sir John Erskine Kennedy-Baird   Francis,
                               2nd Helen Ethel, the widow of   5th Lord Kilmaine
                               Major Richard Cunninghame of Lainshaw

                               Archibald David, 7th Marquess
                               m.
                               Mary, d. of John Burns of Amble

            Elizabeth Helen   **Archibald Angus, 8th Marquess**   David Thomas
            (1955-)   **(1956-)**   (1958-)

Family tree of the Earls of Cassillis and the Marquesses of Ailsa.
This is not comprehensive and does not necessarily include all the children of a marriage.

The drawing of Culzean by S. Hooper in 1791 showing the uncompleted roof of the drum tower.

have cancelled works that had not been started or were not essential. Expenditure was certainly scaled down, falling to just over £2,500 between April 1790 and December 1792 when the Earl died. John McClure, the plasterer, submitted no accounts after 1790, although one and a half tons of alabaster were delivered in November 1792. Moreover some of the chimney pieces that had been delivered were sent back. The contract with Thomas White to lay out the grounds must have been cancelled as no other payments were received. The Earl's final extravagance was to have some of the pictures reframed, including a portrait of his friend Lord Mountstuart, the eldest son of the Earl of Bute.[124] All work definitely stopped at Cassillis and modifications to the house remained unfinished.[125]

It is evident that in all the Earl's building projects, there had been no attempt to control costs. Writing in 1796, Richard Campbell, the factor,

reported: 'In former times things were done without ascertaining *quantity or price* which was bad for either party that meant to act honestly.'[126] He had been appointed factor by his brother William Campbell of Craigie and the other creditors to replace the elderly Captain Robert Kennedy of Daljarrock who, early in 1792, had fallen into the river between the two bridges at Ayr and drowned. With Campbell in charge, any work undertaken from then on would have a strict eye to economy. Moreover, he brought with him new agricultural ideas. He changed the system of rotation in the leases and in June 1792 introduced 'two score of ewe hogs, and a ram' of the Cheviot bread on Tarfessok, one of the highest hill farms on the estate which was tenanted by Mr McHutcheson of Changue. To the surprise of other local farmers who expected them all to die in the severe winter of 1793, the 'long sheep', as they were dubbed, flourished and, even more galling, produced better

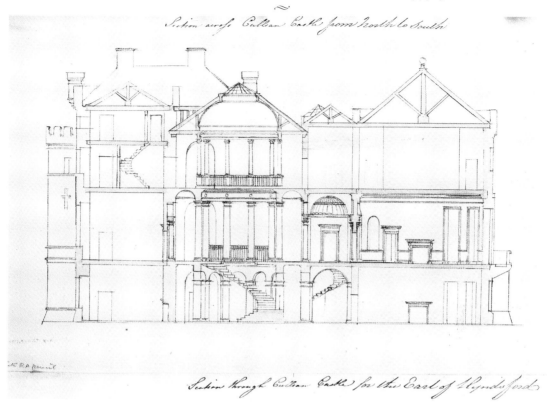

Section across Cullean Castle from North to South

Section through Cullean Castle for the Earl of Glyndeford

quality and more wool than the native 'short' breeds. As a result incomes could be increased with fewer sheep per acre. Overstocking had been a persistent problem on hill farms and the principal reason for high rates of mortality during severe winters.[127]

It was only with the news that the Earl was mortally ill in the spring of 1792 that Captain Kennedy began to take his claim to the estate seriously. He had been in contact with the Earl for some time, and the Earl for his part took an interest in the careers and fortunes of the Captain's children. With the Earl's agreement, Captain Kennedy instructed John Hunter, the Edinburgh family lawyer who was also a partner in Hunter & Co. (the Ayrshire bankers), to research the validity of his claim by examining the papers in Register House. In June Hunter reported on 'my researches in the Records, what has been more troublesome & tedious than I expected & as I could not well commit any part of the

> The original drawings of the great staircase by Robert Adam with the Greek capitals clearly shown in the correct order.

Business to another I have been the longer getting it done than I expected or would have wished'.[128]

Although the Earl, convalescing in Edinburgh, was by July able to go out in a carriage, he was not strong enough to make the journey to Culzean until later in the year. The Captain's eldest son, Archibald Kennedy, who had been gazetted a captain in an independent company of foot the year before,[129] travelled to Scotland in July 1792 maybe to take up his duties, but more likely with his inheritance in view. The majority of recruiting in Scotland at this time was through independent companies which were drafted into regiments as required.[130] On Arran, he rented Spring Bank House, behind the Douglas Hotel near Strathwhillan Bridge, from where he could watch events across the Firth of Clyde at Culzean. The Earl was concerned about the young captain abandoning his profession. Unaware of Captain Kennedy's generous settlement, he instructed Hunter to scold him: 'You are a thought-less extravagant Boy. He does not like you running about that way from place to place.' Hunter passed on the Earl's opinion that he should be 'settled either in the Guards or the Dragoons' – ' he does not like the Idea of any young Man being quite idle who has been bred to a Profession.'[131] Disregarding this advice, Captain Kennedy junior remained in Ayrshire until early December. By then Hunter had travelled with the Earl to Culzean and from an examination of the family papers convinced himself that the captain's claim was sound. When the Earl died there on 18 December, he wrote the next day telling the captain to call himself Earl of Cassillis at once, but adding the disturbing intelli-gence that the estate would remain in trust until the 10th Earl's debts (thought to be in the region of £40,000–£50,000) were repaid. Suspecting trouble, John Hunter on that day arranged for all the Earl's papers to be sealed in the presence of Captain Kennedy junior (now Lord Kennedy, a courtesy title that had not been used for almost a century), Thomas Kennedy of Dunure, Primrose Kennedy of Drumellan, Mr Webster, Dr Gillespie and the Earl's factor, Richard Campbell. The keys were handed to Thomas Kennedy as one of the trustees appointed under the terms of the Earl's will. This was an unusual procedure as in normal circumstances the keys would have been given to the heir; but these were not normal circumstances.[132]

The Earl was buried in the collegiate church at Maybole on New Year's Eve. The following day the charter chest was opened in the presence of Lord Kennedy, Sir Andrew Cathcart, Thomas Kennedy of Dunure, Primrose Kennedy of Drumellan and John Hunter. When the will was read by Thomas Kennedy and the secret deed of entail produced, Sir Andrew was furious and announced that he would contest it. He had every right to be disappointed since as recently as 1790 the 10th Earl had sup-ported him in standing for parliament in Ayrshire, unsuccessfully as it turned out. Unable to get home, the party spent an uneasy New Year's evening at Culzean.[133] On 16 January 1793 John

Hunter wrote to all the trustees with the unwel-come news of their onerous duties under the terms of the deed of entail. He informed them that the debts were at least £65,000, that the rental was only £4,050, and that the value of the land to be sold between £9,000 and £10,000.[134] They could have been in no doubt that meeting these obligations would take a long time if the estate was to be sal-vaged, particularly as Sir Andrew seemed bent on an expensive and damaging law suit. Within a week John Hunter wrote again to tell them that there was no hope of a settlement with Sir Andrew, who had refused an offer of a further £4,000 over and above the £1,000 he had been left.[135] Sir Andrew now tried to gain entry to Culzean to get access to the charter chest. This was locked away in the safe and Thomas Kennedy of Dunure had the keys. The Earl's lawyers cautioned the trustees that all such demands should be rebuffed.[136]

The death of the 10th Earl definitely brought all building operations to an end, as the responsibility of the trustees was to liquidate his enormous debts. It is difficult to know what motivated the Earl's reck-less expenditure on his cliff top palace. After all he had several other homes including Newark, which by all accounts he loved dearly. With only a distant American cousin as heir, there was no one to put a break on his extravagance until his resources were almost exhausted. This still does not explain why he chose to rebuild Culzean on such an ostentatious scale, demolishing buildings which were only just over thirty years old. Was his intention, perhaps, to create a shrine for his brother's collections or simply to assert the power of the Kennedys in the county, throwing down the gauntlet to his brother Earls of Loudoun and Eglinton. He was not alone in Ayrshire in such conspicuous consumption. Colonel William Fullarton of Fullarton, writing about the county in 1794, commented wistfully 'the greatest number of old families have, within the present century, been obliged to sell their property, embarassed by the reigning spirit of conviviality and speculation, dis-proportionate to their income.'[137]

CHAPTER 5
Americans to the rescue:
1792–1816

Captain Kennedy, now the 11th Earl, chose to remain in London while the trustees of the 10th Earl's estate, of whom he was one, set about trying to rescue what they could. Feeling his age, he left his son and heir Lord Kennedy to deal with the trustees on a day-to-day basis while he and his wife had their portraits painted by the well-known American artist Mather Brown who was now resident in London.[1] The 11th Earl had another cause for concern. In 1793 another rival claimant to the title emerged, the Reverend Alexander Kennedy, a Church of Ireland clergyman in Cork, who maintained legitimate descent from John Kennedy of Kilhenzie, the receiver general's elder brother. Lacking the funds to prosecute his case, he effectively blackmailed the 11th Earl and his son for the next twenty-five years.[2]

Sir Andrew Cathcart's case first came to court on 17 December 1793 when his counsel argued that under the terms of the will of his grandfather, Sir John Kennedy, he was entitled to the whole Culzean estate which he contested was not subject to male descent like Cassillis.[3] The case continued throughout the following year with petitions and counter petitions during which the full extent of the Earl's financial embarrassment emerged. As a result, in 1795 Sir Andrew changed tack and demanded the payment of £25,000 in return for which he and his co-heirs would abandon all further claims as heir to his three uncles, John, Thomas and David.[4] He argued that, under the terms of his grandfather's will, some of the property should have passed to himself and his co-heirs at the time of the 9th Earl's death in 1775. There was a political motive to the suit, as Sir Andrew was not prepared to allow an outsider to have any influence in an Ayrshire election. Moreover there had for centuries been no love lost between the Cathcarts and the Kennedys of Culzean. This was a double blow to the trustees. It raised the potential indebtedness of the 10th Earl's estate to £90,000 and at the same time prevented the sale of any property until the case was settled.[5] The estate was completely paralysed. All the trustees could do was to use the surplus from the rental, after payment of interest and expenses, to defray the debt and meet interest charges; just over £1,000 a year.[6] From the outset the trustees regarded their task as a hopeless and were quickly convinced that their only course of action was to break the entail by Act of Parliament, and sell a larger part of the estate than had been intended; but even this obvious expedient could be frustrated by political action. Since the trustees were only responsible for the entailed part of the estate, the income from the unentailed parts came directly to the Earl. This amounted to some £800 a year and was never sufficient to cover the expenditure on the property and some personal and household necessities. With the family resident in London for much of the year, the establishment at Culzean was run down.

The Earl and his Countess visited Culzean in

1793 and set about making the castle habitable. He ordered curtaining, carpets and yards of chintz from the fashionable Edinburgh upholsterers, Young, Trotter and Hamilton, who also sent staff to the castle to hang wallpaper. They supplied two bamboo circular sofas and eight bamboo chairs.[7] While at Culzean, the Earl borrowed six silver candlesticks to grace his Charles Street table in London.[8] His other reason for coming north was to celebrate the wedding on 1 June of his eldest son, Captain Archibald junior, to Margaret, second daughter of John Erskine of Dun, near Montrose in Angus. Archibald had met his bride through her brother Captain William John Erskine, also of an independent company of foot.[9] William was heir to the estate, which produced an income of some £2,000 a year.[10] At the end of December the Earl's wife died in Edinburgh and was buried at Holyrood on 1 January 1794. Her funeral was a grand affair with four black silk flags bearing the family escutcheon flying at each point of the hearse and hatchments on either side.[11]

The 11th Earl only outlived his wife by exactly a year, dying on the same day in 1794 at the age of seventy-six. As agreed, he left nothing to his eldest son, as he had already been well provided for. The Earl's only daughter Anne inherited for her lifetime the lease and contents of his Charles Street house apart from the six candlesticks, which were to be returned to Culzean, and his Lisbon plate, which he left to his eldest son Archibald, who succeeded to the earldom. Anne inherited £10,000 which was to be invested to provide an income during her lifetime and then divided amongst her children, and if there were none was to be returned to the family. She was left £4,000 for her own use. The residue of the estate in England and North America the Earl left to his two surviving sons; John, now a captain in an independent company of foot and resident in London, and Robert, 'share and share alike', with

OPPOSITE AND OVERLEAF

The portraits of Captain Archibald Kennedy, 11th Earl of Cassillis, and his second wife Anne Watts, painted by the American artist, Mather Brown, in London in 1793. The Earl's action against two French warships in 1760 is depicted to the left. These appear to be cut down versions of full-length portraits.

the proviso that one of them continue to live at his New York home, No. 1 Broadway.

Robert by this time had returned to America and was resident at New Ark (Newark) in the State of New Jersey.[12] He was by all accounts American in his outlook and he bought out his brother Captain John's interest in their share of their father's estate in the country with the intention of living there permanently. However, he sold No. 1 Broadway to his Watts cousins in 1801 for £2,500 and the rest of his American property over the next two years. He had returned with his wife and family to London by 1803 but soon found it not to his liking,[13] and went instead to live at La Chartreuse on the shore of the Thuner See in Switzerland. He was sufficiently British, however, to be jealous of his privacy and put up a notice to warn off would-be trespassers. To his chagrin a French visitor scrawled on one 'ce farouche insulaire, ce misanthrope ridicule' – this wild islander, this ridiculous misanthrope.[14] Altogether the 11th Earl's estate in the United Kingdom amounted to about £40,000 before the legacies were paid to Anne,[15] leaving the two brothers some £26,000, which would have produced an income of some £400 a year each. This time he appointed as his English executors Lady Riddell as before, Peter van Schenk, a London merchant, and Francis Adams of Norton Malreward in Somerset.

Settling the 11th Earl's affairs turned out to be a protracted affair. There were problems about settling the debts on the unentailed parts of the estate in Scotland, including Culzean, which his son the 12th Earl assured the trustees could be 'settled by raising rents'. This was, however, easier said than done.[16] At the same time Richard Campbell, who was still factor, advised the Earl to register any future improvements with the sheriff court under the terms of the Montgomery Entail Act of 1770 so that they would become a charge on the estate and not on him personally.[17] In June 1795 the 11th Earl's

daughter Lady Anne married Colonel William Henry Digby, whom neither the 12th Earl nor his brother Captain John trusted. Digby appointed as trustees of his marriage settlement Thomas Coutts and a Dr Langford who turned out to be dishonest. Colonel Digby then asked the trustees to advance him £1,200 to help him buy an estate at West Grinsted in Surrey.[18] Suspecting that Digby had designs on their sister's fortune, the brothers insisted that the estate could not be sold to meet any debts he might incur without their permission, and that if she predeceased him and there were no children of the marriage then he could no longer use her income to defray the mortgage.[19] Their fears were justified nine years later when Digby, seriously in debt, remortgaged the property and demanded the balance of his wife's inheritance from Coutts. By that time Dr Langford was 'now somewhere in jail or lately out' and Coutts 'sadly troubled' resigned as a trustee.[20]

The 12th Earl was just twenty-four and had radical (if not always consistent) political ambitions coloured by his American upbringing. He remained unmistakably American for the whole of his life. His letters gave him away. He wrote in a large florid hand and generously sprinkled his text with capital letters, much underlining and an unfashionable use of parenthesis. Hyperbole was never far away. This became very obvious during the early months of 1797 when invasion threatened. The French fleet had been driven out of Bantry Bay in Ireland by a gale on Christmas Day and the British fleet was taken by surprise, not able to get to sea until 3 January. Thoroughly alarmed at the possibility of an Irish rising, plans prepared by Henry Dundas, secretary of war, were set afoot for the self-defence of the country. The first initiatives had been taken as long ago as 1793 at the outbreak of war, when yeomanry and fencible regiments had been raised, including in Scotland the Western Fencible Regiment with Hugh Montgomerie, the heir to the Earl of Eglinton, as colonel and Lord Kennedy (later the 12th Earl) as Lieutenant Colonel.[21] The fencibles were only a temporary

expedient and the following year lord lieutenants were appointed for the first time in Scotland, with instructions to raise volunteers. Responding to the crisis three years later, Dundas introduced a Scottish militia bill.[22] The lord lieutenants were to play a pivotal role in arming the population and gave the great magnates the power to extend their influence over the gentry through the appointment of deputies and military patronage.[23] The Earl of Eglinton was appointed Lord Lieutenant of Ayrshire and singularly failed to nominate the Earl of Cassillis amongst his deputies. The response to the call to arms was much more enthusiastic than in England, largely because Scotland had a coastline which was long and difficult to defend, as smugglers knew only too well. Again unlike England, volunteering in Scotland remained throughout the war as much a rural as an urban phenomenon and was therefore county based.[24] There were dangers inherent in arming and training the populace, but the government was powerless to prevent it and all Dundas could do was to try to control it through local government institutions.[25] Later in the war the volunteers were to provide a vital source of recruits into the militia and regular army.

On 6 February 1797 Thomas Kennedy of Dunure wrote to his friend the Earl of Cassillis complaining that there were insufficient experienced soldiers to drill recruits. This was to be a persistent problem throughout the war.[26] Kennedy proposed the reconstitution of the West Fencibles:

> The skeleton of the old regiments which the Duke of Portland [a landowner in Ayrshire] mentioned to your Lordship if properly distributed might be of great service in this respect and also in the case of cavalry by mixing them with the volunteer corps who never saw real service.[27]

His real concern was the 'rabble', mostly the Irish 'people we should be better without'. Cassillis responded by suggesting the formation of a cavalry regiment, presumably on the model of the fencibles, composed of gentlemen without pay: ' I am clear that every Gentleman now should be mounted and accoutred.'[28] On 13 February Kennedy reported on a meeting he had attended in Edinburgh convened by the lord provost, with the Duke of Buccleuch in attendance, at which it was agreed offers of 'volunteer corps (not by way of puffins* but such as were most seriously to be useful) should be encouraged'.[29] Three days later Richard Campbell, the factor to the Earl of Cassillis, wrote from Culzean that he had received the promise of one hundred and twenty horses and carts from the tenantry, who had expressed concern that, if they kept guns at home, they might be open to accusations of poaching: 'To convince the world that your Lsh is not *puffing* if ever these horses are required Your Lordship's factor and Baron Officers will take care that every Man is at his station the moment they are wanted.'[30] Captain John Shaw,* the Earl of Cassillis's cousin and a retired professional soldier living in Maybole,[31] eagerly began to train these recruits. He wrote to the Earl urging that the promised fifes and drums be sent as soon as possible, perhaps suggesting that there was an element of puffery in the enterprise.[32]

On 24 February 1797 as lord lieutenant the Earl of Eglinton, who had succeeded to the title the year before, called a meeting of the county, at which the 12th Earl of Cassillis was not present. It was announced that subscriptions 'for furnishing Horses, Carts, etc. for conveying Troops in case of emergency, had been filled up through the County in general'. Hamilton of Sundrum moved:

> That whereas the enemies of this
> country have avowed their determina-
> tion to invade these kingdoms with an

armed force; and whereas, we know that these enemies have carried devastation and destruction into every country that had the misfortune to be invaded by them, and whereas, we have had recent experience of their attempt to invade Ireland, which by the blessing of divine Providence has been prevented from taking effect; the Lord Lieutenant and the Deputies and other Magistrates in it, having met this day and agreed to imitate the laudable example of other counties in England and Scotland in preparing a Volunteer armed corps to resist such diabolical attempts of our enemies, and for the protection of our wives and our children and our laws, of our property and everything that is sacred or dear to mankind.[33]

Following this resolution volunteer companies were raised throughout the county by the deputy lieutenants and the magistrates. This effectively excluded the Earl of Cassillis as he was not a deputy lieutenant. The task in Carrick fell to the five deputies there – Sir Andrew Cathcart, Sir John Whitefoord, Thomas Kennedy of Dunure, Primrose Kennedy of Drumellan and Quinton McAdam of Craigengillan.

Kennedy of Dunure and William Niven, the chief magistrate in Maybole and school-fellow of the poet Burns at Kirkoswald, were not happy about this state of affairs. Dunure encouraged Cassillis, who after all had military experience, to get involved. He was convinced that it was:

> most desirable to have a number of the
> good sort armed, fully as much to keep
> down the rabble as to resist the enemy.
> There are a great number of Irish in all
> the villages employed in the Cotton
> manufacture and also as labourers in the
> county and it is feared that those, added
> to natives of a bad way of thinking,

*A reference to the fondness some volunteers had for dressing up in fancy uniforms rather than taking their military duties seriously.
*The Shaw family were owners of the Great Valley Plantation in Jamaica (Ayrshire Archives Centre ATD 60/8/2).

might very probably in case of an Invasion taking place in the least even temporary appearance of success and in however distant part of the kingdom be disposed to fall on their more peaceable and richer neighbours.

Niven reported on the progress of recruiting a company of a hundred men in the town and offered command of the company to the Earl: 'The volunteers are all respectable Men, mostly Young Men, and I am sure that if their services were actually needed they may be reckoned upon to the fullest extent.' When their enthusiasm ran away with them and they set about getting together another company, he put a stop to it: 'I found two thirds at least were Vagabond Irish Weavers who have lately come over from their country most likely have been guilty of outrages there.'[34] No doubt egged on by Cathcart, the Earl of Eglinton was furious that an offer of command had been made to Cassillis without his authority as lord lieutenant. When news of this disagreement got around attendance at drill practice in Maybole fell away.[35] The dispute dragged on throughout March and was only settled early in April on the direct intervention of the Duke of Portland. With Cassillis confirmed as commanding officer and reports of the mutiny at Spithead, the formation of the company proceeded rapidly. After an inspection on 10 May, the Earl and John Shaw set about choosing a splendid uniform with 'a yellow cuff and cape and blue pantaloons' and at last sending four boys to learn how to play the fife and drums in Ayr. Although arms were promised, these were not finally acquired until 1803 when the danger of invasion returned.

Despite the uncertainty about his ownership of Culzean, the 12th Earl carried out work on the house, such as the decoration of the second drawing room. He also made Cassillis House, which he did own, wind and watertight. The coach house, yard and dog houses at Thomaston were completed in 1793–4,[36] and the Swinton gate and

lodge built in 1796 to designs by the Edinburgh architect John Thin.[37] The pillars supporting the gates were surmounted with recumbent cats made from Coade stone by Coade and Sealy of Lambeth, and as a result were quickly dubbed the Cat Gates. At the same time a foot bridge designed by Hugh Cairncross was erected across the Carrick Lane on Loch Doon.[38] After a final settlement was made with Cairncross (now calling himself an architect) in 1797, he left Ayrshire for Ardgowan in Renfrewshire where he built a new home for Sir John Shaw Stewart, who had been in Italy with Sir Thomas, the 9th Earl, and had also had his portrait painted by Batoni.[39] The design of Ardgowan with its great circular saloon facing out to sea has many resonances with Culzean. Large scale plantings on the terraces and in the policies at Culzean were made in 1797–8. The shrubs and trees included honeysuckles, jasmines, chestnuts, limes, species roses, lilacs, and *rhododendron ponticum*. Also, no doubt reminding him of his native America, the 12th Earl planted azaleas, clethra, kalmia, ledums, tulip trees, scarlet oaks, red cedars and white sycamores, and stocked an aviary with American birds.[40] He also purchased a house in Castle Street in Edinburgh in 1797, presumably because his presence was regularly required there and it was a useful staging post on the way to London via Leith.[41]

The alliance with the Erskines had the additional effect of defusing Sir Andrew Cathcart's political vendetta in Ayrshire. Already the Earl had sounded out the government about the possibility of succeeding his cousin as a representative peer. He had received assurances from Henry Dundas, the political fixer in Scotland, 'that at any time; I should wish to be in Parliament you would make it a point with Mr Pitt to obtain me a seat'. He wrote to Dundas in March 1795 stating 'I am now desirous of comeing in – as one of the sixteen peers upon the first vacancy.'[42] Dundas did not reply and Cassillis wrote again in May believing his letter had gone astray. This time Dundas responded but was non-committal, explaining 'hurry of business' was

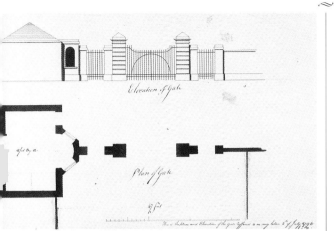

Elevation of Gate

Plan of Gate

the cause of the oversight and adding that 'the feelings of the Scotch peers on the subject of Election are a matter that renders delicacy in that business very material – all I can say at present is that yr family has as good pretensions as any on the list.'[43] Despite the note of caution the 12th Earl was elected as a representative peer in 1796.

Notwithstanding his connection with the government, Sir Andrew Cathcart continued to harass the Earl, testing his commitment to the war against France in 1799 by asking him to sign a petition to the lord lieutenant, the Earl of Eglinton, requesting a county meeting to express loyalty to the commanders in chief on land and at sea.[44] The 12th Earl's ambitions above everything else was to become a Knight of the Thistle, gain a British peerage which gave the holder a permanent seat in the House of Lords, and for office.

Membership of the Order of the Thistle, which had been revived by James II in 1687 and re-established by Queen Anne in 1703 as a Scottish equivalent of the Garter, was restricted to the sovereign and sixteen knights and Cassillis had to wait for a vacancy to come about by death. When a vacancy occurred in 1802 he petitioned Pitt, whom he supported, for the honour.[45] When this was refused, he broke with him and in January 1803

joined Brook's club, whose members were exclusively Whigs and enjoyed gambling.

The first practical expression of his change of political view came the following month when Colonel Fullarton was forced to resign as member of parliament for Ayrshire on his appointment as governor of Trinidad. The Earl wrote to the Ayrshire gentry urging them to endorse the candidacy of Thomas Kennedy of Dunure against the government interest. Kennedy was appalled by this intervention which he was convinced would be counter-productive. He wrote at once to reassure his friends that he had not put the Earl up to writing on his behalf: 'I trust however you will have no difficulty in believing that I have not the most distant idea of what Lord Cassillis's letter to you contained.'[46] Sir Adam Fergusson replied: 'I am perfectly satisfied from what you say yt you neither knew the content of Lord Cassillis's letter to me nor had desired him to write to me. The expressions in his Lordship's letter are perfectly polite considering it is only a letter in favour of a Candidate set up by him.'[47]

Cassillis's approach to Henry Dundas, Lord Melville, who effectively controlled the political machine in Scotland, met with a frosty response: 'many convenient circumstances have induced me to form intimate political connections with the

family of Eglinton.'[48] Cassillis at once wrote to Robert Peel asking his advice and concluded: 'Ld Melville may not be pleased that I, or any Man, shd correspond with you about Scotch Elections or Scotch affairs, but I will continue to do so.'[49] Bruised by this experience Cassillis defected to the opposition to the government and Lord Grenville, clinging to him to like a limpet for the next sixteen years.[50] At this time Grenville was still a close friend of Pitt's, but when he refused to join Pitt's government in 1804, they fell out. Like Cassillis, Grenville could at times be inconsistent due largely to his fear that revolution might spread across the Channel, but like Cassillis he never wavered in his support for Catholic emancipation and the abolition of the slave trade. They shared an enthusiasm for estate improvement and experimentation in agriculture and horticulture. Cassillis regularly sent Gren-

LEFT
Lord Grenville, the earl of Cassillis's closest political friend.

RIGHT
The magnificent Culzean cup designed by the London silversmith John Faithful in 1801 for the 12th Earl. It is now in private hands in the United States. The illustration of the castle shows that by then the upper terrace and central stairway had been removed.

ville presents of game, pedigree cattle, fruit and vegetables. These were not always very welcome.

Grenville responded to a gift of black American potatoes, which were sent in exchange for some 'delicious' Walcheren seed:

I have been very remiss in not thanking you before for the Potatoes which are safe arrived and apparently in good condition. They will I fear degenerate on our poor soil but I will give them as good a trial as I can.[51]

Cassillis and Grenville were both interested in potato cultivation, trying out some years later Iceland cultivars which reputedly stood long in the ground. Although Grenville had no difficulty in believing that they would be 'a most valuable accession to our stock of winter

food for cattle and sheep', he preferred to await the outcome of the trials at Culzean before planting them at Dropmore, his Buckinghamshire home.[52]

The Tories certainly had hopes of retaining Cassillis's support, as Melville stayed with him at Culzean in September 1803. The Earl commented to Grenville: 'I dare say you will be surprised when I tell you that my *Evil Demon*, Lord M. has been here for some days on a visit with his family – not surprising I hope that I received the visit but that he offered it.'[53] On 15 April 1804, Colonel MacMahon, the Prince of Wales's private secretary, suggested that he might be offered some preferment: 'I am commanded by the Prince to say how sensible his R.H. is of your Lordsh. <u>Kindness and proofs of attachment upon every occasion</u>.' He was given to understand that he 'stood high on a list among eleven to be made a British Peer', which would avoid the necessity and cost of election.[54]

With a foothold in Westminster, the Earl spent less and less time at his troubled Ayrshire property and more and more in his London home where he

LEFT
The Ayr Gold Cup, to which the Earl of Cassillis was one of the subscribers. It is now owned by the Western Meeting and is seen here being presented to the trainer of the winner of the Scottish Grand National, Dandy Nicholls with the jockey, his son Adrien, in 2001.

RIGHT
The Earl of Cassillis's horse, Chancellor, outside the Home Farm in about 1804.

renewed his boyhood friendship with the Duke of Clarence, later King William IV. Denied a role in the war with France, unlike his other brothers, the Duke was a focus for moderate opposition. He shared Cassillis's dislike of Melville, supporting his impeachment in 1805. Like Cassillis he was inconsistent and had a tendency to speak his mind without thinking. He had a reputation for boorish behaviour and was often described as vulgar, a fund of salacious stories and regular attender at pugilistic competitions. Clarence had become ranger of Bushey Park in 1797, which carried with it the use of Bushey House not far from Hampton Court. He loved this rural retreat where he became a passionate improver, like Cassillis.[55]

So as to be close to the Duke, the Earl of Cassillis rented a house in Cavendish Square (1802–4) and then in St James Street (1804–8). He too had a taste for gambling. One of his best known wagers, which he won, was for the shortest time it was possible to ride from Culzean to Glasgow and is commemorated in a painting which hangs in the dining room at Culzean. This reputedly took place in 1800 and it is possible that the beautiful Culzean silver cup designed by the London silversmith John Faithful was commissioned as a commemorative trophy. The Earl had begun owning racehorses in the mid–1790s, running *Clementina* at Dumfries and Ayr in 1796.[56] In conjunction with his sister-in-law at Dun, Alice Erskine, he entered his horse *Scaramouche* at the Montrose races in 1799.[57] He won at Ayr with *Pegasus* in 1801 and *Trimmer* in 1802.[58] He joined with thirteen other subscribers to establish the Ayr Gold Cup, to be competed for annually over two miles by horses trained in Scotland. He was victorious in the first race in October 1804 with his horse *Chancellor*, which was trained at Culzean, and repeated his triumph the following year.[59] Although he raced *Chancellor* for a third time in 1806, coming in second, he did not enter a horse in the race again and only occasionally competed in other races at what became known as the Western Meeting.[60]

With little tact or taste the Earl pestered the Prince of Wales, the Duke of Clarence and Lord Grenville whenever a vacancy in the ranks of the Knights of the Thistle seemed in prospect. According to him: 'his Royal Highness Personally assured Ld C that his claims shd not be forgot whenever he had it in his power … that he should not stand worse with him than he did with Mr Pitt.' He claimed to have introduced the Earl of Eglinton to 'Carlton House and he thinks contributed to secure him in his R. H.'s Interest'.[61] This was despite the fact he happily caballed against his interest in Ayrshire in the 1807 election, which elicited the retort from his fellow Whig William Maule: 'Damn Eglinton and all such Rats – N.B. Ld Eglinton writes to Edinbro . that he is determined to support Opposition – Querie – is David Boyle [the Tory candidate] in opposition? !!!!.'[62]

In the meantime the trustees of David the 10th Earl, who included the 12th Earl, were grappling with the enormity of their problems. Newark Castle was let to the parents of the well-known Ayrshire radical, Dr John Taylor, who was born there in 1805.[63] It was widely recognised at the time that entail cases were immensely complicated and open to abuse, as Sir Andrew almost certainly intended. Few were settled in the Court of Session and most, as in this instance, were appealed to the House of Lords with considerable delay and expense.[64] The 12th Earl engaged as his lawyer David Cathcart of Greenfield, one of the trustees and later a judge in the Court of Session with the title of Lord Alloway. On Cathcart's death in 1829, Henry Cockburn, his fellow advocate and also a Whig, described him as:

> an excellent and most useful man; kind in private life, and honest in the discharge of his public duties. Without learning or talent, and awkward in expressing himself either orally or in writing, he was a good practical lawyer, and remarkably knowing in the common business of life.[65]

This certainly proved the case in his handling of the Cassillis defence. He scrupulously examined the title to the estate and the deed of entail and concluded that Sir Andrew's claim to parts of the property was good.[66] He wrote regularly (sometimes daily) to the Earl, offering tactical advice and reporting on the shifting political balance in the Court of Session and later the House of Lords which might sway the outcome of the case.[67] An added difficulty was Sir Andrew's mercurial temperament. He kept changing his mind. Although he at first demanded cash, by 1800 he was wanting 'a part at least of the estate of a family with which I was so nearly connected'.[68] In this instance he announced he was willing to go to arbitration. By the time the case got to the House of Lords in 1805, David Cathcart had hopes that the lord chancellor, the celebrated Lord Eldon, of whom he had 'a very high opinion', would find in favour of Cassillis.[69] He was delighted by the appointment of the Ministry of All Talents in 1806, with the Earl's friend Lord Grenville as prime minister. He wrote from Edinburgh: 'You cannot conceive greater consternation than that the intelligence has produced here to a certain set of Politicians. I allude to the Friends of Dundas who have enjoyed much uninterrupted sway in the country.'[70]

Cassillis himself now had fresh hopes of preferment, particularly the coveted green ribbon of the Order of the Thistle. Within a month of the new ministry taking office in 1806, he was lobbying for an appointment as a lord of the bedchamber and a British peerage which would entitle him to a permanent seat in the House of Lords. He wrote to Grenville on 3 February:

> I consider it but Justice, to myself, when
> mentioning to your Lordsh that at the
> moment, when I took the same line of
> politicks, persuaded by your Lordsh,
> that I stood one upon a list in the pos-
> session of Mr Pitt, for a British Peerage,
> and at the same time had from Mr Pitt a
> promise of the first vacant Green
> Ribbon, these circumstances may not
> and probably are not known to your
> Lordsh but are in the possession of a
> great many of your Lordsh friends and
> known to His Royal Highness the Prince
> of Wales.[71]

Despite the sheer effrontery of this epistle, Grenville replied immediately inviting Cassillis to call the following day, 5 February, to discuss a possible role in his administration.[72] There was little enthusiasm, however, from others for including him in the government 'because he had at one period changed his party and asked for a green ribbon from Lord Melville' – in other words Dundas. Cassillis hotly denied such a suggestion, writing to the Earl of Moira, who had offered to act as an intermediary: 'Your Lords I am convinced will do me the justice to believe that I would not leave my Party and Friends for a Green Ribbon.'[73] Moira was not entirely convinced by these protestations of innocence and drew Cassillis's attention to inconsistencies in his version of events, but he was still willing to support

his wish for a place. Cassillis hurriedly retracted and told Moira he asked for nothing and did not want anything asked for him. However, although he replied by return of post, Moira had already interceded for a British peerage for his friend which he knew he hankered after. This was promised for both him and the Earl of Breadalbane 'as soon as the King might be inclined to add to the number fixed'.[74] Much to Cassillis's irritation, the Earl of Eglinton was given a British peerage with the title Lord Ardrossan of Ardrossan before the end of the month. Grenville, however, did not forget his friend and went out of his way to assure him that no slight was intended, and he would be promoted as soon as a vacancy arose. At his most servile, Cassillis reminded Grenville of his promise on 19 October writing from Culzean.[75] On 24 October Grenville replied with relief from Downing Street:

> The best answer I can give your
> Lordship's letter, which I received this
> morning, is by acquainting you that I
> have this day laid before the King my
> humble recommendation for a British
> Peerage which HH has been graciously
> pleased to approve of.[76]

Cassillis took the title Baron Ailsa, but to add to his annoyance, Breadalbane was created a Marquess. This slight fuelled the 12th Earl's ambition for similar elevation.

On 17 November 1806, only four days after the death of the Earl of Galloway, he wrote again to Grenville asking to be considered for his green ribbon of the Order of the Thistle,[77] but was opposed by the Earl of Lauderdale, who doubted his loyalty.[78] Grenville wrote to Earl Spencer: 'in the course of our conversation, I took care not to give the least ground for his expecting any alteration in our determination on the subject of this ribbon.'[79] His reply to the 12th Earl was less than honest:

> 'I would undoubtedly have had great
> pleasure in recommending your

Lordship to His Majesty to succeed to this vacancy. But your Lordship having so very recently received from His Majesty the high & distinguished favour of a British Peerage, I cannot for a moment doubt that you will at once see the impossibility …'[80]

Cassillis was affronted, penning Spencer a long letter full of injured pride:

'I cannot help feeling extremely hurt at the conversation which took place this morning upon the subject of the Green Ribbon and the more so perhaps from the circumstances of being unprepared to receive such a denial … Ld Grenville promised that I would be one of the first Peers made British. He hesitated whether to propose to the King that the number of G. Ribbons shd be increased in order that I might *at that moment* have one but I understand it as did all those who were privy to the promises that it was settled that I was to have the first ribbon that became vacant.[81]

With the prospect of office in view he purchased a house in Privy Gardens in Whitehall where his neighbours included Lord Sheffield, the Marchioness of Exeter, the Earl of Tankerville, the Duke of Richmond and the Duke of Buccleuch.[82] Here he became a close friend of Earl Spencer, home secretary in the Ministry of All Talents.[83] He asked the nurseryman George Fitcher to look after the garden which was planted with sycamores, planes, limes, alders, laburnums, scarlet thorn, lilacs, gelder rose, euonymus (spindle berry), and dog roses. The borders were decked with pinks, wallflowers, sweet williams, heartsease pansies, catchfly (silene), yellow alyssum, daisies and mignonette (reseda).[84]

The Ministry of All Talents collapsed in March 1807 after the king refused to give his assent to a measure to open the armed services to Catholics, a reform dear to Cassillis's heart confirmed by his long military service in Ireland. Grenville wrote at once to his friend hoping: 'I shall always retain a strong sense of the friendship & support which I have experienced from you.'[85] The Duke of Portland succeeded him as prime minister. At Brooks the Earl of Cassillis laid at least two wagers on the likely survival of the Duke's ministry before Portland decided to stand down on grounds of ill health in September 1809.[86] The king instructed Lord Liverpool and Spencer Perceval to form a new government, and they invited both Grenville and Earl Grey to join 'an extended & combined administration'. Grenville declined and immediately let his friends know of this decision, 'which must indeed I think be apparent to every dispassionate man'.[87] During the year the Earl of Cassillis, somewhat unpatriotically, had ordered twelve cases of claret from Bordeaux.[88]

The Earl tried again in 1810 to become a Knight of the Thistle in return for his support for the Regency bill which was to appoint the Prince of Wales regent during the final illness of his father, George III.[89] He opened his campaign by once more reminding Grenville that 'The Prince of Wales has for a great many years shown me more than ordinary kindness …'[90] In November he came to London from Scotland especially at the prince's request to vote against the clause restricting the number of peers the regent could create. He obtained the prince's permission to return to Scotland 'provided he was in <u>London again</u> at a certain day which 2nd January Ld C. performed' to vote in favour of the Bill.[91] On learning of the serious illness of the Duke of Queensberry in December Cassillis, seeking his green ribbon, wrote at once to the sorely tried Grenville, who rebuked him: 'If you think the P's word at all engaged to you, than cannot I conceive to the smallest objection to you applying to him.'[92] After Queensberry's death, taking this advice he wrote a long ingratiating and convoluted letter to Colonel MacMahon, private secretary to the Prince of Wales, which concluded 'Lord Moira was so good as express to me, of his own accord, before I left London that he thought Nobody more fit for the Ribbon than myself & if the Prince ask'd him on the Subject that he would say so.'[93] Despite this recommendation and his willingness to do the prince's bidding, he was again passed over when the Prince of Wales became regent early in 1811. Cassillis ingratiated himself further with the Duke of Clarence by presenting him with a portrait of George I, which the Duke regarded as 'remarkably fine'.[94]

After Perceval's assassination in 1812, Grenville was again approached about participating in Lord Liverpool's administration but refused because he was convinced of the need to address the related issues of Catholic emancipation and the reform of the government of Ireland. He commented to Cassillis: 'I had much rather they than I had anything to do with the Government in the present state of public affairs.'[95] During that year a motion in favour of considering Catholic claims was carried and Grenville was active in support, badgering Cassillis to come to London from Culzean in May 1813 to vote in favour.[96]

With the change in government in 1806 it had become practical for the trustees of the Culzean estates to consider obtaining an Act of Parliament to break the entail. By July 1807 a bill had been drafted and the Act became law in 1809.[97] Encouraged at the possibility of a settlement, thorns, ashes, larches, Scots firs, elders and planes were planted within the policies at Culzean in 1806 and 1807, along with exotic trees imported from America.[98] Two ornamental stone bowls for the garden arrived by sea from Liverpool, which suggests they may have come from one of the family's American homes.[99] Hugh Cairncross was re-engaged, presumably to supervise further work on the house and to build the coach house directly beyond the old tower gate, which was designed by Robert McLachlan.[100]

By this time the high wartime prices of agricultural produce had allowed the trustees to raise the rental to some £7,500 a year and to reduce the amount of outstanding debt to about £45,000.[101] This was a shared experience. Many landed families assumed that the wartime increase in their income was somehow permanent and improvidently borrowed heavily. As a result when prices fell with the coming of peace in 1815, many estates were sold up to meet debts often at good prices to industrialists and merchants who had made money during the war.[102] Now that it was possible to sell the Culzean and Cassillis estates, the Earl toyed with the idea of disposing of the whole property and moving to an estate on the outskirts of Edinburgh.[103] Presumably as a memento of the family's Ayrshire roots, he invited Alexander Nasmyth to sketch the castle along with Cassillis.[104] He also celebrated by purchasing a complete dinner service of silver plate engraved with the family crest from Rundell, Bridge, & Rundell, the royal family's jewellers and goldsmiths of Ludgate Hill, for the colossal sum of £1,753.[105] This silver travelled with him when he moved from seat to seat. When, however, the trustees following a judgement in the House of Lords in 1810 gave notice of their intention to use their powers under the Act to sell land to clear the debt, their decision was challenged in a further appeal to the House of Lords by Sir Andrew and his co-heirs.[106] Frustrated in his efforts to sell up, the Earl took 'several large farms' near Culzean into his own hands, telling Grenville: 'It will take me, I don't know how long, to shape matters to my mind.'[107]

Suiting his actions to his words, the Earl appointed his own factor, his cousin Captain John Shaw, to replace Richard Campbell. Since the Earl had no need of Maybole Castle as a residence, Shaw took up residence there and it continued to be the factor's home until very recently. He must have had a thick skin as the Earl proved to be an exacting and abrasive taskmaster. His impatient attention to detail was fearsome. This was typical of many landed proprietors, who as a result neglected the overall management of their estates. The staff and workforce on the estates must have dreaded the Earl's visits.

Determined to improve the management of

Culzean, the Earl opened a 'day orderly book' in which he noted instructions to the hapless Shaw, writing on the flyleaf 'All questions, and memorandums in this book are to be answered & settled before Saturday night every week without fail.'[108] His instructions were impetuously direct: 'Is anything done about more lime for the Garden' to which the factor replied 'No Lime at the kiln'; or 'You are <u>to count yourself</u> out to the old men the trees they get to plant & keep a regular memorandum thereof' – the factor noted resignedly in the margin 'will do it'.[109] '<u>You</u> are not to allow any servant to keep more than 4 Hens I won't allow of any Ducks.'[110] He may have said he wanted answers within a week but often his time scale was much shorter: 'I want to know if Dun the carrier or any other carrier will go from Cullean to Leith on Tuesday with the luggage & on what terms. I want <u>immediate</u> Information.'

The magnificent painting by Alexander Nasmyth of London looking east from the terrace of the Earl of Cassillis's town house in Privy Gardens. The figures on the terrace are Lady Cassilis with two of her children.

Captain Shaw explained wearily: 'Will inform your Lordship to morrow in the afternoon. It will be that time before Dun comes home.'[111] The Earl added later: 'I desire that you execute every order in this Book <u>Instantly</u>.'[112] He told the factor that he would prosecute the tenant of Pennyglen, if his cottar's (a subtenant) cow grazed on the roadside.[113] He instructed the gardener on the precise method of making up the new asparagus beds, and told him to go to the garden at Thomaston and protect the fruit trees against hares with thorn trimmings.[114] His only saving grace was that his bark appears to have been much worse than his bite. He could quite quixotically order someone to be dismissed, who years later still appeared on the payroll. The Earl fashionably began breeding pedigree cattle and experimenting with growing new varieties of potatoes, particularly black tubers which he imported from America.[115] During 1811 he

planted 18,000 trees 'besides old plantations filling up'.[116]

Attention to the management of the estate combined with his political activities necessitated regular arduous and expensive journeys between London and Scotland. The Earl made the trip five times between 1810 and 1811.[117] The usual method was to travel to Leith by sea and then take to the road. These overland journeys were like royal progresses with the family in a chariot or state coach escorted by outriders and the servants following in a humble coach.[118] Once the family and domestic servants had embarked, the grooms and the coaches travelled on by road taking about a fortnight to reach Culzean.[119] After the death of his father-in-law, John Erskine of Dun, in 1812, the Earl had to divide his time in Scotland between Culzean and Dun. Captain William John Erskine, the heir, had been killed during the Irish rebellion in 1798 and John Erskine had only two other children who had survived to adult life, Alice, the eldest, and Margaret, the Earl's wife.[120] Since Alice was unmarried, the estate was left to the Earl's second son

LEFT
The beech trees in Piper's Brae photographed by the 3rd Marquess about sixty years after they were planted by his great grandfather, the 1st Marquess, in the 1820s.

RIGHT
The House of Dun, near Montrose, which Margaret Erskine, the wife of the 1st Marquess, inherited on the death of her sister. She and her husband preferred this charming William Adam's house to the much grander Culzean.

John, who changed his surname to Kennedy-Erskine. John Erskine's widow, Mary, and their daughters, Alice and Margaret, were to enjoy a life rent of the property until their deaths. Under the terms of the marriage settlement Margaret was permitted to add £8,000 to the burdens over the estate so as to make provision for the younger children.[121] Young John was just ten and the management of the property fell to the Earl, who came to enjoy the House of Dun, built by William Adam, more than Culzean.[122]

Alice was well-known in the locality for her eccentric manly behaviour. She kept a pack of hounds and hunted regularly with the help of her brother-in-law's old coach guard, who had lost his arm when his pistol blew up.[123] Preferring the company of her horses, she relied heavily on her brother-in-law in running the estate: 'The longer I live the more I feel my own incapacity to manage any thing. I am delighted with my new horse she is by much the handsomest horse I ever had and as quiet as a Lamb at the same time dances & looks pretty when I mount in short she is a piece of perfection.'[124]

The difficulties in managing his properties did not prevent the Earl from purchasing more expensive silver from Rundell, Bridge & Rundell. He bought in 1810 for £321 'two very elegant large silver table candlesticks with three arm branches the shafts richly ornamented with Dolphin flowers & swan in the centre to take out occasionally', and the following year for £374 'two very elegant closed silver vases for wine coolers richly ornamented with festoons of grapes, goats head handles all polished'.[125] It was another five years before this account was paid.[126]

By the summer of 1812 all intention of selling Culzean seems to have passed, for he purchased from the office of ordnance a veritable armoury of obsolete weapons to decorate the hall, five hundred old pistols, four hundred and fifty swords

'whole & broken', one hundred and forty sword blades and one hundred carbine bayonets.[127] These weapons were indeed obsolete, some dating back to the 1730s.[128] They were mounted for display by Mr Bellis, master furbisher of the Tower of London, who commissioned R.E. Pritchett, another gunmaker, to clean them and the wooden wall mountings from Adam & Robertson of Lambeth at a cost of almost £90.[129] The accompanying Cassillis's arms were carved in lime wood by Adam & Co. The wooden mountings were dispatched in seven packages by the *King George* packet by way of Leith. Directly the wooden frames had been erected at Culzean, Bellis sent the 'swords, pistols etc.' in twelve chests along with 'one of the men from the tower with the Arms, who will fix them up in a proper manner'.[130] He described the

finished product as the 'most Elegant Armoury belonging to any individual in the Kingdom', quite justifiably as it was and is the largest collection of ordnance outside the Tower of London.[131] Just as with his silver, the Earl was a bad payer for a year later Pritchett complained 'I have made repeated application for payment of the above amount,* which I have not yet been favoured with and the usual period of Credit for similar work with the Rt. Hble Board of Ordnance is but two months …'[132] The installation of the armoury in the entrance hall was just part of an ambitious plan to complete the interior of the house, particularly the saloon and staircase. It is not known when these were finished but the style suggests it was probably in the late 1810s. In the final execution Adam's original design was changed and the elaborate Corinthian orders used on the first

LEFT
Looking down the main staircase at Culzean, which is universally acknowledged to be a masterpiece of design.

ABOVE
The lawns in what is now the Fountain Court with the conservatory behind, which were conceived by Thomas White.

floor instead of the second, but as Eileen Harris has pointed out, not to his standard of craftsmanship.

Nevertheless she has no doubt that the staircase 'ranks with the gallery and vestibule at Syon and the library at Kenwood as one of Adam's masterpieces'.[133]

During the autumn of 1814 the Earl began large scale planting with a mixture of larch, firs, spruce, alders, oak, beech, ash, and 'thorns'. Altogether 98,300 young trees of between one and four years old were set by old men and women at the rate of three pence per hundred.[134] This was a prudent investment as under the terms of the emergency wartime income tax, afforestation was tax allowable to replace the thousands of acres that had been felled. Even after the abolition of income tax in 1815, extensive planting continued with over 86,000 young trees being set in 1816 and 131,000 the following year.[135] The majority of these plants were supplied by

*The account for the arms themselves does not survive.

either W. & T. Sampson or Foulds & Lymburn, both of Kilmarnock.

These plantings were almost certainly carried out to designs drawn up twenty-five years earlier by Thomas White. He had died in 1811, but his practice had been taken over by his son Thomas White junior (c. 1764–1836).[136] Thomas White junior worked at Bargany in 1802 and after his father's death at Brodick and Mount Stewart in 1814.[137] In the spring of 1814 the Earl noted in his factor's day orderly book: 'If Mr Whyte is in the Country send him word to come to me early next week.' The factor noted in the margin 'Mr White in Fife Shire.'[138]

Since the time of White's father working at Culzean, the Earl had been in discussion with the road trustees about moving the road to Girvan away from the castle to create the new approach.[139]

In 1809 the Earl secured a clause through his friends in government in the private Act of Parliament for the maintenance of the roads in Ayrshire, which allowed him to form a new road from Glenside bridge, to Thomaston, Belvaird, Hogston Hill, Ardlochan, Turnberry Park and Drumbeg at his own expense.[140] It is not clear if this scheme was ever completed as eight years later the road was diverted to its present course from Glenside to Morriston.[141] The construction of the new roadways within the policies as part of the landscape improvements did not begin in earnest until after the Act of Parliament to sell part of the estate had been secured. During that year the Glenside road was completed, a new way made across the burn to Bowmanhill and other paths and tracks laid out. A levelling machine was purchased to help

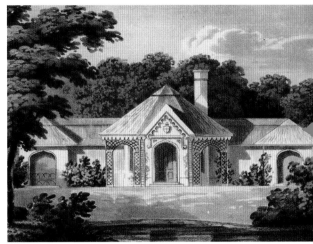

shape the contours.[142] The drama of the now private landscape was to be enlivened by finally creating the Swan Pond to take in the whole of the old Cow Park, very much in keeping with Capability Brown's tradition. Forming such water features was a major and expensive undertaking.[143] The new pond was completed by 1816, as the Earl gave instructions that the small boat 'must be repaired & repainted'.[144]

To enhance the theatrical effect, the park was to be embellished by a number of new buildings, some practical and some entirely ornamental. There was to be a new ornamental battery on the cliffs to the south-west of the castle, an orangery between the walled garden and the castle, an aviary or 'bird house' near the Swan Pond, a pagoda and three Gothic lodges on the side of the new road. These were at Pennyglen, where the old road joined the new road, at Glenside and at Morriston.* There was a smaller lodge in a similar style at the entrance to the policies proper beside a new bridge at Hoolity Ha'. The London architect Robert Lugar,

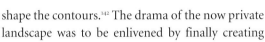

LEFT
Pennyglen on the road to Maybole designed by Robert Lugar.

RIGHT
Drawing of the birdhouse at the Swan Pond by Robert Lugar.

who specialised in rustic Gothic architecture, designed the bird house. He commented:

The spot on which these buildings are placed is a gentle slope, sheltered from the sea by bold rocky grounds, covered with plantations and backed by a connected wood, which is the preserve of pheasants. The buildings themselves stand at the head of a large sheet of water or lake which is entirely surrounded by plantations and wood and the surface of the water is enlivened by swans and various kinds of fowl together with wild fowl which frequent it in considerable numbers.[145]

The bird house also included an aquarium. In the walled garden the central hothouse or vinery, which had fallen into disrepair, was to be rebuilt and an entirely new greenhouse, melon frames and a pine house for growing pineapples were to be built for John Reid who was now gardener.[146]

This work at Culzean seems to have been entrusted to a variety of architects and engineers. Designs for the battery were commissioned from an

*These were all demolished to make way for road widening in the 1950s.

unknown architect and Robertson Buchanan of Rothesay, whose principal interest was the ventilation of cotton mills but who also designed two fine bridges at Inchinnan in Renfrewshire.[147] The idea for the battery stemmed from the Earl's father's quip about being able to capture Culzean with gamekeepers armed with dog whips.[148] Robert Lugar was re-engaged to design all the lodges, the extension to the aviary and probably the pagoda.[149] James Gillespie Graham, the Scottish architect, was commissioned to redesign in forbidding Gothic style the entrance arch to Adam's causeway, which would have completely obscured the majestic view, and other lodge buildings. None of these was built.[150] Richard Crichton, the Edinburgh architect, was retained to design farm steadings.[151] To execute these various projects the Earl employed at Culzean a resident architect by the name of Thompson or Thomson, the Earl spelled his name variously. It is possible that this was James Thomson, the Dumfries architect.[152] At the same time a fishing pavilion was built at some expense by William Ramsay & Company on the shore of the loch at Martnaham to the north-west of Dalrymple.[153] Martnaham Loch had and still has good coarse fishing and was much more accessible and hos-

LEFT
The path from the Swan Pond to Piper's Brae.

RIGHT
The battery at Culzean, which was constructed in about 1815.

OPPOSITE
A plan of the new shooting lodge at Craiglure in the hills above Straiton.

pitable than the bleak but beautiful landscape above Straiton. The Earl also decided to move the hunting lodge from Craiglure to a more convenient situation nearer the bridge over the Stinchar on the road from Straiton over the Tairlaw Rig.[154] This new Craiglure lodge was completed by 1814, as in that year the Earl left one of his guns there.[155] He, however, soon tired of his new lodge, writing to Sir James Fergusson of Kilkerran ten years later:

You are most exceeding welcome to Fish in any of my Lakes or Rivers you Please, you should try The Doon about Cassillis. My Boys – viz. Kennedys, Bairds and John had most Capital sport there last year. Killing Four or Five Salmon a day – when you get to the Stinchar Lakes pray make a Home of my Lodge. I have Built a House up there what I don't know now what to do with. I should like to set [let] it and all my rivers for 5 years – more or less – The Weather here is Dreadful. Hail, Snow and Rain alternately.[156]

Work on Culzean itself progressed more slowly, largely because the Earl was unable to decide whether he wished the completion of the house to take priority over the grounds. When the plans were not immediately forthcoming from Thomson, the Earl became irate.[157] Habitually paranoid, he suspected the tradesmen of trying to swindle him. He commented 'I am certain that they are quarrying more stones than what is necessary for orangery & chimney tops of castle & step from Green at West Door.'[158] The battery was finished by June 1815, just after Wellington's final victory over Napoleon at Waterloo and the cannon were delivered by Thomas Edington of Glasgow at a cost of £74.[159] The hot house and the orangery were more or less finished by the autumn.[160] The lean-to tool sheds and fruit stores behind the vinery bear the date 1815 and the wires for the trellises were delivered in October from the gardener at the House of Dun.[161] However these were still not erected by the summer of the following year.[162] The Earl had hopes that his gardens might soon be free of building work for he told his factor to buy '12 Garden Chairs. Simple Chairs to stand out of doors with <u>Wooden Seats</u> painted Green & neatly made'. The factor could only find ones with rush bottoms.[163] The estate masons also made a similar number of stone seats.[164] During September 1816 the Earl also ordered the baths at the back of the house to be filled up and two larger plunge baths constructed near the shore – one hot and one cold.[165] (This building in a remarkable rustic style can still be seen next to the Dolphin House.) A month later a contract was placed for repairing the walls of the deer park, abandoned since the time of the 9th Earl.[166]

The final defeat of Napoleon in 1815 was followed by a long period of reactionary government troubled by increasingly popular discontent in response to the sharp downturn in the economy coupled with demands for parliamentary reform. Whigs, such as the Earl of Cassillis, were in a dilemma. They supported some measure of reform but, with events in France still fresh in their minds, they were deeply disturbed by the possibility of revolution. Lord Grenville, Cassillis's friend, was increasingly worried by the popular disturbances,

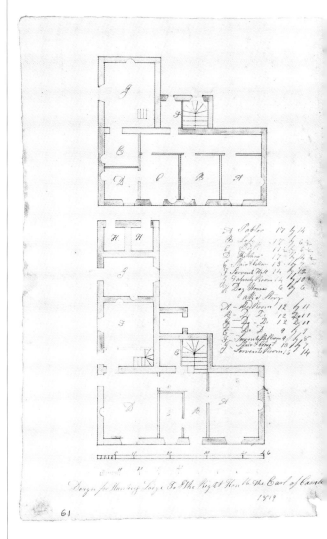

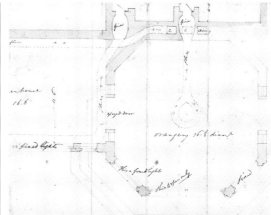

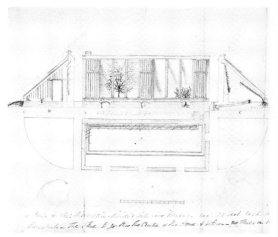

which he first attributed to economic hardship. In 1816 he wrote to Cassillis:

> The distress of the country is I fear quite universal, & is certainly in short alarming. It is I believe the necessary & inevitable consequence of the obstinacy with which Government maintained a system of [bank note] circulation in direct opposition to every principle of political œconomy … As it is, I believe there is no other remedy but to restore the currency to its true level as fast as so great a change can safely be made, & in all other respects to trust to the

TOP

The orangery at Culzean, now known as the Camellia House, as it is today, with the original drawing.

BOTTOM LEFT

A drawing of the proposed vinery for Culzean.

BOTTOM RIGHT

The plunge bath house on the shore, next to the Dolphin house at Culzean.

natural operation of Peace for setting things right.

> But then Peace must be accompanied by a reduction of military establishments, & a consequent repeal of War taxes.[167]

This happened, but it left the government with the county-based militia and the yeoman cavalry as the only means of dealing with popular disturbances.

During 1816 Alexander Nasmyth executed two large panoramas of Culzean to hang in Privy Gardens, the Earl's London home. Patrick Nasmyth referred to these in a letter to his father and sisters on 29 March: 'Your two Magnificent

Pictures are arrived ten days ago, they are at Lord Cassills [*sic*]. I was at Cribbs* today and the Splendid frames will do him honour as the Pictures do you, I dare say for I have not seen them yet.'[168] Over the next twenty years the Earl was to commission no fewer than ten more paintings of Culzean from Nasmyth, along with paintings of Cassillis House, Dunnottar Castle in Aberdeenshire, a view from the balcony of his London home, and Edinburgh.[169] None of these was intended to hang at Culzean but were either wedding gifts to his children or to hang in his London homes. Two of the views of Culzean adorn the walls of the castle today, and four others are in the possession of the family.

The appeal to the House of Lords by Sir Andrew Cathcart dragged on. The Earl's lawyer, David Cathcart, became increasingly concerned that, with allied victory in sight, by 1813 agricultural prices would plummet and the value of land collapse: 'less prices would be taken than a few years

ago'.[170] Although the creditors were now becoming very impatient, nothing could be done until a settlement had been reached with Sir Andrew, who persisted with his claim. After further petitions and counter petitions, Sir Andrew was finally awarded in 1825 the value of the farms of West and North Enoch on the road between Maybole and Culzean, which he was deemed to own; £4,852 along with back rent of £2,359 – far short of his original claim of £25,000.[171] Sir Andrew was now eighty-four with only three years left to live. As prices had fallen in the way David Cathcart had predicted, rather more of the estate had to sold than intended when as a result of a judgement land was on the market in 1819 and 1820. With this costly suit behind them the trustees could now dispose of the land and be discharged after almost thirty years of service. Some had died in the intervening period. Now the debts were cleared, David Cathcart could not think of 'a more rising estate in Scotland'.[172] Throughout the whole of this time the 12th Earl had had little difficulty in supporting himself, as his father had made generous provision for his eldest son.

*A reference to Tom Cribbs, the prize fighter, who after he retired from the ring became a successful London publican.

CHAPTER 6

Gambling and green ribbons:
1816 – 46

Having finally taken possession of most of his patrimony, the 12th Earl indulged himself by travelling on the Continent, visiting the battlefields and collecting memorabilia of the war. He took with him a servant who travelled armed in the rumble seat of his coach.[1] His purchases included a full length portrait of Napoleon by Robert Lefèvre and the uniform coat worn by Marshal Blücher at the battle of Leipzig in 1813.[2] The portrait of Napoleon hangs today in a bedroom at Culzean and Blücher's uniform was given by the Earl to Madame Tussaud's. In making these acquisitions he was almost certainly helped by his factor's son, adjutant-quartermaster Shaw, a hero of Waterloo, who was in charge of the port of Calais during the occupation.[3]

The rather stylised portrait of Napoleon by Robert Lefèvre in 1813, which the 1st Marquess directed in his will to be hung at Culzean.

On these expeditions he visited his brother Robert, who was still living in Switzerland. During the war of 1812 between the United Kingdom and the United States, Robert had been described by his other brother Captain John, who now lived in Bryanston Square, as 'an Englishman he is not'.[4] The Earl took a particular interest in Robert's eldest son John, a brilliant scholar whom he helped to enter the British diplomatic service. At this time he also seems to have helped finance Admiral Lord Exmouth's expedition to North Africa in 1817, ostensibly to suppress Christian slavery but also, it seems, in search of booty. The Earl Spencer wrote

to the Earl of Leven in June: 'I have not heard of any discoveries made by Lord Exmouth's voyage to the Barbary State of the description you allude to and I shall be very sorry if my friend Lord Cassillis is the sufferer by them.'[5] The expedition ended in August with a two-day war against Algiers in which all the Dey's (ruler of Algiers) navy, storehouses, arsenal and half his battery were completely destroyed by naval bombardment.[6]

Whatever his losses might have been, Lord Cassillis could still afford to buy the magnificent Lacy House in Twickenham Park, on the banks of the Thames, from the estate of the London banker, Francis Gosling. He renamed the house St Margaret's (which survives as the name of a railway station), making it his principal home for much of the year.[7] Grenville wrote to congratulate him, and at the same time enquired if Cassillis could supply him with four Ayrshire cows for Dropmore, his country seat in Buckinghamshire.[8] These cattle, sometimes referred to as 'the poor man's cow', evolved in the late eighteenth century and were bred to produce high yields of milk rich in butter fat from relatively poor feed. In about 1808 farmers around Kilmarnock inaugurated a show for the breed to help encourage further improvements.[9] They were to play a significant part in the future prosperity of the Culzean estates.

In October Grenville, having spent the

summer on his wife's property in Cornwall, thanked his friend Lord Cassillis for the cows which had arrived safely after being driven on foot. Responding to an enquiry from Cassillis about the political landscape, he was tempted to duck the question, 'but I should be wholly unworthy of that steady & flattering friendship on your part which I so highly value, if I had the least reserve in expressing to you all that I feel on the subject'. He reflected:

> I am confident that we enjoy a free & most happy form of Government & Law – not merely that we are <u>entitled</u> to it, but that we are actually in the <u>enjoyment</u> of it. I firmly believe we want nothing but a continuation of Peace abroad & Peace at Home to make us still what we have never ceased to be for more than a century, the happiest, & best governed people, (taking all things together) that ever existed on earth. For Peace abroad our best remedy is the inability of any power European or American to indulge in the expensive amusement of War. It is therefore to the maintenance of Peace at home that all my <u>wishes</u>, in they are now <u>wishes</u> [rather] than <u>endeavours</u>, are directed.
>
> In the means of attaining that subject here in Great Britain I believe I agree on the whole more with Government than with opposition, tho' not entirely with either.

His change of heart towards Lord Liverpool's government was undoubtedly due to the civil unrest, which had begun with the Spafield riots in December 1816.[10] He believed, however, that the problems in Ireland could not be resolved until some measure of Catholic relief was introduced. He concluded: 'This is the best map I can give of the road I am on, but it signifies little what the remaining course is of a public life so near to its close.'[11] When the government agreed later in the

year to open the army and navy formally to Catholics, he gave his tacit support. By the autumn of 1819 he had become a Tory in all but name, declaring to Cassillis his 'unshaken attachment to the existing form of Govt. & Law, & my horror of those attempts to overthrow them by popular tumult & insurrection'.[12]

In 1818, Cassillis gave notice of his intention of quitting county politics in Ayrshire and spending most of his time at his London homes and the House of Dun.[13] He was still, however, prepared to lavish money on the estate. In 1816 Captain Shaw, tired of his cousin's demanding ways, had resigned as factor to manage the family's Jamaican property.[14] The Earl wrote to John Hunter seeking a replacement. Hunter had approached one of his able young clerks, Charles D. Gairdner, who hailed from Ayrshire, with the warning: 'You must know well the character of Lord Cassillis from his correspondence.'[15] Gairdner, who was just twenty-two, accepted on the understanding that he could live in Ayr, have two sub-factors to help him and could also undertake other business. He found the estate in considerable difficulty, very largely because the Earl had convinced himself that his tenants were trying to deceive him. He had forced Shaw to commence sequestration (bankruptcy) proceedings against thirty-six tenant farmers. Gairdner persuaded the Earl, whom he described 'as very quick in temper', 'for one twelve month to adopt my own plan of management with which he would not interfere'.[16] Although the next three harvests were deplorable, his strategy paid off and by 1821 arrears had been reduced from £5,000 to £3,000.[17]

At much the same time that Gairdner was appointed, Thomson was joined as resident architect by James Donaldson, who practised in Bloomsbury but whose family came from Williamshaw in Stewarton in north Ayrshire.[18] He was already familiar with Culzean, as he had produced a scheme for the coach house in 1808.[19] His tasks were to complete the outstanding contracts, particularly an extension to the bird house, to build a new house beside the battery, to enlarge the walled garden, to improve the castle drains and to rebuild the perimeter wall. Adam's garden gates were to be retained, but widened to allow access by carts, so reducing the amount of labour required to cart manure and soil. The extension required the creation of new beds beneath the walls by the gardener James Walderton, all of which had to be laboriously double dug and manured.[20] Double digging improves drainage and thus the fertility of the newly opened ground. The enlargement of the walled garden allowed a new flower garden to be created within its perimeter. The orangery was a disappointment as the trees refused to fruit and the heating apparatus was eventually dismantled and sent to Dun.[21] As a result the building was to serve as a conservatory and the area in front used for setting out plants during the summer months. Nevertheless oranges and lemons continued to be grown at Culzean.[22] The drains in the castle proved troublesome and the Earl complained: 'There is such a smell comes from the New water Closet that it is utterly impossible that there can be proper Cess Pools & Stink traps.'[23] He later complained: 'The one in my room has of late and only of Late Become so bad with wind, when it Blows from the North that it is utterly unserviceable … The pipes up the side roar like Cannon.'[24] The bird house was still not complete by early 1820 and the estate mason and carpenter were told to complete it 'and then go to the Castle about which there is no hurry'.[25] The Earl was impatient because he wanted to begin breeding that season and his wife to introduce black swans.[26] As work on the castle drains resumed in June, it must be assumed that the work at the bird house was now finished.[27]

The tree planting continued on a massive scale with the delivery of almost 635,000 young trees in 1820 alone, including larches, Scots firs, black poplars, Huntingdon willows, Canadian poplars, filberts, privets, *rhododendron ponticum*, laurels, and crab apples.[28] When at Culzean the Earl was in the habit of inspecting his plantations and he instructed the old men (pensioners from the army), who planted and tended the trees, 'to cut

The Thistles in all the Parks & Rag Weed'.[29] Towards the end of his life the factor Charles Gairdner recalled an amusing consequence of this order. One day he found three young spruces had been inadvertently cut down with sickles and 'broke out with some violence and threatened most lustily to disband them all if such a mistake should again occur'. A few days later he discovered the same thing had happened again and was about to suit his action to his words when the leader of the pensioners approached him. He was Irish and he took off his hat and scratched his head 'Well, my Lord, a poor man does not know how to please people in the world. In the Garden of Eden there was only one tree forbidden but by St Patrick they are all forbidden here.' The Earl was much amused and 'ran away laughing'.[30]

When the lord lieutenant of Ayrshire, his rival the Earl of Eglinton became mortally ill in November 1819, the Earl of Cassillis could not resist seeking his position. Five days before Eglinton's death, Cassillis wrote his most servile and tactless letter to Grenville: 'The LL of the County and the Green Ribbon! By his Death! Becomes vacant – My Landed Property in the County (If that gives any Claim) exceeds I dare say any other Individuals by four fifths!'[31] The letter rambled on over several pages and concluded gratuitously: 'How can a country be quiet with Forty Thousand Starving Irishmen of the worst description in it! I employ a great many at present about here.'[32] Perhaps because he thought he had over-reached himself, he wrote again the following day, seemingly contradicting his request to be considered for the lieutenancy: 'I really have only enjoyed myself since I gave up County Politics and the Society of Voters.'[33] Grenville replied with great discretion the day after Eglinton died: 'With respect to myself my own resolution has, as you know, been taken some time since to withdraw myself from all active concern in political business.' He went on to say that since the massacre of Peterloo in 1819 and the passing of the Six Acts, designed to repress sedition: 'If I continued to take part in politics I think the result of this state of things would probably lead me to concur more generally with the measures than I had hitherto done with the measures of the present Government.' Nevertheless, he still disagreed fundamentally with the existing policies towards Ireland. He unequivocally advised Cassillis to take the lieutenancy:

> I can see no possible reason which should deter you from making an immediate and direct application to the Ministers to recommend you to the situation to which you have both by station and character so many powerful claims. The wish of receiving, at the same time with this mark of confidence, the distinction of the Green Ribband, is one which, I am sure you will allow me to say truly, I do not think likely …
>
> I hope you will succeed in your endeavours to keep things quiet in your immediate neighbourhood, & with respect to the general tranquillity of the Country I have great confidence in the measures now adopted, & much more in the spirit & dispositions of Parliament, which have been manifested on this occasion in a manner exceeding my expectations. The thing has been suffered to go much further than it should have been, but I do believe we are yet in time to check, & to suppress it.[34]

Cassillis remained undecided and Grenville wrote again on 15 December:

> With respect to the preference between the two objects you are much the best judge – as matter of advice I should recommend the application for the Ltcy (with a reference to *future* claims to the other object) – that if you feel otherwise there can be no reason why you should not distinctly say so, either to Ld

Liverpool or to Lord Sidmouth, as may be most agreeable to yourself.[35]

Having finally decided to rule himself out, Cassillis was, nevertheless, furious when it was proposed to transfer the Earl of Glasgow from Renfrewshire to be lord lieutenant, condemning it as 'too flagrant an act of Scotch jobbing', 'motivated by the fears of the Scotch ministry' that 'such an appointment to me would throw the county into my hands altogether at the next election'.[36] He wrote immediately to Sidmouth, the home secretary to register his complaint:

> I speak now for the County; for the Great Familys in it out of whom its surely possible to choose a Lord Lieutenant & not so to displace one from a Neighbouring County for us. The Political Proceedings /Provincial/ of course at once strikes every man, it cannot fail to do so.

He continued by giving voice to his own hurt feelings: 'Why has Govt passed over the pretensions of one of the very oldest peers in Scotland/ supporting Government/ with one of the largest, & most independent propertys …'.[37] He received a brief response, denying the appointment was a 'job' and fully supporting Lord Glasgow: 'It is upon public grounds that he has been approved of by the Prince Regent.'[38] Dissatisfied, he turned his back on Ayrshire. He maintained only a small establishment at Culzean of about four staff, bringing his butler, his cook and other personal staff with him when he visited during the autumn. He always employed foreign cooks. In 1818 his son Lord Kennedy wrote: 'I am trying every where for a Cook for you but have not yet succeeded. I have heard of several – One seemed likely, but was so enormously fat that she could hardly have turned even in your Kitchen.'[39]

By this time the Earl was planning to build a new house for himself at St Margaret's, on the site of a house immediately upstream of Lacy House

which he had acquired and pulled down. In December 1823 he again engaged the Bloomsbury architect James Donaldson to help him on strict terms:

> I pay you by the day /£1.1/ for the time it takes and no more and in like manner in going over accounts and reporting thereon … in short no <u>percentages at all</u>. – I am thus particular, because I wish to have a clear understanding about my business in order to prevent disputes afterwards which are perpetually arising about the Works here and which never happens anywhere else.[40]

When the new house was complete Lacy House itself was demolished. A visitor in 1824 described the house as 'the chief ornament of Twickenham Park' and continued:

> In the interior arrangement, fitting-up, and combination of furniture, it vies in

St. Margaret's from the Thames drawn and engraved by Frederick Swan in 1832. The 1st Marquess was no doubt rowed down the river in a barge such as this to his town house in Privy Gardens.

elegance with any thing of the kind in the kingdom. In fact, it is so exquisite and chaste, that in admiring the suite of apartments, we forget the splendour that pervades it. The Dining-Room occupies the east wing, extending along the south front: it is a fine room, lofty, and finished with a dome, from which is suspended a beautiful chandelier. Several fine pictures by old masters ornament this apartment, as well as the charming ante-rooms which connects the suite of apartments.

The author extolled the beauty of the grounds and even the kitchen garden, which was described as 'extensive, well walled, and abounding in fruit-trees, also a handsome range of hot-houses and lime pits'.[41] The Earl's new home soon became well known for the quality of the hospitality. At the time of the Reform bill the prime minister, Earl Grey, when he was forced to cancel a visit, commented, 'but I believe I shall be better for avoiding the

temptation of your good wine'.[42] Its kitchen garden was soon legendary,[43] with melon frames and vineries.[44] The Earl was proud of his garden, writing to Lord Stanley in 1834 'You shall manage the State Affairs and I will look after Corn & Cabbages.'[45] When Stanley requested some melon seeds, he boasted:

A rustic lodge for St. Margaret's designed by the architect Robert Logan.

> If there is anything in my gardens
> here or elsewhere you would like to have
> name it only – I have all the finest sorts
> of pears, apples, grapes etc./at least I
> think so/that are going & you may have
> cuttings of all or any indeed part of any-
> thing. I am much more of a
> Horticulturist than Politician.[46]

Stanley replied accepting the offer of a 'small vine plant of the black keeping sort', and adding:

> I do not doubt your finding
> Horticulture a more agreeable occupa-
> tion than Politics – but I fear that times
> are at hand in which it will be necessary
> for every man possessed of influence

and property and desirous of serving the Country to be at the Post, not which

> he may find the most agreeable,
> but where he may think he can be
> most useful.[47]

The grapes did not keep as well as was claimed for by the time they arrived at Knowsley Hall, Stanley's home in Lancashire 'they had become quite mouldy'.[48]

During the so-called 'Radical War' of April 1820 the Earl took draconian action to defend Culzean. While in Scotland in November and December 1819 he had taken steps to raise additional yeomanry in Carrick, suspecting that the fall in wages and consequent economic hardship might result in trouble. He had been kept informed of the progress of events in the south by his friend and fellow moderate, the Marquess of Buckingham.[49] Although Buckingham had some sympathy with tradesmen who had lost their jobs, he had no truck with the radicals: 'still if we have stout hearts & can silence Hunt* and his crew we still shall weather the storm'.[50]

* Henry Hunt, the mob orator.

Back in London in the spring, Cassillis replied to his factor's urgent appeal in April as to what action he should take:

> In answer to your letter about the Rebels, I have no doubt when those in the west find that those in the south can make no head that the greatest proportion of them will return to their work. But in the meantime every precaution must be attended to to prevent surprise & depredation as most likely thro' thieves. I mean those whose object is plunder will be at work to take advantage of the general confusion and lay their hands on all they can. Some additional people must sleep in the Castle … And the whole of them must be well armed and well served with ammunition, Chiefly with blunderbusses & plenty of Balls in them … And if any man or men attempt to enter the castle by force to instantly fire upon them, And the same of breaking into any of my houses or office houses, not to spare them for a single second and repeat it as often as is necessary. Any attacks of the rebels for they are nothing else is to be met with my people with the severest chastisement.[51]

He promised to come north should the need arise, travelling day and night. As things turned out his presence was not required. Like other moderates who were moving towards the Tories, he had to steer a difficult course.

He was uncertain if his conscience would allow him to support the Bill of Pains and Penalties in November of that year which was intended to end Queen Caroline's marriage to the Prince Regent. Only in 1819 he had used the good offices of her physician, Dr William Muton, to secure his election to the Royal Society.[52] He wrote to the prime minister, Lord Liverpool:

> I feel it proper to state the strong objections existing in my mind to the Bill now pending in the House of Lords and that my desire at present [is] not to pronounce, when it comes to a second reading. At the same time those sentiments of real esteem which I feel for you would reduce me to forego my own opinion and vote for the second reading.[53]

Liverpool replied by return, gently seeking his support:

> All I feel I have a right to ask of you, is to suspend your first determination until you have heard the Chancellor's speech, If after hearing that speech you entertain any doubts of the Queen's guilt, you are correct in Duty to vote against the second Reading of the Bill.[54]

Despite his concern that the measure might stir up popular protest, Cassillis was persuaded and supported the government. His change of heart was in part due to the outcome of a long meeting in late November between the King and Grenville, which was reported to Cassillis by Buckingham. The Marquess was critical of the ministers' lack of foresight:

> give us good Lord our daily bread seems to have been the extent of their prayer & the limit of their humble desires. Instead of leaving futurity to take care of itself, they have always looked to futurity to take care of them … What this is to end in, it is impossible to say. What I dread the most is that the King, if he feels this present Ministry cannot go on, will in despair throw himself upon the Whigs … The Queen is <u>playing the whole game</u>.[55]

As a reward for his loyalty and to ensure his continuing support, the new King George IV in 1820 at last made the Earl of Cassillis a Knight of the Thistle without reference to ministers. Arriving at Culzean not long afterwards, Cassillis was relieved that rumours of protest following the government's decision to abandon the Bill of Pains and Penalties were exaggerated: 'not a single soul attended the meeting of <u>Radicals</u> in Ayr'. He was concerned at the obvious signs of distress in the local community: 'The weavers in this quarter are literally starving' and expected strong action from the government.[56] Towards of the end of November he was less confident: 'Things are certainly not in a good state but they are not in such a position as to cause any fear of an <u>overturning of the State Coach</u> … I am thoroughly satisfied that nine tenths of the People are Loyal.' He added, however: 'How can we be quiet when in Glasgow alone, I dare say there is nearer to 30,000 than any other number of the <u>Idle Irish of the Worst Class</u> … God help us, as the saying is, for what is to become of us.' Nevertheless he believed a troop of dragoons at Ayr would keep the surrounding towns quiet.[57] After the great public meeting at the Pantheon in Edinburgh on 16 December he described himself as a 'gloomy dog'; 'I cannot see daylight in any direction.' He was convinced there would be revolution if the army was reduced and that the 'opposition will take the King by storm, backed as they are and will be by the People, as they are called'.[58] Despite his concerns about the Irish, he employed them at Culzean and remained an active supporter of Catholic emancipation and voted in its favour in 1821.[59] Illness prevented him from being in Edinburgh at the time of the King's visit in 1822.[60]

During that year Sir Robert Peel, who had succeeded Sidmouth as home secretary, moved into Privy Gardens and Cassillis seized the opportunity to make friends: 'I have many useless horses here at your service.'[61] In 1824 the Earl's youngest daughter married Sir Robert Peel's younger brother, Colonel (later Lieutenant General) Jonathan Peel, MP, who owned a string of successful racehorses in partnership with the Duke of Richmond.[62] This familial tie was not always respected. Cassillis complained in 1826: 'I can get into every <u>Ministers' House</u> but yours. I rather think your Porter looks upon me as a suspicious sort of Fellow one that wants of a place from my dress and gouty appearance.'[63] After the prime minister, Lord Liverpool, suffered a stroke early in 1827 he was succeeded by George Canning, who had agreed on taking office not to press the question of Catholic emancipation, even though he depended for support on the Whigs. Furious, Cassillis shifted his allegiance to Peel, writing in April:

> I ask no questions, I seek no Favour and I beg that this letter may not receive any answer. With these Preliminaries, I proceed to state that I have heard/and from authority which I consider good/that Mr Canning is to succeed Lord Liverpool! Perhaps with your consent! Be it true or be it otherwise. Be you out. Or be you in. <u>I go with</u> you … I have for the most part of my Political Life born <u>Strict Allegiance</u> to my Friend Lord Grenville and he has requited my attachment in manner most pleasing to a Man with much feeling namely by taking me into his confidence both in matters personal and political.[64]

It is doubtful if Grenville saw their relationship in quite this light. The Earl explained his erratic voting behaviour in the Lords by claiming that he had been 'educated in The Catholic School and perhaps have some times voted against my opinion, but I <u>am committed</u> and you must allow me to Tread The beaten path – consistency "in my view" requires it.'[65] He pledged his support to Peel in his proposal to repeal the Test and Corporation Acts. Peel replied generously: 'There is no part of your letter which gives me so much pleasure as that which convinces me that I have acquired a claim to your personal friendship and esteem.'[66] The tone of the letter was no doubt influenced by Cassillis's close friendship with the Duke of Clarence, who became heir to the throne on the death of his elder brother the Duke of York in June 1827. For the only time in his life Cassillis was in a strong political position. Not only could he provide reformers of either party, such as Peel for the Tories, with information about the mood in the Duke's household, he could also help influence his opinion. In the summer he distanced himself from the Duke of Buckingham,* a supporter of Canning:

> I hold [him] utterly unfit to stand Helmsman of the *Royal George*, both old and recent events, disqualify him in my notion for being the first Minister of this country … If he has said to the King that he entertains not the Catholic Question or said to the King <u>anything like it</u> in my opinion he has a very awkward case to square with the people who have so often heard his declarations for emancipation … My intention is to embark in the same Boat with Mr Peel as a friend. I love the man. As a statesman I hold him to be <u>upright, able & Honest</u>.[67]

On Peel's return to office in 1828 under the Duke of Wellington, the Earl brazenly proposed: 'Why not give me the Great Seal of Scotland?' on the understanding that that he would use the income to buy seats for both his sons so as to 'strengthen <u>permanently both of our families</u> and I consider myself belonging to you. I don't see why I should not be distinguished in some manner by you as well as others who do not belong to you.'[68] Peel responded that despite their friendship: 'If I was called upon to give advice in the exigencies of the present moment with respect to any great offices of the State, I should be bound to say, Dispose of it in such a manner as may be calculated to give the greatest strength to the government.'[69] Entirely within character Cassillis hurriedly backtracked: 'I have

---

* The 2nd Marquis of Buckingham had been created a Duke in 1822.

nothing to ask for myself of Any Man. Happy by the King's Kindness is my lot – No it was for you and not myself that I made venture about the seal.'[70] Within a week he had concluded: 'Tho' I could screw up my courage to a pitch that would not prevent me exposing myself when erect before their Lordships in Bag and Sword I think it is a Task more fit for a younger member of the Lords than a Man of my Standing there.'[71] He wrote later:

> A few words of explanation, & my Little adventure ends – when I found Ld Aberdeen placed and D of Gordon likely to be promoted in the line of his profession, I considered all the <u>Old</u> Candidates for the Seal out of the Field saving Lauderdale. Whose Political bearing was for me a matter of doubt – thus having Cleared away in my own mind the Old Gentlemen in waiting upon the Seal, I believed next that <u>I might be</u> thought even in the Cabinet of the Premier had I proposed myself there for <u>my adhesion</u> as <u>Warrender calls it</u>. As good in my pretension as any <u>New Comer</u> for the Seal … but no matter it is at an end.[72]

During these years he had also used his relationship with Peel to try to advance the career in the diplomatic service of his nephew John, his brother Robert's eldest son. He seems to have kept in touch with his brother's family. In 1821 his niece Anne married Edward Disbrowe, who had been British minister in Switzerland for a year. He was appointed minister to the court of Tsar Alexander I at St Petersburg in the spring of 1825, taking the dangerous overland route in April. His wife followed by sea accompanied by her father and her brother John. They were no sooner settled in St Petersburg than the Tsar died, on 1 December. There followed a period of uncertainty as the heir apparent, Constantine, had resigned his claim to the throne and Tsar Alexander had nominated his younger son Nicholas his successor. Anne wrote regularly to her mother and sisters describing her life in Russia and her father had nothing to add:

> I do not regret not entering more par-
> ticularly into the picture of Russian
> country amusements as your sister's pen
> is so brilliant and correct in description
> and she is none of those sulky islanders
> who think that nothing is good out of
> their own country and think all civilities
> their due, nor does she overrate what
> she sees and receives, to deprecate her
> native lovely island.[73]

After her father and brother had left, Anne and her husband attended the coronation of the new Tsar. Her letter to her parents describing this event is one of the best accounts in English of the Russian court in the early nineteenth century. When her correspondence was edited and published by her eldest daughter, Charlotte Anne, in 1903, the 3rd Marquess of Ailsa subscribed for two copies.

In December 1811 the Earl of Cassillis had asked the advice of Lord Grenville on 'how to dispose of my son Lord Kennedy', who had just left the University of St. Andrews where he had been boarded with his former tutor, James Ferrie, professor of Civil History.[74] Claiming he was 'one of the best scholars of his day in this country' and 'that he has read a great deal upon most subjects I understand both modern and ancient history in an uncommon degree well for his time', his father proposed sending him to Oxford or Cambridge after two years studying with a private tutor. He ended by saying that his son was 'extremely ambitious to become a man of some character in Parliament. I mean to get him into the Hs of Cs as soon as the frame will permit …'[75] He boasted 'money is no object' and pledged that he would 'not spare … any expense which can contribute to turn him into the world a good and able man'.[76] Grenville replied:

> I lose no time in replying to your letter,
> and I should be truly happy if I could

suggest anything likely to be of the smallest use to you in a matter so interesting as that about which you write. It is natural that you should feel the greatest possible anxiety about the mode of completing an Education so well begun.

He entirely concurred with the Earl's plan but was unable to recommend a tutor. He was, however, willing to take soundings.[77]

The plans for the boy's further education were never fulfilled and in 1814 when still only nineteen he married Eleanor, the seventeen-year-old daughter and heiress of Alexander Allardyce of Dunnottar in Kincardineshire, who until his death in 1801 had been MP for Aberdeen Burgh and Dundas's chief agent in the north-east. He had made a great fortune in the slave trade while living as a young man in Jamaica.[78] There is no doubt this was an opportunistic match, which was aided and abetted by the Earl. Lord Kennedy entertained Eleanor and her mother, Hannah, at the House of Dun in December 1813. After they left he reported to his father:

> Mrs & Miss Allardyce left this yesterday
> Morning – You cannot but suppose that
> after all which has been said and done I
> should be very anxious to get
> acquainted with her – I paid her every
> Attention possible in the time – I rode
> with her twice out with the Harriers
> danced with her frequently and in the
> course of the time have had a great deal
> of conversation with her – She is shy
> and says little to any Body but upon the
> whole, I without any prejudice (which I
> have attempted to avoid) think, that she
> is one of the most sensible & unaffected
> girls I ever met with, in which opinion I
> have been joined by my grandmother &
> all who saw her – In some people's
> opinion, she is plain, in others good
> looking. There is something exceedingly

agreeable in her look and for my own part I have never seen anyone whose appearance is more engaging – In her manner she is perfect Nature itself, without the smallest tincture of anything allied to Affection … I think the Fortune, which I believe to be <u>fully equal</u> to what we talked of being joined to such a person is uncommon, and would render her as far as I can judge a very good companion for life – I will now speak a little of the Mother – I do not like her altogether so well as the Daughter, although I have not the smallest doubt that she is a very good sort of Woman – She has evidently not been brought up in the first Circles, but is certainly in spite of a little Affectation in her manner, perfectly passable in the strictest sense and one with whose connexion you could never feel the least ashamed.[79]

Mrs Allardyce, who in fact came from a relatively humble background, was troubled by the proposed union, confiding to the Earl:

> I would not on any account that his attachment to Miss Allardyce should be the means of interrupting your plans for the completion of his Education … From what I have seen of Lord Kennedy as far as I can judge I must freely own I think him worthy of the excellent character you have given him … It will certainly become the duty of my Daughter's Guardians to see that any connection which she may form shall be prudent and proper in point of pecuniary arrangements …[80]

Had she known Lord Kennedy's opinion of her and the Earl's matchmaking intentions, she would have no doubt formed a very different first impression.

Eleanor's guardians had their suspicions, believing the Earl was 'desirous of getting the whole of Miss Allardyce's property <u>into [his] own disposal and management</u>'.[81] The Earl, with his eyes on the fortune, hurriedly reassured her and by 17 January 1814 they were engaged 'both in one another's eyes and in those of Mrs <u>Allardyce</u>'. An added attraction of this alliance was 'the very considerable political interests attached to the Kincardineshire Estate, which under Lord K's management would command that county'.[82] The hostility of the guardians to the marriage almost certainly derived in part from a reluctance to allow the county to fall into Whig hands. Lord Kennedy wished for an early wedding 'as there is certainly too great an intimacy between us to remain long separate – You may therefore be sure that any <u>being off now</u> is entirely out of the Question'.[83] Her guardians tried to make the marriage conditional on their approval.[84] The Earl used his mother-in-law, Mrs Erskine, as a go-between with Mrs Allardyce, whom she described as 'a good well meaning body and has no view upon earth but to act right'. Mrs Allardyce was persuaded to agree against the advice of the other guardians, including their chairman, her brother John Innes of Cowie, an Edinburgh lawyer. She found it difficult when Lord Kennedy described her brother as 'a damn'd rascal' but, nevertheless, she gave her consent. Mrs Erskine encouraged Mrs Allardyce to let her daughter go to London unaccompanied so that, as she reported to the Earl, it 'puts it in your powers to lift the Lassie completely from amongst the set'.[85] The Earl also enlisted the support of his friend David Cathcart, Lord Alloway, to make discreet enquiries about the Allardyces and any other possible contenders for Eleanor's hand. He advised:

> My thinking most decidedly is that the higher the Rank of the Gentleman the greater is the chance of his happiness by an early marriage … . In point of Fortune this Lady is certainly equal to your wishes and if she possesses good

qualities, and good sense … I cannot conceive a greater prospect of Happiness.[86]

Since her father was dead, the wedding took place in early May at the House of Dun where 'the most furious festivities took place … and raged for three days. People of all classes were entertained, and one man is said to have lost his life as a result of the overeating that went on.'[87]

The bride was worth about '£50,000 in Bank stocks over and above the estates of Dunnottar and Barras of some 6,000 acres, then free of encumbrances [mortgages], and worth above £200,000'.[88] Dunnottar House, which had only been completed after her father's death, was exquisitely appointed with the best French furniture and fittings. She also had a home in Aberdeen along with several other properties in the city and a London house. In fact she had inherited on her father's death in 1800 £126,222, which it was now estimated was worth over £250,000.[89] It was reckoned that the rental of the estate alone could be raised easily from its existing £4,000 to £10,000 a year.[90] It was normal practice to contract a marriage settlement before the wedding to protect the bride's property from an avaricious or reckless husband and to make provision for younger children and for her after her husband's death.[91] As Lord Kennedy and Eleanor Allardyce wished to celebrate the marriage without delay,[92] no ante-nuptial agreement could be reached between her guardians and the Earl. The guardians thought the couple should have an income of some £8,000 a year. David Cathcart had misgivings, rightly as it was to turn out: 'I did venture to throw out some hints of the danger of too large an income for persons so very young, & whose characters might in some degree be proved either to profusion or prudence …'[93] He also had doubts about their being left to their own devices in Dunnottar, suggesting 'fitting up Cassillis as a proper place of residence'.[94]

The Earl, whose own equally wealthy father had expected him to live at first on his army pay,

was reluctant to settle a 'farthing' on his son. Appalled, Cathcart advised:

> You would not allow your eldest son and the Representative of your high Person & great Estate to settle in life without some provisions out of the most ample Fortune which if he survives he must inherit, and especially as he is a son of whom you have such just cause to be proud, and who has hitherto conducted himself, even with regard to this very matter, as the fondest father would desire – Whether Lord K. is married or unmarried you must have given him a handsome establishment suitable to his Rank & your Fortune; You could not have put him to any of the Universities, nor could he have gone abroad but at greater expense than is now demanded for his complete establishment in Life and when instead of ever after costing you a Farthing he will be entitled to live with all the splendour you could wish him and also add prodigious wealth to the Family.[95]

He went on to suggest that the £4,000 a year that Innes and his fellow guardians demanded was entirely reasonable, given that the Earl's income was now some £25,000 a year. He feared that breaking off the engagement at such a late stage might unhinge Lord Kennedy as had happened with disastrous consequences to the Duke of Roxburghe 'which prevented him ever afterwards marrying'. Chastened, the Earl did agree in a draft ante-nuptial settlement to pay his son an annuity of £2,000 a year in ten years' time.[96] Her guardians objected to this state of affairs as they were looking for £4,000 and threatened legal action. The Earl and his son were advised to settle 'extra-judicially' to avoid expense.[97] Under the law of Scotland on marriage:

> the whole personal property of the wife

would instantly become the Husbands & the Landed Estate would remain the property of the wife subject to such settlements as she might afterwards think fit to execute, the rents in the meantime belonging to the Husband.[98]

The guardians claimed that since Eleanor was a minor they should still control her large personal fortune and insisted that it was only equitable that the Earl should match her income pound for pound in any settlement. This he refused point blank to do. After protracted, and at times bitter negotiations, the guardians raised an action in Chancery against Lord Kennedy, declaring the marriage null and void as his wife's guardians had withheld their permission.[99] His father the Earl was incensed, noting angrily to his counsel: 'I think that the [Lord] Chancellor is not made sufficiently aware of the Character & Situation of Mr Innes! – he does not know that Mr Innes is carrying on this action against the opinion of all the Trustees & Mrs Allardyce.' Lord Kennedy and his wife countered by raising an action in the Court of Session against Innes alleging 'for Misapplication of the Trust Funds: a sum – not less than £50,000'.[100] It was finally agreed that the 'ante-nuptial' settlement, which had been drawn up, should at least be ratified as a post-nuptial contract. Such contracts had little legal force and gave 'no right of credit, either to a wife or children' and were 'revocable at pleasure'.[101] Under its terms her husband was to enjoy her property for his lifetime when it was to pass to the second son of the marriage in the same way as the House of Dun estate. Lord Kennedy was only allowed to burden it with mortgages not exceeding £10,000 so as to make provision for other children of the marriage.

At first they made their home in Edinburgh where they were well thought of. John Smith, the Erskine family lawyer, reported to the Earl in October 1814:

I cannot help saying that both Lady
Kennedy and he are very much thought
of in East Lothian from the prudent and respectful manner in which they go on & it was very gratifying to me to hear so from people well qualified to form such an opinion.[102]

David Cathcart had a similar opinion: 'I think Lord Kennedy one of the most promising young men I ever saw.'[103] They spent the summer at Dunnottar. When their first child was due in the autumn of 1815, it was confided in the Earl that: 'The affection and anxiety of Lord Kennedy is most amiable & honourable to him.'[104] While in residence Kennedy set about resolving a long standing dispute over the construction of the monumental walled garden which had been designed by the Edinburgh architect John Paterson and completed in 1810. Built by Andrew Smith, a mason and architect at the Burn, it had cost the colossal sum of £3,874, which was £1,900 over budget. Lady Kennedy's trustees had refused to meet the difference and her husband was just as robust in rejecting Smith's claim. As a result both Smith and his cautioner, his uncle-in-law George Austin of Nether Thanestone, became bankrupt.[105] Taking his responsibilities as a local landowner seriously, Lord Kennedy presided at the inaugural meeting of the Stonehaven Savings Bank on 17 June. Given his subsequent improvidence this was perhaps out of character but he was still very young.[106]

Although Lord Kennedy's debt to John Smith was over £5,000 by 1816, he could attribute his financial problems to unpaid rents in marked contrast to the previous year, a consequence of the sudden post-war recession: 'the Arrear was upward of £1,600 – an immense sum.'[107] He pleaded with the Earl: 'So my Dear Father you must yourself see that not only œconomy, but the greatest frugality have been used … we amongst others have therefore to complain of the hard times.'[108] His father agreed to provide surety for a loan of this sum so that his son would no longer have to pay Smith's exorbitant rates of interest. Smith in turn was grateful and had no doubt that Lord Kennedy: 'will

continue to go on in the same respectable & proper manner as he has always done'.[109] This was sadly not to be the case. Charles Kirkpatrick Shaw, an Edinburgh antiquary, in 1817 mourned Kennedy's early marriage, which had brought to an end his scholarly pretensions.[110] Instead he had become an enthusiastic pedestrian and rider, race horse owner, a good golfer, one of the best shots of the day, a skilled fisherman, an inveterate gambler and a prominent member of what was known as the 'Fancy' – a fast set of sportsmen.[111] Dr Johnson's 'Short Song of Congratulation' of fifty years before could almost have been written for him:

> Wealth, my lad, was made to wander,
> Let it wander as it will,
> See the jockey, see the pander,
> Bid them come and take their fill
>
> Call the Bettys, Kates and Jennies
> Every name that laughs at care;

The massive walls of the garden at Dunnottar, which were, no doubt, modelled on the ruins of nearby Dunnottar castle.

> Lavish of your grandsire's guineas,
> Show the spirit of an heir.

Lord Kennedy kept a pack of hounds and racehorses at Dunnottar, with which he competed at Aberdeen and Montrose where racing was revived in 1821. These included *John Knox*, *Vestris*, *The Captain* and *Habeas Corpus* (1816), *Bolivar* (1820), *Hospitality* (1822), *Neil Gow* (1823), *Negotiator* (1824), *Grecian Queen*, *Skiff*, and *Caccia Piatti* (1826).[112] He also had horses at training in the north of England, which were raced at York, where he won the King's purse of one hundred guineas in 1825 for a four mile race.[113] Like those of his father and other members of the Fancy, Lord Kennedy's wagers were usually for feats of sporting prowess. In August 1822 he backed himself for 40 to 1 in £50 notes to shoot forty brace of grouse and ride from his shooting box at Feloar in Perthshire to Dunnottar and back to Feloar in a day – a round trip of some one hundred and forty miles in under twenty-four hours. Despite the fact that 'a

great deal of rain had fallen in the night which made the hills very wet and birds very wild', he set out at four o'clock in the morning 'attended by a great body of Highlanders' who had turned out to see the sport. He killed his first bird after quarter of an hour and reached his target just before nine. He changed out on the moor and mounted a sure-footed hack which he rode for the first seven or eight miles over rough ground. When on the road he had relays of horses waiting for him and arrived at Dunnottar at two in the afternoon. He was back at Feloar by eight in the evening and was described 'as not the least knocked up'. His neighbour, Captain Barclay of Ury, the great pedestrian and one of his wife's relatives, was the umpire and thought it one of the best physical feats ever recorded.[114] Later in the year Kennedy wagered that Captain Barclay could not find a man to throw a cricket ball one hundred yards both ways. The match took place in Hyde Park in December and Kennedy won.[115]

The following year he bet William Coke, Earl

The ne'erdowell Lord Kennedy, later 13th Earl of Cassillis, hunting near Dunnottar, painted by John Fernley.

of Leicester and a noted shot, two hundred sovereigns that he could shoot in two days (a week apart) more partridges in Scotland than he could on his Norfolk estate at Holkham. Kennedy chose the moors at Monreith in the mild Wigtownshire climate of Sir William Maxwell, another well-known sportsman. This well-advertised wager attracted a great number of spectators at both venues and heavy betting. Coke killed three hundred and eighty-four birds with seven hundred and fourteen shots and won the match by forty-two brace. Sir William vowed he would never allow such a competition again as 'the ground was strewn with crippled and wounded birds for days afterwards'.[116] In a return match in 1824 at Coke's Norfolk seat, Kennedy won.[117] During the summer of that year he took part in a pigeon shooting match on the New Subscription Ground next to the Red House tavern in Battersea, one of the favourite resorts of the Fancy during the London season for such 'trials of skill'. These were the:

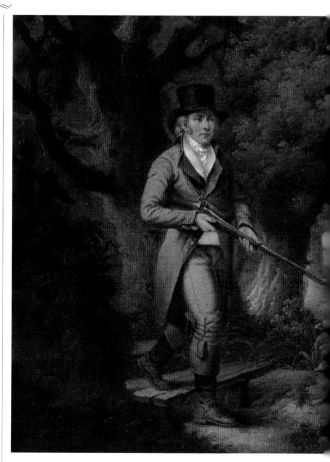

occasion of several public breakfasts, capital dinners, and some little *betting* – which latter circumstance, to the sporting man, may be viewed as a kind of food to feed upon, not only to give him strength, but to increase his exertions.[118]

His team mate was his friend James Cruikshank of Langley Park, near Montrose, and his opponents were the celebrated sportsman George Osbaldeston, the master of the Quorn Hunt, and Captain Horatio Ross of Dibdale Lodge, Bonar Bridge, another notorious member of the sporting fraternity. The match lasted for two days, attracting huge crowds and large bets. Each competitor was allowed to fire thirty-eight balls and, although the

LEFT
Alexander Allardyce, father-in-law of the 13th Earl, who began building Dunnottar house and who died in 1801.

match was drawn, Kennedy won on side bets.[119] The *Sporting Magazine* commented: 'Nothing can be more elegant than Lord Kennedy's style of shooting.'[120]

These pigeon shooting matches at the Red House became annual events, with Kennedy often the winner. In a match in the spring of 1825, however, Ross beat him. Kennedy, according to Ross, was a bad loser: 'he did not so easily get over betting. He brooded over it and turned over and over in his mind how he could have his revenge.' Riding shortly afterwards with him to the Derby, Ross was warned to be 'wide awake and prepared for all sorts of wild proposals from his Lordship'. After declining various wagers including a cock-fight, there was an argument about whether a 'tip top <u>provincial</u> rider will gen-

erally be found <u>in the crowd</u> in a Leicestershire [hunting] field'. As the editor of the *Sporting Magazine* commented: 'a truism which can never be doubted'. Goaded on, Ross accepted a challenge to ride a steeple-chase against Captain Douglas over four miles of Leicestershire countryside from Barby Hill to Billesden Coplow for £1,000. The stakes were later raised to a colossal £2,300. The two opponents immediately went into serious training. At Dunnottar Kennedy kept an eagle eye on Douglas to such an extent that when he found him eating a potato, he exclaimed: 'What are you about? Surely you forget the steeplechase.' The training regime was clearly stringent, as Douglas got his weight down from fourteen stone to twelve stone nine pounds and Ross from thir-

LEFT
The 13th Earl of Cassillis out shooting.

RIGHT
A pigeon shooting competition in the 1820s. This was the precursor of clay pigeon shooting.

teen stone five pounds to eleven stone eight pounds.

Ross was well known in Leicester-shire and had the offer of several horses. Finally he accepted *Clinker* which was owned by Kennedy's brother-in-law Lieutenant General Jonathan Peel, a well-known judge of horseflesh. Ken-nedy brought two horses for Douglas, *Whynot* from Colonel Wallace for £400 and *Radical* from Thomas Assheton Smith for £500, and tried to buy a third, *Whitestockings* from Lord Lynedoch for £800. By the day of the race the course was much knocked about by the constant practice and many of the fences were broken and 'in a state not to have stopped the commonest hack'. The event attracted widespread interest. 'People came from all parts of the country to see it' and many followed the contestants on horseback. So confident was he of victory that, moments before the race, Kennedy insisted that the normal courtesies of the racetrack should be ignored. Douglas led for the first four fields but then *Radical* refused a fence. Douglas was thrown but since one of his hands was tied to the reins he still had hold of his horse. Heeding Kennedy's caution to abandon the normal rules of racing, Ross rode Douglas down. In so doing he got caught in Douglas's reins, throwing him and *Radical* to the ground. Although Douglas remounted and pressed his horse hard, he was unable to catch up and *Clinker* won taking just eleven minutes fifteen seconds to complete the course.[121]

The conduct of the race was not without its critics, and some suggested that Ross had been unduly helped by riders pointing out the route. There was sympathy for Lord Kennedy, who was described as 'a never failing supporter of all field sports' and suggestions that there should be a rematch: 'Let no fences be broken, no roads made, no horsemen be placed like so many finger-points to direct the route.'[122] Ross later exaggerated his triumph, claiming to have ridden down *Radical* sending him 'heels over head' after he refused the first fence.[123] After this encounter the editor of the *Sporting Magazine* commented: 'Lord Kennedy is as true a sportsman as any in Britain. His Lordship keeps hounds and is one of the finest shots in England. Few, very few, can say as much.'[124]

At the next pigeon-shooting context at the Red House later in the year, Kennedy, still licking his wounds, was described in the press 'as being a burnt child upon the turf'. The hope was that he might reverse his fortunes, as indeed he did, winning six hundred guineas in a competition to shoot one hundred balls over two days.[125] In 1827 with Osbaldeston and Mr Anderson, he defeated Captain Ross, Lord Anson, and Mr Furness so resoundingly that a volley of seven guns was fired in his honour. For his personal performance he was

Sir Andrew Leith Hay who was Lord Kennedy's challenger in one of his best known walking competitions.

awarded the club's gold cup and prize rifle.[126] Osbaldeston later recalled that Lady Kennedy sometimes attended such matches, when she was accustomed to tie a piece of paper round a leg of the pigeons to make them fly with a zigzag motion, which she hoped might make them more difficult to shoot.[127] On 5 June of that year her husband shot a grand match against Mr Arrowsmith at the Red House for six hundred guineas, when the betting was 5 to 4 on his opponent. After a very close competition over two days, the outcome was a tie with level scores of fifty-seven kills out of seventy-five shots apiece. At the end of the month he took part in a remarkable engagement with Captain Ross at the Haymarket shooting gallery, another popular venue for sportsmen. Although Kennedy was armed with a rifle and Ross with neater pistols, Ross won.[128] On a further occasion he was so indignant at losing to Ross that he wagered £100 to £1 that he would 'never shoot another match as long as he lived'. Sometime later complaining at the 'slowness of the sporting world and expressing a wish for something going on', Captain Grant wagered him £50 to shoot pigeons. Kennedy accepted and won, but on accepting his takings, Ross asked for his £100.[129]

Kennedy shot a match at the Red House in June 1828 against Osbaldeston for the princely sum of two thousand guineas, which lasted for five days. The wager was to shoot at one hundred pigeons each day with double-barrelled shot guns. The competition was very close, keenly watched by a large crowd. Osbaldeston triumphed on the final day, having killed four hundred and thirty-seven birds to Kennedy's four hundred and eighteen. Nevertheless the correspondent of the *Sporting Magazine* believed Kennedy the better shot, displaying 'coolness and firm judgement' in handling the gun.[130] Ross had agreed to take on the winner on the same terms, but, respecting the skill of his would-be adversary, wisely withdrew and paid a forfeit.[131] The Red House also boasted a sparrow club where contestants had to shoot a dozen spar-

rows at eighteen yards. Kennedy won this dubious competition in 1831.[132] It was said of Kennedy, Osbaldeston, and Ross that they had 'merely to hold up their guns as it were when destruction and *death* follows the sound of their pieces to the feathered tribe.'[133]

When at home in Scotland James Cruikshank and Captain Ross were frequent adversaries. In July 1823 Kennedy and Cruikshank played two twenty-one hole golf matches at Montrose in front of a large crowd. In the first match Cruikshank won every hole. The second was drawn and settled in a ten-hole play-off in which Cruikshank was again victorious.[134] In September 1824 Kennedy challenged Cruikshank to the best of eleven seven-hole games of golf at St Andrews. In an exciting contest, which was again thronged with spectators, Cruikshank won six games to five. Kennedy replied by betting him he could not shoot ten brace of grouse with single balls in one day. Kennedy won, killing his ten brace with one hundred and seventy balls.[135] On another occasion, after dinner one night at Dun, he bet Cruikshank £500 a hole for the best of three holes of golf played there and then. No light was allowed except one placed on the

LEFT
Lady Kennedy's swimming pool above the Glasslaw Burn at Dunnottar, restored in 1999.

RIGHT
Cassillis house, with at the front the addition designed almost certainly by the architect William Burn for the 13th Earl of Cassillis in 1829.

hole and another carried by the players. Boys were engaged to listen for the flight of the ball and then search for where it landed. Kennedy won by a hole in the same number of strokes in which he had in daylight. Another time he bet Ross £20 that he could not kill twenty brace of swallows on the wing in a day at Rossie Castle near Montrose. Ross triumphed, 'I sent him the twenty brace in a box and they arrived while he and a party were at dinner and were brought into the dining room. He sent me the twenty pounds and said in his note it was "the most expensive entrée ever handed to him".'[136] While at Culzean he challenged Lord Kelburn, the heir to the Earl of Glasgow, to a midnight coach race from Ardrossan to Ayr. Kelburn took a wrong turning and ended up in the sea, only narrowly escaping being drowned.[137]

Kennedy's endurance was renowned. George Osbaldeston remembered spending an evening dancing with him and Ross in Perthshire and then leaving to go stalking at four o'clock in the morning. They bagged only one stag and did not return to their lodgings until seven that night.[138] After spending a day snipe shooting in September 1826 with Ross, Major (later Sir) Andrew Leith Hay,

and Captain Barclay at Archibald Farquharson's home at Blackhall, Aberdeenshire, there was a disagreement after dinner about the quickest route to Inverness. Kennedy challenged Major Hay to be in Inverness before him. The wager was for five hundred guineas although in later accounts the sum was doubled. Barclay undertook to be umpire and Ross to be Hay's referee. Kennedy set off at once across the Grampian Mountains in his evening dress taking Ross with him as his second and accompanied by Farquharson. Ross recalled: 'We walked all night and the next – raining torrents all the while. We crossed the Grampians making a perfect straight line and got to Inverness at 6 a.m.' Hay went by the high road and arrived four hours later. He protested, however, that Kennedy had leaned on Ross's arm descending from the mountains and had disqualified himself. Kennedy, who had arrived barefoot, was not to be denied his triumph by such a trivial complaint and Barclay declared him the winner.[139] As well as walking, Barclay prided himself on his skill at long-distance coach driving. Believing his claims to be exaggerated, Lord Kennedy wagered a large sum that he could not drive the Royal Mail coach from London to Aberdeen (five hundred and twenty-six miles) under the scrutiny of an umpire, without breaks, other than those allowed the passengers for their comfort. Barclay took him on and, after almost sixty hours driving, arrived in Aberdeen 'so little exhausted' that he offered to double or quits by returning there and then. Kennedy prudently admitted defeat.[140]

Having run through his wife's cash, Lord Kennedy borrowed heavily to feed his gambling habit. Seriously in debt, he prevailed on her to mortgage her Dunnottar estate for £85,000, contrary to the terms of the marriage settlement and borrowed £22,000 on his own personal security from his family lawyers, Hunter, Campbell and Cathcart, WS, of Edinburgh. Unable to provide security for this immense sum, in 1829 he persuaded his wife to take out another mortgage, but he did have the good grace to take out a life insurance policy for £20,000 to redeem part of the loss to the estate. He instructed his lawyers that the proceeds were 'to be applied in payment of any debts which I may leave; in the second place for the benefit of Lady Kennedy and my children'.[141] To be fair to him, he had made improvements to the estate and policies, commissioning for his wife a delightful shell house in the grounds and a swimming pool beside the Dunnottar Burn.[142]

With such colossal debts to service, Dunnottar was let and Lord Kennedy and his wife moved in 1829 to Cassillis House. This was finally completed for them almost certainly by the architect William Burn, with an elegant Gothic addition to accommodate their growing family and a new walled garden.[143] Alexander Forwalt, the aviary man at Culzean, was sent off to Dunnottar to bring three deer to Culzean.[144]

Even in an age of heroic gambling £150,000 was a fantastic sum to have run through in not much more than a decade, dwarfing the £50,000 loss of the vastly richer Georgina Duchess of Devonshire a generation earlier.[145] George Harley Drummond, the heir to a banking fortune and a neighbour of Kennedy in Aberdeenshire, fled the country for less.[146] The sheer scale of his son's improvidence was a bitter blow to the Earl of Cassillis who had spent so long trying to extricate his estates from similar embarrassment.

Although Richard Campbell had advised the Earl to register improvements on the Culzean and Cassillis estates with the sheriff court under the terms of the Montgomery Act, none was registered until 1820, presumably because the trustees were prohibited from any improvement expenditure under the terms of the Earl's will. Thereafter until the passing of a new entail Act, the Rutherford Act, in 1848, which simplified the process, improvements were registered every year.[147] Altogether improvements of some £39,000 were registered between 1820 and 1841.[148] By 1820 after years of neglect the properties by all accounts were dilapidated and the outlook was uncertain. The sub-factor Quintin Jamieson reported during that year:

There certainly never was a time more difficult than the present to value lands than the present state of markets and alarm to the tenants to guide a valua-

tion. I do not know how it could be done. I am certain so soon as our Manufacturing Trade improves our markets will also rise, and had it not been for the depressed state of Trade our markets would have been high particularly for butcher meat and dairy produce these I think would have been beyond what we have ever seen.[149]

Charles Gairdner resigned as factor in 1821 to pursue a career as a banker and to become the factor to the Earl of Eglinton.[150] He was succeeded by William Craig, who continued to have two sub-factors to assist him. With signs of an upturn in the economy he initiated a programme of improvements. On Jamieson's advice sketch plans were made of every farm 'with the fields numbered and the contents stated' and new leases included details of the liming, manuring and rotation regimes to be observed.[151] Over the next twenty years new shelter belts continued to be planted along with miles and miles of thorn and beech hedges. For example, over three hundred thousand trees were set in 1825 and over two hundred thousand in 1828.[152] Miles of drains were laid and in 1839 a tilery was opened at Knockjarder for this purpose.[153] New farmhouses, byres, milk houses and barns were constructed, often under the terms of new leases. In 1829 new farmhouses were built at Highgate and Culdeoch, North Balloch, and Brae and Lindstone and in the following year at Bowmanston.[154] The intention seems to have been to improve the hill lands, which made up the majority of the estate, for dairying and sheep husbandry.[155] This was an odd time to invest in agriculture which was seriously depressed in the aftermath of wartime prosperity, but after such a long period of neglect the Earl had little choice. There is evidence, however, that his enthusiasm for tree planting soon waned, as a visitor in 1833 found the plantations in a ruinous state from want of thinning.[156]

The effect of such improvements on the rents could nevertheless be dramatic. In the early nine-

teenth century Colonel Fullarton improved his estate between Irvine and Troon, raising rents to '27s. 6d. per acre, a remarkable change, surely, from the two or three shillings per acre of a half century earlier'.[157] The Earl's income did not rise quite so spectacularly, largely because much of the estate was poor hill ground, but even with the much reduced estate, his rent roll climbed to almost £25,000 by 1829, with game, fishings and the sale of wood contributing a further £814. On moving from Dunnottar in that year, his son Lord Kennedy, reputedly a reformed character, took an active interest in the improvement of the ground rented to him. According to the minister of Kirkmichael, who was almost certainly gilding a far from white lily, 'The whole appearance of the lands under his management was changed; new breeds of cattle and sheep were introduced; the most approved modes of farming in all its branches adopted, and improvements, in a style and to an extent not before attempted in Carrick, were skilfully and successfully proceeding …'[158] Yet despite all the improvements the rental of the whole estate did not increase, and in fact by 1836 there was over £15,000 outstanding in arrears in rent.[159]

No building work was carried out within the

Culzean policies for some six years after the completion of the extension to the bird house in 1820 when Thomas White returned to offer advice. Possibly on his recommendation a 'new mortar battery' was constructed in 1829 on the forecourt of the castle with a spectacular view across to Arran.[160] This was furnished with some remarkable weapons of considerable antiquity. As part of this programme of improvement a new peach house and trellis were installed in the walled garden.[161] To help him with his duties Thomas White left the gardener, who was now Bartholomew Hepple, *The Botanical Dictionary*,[162] *The Gardener's Calendar, A Treatise on the Culture of Pinks, Directions for the Culture of Pine apples*, and a copy of the *Journal of the Caledonian Horticultural Society*.[163] This may have been an insult as he came from a distinguished family of gardeners, whose progenitor had been brought to Kilkerran by the Fergusson family in the eighteenth century.

Between 1833 and 1836 the garden wall was again enlarged, the walks in the pleasure gardens laid out, presumably including landscaping the old garden beneath the terraces,[164] and the new coach roads and approaches constructed.[165] In 1834 the park and gardens were embellished by the planting of some three hundred specie rhododendrons and

twenty-five hybrids.[166] From 1834 to 1836 repairs were carried out on the castle, and in 1836 a coach house and a keeper's house were built at the shooting lodge at Craiglure.[167] In that year the Earl gave notice that extensive repairs were needed at Culzean Castle, in the policies and gardens and elsewhere on the estate.[168] These included the construction of Enoch Lodge in 1837, the extension to Martnaham Cottage (renamed Martnaham Lodge) to create a large dining room in 1838 and the building of the new laundry (now known as the Dolphin House) at Culzean in 1840 alongside the bath house.[169] Unlike previous building on the estate, these were a self-conscious attempt to replicate Adam designs. They were 'measured' by a Mr Reid, possibly William Reid, the Glasgow and Paisley architect.[170] It is unlikely that much work was undertaken after these projects, as the Earl and his wife were overwhelmed by a succession of calamities. The Earl's trustees did, however, buy the Dunure estate along the coast in 1849 for some £16,650.[171]

In 1829 the staff at Culzean comprised Mr Rodgers, the steward; Mrs Rae, the house keeper; a maid; William Galloway, the porter and post boy; Alexander Simpson, the house carpenter; James

LEFT
The mortar battery constructed in 1829, possibly on Thomas White junior's initiative, to give spectacular views of Ailsa Craig and Arran.

RIGHT
The restored laundry at Culzean, now called the Dolphin house and used as an outdoor educational centre.

Brook, the gamekeeper; James Forrest, the under gamekeeper; Alexander Fawcett, the aviary man; four baron officers (William Law, James McIlwraith, Hugh McCrorie, and Thomas Rewcastle) along with seven gatekeepers. The house keeper and gamekeeper were paid £80 a year and provided with accommodation. The post boy's duties were extensive. He had to split the logs for the house, fetch the coals, mow the battery and keep the gravel clean, keep all about the washing house clean, rake the gravel on the bridge and coach road, keep the new mortar battery in good order, keep off beggars and stragglers, and lastly go to the post if required.[172] The gardener, Bartholomew Hepple, was effectively an independent contractor selling produce and plants and charging the estate about £100 a year for his services. The baron officers, who were responsible for general maintenance on their section of the estate, were paid about £20 a year. Altogether the total cost of this relatively small establishment for such a large house and estate was about £500 a year including consumables. John Claudius Loudon, the distinguished horticulturist, described in 1833 Hepple's heroic efforts in maintaining the gardens:

Nothing can exceed the grandeur of the situation and the buildings, taking them as a whole and speaking without reference to the correctness of the architectural details, are varied and picturesque. None of the approaches are, however, judiciously conducted either for displaying the beauties of this place, or for easy conveyance. There is a great extent of garden scenery and a very large kitchen garden. The whole is remarkably well kept by the gardener Mr Hepple, though evidently with the greatest difficulty from a deficiency of hands. Mr Hepple had his hothouse crops of pines, grapes and peaches which were not surpassed by any we saw in Scotland.[173]

This was praise indeed from a man who had complete contempt for the work of both Thomas Whites, father and son.[174]

After the accession of the Duke of Clarence as King William IV in 1830, the Earl clearly expected preferment from his friend. His family had already cemented the alliance with the new king on 5 July 1827, when the Earl's second son, John Kennedy-Erskine of Dun, a cavalry officer stationed at Windsor, had married Augusta Fitzclarence, the daughter of the king by Mrs Jordan. When he learned of the courtship the Earl was deeply troubled and penned an extraordinary apology to the Duke:

I venture to address your R. Highness upon a subject that has recently been communicated to me, as early as I well can after the communication, in order, that no respect upon my part may seem wanting to Yr R. Highness's family. For I hope Sir you will do me the justice to believe, that I allways have been, and I assure you allways shall be, under every possible case, most devotedly attach'd to Your Royal Highness Personally and to all your Family. I may say so Sir because my tie is disinterested and sincerely void of all selfish feeling or Personal views – I find that my son, has put himself in Communication with Lord Errol: upon a most delicate & highly interesting subject, it was perhaps natural in him to endeavour to ascertain Miss Fitzclarence's sentiments after so long an absence before he proceed to take any serious steps, or even ask to see her at the same time he should have communicated to me ...[175]

He need not have worried as the Duke was delighted at the prospect of such an alliance.[176]

On his marriage John Kennedy-Erskine resigned his commission with the intention of living near London and at Dun (where he spent his honeymoon). The Duke gave the young couple a yellow carriage with a pair of dapple grey horses and a fat coachman. He also presented them with 'a very solid mahogany four poster bed'.[177] The Duke had quickly shown himself to be a doting father and later grandfather, commenting only three weeks after the wedding 'have received several letters from dear Augusta who seems very happy ... I trust and believe your man and herself will be comfort to each other and I hope my daughter will merit the kind friendship and regard of your Lordship'.[178] He wrote solicitously on 8 July 1828 from his yacht after news of the birth of her first child: 'I have only to observe for God's sake do not bring her <u>too soon</u> down to St. Margaret's ... <u>before</u> 29th of this month she <u>might</u> not in my opinion leave London',[179] and again on 30 July – 'She <u>must not</u> do <u>too much</u> at first.'[180] He wrote again a few days later:

At first Augusta may regret very naturally she being obliged to give up nursing I am glad she has as I do not think mothers in general <u>can</u> live the <u>proper</u> life to do their children justice.

I trust in God the infant will do permanently well and thrive. I am glad the nurse is an intelligent woman and the <u>wet</u> nurse appears to answer.[181]

In May 1829 on the birth of their daughter he was overjoyed that 'our young friends at Dun are as happy as possible'.[182] Despite his original Whiggish attitudes, the Duke by this time favoured strong government and disapproved of any suggestion of reform: 'I want a strong and lasting government and conceive the Duke of Wellington the fittest man to be <u>the</u> Minister.'[183]

John Kennedy-Erskine was a good horseman and a great road runner.[184] In the autumn of 1829 he developed a haemorrhage in his lung during a close run foot race at Windsor. He was nursed by his wife and his mother at St Margaret's, while the Duke and his Duchess cared for his infant son. In the spring of 1830, he and his wife travelled north to Dun. At the time he was keen, providing he made a good recovery, to follow his brother into parliament and the Duke, solicitous about his health and future, approached Thomas Burnett, the agent of his close friend the Earl of Errol, to enquire if any seats might become vacant in Scotland at the next election. He reported that the radical Joseph Hume was unpopular in Aberdeen and that Kennedy-Erskine might have a chance against the Tory candidate, Sir James Carnegie.[185]

In the spring and early summer of 1830, the Duke and the Earl were regularly in each other's company, planning a family holiday to the Continent in the autumn, taking both Lord Kennedy's and John Kennedy-Erskine's family with them. By April Kennedy-Erskine's condition had worsened and the Duke became very anxious about his health, writing to Cassillis: 'It is with real regret I mention I cannot like the account Augusta writes of Mr Erskine and I wait with real anxiety the opinion of the celebrated physicians of Aberdeen.'[186] By now the Duke's brother George IV was seriously ill and there was every prospect that he would shortly succeed to the throne. He rode over to St

Margaret's on 28 April: 'when a great deal of general talk took place about public matters & the King's health'. The Duke: 'thought the D of W [Duke of Wellington's] administration wanted strengthening & that Lord Grey wd add to their strength'. Cassillis responded that: 'Grey [was] a troublesome man in the Cabinet & knew so in the case of the Talents Administration'.[187] By now he feared: 'a Political Breeze seems to be Blowing up', since 'There has been several meetings of the Whigs it is said at Lansdowne House & that Grey has agreed to head the Opposition.'[188]

On 24 June only two days before George IV died and he succeeded to the throne, the Duke wrote to Cassillis, seeking the latest news of his son-in-law and summoning him to lunch at Bushey House on the following Sunday.[189] Instead, the Earl was summoned earlier in the week to witness the proclamation of his friend as king by the Duke of Norfolk and to swear fealty himself as Knight of the Thistle.[190] Cassillis wished for preferment in the Royal Household and wrote to his neighbour Robert Peel, the home secretary. He was to be disappointed, as the Duke of Wellington, despite the king's intervention, did not consider him suitable. On being told that there might be speculation if he was overlooked, the Duke rejoined that if the king wanted to know the mood of the country he should consult his ministers.[191] Peel was more circumspect in replying to the Earl: 'So far as the great offices of the Household are concerned, I understand that the King in the handsomest manner left it to the Duke of Wellington [the Prime Minister] … His Majesty waived all private feelings.'[192]

At the time of his accession, the new king appointed his son-in-law, John Kennedy-Erskine, one of his equerries. Not long afterwards tuberculosis was confirmed and John was advised to winter abroad. He travelled to Italy where he was visited over Christmas by the Earl and his wife, who at first found him improving.[193] By mid-January, however, his condition had deteriorated, and Lady Augusta sent news to her father by way of her brother Lord

Enoch Lodge after the devastating gale in 1884.

Adolphus Fitzclarence. The king's heart went out to those who were 'watching the melancholy progress of a disease which has unfortunately not responded to changes of climate'. Such was his anxiety that the queen and her sisters wrote almost daily.[194] He died in Pisa on 6 March 1831. The diarist Charles Greville noted that: 'On learning the news the King put off going to the Opera … appeared in mourning (crape that is) which is reckoned bad taste; the public allow natural feelings to supersede etiquette, but it is too much to extend that courtesy to a [bastard] 'son-in-law'.'[195] Kennedy-Erskine's distraught father-in-law sent the royal yacht to the Mediterranean to bring home his body and his grieving wife, who was expecting her third child. She returned to Windsor and gave birth to her second daughter in May.[196]

The Earl and his eldest son, Lord Kennedy, were supporters of parliamentary reform. In the general election following William IV's accession, the Tories returned to power but only remained in office for a few months because of their determined opposition to reform. The Whigs, who were committed to reform, took office and the new government led by Lord Grey included many of the Earl of Cassillis's friends including Lord Althorp (later Earl Spencer). Grey was quick to recognise how useful

Cassillis could be both in passing information to the king and in helping to gauge the temper of the royal household. The king's private secretary, Sir Herbert Taylor from the outset used Cassillis as a conduit for his master's opinions. He already knew the Earl well and was distantly related by marriage. His wife was a sister of Edward Disbrowe, who was married to the Earl's niece Anne, the daughter of his brother Robert.[197] Taylor rightly sensed that the Earl was flattered by the appearance of being close to the seat of power at a critical time. In the election Kennedy, who had broken his ribs in a fall from his horse, stood for the 'open' borough of Evesham, to which he had been introduced by Benjamin Rotch, a barrister. Returned in second place after a brisk contest with a Catholic, he was listed among their 'friends' by ministers in Lord Grey's new Whig government. He gave notice in November that he intended to introduce a bill after Christmas to allow Scottish peers, who had not been elected as representative peers, to sit in the Commons.* He presented petitions for the abolition of slavery from

* Under the terms of the Act of Union Scottish peers were represented by twelve of their number in the House of Lords but those who were not 'representative peers' were not allowed to stand for election to the House of Commons unlike Irish peers, who enjoyed no right of representation.

two Baptist congregations in Evesham on 15 November. He was, however, unseated on bribery charges a month later. Although he stood again in the general election in April 1831, he did not campaign and remained at Cassillis. Nevertheless he finished a creditable third behind the reform candidate. He was, however, to be rewarded by the government by inclusion in the list of so-called 'Reform Bill' peers to be created if the Tory dominated House of Lords voted it down.[198]

Early in 1831 with the battle for parliamentary reform joined, Taylor hinted that the king, who liked order but also considered himself liberal-minded, was coming round to the need for change:

> This country is getting more quiet and the Special Commissioners have done and are doing their Duty well. A better spirit is getting afloat, the well disposed are in better heart and more inclined to exert themselves and the mechanics, if not cured, are at least cowed.

Lady Augusta Kennedy with her three children, Williamina, William Henry and Millicent by Sir George Hayter. This painting hangs at the House of Dun.

He went on to say that the militia was being called out ostensibly to deal with the situation in Ireland: 'It is however quite right to take these precautions & they will give employment to a Portion of our superabundant and restless population.'[199] Cassillis was being treated for rheumatism and gout at Buxton at the time of the reading of the second Reform Bill, but gave his proxy via the king to Grey. Taylor thanked him and commented:

> It is odd how much uncertainty that persists with regard to the probable decision different opinions arguing as to the Number of the Majority from 29 to 33 without the Bishops, with some go so far as to say not more than 15 & some say that the second reading will not be opposed but that the question will be fought in Committee.[200]

Although the king refused to intervene in the appointment of members of the royal household, he was willing to accede to his friend's plea for a marquessate, raising the matter with Earl Grey directly. Even this honour was not enough as the Earl wished: 'his promotion in the Peerage should be a distinct act and unconnected with any others of the same description which may be contemplated'. This was too much for William IV who replied:

> The King could, however, not have sanctioned this without placing himself and His Ministers under Embarrassment while, on the other hand, he is persuaded that the Distinction will whenever conferred be reward (for indeed it is intended) as a mark of his Majesty's Personal regard.[201]

Like it or not, in the coronation honours in September, the Earl was created a marquess, taking the title Marquess of Ailsa. He immediately named his home in Privy Gardens 'Ailsa House' in imitation of other members of the aristocracy. Any satisfaction he may have had at this public recognition for his years of pestering was overshadowed by the death of his second son John Kennedy-Erskine of consumption earlier in the year. Not long after her husband's death Lady Augusta, as she now was since her brother had been created Earl of Munster, moved out of the House of Dun to make her home in London. The Marquess loaned her £8,000 (to be repaid within two years by the king) to buy Railshead, a villa at Isleworth belonging to Lord James Hay, whose grounds adjoined those of St Margaret's.[202] The gates between the two were 'kept unlocked so that the two households might have access to each other at any time'.[203] Sir Herbert, the king's private secretary, wrote to the new Marquess from Brighton on 27 November:

> His Majesty goes to London next week & will be very glad then to see you & to

assure you in Person how sensible he is of your constant kindness to his daughter Lady Augusta Erskine & of your affectionate & liberal proceedings in the recent instance. He is truly rejoiced to hear that she is so happy in the Possession of her new residence, which must be rendered truly comfortable to her by the neighbourhood of such kind friends.[204]

To be near her father Lady Augusta also had a home in Brunswick Terrace in Brighton overlooking the sea.[205] The Marquess was bidden to an audience at St James's Palace on 8 December, no doubt to discuss the political situation, particularly the third Reform Bill.[206] When it came to the crucial vote in the House of Lords in May 1832 Ailsa, stricken with gout, was carried to the chamber.[207] The following year the government again needed Ailsa's support in the Lords for the abolition of slavery.[208] In the uncertain mood of the country he instructed his gamekeepers at Culzean to be especially vigilant and to organise night patrols with the help of the grieve, the gatekeepers, the gardeners and ploughmen, all of whom were to be armed with swords and pistols: 'The arms at all times to be kept in perfect order and inspected once a month by the Head Keeper.'[209]

In August 1832, his eldest son the spendthrift Lord Kennedy died, a month after his wife had given birth to their tenth child, Adolphus Archibald. Since 1829, when he had insured his life, he had notched up a further £10,000 of debts.[210] He reputedly came to his premature grave by impetuously going salmon fishing in the Doon when suffering from a fever. His doctor, who arrived too late at Cassillis to prevent him going, reportedly declared: 'Then he's a dead man.'[211] His widow, Eleanor, was left in possession of the heavily mortgaged Dunnottar estate for her lifetime. (The debt secured over the estate now totalled £124,500.)[212] On her death the estate would have passed to her second son, Alexander, but in October he too died.

Eleanor herself died on 16 November, worn out by childbirth and her husband's gambling. She left her estate to her third son John, born in 1819. In her will she appointed three trustees until he should come of age in 1840, her father-in-law the Marquess, her brother-in-law Colonel John Peel and the Kennedy family Edinburgh lawyer, Alexander Hunter, John's son and like him a partner in Hunters & Co. The Marquess and Colonel Peel refused to act because the scale of Lord Kennedy's debts could easily have engulfed the whole family. Hunter was left to carry on alone with this formidable task which made the financial problems left by the 10th Earl seem trivial. His objective was to try to preserve sufficient funds to provide for John and his brothers and sisters (apart from Archibald, the eldest and heir to the marquessate) as well as Mrs Allardyce. He soon found the estate was much more burdened with debt than he had appreciated. Taxed later by the Marquess for his failure to keep an accurate list of mortgages, he rejoined: 'I really think it would have been more surprising if I had recollected considering the multiplicity of sums lent out on Mortgages by him [the Earl of Cassillis].'[213]

The post-nuptial marriage settlement was revoked and the Dunnottar estate sold along with all 'the other means, estate and effects' of the Countess. Hunter also collected the £20,000 proceeds of Lord Kennedy's life assurance policy which was used to make provision for the children other than Archibald, the heir to the marquessate, and John, the heir to Dunnottar.[214] After discharging the mortgages he was left with a total of about £53,000. He invested just under £28,000 for John Kennedy when he became of age and the remainder for the younger children.[215] Ironically Cassillis House was let to the Earl of Glasgow, who had been preferred to the Marquess as lord lieutenant.[216]

The Marquess and his wife were left with nine grandchildren to bring up. The House of Dun was altered to accommodate them all and their daughter-in-law, Lady Augusta with her three children when they wished to visit. The family seem to have passed the summer months at Culzean, moving to

the House of Dun in the autumn. The rest of the year was spent in some style either in Westminster or at St Margaret's, Twickenham. In October 1837 Sir Thomas Rutger described the extensive gardens there, making one wonder why the Marquess bothered to garden on such a large scale at Culzean and the House of Dun:

There is a considerable length of wall in this garden. One of the walls is devoted to pears: the trees are fine, and the walls well filled. In the border in front of this wall, a fanciful mode of pear training is carrying on, by training the trees to circular iron trellises, of about 7 ft. in diameter, formed exactly in the shape of an inverted umbrella … There being no pines grown here, the forcing-houses

LEFT
The 12th Earl of Cassillis and 1st Marquess of Ailsa, painted in his coronation robes by William Owen. He was reputed to be one of the most good-looking men of his generation.

RIGHT
Railshead or Gordon House as it is today.

are all devoted to peaches, grapes, etc., of which there are several ranges placed in different parts of the garden … At the extremity of the lawn on the Isleworth side, stands an opaque-roofed green-house, which is now (Oct. 12) furnished with hybrid rhododendrons in large pots. Nothing can exceed the beauty of these plants, as respects their handsome growth and luxuriancy of foliage … At the back of the flower-garden, the shape of which is the segment of a circle, stands the orangery, consisting of a centre and two wings, the centre running back some 30 ft. beyond the back line of the wings. There are some orange trees, with the finest heads I have seen for some years … The flower-garden,

153

with its conservatory, has a striking effect; and, at the moment of entering it, my thoughts were involuntarily led to Dropmore.*[217]

Another visitor some years later noted:

As there is neither extent nor variety of surface in the park, it is indebted to the trees for all that is interesting in the landscape; but the cedars of Lebanon, horse chestnuts, and beeches, are of such large dimensions, and of such beautiful forms, that they compensate in a great measure, by the variety of outlines and contrasts of foliage, for the want of variety in the ground.

This beautiful ferme ornée, stuccoed, is … encompassed by pleasure

LEFT

King William IV, a close friend of the 1st Marquess. The King's illegitimate daughter by the Mrs Jordan, Augusta, married the Marquess's second son, John Kennedy.

RIGHT

St. Margaret's from the garden, with the huge conservatory on the left where the Marquess grew oranges.

grounds of novel and varied character. The ground appears to have been scooped out and raised into high mounds, by which a concave of the most elegant shape, and of pretty considerable dimensions, was formed. This interesting scene of greensward is planted in a manner to represent a Roman amphitheatre, closed at one side by a huge massive wall, begrimed by time, with an archway, when the wild beasts enter from their lairs, and then sports begin. The area is surrounded by trees to represent spectators.

Like Rutgers, this visitor was struck by the huge glasshouse, '160 feet long by 25 wide' with a transverse greenhouse attached to the centre 54 feet long and 27 wide'. He commented on the Marquess's success in breeding horse chestnuts and verbena and remarked on the four life-size figures of Tam O'Shanter, Souter

* The home of the Marquess's friend Lord Grenville and noted for its greenhouses.

Johnnie and the Landlord and Landlady to be seen in the gardens.[218] These were carved by James Thom and were replicas of those made for the Burns Monument in Alloway.[219] At about this time part of the St Margaret's estate was developed, with the construction by the Marquess of Ailsa of Park Villas, where Charles Dickens lived in the summer months of 1838 and wrote part of *Oliver Twist* and some of *Nicholas Nickleby*. While there Dickens 'had many friendly days' with such men as Thackeray and Landseer, whose engravings the Ailsas were to collect.[220]

The Marquess continued to collect pictures for his London homes. In December 1833 his friend, the Countess Münster (not to be confused with the Earl of Munster in the Irish peerage), wrote to him from Dernebourg, near Hildesheim in Hanover, offering him a huge canvas by Ruhl, the director of the picture gallery at Cassell, depicting James II and VIII being introduced to his future queen, Anne of Denmark by Louis XIV. She

enthused: 'It is painted in Netcher's best style and excited great admiration at the exhibition at Hanover.' If the Marquess was not interested in it, she hoped he might find someone else who was.[221] He had probably got to know the Münsters when visiting his brother Robert, who in 1830 had moved from Switzerland to Ludwigsberg, outside Stuttgart, to be near his daughter Anne. Subsequently Robert rented the old palace of the Margrave of Baden in Karlsruhe where he lived in some style until his death in 1843.[222] Ruhl's canvas was delivered in 1834 and displayed in the Pall Mall Gallery. When it failed to make the offer price, the Marquess bought it for £100.[223]

The Marquess and King William remained firm friends and were often to be seen in each other's company. Lady Augusta's eldest daughter Wilhelmina, later Countess of Munster, recalled in later life that the king used to drive out to Isleworth to see his grandchildren.[224] In the summer of 1835 the Marquess threw a great party for the king at St Margaret's which the Duke of Wellington attended.[225] He had to call on his neighbours to help out. The Duke of Northumberland replied from Syon House: 'We have little here to offer for your Dinner Party on Tuesday; except Upper Servants & three tents of the same size as those before the House which were occupied occasionally by the band.'[226] The Marquess commented that he hoped his catering arrangements would be 'better than Lady Mansfield did for my guests' sake … she ordered dinner for 250 and had a party of 800'.[227]

By this time relations between the Marquess and his wife and Lady Augusta had become strained largely because she was courting Lord John Frederick Gordon, the third son of the 9th Marquess of Huntly, whom the Marquess of Ailsa regarded, like all the Huntlys, as extravagant. He did his best to ensure that his daughter-in-law had no control over the inheritance of her three children by setting up a trust which they could benefit from only when they reached the age of twenty-five.[228] Wilhelmina, Countess of Munster recalled: 'Railshead became a scene of squabbling and family bickering between her [Lady Augusta] and the old Lord and Lady next door.'[229] In the summer of 1836, Lady Augusta became engaged to Lord John, who was subsequently to change his name to Hallyburton on inheriting the Hallyburton estates in Angus. According to the Countess of Munster, on the morning of the wedding her mother, Augusta, left Railshead unaccompanied for London, and immediately Wilhelmina was summoned to St Margaret's by her grandmother. On learning where her mother had gone, the Marchioness seized the arm of the future Countess of Munster and pointed at a portrait of her father, John Kennedy-Erskine, and exclaimed 'There's ye father and he's dead poor fellow and I want ye to promise me ye'll never love this new man and never call him 'Father'.'[230] This story is almost certainly an exaggeration, as well before the wedding Lord Ailsa had been in contact with Sir Herbert Taylor in an effort to quash gossip.[231] On 15 August Lady Augusta

wrote from Windsor informing Lady Ailsa that she and the Marquess were bidden to the wedding. The Marquess replied somewhat frostily: 'We have not received any Command from His Majesty to attend it – And all things considered – it is perhaps better that I should not attend – Lady Ailsa is not well enough to do so.' He condemned the gossips and excused his non-attendance at court on the genuine grounds of ill health.[232] Nevertheless, he was summoned to the wedding at Windsor, and left his wife at home supposedly ill in bed.[233]

Relations between the Ailsas and their erst-while daughter-in-law went from bad to worse. The Ailsas convinced themselves that, remarried, Lady Augusta was no longer fit to be the joint guardian of her children. At her new husband's bidding she tried to burden the Dun estate with a further £10,000 to make provision for her two youngest children. The Marquess was furious and wrote intemperately in March 1837: 'I am perfectly certain that Lady Augusta's friends/connections/ would be much more likely to come at once to our arrangement if they knew we were determined to proceed by law if fair means would not do.'[234] Wise Alexander Hunter, the family lawyer, advised that there was little they could do about it unless they were willing to have her condemned as a lunatic.[235] The Ailsas were not to be thwarted, and in December instructed their London lawyer C.G. Bannister to retain Henry Pemberton MP, one of the leading equity barristers of the day. Bannister, following Hunter's sanguine approach, advised against haste, suggesting it would be sensible to find out how much legal proceedings might cost. Nevertheless he had no choice but to instruct Pemberton. On 18 January Lady Augusta's lawyer approached him 'to express his regret at what had occurred and to see if any satisfactory arrangement could be made through some influential friend' – no doubt a reference to the king. This overture was rejected outright by the Ailsas and by 23 January there was no alternative but 'the Court must be applied to'. In mid-February the king and his good-natured wife Queen Adelaide, sensitive to the situation, took action and appointed Lady Augusta to the post of 'State Housekeeper' at Kensington Palace with a suite of rooms for herself and her husband.[236] They made it clear through Lady Augusta's lawyers that the matter was to be kept out of court and in May a settlement was reached.[237] Relations with the Ailsas, nevertheless, remained very strained, particularly over the custody of the eldest son Willy, heir to the Dun estate, who under the terms of an agreement spent some of his time at St Margaret's with his grandparents. There was family contact with Lady Augusta, as Sir Edward Disbrowe, as he now was, and his wife often met her whilst visiting his brother-in-law Sir Herbert Taylor at Brighton. Their daughter Charlotte was puzzled as to why the daughter of the king should only be a lady and not a princess![238]

Having gained honours but not office, the Marquess continued to play a peripheral part in politics, but was still distrusted because of his lack of consistency. Although he supported the Reform Act of 1832, he believed that any 'further extension of the elective suffrage is to be opposed'.[239] In such an opinion he found a ready ally in Earl Grey who confessed to him during the heady general election campaign in January 1835:

> It can hardly be necessary for me to say to you that, since the passing of the Reform Bill, it has been my constant endeavour to bring back the Government to a regular course of action … & to put an end to the agitation which prevailed in the country. I pursued the same course even after I left office [in 1834], in proof of which I can refer to all my speeches at political meetings and to my answers to the addresses which were sent to me. How I was thwarted & ultimately defeated in these endeavours you cannot fail to have observed the opposition of the Tories, & their majority in the House of Lords not only embarrassed & cramped me with

input to the measures which I wished to propose, but added to my difficulty in controlling the unreasonable and unreasoning pressure of those, who urged Reform both as to time and extent which I deemed inexpedient.

> I still, however, kept off the collision which I dreaded, but which has now been produced by the abrupt & unexpected dismissal of the late ministry [Melbourne's] by the appointment of that of Sir Robert Peel, & by the dissolution of Parliament.[240]

No doubt Grey hoped Cassillis would pass these opinions on to the king, but he did not share Grey's pessimism. He had already remarked very perceptively to Lord Stanley, who had resigned from Grey's administration the year before to form his own independent party:

> I do not believe the country to be in danger or that it is likely to arrive at that State – The Middle Classes of Great Britain enjoy too much Happyness nay luxury: and know that they do so to venture the whole for an ideal good: and there is your security they will go certain lengths but not the whole Hog' & that will be seen – they are fully aware; that they would be the first to go & live no more – your little Strand & Fleet Street Fellow and those who have Property from one to five hundred a year depending upon others annually who are the chief mass of the people! [They] will stand in the gap on the day of trouble. If it ever comes upon us they read and know that in all Revolutioned countrys – where Mobs have led that their order have been swept away entirely – in France for instance in the second rate towns/in many instances/ & in all minor towns & villages there

remains, but the douanier & Post Master nearby – while at this moment a great proportion of the old Noblesse/who did not take conspicuous parts in the various revolutions and the great landowners/owners of Land/not only hold on but are actually in a quiet way buying up all the Land as it comes into the market.[241]

Ailsa was critical of Peel, who had become prime minister in December and called the election in the hope of improving his Commons' majority: 'It is very well for the <u>Chief</u> [Peel] to mount that Old Trusty Nag <u>Expediency</u> that served him so well in the Catholic Case [a reference to Peel's Catholic Emancipation Act] and try to strike a trot at the Head of a Reforming Govt but he will do it with bad grace in my opinion.' This was a very different tune from the one he had sung in 1827. As Ailsa correctly judged, the mood of the country would deny Peel a majority since the Reform Act made it much less possible for landowners to influence the outcome. For his part he declared: 'In the three counties where I am concerned I have left the tenants to do as they please.'[242] Ailsa was concerned that the Tories may have gained an undue influence over the king and that if Peel failed then the Duke of Richmond, who had shifted his allegiance, would be employed to broker a deal: 'I have, however, no doubt of the King's <u>Tailor</u>* having <u>tried on</u> a Conservative Coat to one man at least mind: all that passes between us on Court affairs is/as we agreed upon/strictly confidential.'[243] Although he admitted little now separated Grey and Peel in their attitudes to reform, he was determined to remain a 'Moderate Whig'.[244]

Nevertheless he continued to conduct a desultory correspondence with Peel, who was after all a neighbour. In 1842 his complaint that the reduction in the price at which oats could be imported was hurting his tenants drew a stinging rebuke:[245]

Whatever the facts may be – no one can think the present state of things very satisfactory. If I were a landed proprietor in the west of Scotland and saw 17,000 persons supported during the winter as 17,000 persons have been in one Scottish Town viz. Paisley by charitable contributions – I should sincerely enquire whether the continuance of such a state of things was quite compatible with the security or at length the enjoyment of property.[246]

It may have been in response to Peel that the Marquess decided to open the grounds of Culzean to visitors on Wednesdays during the summer by cards obtained from the estate office.[247]

By this time the Marquess was ill and beset with family problems; and since the death of William IV in 1837 such influence as he had had ceased. On attaining his majority in 1841 John, his grandson and heir to the Dunnottar estates, decided to challenge the settlement of his mother's estate, which had largely been devoted to meeting his father, Lord Kennedy's gambling debts. He was advised by his lawyer, Alex Smith, 'that the Funds held by your Father & Mother, having only been derived from the Estate of Dunnottar, which was Destined to you, was only subject to the Provision of £10,000, which your Mother was entitled to settle on your sister & brothers & that the Ballce [balance] was wholly yours'.[248] Alexander Hunter was outraged at this attack on his professional judgement and was concerned about the possible effect any legal proceedings might have on the provision for the younger children.[249] Although John assured him that he had no intention of disturbing their settlement, Hunter remained distrustful: 'I see no reason for them at all throwing themselves on his *tender mercies*.'[250] Despite having being allowed access to all the executory papers and accounts, John Kennedy commenced proceedings in the Court of Session in November 1843.[251] Hunter was saddened by this turn of events 'as it publishes to

---

* A reference to the king's private secretary Sir Herbert Taylor.

the world a disagreement between the members of the family … I would rejoice that litigation was avoided as it necessarily incurs a heavy expense and much unpleasantness amongst the parties.'[252]

This action was almost certainly motivated by the news that John's eldest brother Archibald, the titular Earl of Cassillis, had succumbed to his father's weakness for gambling. In 1833 his grandfather purchased a commission for him in the Rifle Brigade and five years later obtained for him a captaincy in the more fashionable 17th Light Dragoon Guards. He was persuaded, almost certainly against his grandfather's better judgement, to take the part of the Knight of the Dolphin in the ill-fated Eglinton tournament of 1839. This remarkable anachronistic event was the product of the fevered reactionary mind of Sir Charles Lamb, who was peeved that in the more economical coronation ceremonies for Queen Victoria, he had been denied his hereditary privilege of acting as queen's champion in his hereditary role of Knight Marshall of the Royal Household. His naïve and impressionable stepson, the young Earl of Eglinton, willingly

LEFT
Honourable Robert Kennedy in old age. He was the great grandfather of Sir Ludovic Kennedy.

RIGHT
The vinery at Culzean photographed by the 3rd Marquess in 1885.

agreed to host the event towards the end of August in the grounds of Eglinton Castle, his Ayrshire seat, which was already a well-known sporting venue. A month before the event, a practice was held near Regent's Park in London, where the Earl of Cassillis distinguished himself by being dismounted by the dummy which the would-be contestants had to charge.[253]

The tournament itself attracted enormous interest and huge crowds, but was spoiled by torrential rain. For the participants it was ruinously expensive; the armour and costumes cost a fortune.[254] The Earl of Cassillis appeared in a suit of engraved steel armour inlaid with gold on a Barbary charger all decked out in livery of scarlet, black and gold. He was accompanied by three men at arms in half armour, possibly his brothers. His purse unlike that of other participants did not run to esquires and pages.[255] The Marquess was forgiving and attended with a party, only to see his grandson fall off his horse weighed down by his armour.[256] He was proud of his grandson, writing in September 1841: 'He is clever, well behaved and I think will turn out a good gentleman.'[257] This was, however, before the Earl of Cassillis made his disastrous debut as a racehorse owner in May 1842 at Bogside races in Eglinton Park where three years before steeple-chasing had had its origins in Scotland. The Earl entered three steeple chasers and had no more luck than his father had racing twenty years before.[258] Only one of his horses, *Roderick Random*, gained a place, coming second in the Curraghmore Cup.[259] The Earl and his other brothers seem to have lost something in the region of £100,000.[260] Such wagers were not unusual. The Earl of Glasgow bet of £100,000 on the Derby of that year.[261] The horses were sold and the Earl never owned a racehorse again.

By the autumn of 1842 the Earl of Cassillis had such gigantic debts that Alexander Hunter believed the whole of the Culzean and Cassillis estates where threatened, writing to the Marquess of Ailsa:

> Your Lordship cannot be more desirous
> than I am that your Lordship's successor
> shall make no inroads on the property
> which he will receive much enhanced in
> value by your Lordship's extensive
> improvements and it was with that view
> that I have interested myself so much in
> Lord Cassillis's affairs and you have my
> best advice on all occasions …[262]

There had already been similar catastrophes. Just three years before, Lady Augusta's father-in-law, the Marquess of Huntly, had been in the bankruptcy courts because of his addiction to the turf. True to his word, Hunter quickly devised: 'a plan of paying his debts thro' the intervention of friends without incurring the ruinous expenditure of raising money from an Insurance Co. in <u>post obits</u>'. He added: 'At this moment Lord Cassillis is so impressed with the folly of his conduct that were he to be in possession of the estates tomorrow, he would live abroad until he got clear of his difficulties and was able to resume his place in society.' Hunter was not convinced this course of action was practical, even if laudable, and feared that in the event of Lord Cassillis's succession the estates might be 'torn to pieces' by his creditors.[263] Hurriedly the whole rental of the entailed parts of the Culzean and Cassillis estates were assigned to Hunter so as 'to keep Lord Cassillis in check' by preventing him borrowing any more money against his expectations.[264] Expenditure was reduced to a minimum. Lord Cassillis was forced to resign his captaincy in the 17th Light Dragoon Guards and fled the country.[265] This must have been a bitter blow to the Marquess; here was history repeating itself with a vengeance.

As heir of entail under the terms of the Montgomerie Act the Earl had agreed that the costs of the improvements undertaken by his grandfather should be charged against the estate. Since he would not now benefit from this arrangement, it was decided that a sum equivalent to the whole cost of the improvements since 1820, some £40,000, would be paid to him to help reduce his debts. This had to be approved by private Act of Parliament in 1844.[266] To make this provision and to cover additional advances to his grandson, the Marquess raised £29,000 from family friends, particularly from the marriage trustees of his daughter Alicia to Lieutenant General Jonathan Peel. It proved impossible to raise the whole of the funds required in this way and the Marquess was obliged to seek a loan from an insurance company for an equivalent amount. Hunter negotiated what was termed a redeemable annuity from the City of Glasgow Life Assurance and Reversionary Co.[267] Redeemable annuities had been pioneered in the insurance industry by the Pelican Life Assurance Co. as a means of advancing money to the landed gentry whose estates were entailed. Under their terms a capital sum was advanced to a landowner, which was repayable after a fixed period and was secured against the proceeds of a whole-life without-profits assurance policy. Since such policies were not considered in law to be 'an absolute security for repayment of the principal [as] the policy may be forfeited by suicide and the like',[268] they were not subject to the usury laws which prohibited the charging of rates of interest above 5 per cent. It was understood that the Earl of Cassillis would take over these debts when he inherited the estates from his grandfather.

Under the terms of the trust the Marquess was able to make provision for his other children and grandchildren, some of whom were in danger of being left destitute by John Kennedy's legal action over the settlement of his mother's estate. Hunter did his best to repair relations between grandfather and grandson:

> I think his Lordship has now got a
> lesson & sees fully the folly of his
> conduct and will now do well, but after
> your Lordship has made up your mind
> as to the cause of procedure I think it
> might be immediately communicated to
> Lord Cassillis that he may be fully aware
> of his position & it will be an induce-
> ment to him in future to be cautious.[269]

Taking Hunter at his word, the Marquess made over Cassillis House and four adjoining farms with a rental of about £650 to his grandson's trustees to provide him with a modest income.[270]

In the midst of these troubles the Earl of Eglinton suggested to the Marquess that Cassillis might succeed Lord Kelburn, whose father the Earl of Glasgow was at death's door, as MP for Ayrshire: 'I can answer for his being universally acceptable to the county.'[271] Panic-stricken, the Marquess hurriedly penned a note to Peel:

> I have no desire whatever to let him
> come forward – for one good reason
> because I can't afford/doing justice to
> my other grandchildren/to increase his
> income much & pay his Election
> expenses. I have long ceased to meddle
> with Ayrshire Politics beyond telling my
> tenants/some of them/whom they
> should vote for – Because one's House
> becomes an Inn; – I was put to all sorts
> of trouble and expense.

> Can anything be done for Lord
> Cassillis in any way?[272]

He was relieved when Peel replied he was unable to offer any help. Earlier in the year Ailsa had approached Peel about getting his grandson an appointment as an equerry to Her Majesty – a paid office, only to be told that Queen Victoria would consider no one less than a Lieutenant Colonel.[273] He often repaid these pleas for preferment with his hospitality. In July 1842 he read a report in the newspaper that Peel intended to holiday in Scotland. He at once offered Culzean as he was going to Buxton to take the waters. His letter gives a glimpse of what the house must have been like for most of the year:

> The house shall be prepared for you/it is
> just a matter of uncovering the
> Furniture, and you will find a well-
> stocked garden – Plenty of Cows and
> poultry entirely at your service and I
> will tell you where to find the key to the
> cellar and further my Fishers will supply
> you with the greatest abundance of
> fish.[274]

He was disappointed to learn that the newspaper report was inaccurate.

By May 1843 the indefatigable Hunter had reached agreement with all but one of Lord Cassillis's creditors.[275] To add to his problems a venture in Australia, in which the Marquess had a large interest, got into difficulties. Implicated in the Earl's gambling were his brothers David and Gilbert and their grandfather the Marquess was determined to get all his grandchildren out of the country where they could not be pursued by their creditors and might make their fortune. Writing about his youngest grandson, Fergus, in 1843, he explained:

> I do not wish my grandson to become a
> Diplomatist. It is an Idle Life/The First
> stages of it/and promotions very slow &

very uncertain the last few years – No Profession at all for a young Man … I want to get him out to India, in a Situation where he can show his capacity – <u>and make his Fortune</u>.[276]

David, the fourth son, was sent to India in the service of the East India Company and Gilbert, the fifth son, went out to Australia in 1840, largely on the advice of his doctor, to manage a sheep station in which his grandfather was a major shareholder. This investment had been recommended by Alexander Hunter, whose nephew John was a partner in Watson Hunter & Co., who factored the station. Alexander Hunter's sons were also well-established in the colony along with those of Charles Gairdner, who had briefly been factor to the Marquess and was now a partner in Hunters & Co., bankers in Ayrshire. Gilbert was accompanied on his journey into exile by one of the sons of William Craig, who had retired as factor to the estate in 1838 and was now living at Logan House, Cumnock.[277]

The ranch was obviously a large affair as on arrival they were looking to buy 7,000 head of cattle.[278] The venture was not a success from the outset due to a combination of a fall in commodity prices, the abolition of convict labour and a mixture of incompetence and fraud. When Watson Hunter & Co. were declared insolvent by the court, the future looked bleak. William Craig volunteered to make the arduous journey to investigate, arriving early in 1843. In his first letter after his arrival Craig commented: 'The Colony since then has been getting worse and worse in Mercantile as well as in Agricultural matters & when it is to end I know not. We have had a succession of failures lately & the parties will pay nothing whatever.' He spent three days in the Insolvency Court with counsel and solicitors in the hope of being able to examine one of the partners in Watson Hunter & Co. whom he suspected of conspiracy to fraud, but to no avail.

By chance at a cattle sale he met Judge Willis, who promised to provide time in his court. After nine days examination the extent of the fraud was revealed. The partners in the United Kingdom had been either vastly overcharged for stock or asked to pay for stock which simply did not exist. Moreover Watson Hunter & Co. had then sold the stock as if it was their own. Alexander Hunter wrote to Craig from Edinburgh: 'From what I have seen of Judge Willis's Decision in the Newspapers I have no doubt he will view the assignment as a case of <u>fraud</u> as under the agreement we never could by any possibility ever be in Watson & Hunter's debt.'[279] At the end of the examination Judge Willis handed over to the Crown prosecutor, who was too frightened to do anything. Craig commented ruefully: 'We will have false swearing, embezzlement & all manner of villainy going on among the higher classes here, & our own Crown prosecutor, who is very slow & wants mettle, will not prosecute the cases.' This impression was confirmed when Judge Willis was summarily suspended with no explanation and sent home. Craig lamented:

> He has done much for this Colony by his decided determination to root out and expose the dishonesty and intrigues that exist here, no matter by whom, Government men & everyone else when they deserved it; In fact it is the Opinion of all respectable men that the state of things here is now such that since the Judge is removed no honest man will be able to stand his ground.[280]

Charles Gairdner came out to assist Craig in rescuing the business. He gave the young men sound advice 'never to invest above 3/4ths of their capital & retain a 4th in cash to meet a <u>wet</u> day' and to stick it out. By June 1845 commodity prices had recovered and the corner had been turned.[281]

The Marquess's relations with his daughter-in-law, Lady Augusta and her second husband, Lord John Frederick Gordon, had deteriorated even further over the education of her only son Willy, the heir to the Dun estates. Lord John insisted that at the age of nine Willy should be sent

to Eton. The Ailsas strongly disagreed. The Marquess, as one of Willy's guardians, protested:

> I find the enclosed letter of Lady Augusta Gordon written when the Boy was put to school. <u>It acknowledges</u> my right of guardianship <u>and acquiesces</u> in the <u>arrangement about the money affairs</u> after which; the <u>stealing</u> away the child in the face of the agreement and acknowledgement must appear to everybody a most Ignominious Act.[282]

The Eglinton tournament, 1839.

He was forced to give way, writing grudgingly the following year: 'The Boy May be sent to School if it is thought proper – I <u>never shall in the most remote degree – interfere with him when there</u> in no manner of way.' Earlier in his letter he had vowed to have nothing more to do with his Dun grandchildren: 'It is long since my mind has been made up to cease all communications, and banish from it all that has ever taken place – I have done with the Children.'[283]

Willy, however, was unhappy at Eton and Lord John and Lady Augusta went to the school to 'see & ascertain how Willy was behaving & very sorry I was to find that he was in great disgrace & not doing or going on well'. The Headmaster advised his anxious parents 'to scold & admonish him', adding that 'should there be no change for the better after a further trial of a week or Ten days he would strongly recommend his Removal'. There was no improvement and Willy left. Lord John was sympathetic with his plight: 'My own opinion is that the sudden change from home to so large a School where he is frequently left to himself & his own Masters, has been too much for the Boy's mind.' As a result he and his wife placed him in the charge of Mr Jackson, the chaplain at Kensington Palace, their London home, while they searched for a smaller school.[284]

If this catalogue of calamities was not enough, in March 1845 the Earl's brilliant nephew John, who had recently been promoted from secretary of the legation at Naples to a similar position in Washington, died at Brighton before he could cross the Atlantic.[285] His four sons were to become close friends of the 3rd Marquess. In October 1845 the family was struck by a further tragedy when two of the Marquess's young grandsons were drowned in a boating accident. They were the eldest sons of his daughter Anne and her husband Sir David Baird of Newbyth. In his grief Sir David, who was short of money, wrote to ask if their funeral expenses could be charged against the children's provisions under the marriage settlement. The Marquess was still trying to find positions for his wayward grandchildren. He wrote in desperation to Peel in May 1846 enquiring about a post in Ceylon: 'I have <u>never yet</u>

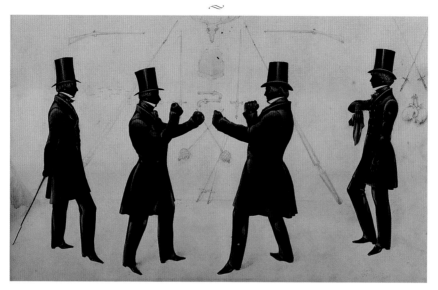

got <u>anything out of you</u> for any of my sons.'[286] Peel was disposed to be helpful, but on learning that there would be exams in Latin and Greek, the Marquess packed the grandson off to Bengal.[287]

Surrounded like Job with troubles, his health suffered and from 1842 the Marquess was frequently at Buxton taking the waters. In the summer of 1846 he became seriously ill and died at St Margaret's on 8 September, just five days after the death of his grandson John, the heir to Dunnottar, who had caused him so much trouble.[288] Apart from the landed property he owned, John left £17,903 to be divided equally amongst his brothers but with the express instruction that his brother, the Earl of Cassillis was to receive not a penny.[289] The *Ayrshire Advertiser* commented with no intended irony on the Marquess's death: 'The deceased nobleman was one of the finest looking men of his day. Throughout his life he was remarkable for the clearness of his judgement and decision of character.'[290] He was not buried with his ancestors in the collegiate church in Maybole but in the chapel at the House of Dun. Within a week of his death the Culzean lodge keepers at Morriston, Low

A silhouette of William, Fergus, John and Nigel Kennedy, brothers of the Earl of Cassillis, taking part in a mock boxing match in about 1840. In the background are the lances used by the Earl at the Eglinton tournament. The silhouette was drawn in an Edinburgh gymnasium after they had put their clothes on

Whiteston, Swinston, Pond Cottage, Ardlochan, Thomaston gate, and Glenside were supplied with mourning dress.

Despite all the trappings of wealth and status, the 1st Marquess died a disappointed man. He had lived for almost fifty years cheek by jowl with the movers and shakers of the age, even counting himself amongst their friends, but he had never really been accepted. He was too strong meat for most of them and yet despite, or perhaps because of his, bombastic personality, he could be generous to a fault. Like many of his fellow Americans, he had a good head for business and succeeded in improving his still vast properties in a way which had eluded his cousins. In the adversity of the last years of his life, he had with Alexander Hunter's help skilfully rescued the family from certain ruin. He left an estate valued at some £191,420.[291]

He left unusually specific instructions about the disposition of his picture collection, which strangely included none of those purchased by the 9th Earl Thomas on his expeditions to Italy. The Marchioness was to have the use of all of them during the remainder of her life with the exception

of the full-length portrait of Buonaparte painted by Robert Lefèvre in 1813, which was hanging in Twickenham. This was to be dispatched immediately to Culzean. After the Marchioness's death the following pictures and portraits in London were to be hung in Culzean: *The Lioness in the Net*, *Mary Queen of Scots*, *James her Father*, *Gilbert Earl of Cassillis*, and *Louis XIV introducing King James to his Queen* by Ruhl. He left two Nasmyth paintings each to his son-in-law Colonel John Peel and to his daughter the self-styled Countess of Newburgh, and four to his son-in-law Sir David Baird of Newbyth. He left a portrait of Lord A.J. Peel to the Countess of Newburgh and a piece of plate representing hawking to Lord A.J. Peel. He declared the plate of 'my father's battle' off Lisbon a family heirloom which could never be sold.[292] The Marquess had agreed, also, at his death to make marriage portions to his four daughters totalling £38,000. He also made generous provisions to his sons and grandchildren.

To meet these benefactions his household furniture in Ailsa House, Privy Gardens, was sold in July 1847 and that at St Margaret's in June 1848, six months after the Marchioness's death. His plate fetched £3,355, his furniture at Twickenham the colossal sum of £8,403, and that in

Ailsa House £4,251. The furniture at Culzean, which remained in the family, was valued at only £3,337. The inventory of the castle suggests it was sparsely furnished and that much of the furniture was old and worn. There were just a thousand volumes in the library, valued at £52. The only part of the castle that was well-stocked was the wine cellar, the contents of which were valued at £370.[293] St Margaret's was sold for development to Henry Petre and the South Western Railway Co. for £23,425 and the house demolished to make way for new terraces including Ailsa Terrace. Part of the property was subsequently purchased by the very eccentric Earl of Kilmorey who built an enormous replacement house on another site. The Marquess's stables in Whitehall were sold to the tenant, Mr Green MP, for £2,200 and the Citadel in Ayr for £1,700. As part of the agreement to meet the now 2nd Marquess's gambling debts, permission was granted by the Court of Session in March 1849 to sell a further portion of the estate, valued at £45,817.[294] The property was put on the market the following year.[295] Altogether the 1st Marquess's executors after realising as much of his property as possible and meeting all his provisions were left with only £970 in hand.[296]

CHAPTER 7
Nothing to do but hunt:
1 8 4 6 – 7 0

On inheriting the title the 2nd Marquess, with neither the inclination nor the money to dabble in national politics, decided to devote himself to his two passions: hunting in the winter and yachting in the summer. There is no record of how long he was abroad or his whereabouts. However on his travels he met and fell for Julia (Judy), the second daughter of Sir Richard Jephson, who had been a colonial judge. (fig. 1) They were married at Culzean on 21 October 1847. James Paterson, the editor of the *Kilmarnock Journal*, recalled the occasion vividly:

Julia, the wife of the 2nd Marquess of Ailsa.

I took the road pretty early in a phaeton from Ayr, driving to Dalrymple, in the first place, where it was understood, the Marquis and his lady were to arrive in the forenoon. They came pretty punctually to the hour, in their own travelling carriage. Following at some distance in the rear, I proceeded along the Maybole road, through the grounds of Cassillis, and had a fine view of the Cassillis Downs, as well as the house of Cassillis, the Doon rolling past its base, and its towers inclosed in the variegated colours of a woodland foliage in December. We had scarcely passed the house, when the Marquis and his lady were met by the Carrick troop of yeomanry, and con-

ducted into Maybole, the ancient capital of the district. Some time was passed here. The burgh was unusually sprightly on the occasion, bonfires blazing in various quarters, and the inhabitants generally dressed in their best attire. At length the cavalcade got on their way to the Castle of Culzean, about four miles distant, situated on the rocks overlooking the sea …

It had been arranged that the tenantry should be entertained in the hay-loft above the stables, under the presidency of the factor [agent], A. Hunter Esq., W.S., Edinburgh. The troop of cavalry were supplied at the Town Buildings, in Maybole, there being no apartment suf-ficient to accommodate them at the castle. Mr Hunter proved to be an excel-lent chairman and kept the company well in hand. Between speeches, toast, and song, a very happy night was spent.

Returning home for both the guests at Culzean and the troop of yeomanry at Maybole proved haz-ardous, as the night was dark and the travellers were none too sober. For many days afterwards fishermen collected the helmets of the yeomanry around Ailsa Craig which had been washed out to sea after their owners fell in the River Doon.[1]

Despite the sale of a further part of the estate, as a result of his folly the 2nd Marquess inherited an estate burdened with debt. There was still a loan of £18,500 outstanding from the borrowings made by his grandfather to cover his gambling debts in 1844 and he was forced to borrow a further £30,000 from family and friends in 1847 to replace his grandfather's loan from the City of Glasgow Life Assurance and Reversionary Co.[2] Even these advances were not sufficient to meet his liabilities. In July 1849 his debts totalled over £140,000 against which he had assets of only just under £75,000. Further life assurance cover was hurriedly arranged.[3] Immediately after his grandfather's death, some of the staff were sent north from

A photograph of the 2nd Marquess as a young man.

London to live at Culzean, travelling by train to Fleetwood and then by steamer to Ardrossan. These included William Furrell, the under butler; Richard Lidsey, Lady's footman; Alfred Mould, Lord's footman; William Jordan, the coachman; Henry Smith, Lady's groom; and Frederick Crichmore, Lord's groom. Mrs Jones, the cook, arrived in 1847 and a new housekeeper, Mrs Hull, was appointed. Altogether there were now seventeen permanent staff in the house, although the family was hardly ever there. After St Margaret's was sold, Thomas Squires, the butler, also came to live at Culzean. All this staff at Culzean was unnecessary as neither the Marquess nor his wife intended to stay there. He followed his father's example by allowing the public access to the grounds on Wednesdays. Its popularity surprised him. The Marquess noted in his diary on 25 August 1851: 'Beautiful day an immense number of people to see the place.'[4]

Sharing a passion for hunting and sailing, the newly married couple made their home at first at the Priory in Reigate, a magnificent house which was rented from Earl Somers. They lived in some style with a total of twenty servants to care for them and their family including a butler, an under butler, a footman, a housekeeper, a lady's maid, a nurse, eight maid servants, a coachman and five grooms.[5] This was Surrey Union country, a hunt made popular by R. S. Surtees in his stories about Mr Jorrocks, the sporting London grocer. It was also convenient for Dover where the Marquess kept his 76-ton schooner *Cayman*, which he purchased in 1848. He seems to have learned to sail with Sir Andrew Cathcart, the nephew of the Sir Andrew who had taken his grandfather to court. This Sir Andrew was an intrepid long distance sailor and was married to the Marquess's sister, Lady Eleanor. The 2nd Marquess's first child Archibald, Earl of Cassillis, was born in September 1847. Two daughters followed, Lady Julia Alice and Lady Evelyn Anne, and then another son, Alexander, and finally a further daughter, Lady Constance Eleanor in 1855.

The 2nd Marquess was not interested in competitive sailing, unlike the Earl of Eglinton or the Earl of Durham. What he liked best of all was cruising around the south coast and in the Firth of Clyde, preferably in a good blow. During these early years he was more often at sea than on land in the summer months. On 9 September 1850 he sailed from Culzean to Loch Ryan and round to Stranraer the following day. He left for Rothesay and Inveraray on the twelfth. He was becalmed off Pladda and did not arrive at Rothesay until the next day. He returned to his moorings off Culzean on the nineteenth. The following year he was regularly cruising in the Channel with occasional trips to France. A cruise in early July was eventful. He got under way from Dover at about noon on 7 July and headed for the Thames estuary. He brought up at

the Spaniard White Buoy at about nine in the evening. He was under canvas again at three in the morning, arriving below Gravesend by ten that night to wait the tide to take him upstream to Greenwich. On the ninth he took the 11.00 a.m. boat for London, returning in the late afternoon. The following day he sailed with the tide to Southend in heavy squalls of rain. He noted: 'After bringing up came on to blow a hurricane from N.E. several vessels driven on shore, with loss of sails, one schooner, carried away main boom, moderated towards evening.'[6] Undeterred he was off again with the flood and was back at Dover by the twelfth. When he was not sailing he was usually to be found at the races or in his stables. His days were dominated by physical exertion, and he rode or walked often great distances, even when in London. At Culzean he would think nothing of walking to church in Kirkoswald or over to Cassillis.

The winter months were dominated by hunting either with foxhounds or staghounds. He could be in the saddle for nine hours at a time, posting to the meet, hunting and hacking home. Remarkably he did not change horses. His diary for the first week in December 1850 was typical:

> Sunday Dec 1st No frost but hazy wind N.E.
> 2nd Crawley Hounds at Pound Hill a good fresh run & killed in the open. 'Contract'* David [his brother] 'Fireking'* fine
> 3rd Mr Lee Steere's Hounds at 'Ockley' found a fox & had a surprising run about noon & left them still running at 3 o'clock very long day, not home till near 6 o'clock horses out nine hours 'Sharmon'* David 'Kilmore'* fine.
> 4th wet day.
> 5th Surrey Foxhounds Godstone found a fox after discouraging

*The names of hunters.

blank till 2½ ran him into a drain & bolted him & lost him between Smallfield & Westeryear after a quick run horses had quite enough. 'Fireking'* foggy morning but fine p.m.

6th Went to town (fog like peasoup).

7th [Surrey] Union at Mogader mother in for a death found two & three more at Broxford but did nothing a most unsatisfactory day 'Contract' & 'Fame'.*[7]

ABOVE
The bells in the servants' hall at Culzean, which is now just a passageway.

RIGHT
Four of the children of the 2nd Marquess and his wife, from left to right, Alexander, Julia, the Earl of Cassillis and Evelyn, painted in 1855 by Kenneth Macleay.

During these years the 2nd Marquess and his wife were rarely at Culzean, regarding the Priory as their home. When he went north, he usually went alone taking the newly available express train to Glasgow. At Culzean he shot and fished, spending a good deal of time at Craiglure. Although absent, he was keenly interested in his estates. Knowing little about their management from his grandfather, he was shocked to discover and, perhaps a little remorsefully, to find how run down some of the properties were and how badly

paid many of the staff were. John Davidson, who had succeeded Bartholomew Hepple as gardener in 1836, discharged his duties for about £60 a year. He continued to cover most of his costs, which totalled about £250, through the sale of produce. The gamekeepers, such as James Haldane at Turnberry or Quintin Muir at Martnaham Lodge, were paid about £50 a year.

On coming into the property the 2nd Marquess immediately began to make changes, much to the discomfort of Thomas Dykes, who had succeeded William Craig as factor in 1838 and was only too aware of the scale of his new master's financial difficulties. He instructed John Davidson that he wanted the gardens, which had always excluded the policies, kept to a far higher standard than before and personally told him to put the hot-houses and conservatories into good repair.[8] He not only put up the wages of his gamekeepers but also increased the establishment. As a result costs escalated. Expenditure on the gardens soared to £540 and on gamekeepers and baron officers from £200 in 1845 to £732 in 1849.[9] The factor noted rue-fully: 'In every instance in which the wages of a gamekeeper have been increased it was done on Lord Ailsa's own instructions.'[10] The most striking

*The names of hunters.

change was the huge increase in the cost of running Culzean with many more staff resident than ever before. In the last year of the 1st Marquess's life it cost £419 to run Culzean including the gardens; two years later the cost had escalated to £3,840. All the additional staff had, of course, to be housed, necessitating a good deal of expenditure on cottages and other property, which had been uninhabited for some time. For example the Old Tollhouse at Hallowshean was done up for a gamekeeper.

The 2nd Marquess expected to meet some of these additional costs by increasing his income through a variety of improvements. Cassillis House was refurbished and refurnished and let to John Cogan. The gasworks was built on the shore at Culzean in the hope of reducing the enormous fuel bills in the house and offices. David Cousin, the Edinburgh aesthetic architect, was retained to modernise both Newark Castle and Maybole Castle. Newark Castle and Mains were rented by Alexander Hunter, the Edinburgh lawyer and now trustee of the estate, so that he could keep an eye on the management of the property, and Maybole Castle con-

The Priory at Reigate, which the 2nd Marquess made his home for almost eight years after inheriting the title and estate.

tinued to be the factor's house and office. Cousin also designed a chemical works at Douglaston by Maidens to manufacture pyroligneous acid by the dry distillation of wood for making mordants or fixatives used in dyeing cloth. The biggest investment was in drainage, particularly on the Home Farm and Castlehill, with a government loan of £10,000 secured by the Edinburgh life assurance company, Standard Life.[11] Such loans had become available in 1846 to sweeten the pill of the repeal of the Corn Laws, which had provided a measure of protection for British agriculture. Although other Ayrshire landowners such as Marquess of Bute and the Earl of Loudoun took advantage of such loans, the Marquess of Ailsa's was one of the largest.[12] William White was appointed as an additional land grieve to oversee the drainage projects. This further irritated the factor as he had 'charge of all the farm buildings and prepares the plans and specifications for new Buildings and superintends the erection thereof as well as the execution of all repairs and improvements'.[13] It was anticipated that these would make the Home Farm more profitable. The Marquess, however, kept inter-

fering, resulting in a loss of over £1,000 in 1850. Hunter and Dykes came to an agreement with him about the future management, which 'if adhered to … will in future years yield a good return. If such arrangements are not adhered to, the sooner the farms are let the better.'[14]

By the end of the year, Alexander Hunter was becoming seriously concerned about the 2nd Marquess's improvidence, remarking on the accounts:

The ordinary and extraordinary expenditure in the account when contrasted with the last year is very greatly on the increase; and on examining the factor's account current from 1 October to 31 December 1849, the balance due to him appears to be £8,226, which will nearly exhaust the whole half year's rent payable at Martinmas and thus will leave very little for Lord Ailsa. There is an absolute necessity for immediately curtailing the expenditure so far as lies in the Factor's powers. In conse-

LEFT

Martnaham Lodge, near Dalrymple, which was used for coarse fishing and duck shooting, photographed in the 1880s.

RIGHT

Martnaham Loch today.

quence of the steady increase of the poor and other assessments and the fall in fiars prices* which may be anticipated, it is quite impossible that the agents can provide for the heavy payment of the interest of debts unless greatly increased remittances are made.[15]

After meeting interest payments and discharging some of the debts, by the end of the year Hunter only held £100 on account for the Marquess.[16] He called for immediate economies and set a strict budget for all the activities on the estate in the coming year, based on the expenditure in the last years of Ailsa's grandfather. The Marquess, to his dismay, simply ignored this call for self-denial. At the year-end the cost of running Culzean was £1,948 compared to the budget of £800 and of the

*A reference to the rise in parochial burdens to pay for poor relief and the fall in prices of grain consequent on the repeal of the Corn Laws. Fiars prices were struck in every county each year after the harvest by the sheriff at the fiars court and used to calculate parochial and other burdens.

garden £490 compared to £240. Some of the overrun could be explained by the fact that the 'system of retrenchment' was only introduced part way through the year. The factor was confident that by early 1851 he had all the costs, for which he was responsible, under control.[17] Nevertheless much of the expenditure was outwith his authority. He commented of the gardens:

'There can, however, be no doubt that if Lord Ailsa will give orders to have the gardens reduced to the same extent and managed in exactly the same way as they were in the late Marquess's time the expense will be within the probable estimate. The Gardener takes his orders from Lord Ailsa and it would be great presumption in the Factor to interfere.'[18]

The factor pointed out that the Culzean accounts included items for which he could not conceivably budget, such as a fishing boat and subscriptions to various clubs and societies.[19, 20] He took unkindly to criticism of his management, pointing out that since he became factor in 1838 the rent arrears had been substantially reduced, claiming 'as much rent used to be lost every year as is now lost in five'. He was opposed to any curtailing of the programme of improvements: 'The stoppage of drainage work is a great evil and must cause a heavy direct and indirect loss to Lord Ailsa.'[21]

The situation was much more serious than the factor realised. The Marquess's account for the year to July 1851 showed a deficit of almost £7,000.*[22] Alexander Hunter, well aware of his duty to the infant Earl of Cassillis as a trustee of the entailed

*The factor remitted any profits to Alexander Hunter as trustee and agent for the estate, who passed them on with any other accruals to the Marquess. Edinburgh lawyers, who acted in this capacity, were quite prepared to allow their aristocratic clients to overdraw their current accounts (charging them accordingly) as they knew they could raise capital against the security of the rental which could legitimately be charged against the heir of entail.

estate, imposed strict conditions on the wayward Marquess, who was compelled to give up the lease of the Priory at Reigate in April 1852. At first he moved to lodgings in London at 9 Cadogan Place and then at 26 Grosvenor Street West and on 1 June the family went to Culzean for good.[23] The management and staffing of the estate was to return to the level of his grandfather's day. The cost of the household staff and any additional expenditure on the gardens were to be the direct responsibility of the Marquess and not a charge on the estate. His personal expenditure was, however, also to be carefully monitored by Hunter to avoid any further overrun. Although some necessary alterations had to be made to accommodate the horses and dogs sent up from Reigate, expenditure was restrained. At Culzean the total costs fell back to less than £1,800, while the expense of running the gardens was restored to less than £240.[24]

The chemical works at Dougalston, which Hunter described as unfortunate, were closed because they were completely unprofitable. The only increase in expenditure was for improvements at Castlehill, which still formed part of the Home Farm. This still continued to operate at a 'very heavy' loss. The factor commented: 'Unless Castlehill and Culzean Farms pay a good rent for the year from Whitsunday 1853 to Whitsunday 1854 it may safely be assured that they will never do so …'[25]

Despite this evidence of restraint, the Marquess's financial position deteriorated even further. His debts now stood at a colossal £145,000 of which £80,000 was covered by a life assurance policy. Servicing these debts and meeting the insurance premiums accounted for £9,000 a year, a third of the gross annual income of the estate.[26] The Marquess no longer had his grandfather's income from investments as these had been sold to meet the legacies to other children and grandchildren. He was left with £4,000 to meet all his personal expenses. Further economies were essential to ensure that any surplus was used to reduce exposure, otherwise there was a real danger that, as Hunter had feared, the estate would be broken up.

The receipt of proceeds from the sale of property by the 1st Marquess's executors allowed the debt to be reduced to £127,000 in 1854.[27] Prevented from having any real involvement in the running of the estate, the Marquess spent his time at Culzean shooting, fishing, riding and walking, often in the company of his brothers William, who was living at Cassillis, and David, who was a frequent guest. Being of a practical bent of mind, he had a workshop fitted up for himself when he was confined indoors by the weather and ordered a new billiard table. He also laid out a bowling green on the lawn below the terraces.[28] Typical entries in his pocket diary for 1853 include:

> 23rd [August] went to Martnaham killed
>   36 pike weighing 173 lbs.
> 20th [September] shot on Turnberry
>   26 partridges Fine and hazy & overcast
>   5 hares
>   2 rabbits
> 29 [September] Heavy gale with showers
>   out with rifles in afternoon
>   2 Bucks Very heavy squalls with
>   rain during the night
>   2 does
>   1 fawn

His interest in game extended to keeping exotic animals and in September 1854 gazelles were delivered to Culzean to join the deer in the park.

Since the only local hunt was the indifferent pack of Tait's Harriers, the Marquess bought some of his own in November 1853 to hunt the hares which abounded on the estate. They arrived on the thirteenth and for the next few weeks he spent hours at a time exercising them around the estate. They sometimes broke away and at other times put up foxes which he shot. He first hunted them in the Nursery, just beside the kennels at Thomaston on 1 December, when they killed one hare and lost another. Four days later he took them to Corriestown, just outside Kirkoswald, where they 'killed one hare and a fine run with another when we got on to several fresh ones'.[29] The pack now began to meet about twice a week on Mondays and Thursdays at farms and villages on the estate. These were family affairs with his wife and children on their ponies. Within a couple of months he decided that he needed some better hounds and he ordered a new pack from Ayton in Berwickshire. They were hunted for the first time on 13 March 1854. When it was too cold to hunt or do much farm work and the ponds were frozen, everyone turned out to curl, often all day.

The Marquess fished the Doon at Cassillis regularly in the spring. On 3 March 1854 he rode over and caught a twelve-pound salmon. He fished for trout in the Swinston ponds and Mochrum Loch. Occasionally he drew a net in Maidens and Turnberry Bay for flat fish, bass and sea trout. He laid long night lines from the castle for white fish. Martnaham Loch was reserved for coarse fishing – pike, eels and perch. With the coming of the warmer weather in May, he could be found fishing the hill lochs above Straiton. He would leave Culzean after an early breakfast, ride the twelve miles to Craiglure and fish until nightfall.

He sailed occasionally in the summer, mostly day trips to Ayr or out to Ailsa Craig, as for much of the time *Cayman* was chartered out. On Ailsa Craig he shot wild goats and sometimes cruised around shooting sea birds.[30] He still enjoyed a storm at sea with the mainsail reefed down. In September 1854 he was storm bound in Campbeltown Loch on passage to the Giant's Causeway and was forced to turn back. He found shelter in Loch Ranza in the north-west of Arran, not the most hospitable anchorage. He noted in his diary for the '18th Blowing a very <u>heavy gale</u> & rain in torrents

LEFT
The elaborate kennels at Thomaston as they are today.

RIGHT
The 1st Marquess out riding with his greyhounds and a retriever. His grandson followed his example.

with heavy sea rolling in 50 fathoms cable out'.[31] Apart from Lord William and his wife, his other brothers Lord David and Lord Nigel and his uncle General Peel and his family, there were few guests. Lady Constance, his youngest daughter, recalled in her old age that 'they so seldom saw visitors at Culzean that if they happened to hear a carriage come down the driveway, they would all run and hide'.[32] An exception was a visit by the Duchess of Cambridge, the widow of King William IV's brother Augustus, and the Grand Duchess of Mecklenberg, accompanied by the Earl and Countess of Eglinton early in September 1853.

There was also a brief respite to their usual routine when the family went to London. During 1852 they went south in November so that the Marquess could hunt and take his seat in the House of Lords. Although he attended a few times thereafter he was in no sense a serious politician. While in London on 18 November they watched the procession for the Duke of Wellington's funeral pass by the Army & Navy Club on its way to St. Paul's. They were back in London in May and June 1853. They spent their time visiting family and friends, riding in the Park and visiting the Zoological Gardens.[33]

Such London sojourns in the early summer became annual events and, since they no longer had a London home they stayed in hotels or rented a house.

The cost of managing the estate was kept to a minimum except for some improvements associated with increases in rent on the entry of new tenants. Any such exceptional expenditure had to be justified and explained in the annual accounts. The rental was indeed raised from £24,292 to £26,881 in 1855. A new tenant, Turnbull & Co., was found for the chemical works which reopened and the whole of the Home Farm was put down to grass to avoid the cost of ploughing and seeding.[34] Only necessary repairs were made to Culzean and Cassillis, such as the installation of a new reservoir and water supply in 1855. During the following year a clerk of works, John Bowman, was engaged with the specific remit of monitoring all building projects. Meanwhile the Marquess and his wife and family continued to live quietly at Culzean, drinking sherry, Spanish red wine and claret and champagne when the occasional guest came to stay.[35]

Life went on much as before. On many days the only thing the Marquess noted in his diary was the weather 'very fine' or more usually 'wet all day'. He began a game book in which he recorded his daily bag and the names of his shooting companions. At the beginning of the 1855 season on 14 August, he was at Craiglure where he accounted for four grouse, seven black game, a hare, and a snipe. It was the partridge shooting in September that was particularly good, with David and he shooting fifty-seven on 24 September alone at Drumdow and Drumbeg. In that month he was out with his gun on no fewer than thirteen days. By the end of the season in February 1856 the total bag was 2,367 – 97 grouse, 55 black game, 299 pheasants, 529 partridges, 694 hares, 584 rabbits, 25 roe deer, 38 woodcock, 16 wildfowl, 3 plovers, 14 pigeons, and 5 other birds. The cost of running the whole game establishment, excluding the fishing, for the year was £944. William Nicholson was the gamekeeper and was based at Culzean. He had ten assistants at

Enoch, Balvaird, Turnberryhill, Hallowshean, Thomaston, Rowantree, Craiglure, Craigmalloch, Martnaham, and Knockjarder. In addition there was a keeper on Ailsa Craig and two rabbit killers in the policies at Culzean.[36] Disaster struck in January 1859 when Richard Jones, the assistant gamekeeper at Turnberryhill, was shot and killed by Thomas Ross, a noted Maybole poacher. He was buried in Kirkoswald churchyard with a tombstone erected by the Marquess, who paid a pension to his widow for the rest of her life. The Marquess hankered after fox hunting and on 20 January 1856 Mr Montgomerie of Annwick Lodge, near Irvine, 'called to ask what I would do about fox hounds'.[37] They agreed to set up a scratch pack with the subscribers each keeping a hound or two.

With the finances of the estate more firmly under control, Hunter gave the Marquess permission in 1855 to order a small cutter from Smith's yard in Ayr for use as a work boat, and a large new yacht from Alexander Hall & Co. of Aberdeen, well-known builders of fast sailing ships. The forty-foot cutter of twenty-four gross tons was launched on 12 July and named *Tammie Norrie* after the local name for puffins, which, like gannets, nest in profusion on Ailsa Craig. Two days later the Marquess sailed her down to the Maidens. There were various teething problems and she had to go back to the builders. She was in commission by the end of August, drawing nets in Turnberry Bay.[38] The Marquess used her for fishing throughout the winter. Perhaps because he was grateful for these rewards for his new found prudence, he noted somewhat emphatically in his diary on 11 February 1856: 'I sent all my bills to Hunter'.[39]

Named *Kittiwake*, the new yacht, a one hundred and fifty-ton schooner which cost £4,110, was launched on 5 April in the presence of the Marquess and Thomas Dykes, the factor. The Marquess was back in Aberdeen at the end of the month for sea trials. Well satisfied, he returned home while the final adjustments were made before delivery to Southampton. He was in London in late May and early June, anxiously awaiting intelligence of her arrival. He spent much of his time riding in Hyde Park, and also ordered a new brake phaeton for Culzean. News came of *Kittiwake*'s arrival on 10 June, having made the passage from Aberdeen in just six days. The Marquess immediately boarded the express for Southampton. A week later he took her for a short cruise round the Isle of Wight with Alexander Hunter and his cousin Captain (later Sir) Reginald Cathcart, who had been a fellow officer in the Coldstream Guards and was himself a distinguished sailor. He returned to town, attending the Caledonian Ball on 20 June, Her Majesty's Levy at Buckingham Palace on the twenty-fifth and the Crystal Palace on the thirtieth, but his mind was on the *Kittiwake* and he regularly dashed down to Southampton to attend to some detail or other.

On 4 July, appropriately for a man of American descent, he weighed anchor for Culzean. During the night three days later between the Isle of Man and the Irish Coast, he ran into heavy weather. Storm reefed he hove to. The goosestay and mizzenmast were carried away, followed:

> directly afterwards by the main sail with
> its boom & gaff … & had to be cut
> adrift at this time it was blowing a
> perfect hurricane & we had nothing else
> to do but let the vessel drive with the
> wind anchor bare poled during which
> time a sea struck us & carried away our
> jinny boat, at day light we got the gaff
> foresail set again.

He made for Holyhead where he anchored in heavy seas. After making emergency repairs and waiting for a wind, he arrived at Culzean under jury rig on 11 July. The *Kittiwake* was sent to the Duke of Portland's shipyard at Troon and Mr Hall was summoned from Aberdeen immediately to inspect the damage. He took her back to Aberdeen for repair. Despite his eventful voyage, the Marquess was fit enough to go to the Militia Ball in Ayr on 15 July.[40]

The *Kittiwake* arrived back on 9 August when

Culzean was full of family holidaymakers: the Peels, the Bairds, and the Marquess's brother, Lord William. The men were away the following week at Craiglure, shooting and fishing. The first opportunity they had to take the *Kittiwake* out was on the twentieth when they went to Ayr for the day. The Marquess noted ruefully in his diary it 'came on to blow hard at evening had some difficulty in picking up moorings', no doubt to the frustration of his passengers. To relieve his annoyance, he went to Martnaham the following day and killed eighty-four pike, weighing two hundred and eighty-four lbs. His next trip to Brodick on Arran on the twenty-second was equally unsuccessful, as they 'got a headwind coming home so got boat out & rowed got in about 9½'. Culzean Regatta was held on 30 August on a grey wet day, but it cleared at seven in the evening in time for the participants to enjoy 'Pig on the Pole' 'for first time in Scotland'.[41]

On 2 September all the remaining house guests left and the Marquess and the family went on board *Kittiwake* for their first cruise. They made for Loch Ryan to take part in a regatta where their gig won two races. Leaving on the fourth they immediately ran into a gale and, reefed down, made for Belfast Lough where they stayed for a day waiting for the wind to moderate. They then sailed down the Irish Sea to Kingstown, spending the eighth and ninth in Dublin. Under way again on the tenth, they cruised around Land's End, making for Jersey where the Marquess's younger brothers Gilbert and Nigel were staying. They arrived in the outer roads of St. Aubin's Bay on the thirteen and went ashore for a drive up St Peter's Valley. The following day they were warned not to go ashore because of an outbreak of cholera. Ill discipline broke out and the Marquess was forced to sack Henry Blackburn, the cook, and Jack Stuart, one of the crew, for drunkenness. They were presumably put ashore, cholera or no cholera. The family did go ashore on the seventeenth when they drove across the island to Boulay Bay. They left Jersey on the twenty-first. Off Pleinmont Point on Guernsey, while taking in the top gallant sail, the topsail yard

carried away and on inspection it was found that the fore mast had 'sprung'. They made for Guernsey to carry out repairs but left again the following morning. Off Alderney a storm got up and in heavy seas they made for Rye and then to Southampton where the boat was laid up for the winter.[42] The Marquess noted in his game book: 'No shooting all September we being away in the "Kittiwake" on a cruise to Channel Islands. We had very bad weather & left yacht at Southampton arriving home just at end of September.'[43]

There were no more equinoctial cruises. While they had been away a most significant event had taken place for the future of the estate with the opening of the new railway line from Maybole to Ayr for goods on 15 September. This gave the tenants direct access for their produce to the fast expanding markets in Glasgow and its surrounding towns. In the future it would also make possible the development of the

LEFT
A picnic on Ailsa Craig, a favourite summer expedition by boat of both the 2nd and 3rd Marquess.

RIGHT
Lt Colonel Heneage, Lord Cassillis, Mrs Heneage, and the retriever 'Neptune', posing before a days shooting at Culzean in the late 1860s.

Ayrshire coast as a tourist resort.

The Marquess's mind returned to horses and from 7 to 11 October they were resident in Wellington Square in Ayr for the Western race meeting. He spent the rest of the autumn shooting mostly in the company of Captain Reginald Cathcart and his brothers Lord David and Lord William. The weather and the monotony of life at Culzean bored him and his wife and on 6 January 1857 they went to London for a month, entertaining and occasionally hunting. While there he bought two hunters, so as to be able to follow the scratch pack which he had agreed to set up the year before.

They returned to Culzean a month later, when he began energetically to ride to hounds until the end of the season, spending the rest of his time fishing the River Doon at Cassillis. The *Kittiwake* did not arrive from Southampton until 28 April and he did not take her out until 8 May

The Kittiwake *at anchor in Aberdeen. The very long booms were fashionable at the time, but very dangerous if the boat gybed.*

when he sailed round Ailsa Craig. He still found handling her difficult, particularly in light airs. She did not remain long at Culzean and sailed for Southampton on the twenty-fifth. The family departed for London the following day. Apart from two days sailing in the middle of the month, they spent the whole of June and the first half of July in town. They left Southampton on 15 July and were back at the moorings at Culzean by the twenty-first after an uneventful cruise.

In mid-August the shooting season began again, but this year there were few visitors. By early November he and his wife were bored. They took 14 Portman Square in London, stabled their hunters in Leighton Buzzard and remained there until June 1858. It is not known how much use they had of the *Kittiwake* that summer but she was sold early in 1859 by Clark & Price at Southampton for a knock down price of £593.[44] Although the family were never away for so long again, it became their custom to spend much of February and March and May and June in London. They travelled by way of Cumnock, taking their horses with them by train.

The estate continued to be managed on a tight rein. Although little debt was repaid, the total did not increase significantly. Alexander Hunter died in 1859 but his firm, Hunter Blair & Cowan, continued to act as agents and trustees. The only major expenditure was on the replacement of the vineries and conservatories in the walled garden in 1859 for William Greenshields, who had taken over as gardener on John Davidson's retirement.[45] These cost some £2,700 and were supplied by Taylor & Sons of London.[46] The new glasshouses also contained an aquarium for studying the behaviour of freshwater fish. With Greenshields's arrival and the new hothouses, the Marquess began to take more interest in the garden, visiting shows in the Royal Horticultural Society's hall in London and buying plants from Veitch's celebrated nursery.[47] He and his wife also encouraged the formation of the Carrick Cottage Garden Society to promote both flower and vegetable gardening on the estate. Greenshields did not stay long and by 1867 he had been replaced by John Garrett. He in turn left the following year and was succeeded by

John Thomson. He lasted just a year when William Baxter was appointed gardener.[48]

Probably much to his surprise, the 2nd Marquess was made a Knight of the Thistle in 1859. He almost certainly had his friend the Earl of Eglinton, the lord lieutenant of Ayrshire, who was also lord lieutenant of Ireland, to thank for this honour which he had done nothing to seek or deserve. At first it made little difference to his sporting life, although by now he had given up his harriers and ceased to keep foxhounds. He was, however, required to attend Thistle chapter meetings and probably as a result of these contacts with his fellow peers he began occasionally to put in an appearance at the House of Lords. He also had to be present in the Order's chapel in St Giles in Edinburgh on the day of the funeral of Prince Albert in December 1861. With his eldest son, the Earl of Cassillis, a brilliant king's scholar at Eton, there was an incentive to make short visits to London. His son shared his passion for sailing and for sport and had a similar inventive turn of mind. The Earl of Cassillis spent much of his summer holidays at Culzean with the fishermen

A fishing boat on the shore at Maidens where the Earl of Cassillis, later the 3rd Marquess, learned to sail as a boy.

at Maidens, learning to handle their heavily built nabbies and sailing single-handed his little yacht *Julia*.[49] Early in 1861 his father, the Marquess, became much more involved in local affairs when he was invited to become colonel of the Ayrshire Yeomanry when it was formed in the absence of the Earl of Eglinton in Ireland. This involved much journeying around the county to inspect troops, and a good deal of administration, which he seemed to enjoy. He revelled in the contacts with senior officers, many of whom had been his contemporaries when his youthful indiscretion had forced him to resign his commission.[50] With this experience of county affairs it was, perhaps, not surprising that he was appointed lord lieutenant when the Earl of Eglinton died unexpectedly in October 1861. This position, which had so eluded his grandfather, was now largely ceremonial involving representing the queen at events in the county.[51] So as to discharge these duties more easily he rented, in December 1864, 16 Wellington Square in the centre of Ayr for £64 a year from Mr Kennedy of Daljarrock whose grandfather had been factor at Culzean.[52]

All the flurry of activity at the time of the formation of the Ayrshire Yeomanry had subsided by 1862 and life returned to a humdrum monotony. Even shooting was not a pleasure. The summer of 1861 was 'very wet & cold & there were consequently hardly any young pheasants in fact all game with exception of hares & rabbits had failed'. Altogether the Marquess and his guests killed 1,296 hares and 2,339 rabbits during the season, but only 78 grouse. The summer of 1862 was no better. By the end of August 'hardly any of the crops had been cut', there were however no young partridges 'what were hatched having all been killed by rain & cold'. The weather in the autumn was appalling and December was 'dreadfully wet with very strong gales'. The Marquess concluded: 'This has been perhaps the worst season for years ever known. The grouse has almost disappeared from disease & there were no young ones. Neither pheasants nor partridges had bred on account of the cold & wet.' If this was not bad enough, 1863 was even worse. It was very cold and rained almost continuously from August until early January 1864.[53] The fishing was equally bad. The Marquess's diaries are catalogues of the miserable weather 'wild & stormy', 'rain almost all day', 'very strong south westerly gale', and 'very dark & gloomy'. Even the formation of a pack of foxhounds by the new Earl of Eglinton failed to lift his

A liveried coachman holds a horse in front of the mortar battery at Culzean in the 1880s.

spirits. They met at Culzean on 3 March 1863, when he simply commented 'but had not much to do'.[54]

The weather even effected the fox population, which by December had almost disappeared.

The Marquess made the best of a bad job by summoning Charles Lutyens, an army officer turned portrait painter and a cousin of his wife, to come to Culzean in November 1863 to paint him in the uniform of the Ayrshire Yeomanry.[55] Lutyens was a man after his own heart, a first class shot, an excellent horseman and a master of fox hounds.[56] With such credentials it is not surprising that they spent as much time outside as in. Lutyens had intended to stay longer but was summoned home because one of his children was ill.[57] He returned in March 1864 to deliver the portrait which cost a modest £70. He was back for an extended stay in August and September to enjoy the sport and to paint the Marquess's third son, Lord John, with a donkey for £50.[58] Purchases of engravings both by Lutyens and by Landseer, for whom Lutyens worked, followed. With an improvement in the weather in the spring of 1865, the Marquess began to go out more regularly with the Eglinton hounds. However, he also spent an increasing amount of time in his workshop, buying expensive precision machine tools from Holf-zapfell.[59] By all accounts much of his attention was devoted to improving the accuracy of his guns which were made for him by the well-known London gunsmiths, Purdeys.

For most of the year the Marquess and his wife were alone at Culzean, with the odd visitor to lunch or dinner. They continued to drink sherry, claret and Italian red wine with champagne for visitors. There were usually family visitors after their return from London in July and August and shooting parties in October and November. Apart from immediate family, the most regular visitors were the Cathcart cousins of Killochan, the Earl and Countess of Seafield, the Earl and Countess of Eglinton, Lord and Lady Dalrymple, and Sir Michael and Lady Shaw Stewart from Ardgowan. The Marquess was also visited by his brilliant cousins, the grandchildren of his grandfather's brother Robert including John Gordon and William Robert Kennedy.* Apart from the annual visits to London, the Marquess and his wife sometimes made brief excursions to Eglinton Castle and Blythswood House at Renfrew.[60] He still kept a yacht called *Weerit*, but he seems to have made little use of it. During the terrible winter of 1863 his yachtsmen distinguished themselves by rescuing all the crew of the stricken brigantine *Hope*.[61]

The bad weather understandably affected the estate. The grass parks became waterlogged. The factor reported in 1863 of St Valley Holm: 'The grass was not promising and it could hardly be let at all … The grass on this Park and also on the [Cassillis] House Park having become almost useless.'[62] Some tenants, such as James Logan at Lindstone, had gone bankrupt and others, such as John Niven at Potterston and William Kirkpatrick at Whitehill, were forced to renounce their leases.[63] During 1864 the 'Tenants of various Farms … intimated to the Factor that unless they got a reduction of rent they could not go on'.[64] Thomas Dykes, the factor, advised the Marquess that there was little alterna-

tive in the circumstances but either to accept or to find new tenants. He had prided himself on keeping arrears to a minimum, in marked contrast to many other estates in south-west Scotland.[65] Between 1854 and 1858 there were no arrears, but by 1863 they stood at £1,233 or just under 5 per cent of the total rental, which remained stable at about £25,000.[66] Many leases were, however, due to be renewed in the near future and it was proving difficult to find new tenants willing to pay the existing rents even when advertised on the open market. Seven farms were relet during 1865 at 18 per cent less rental than before. The factor noted that in every case the lease had been given up because the tenants were 'unable to go on and pay the rents'. He considered: 'There can be no doubt that the chief cause was a series of bad seasons accompanied with low prices and which operated most seriously on the Tenant Farmers of Ayrshire.'[67] There was plenty of evidence that other landowners were in similar difficulties. The estate of the 13th Lord Elphinstone, who died in 1861, was declared bankrupt the following year and in 1865 the creditors of the Earl of Buchan foreclosed on his property.[68]

The grim outlook prompted a review of the management of the Culzean and Cassillis estates in February 1865 from the time the 2nd Marquess came into possession in 1846. This showed that over this period when there was little or no inflation, income had risen by £6,476, explained largely by increased rents (£3,225) and interest paid by tenants on drainage improvements (£2,885).[69] Expenditure had also increased by £4,137, explained largely by the cost of drainage (£3,233) and the game establishment (£757), as well as arrears. The net result was that the factor had been able to maintain payments to the agents, Hunter, Blair & Cowan in Edinburgh at about £18,000 a year, out of which interest payments had to be met and all the Marquess's own expenses.[70] These had continued to be constrained by the agents, but, with the Earl of Cassillis leaving Eton in December 1865, they were likely to rise.

As a result of the review it was decided to let

*Sir John Gordon Kennedy was a diplomat who was envoy extraordinary to the King of Romania from 1897 to 1905 and Admiral Sir William Robert Kennedy was commander-in-chief in the West Indies from 1892 to 1895 and the Nore (Harwich) 1900 to 1901.

Castlehill Farm for a rent of £360 from Martinmas 1866, but to take in hand Morriston, Hogston and Ardlochan farms on the Culzean estate and Lindsayston on the Cassillis estate. Lindsayston was to be laid down 'permanently in pasture' and let annually, along with Cassillis Park, as grass parks for summer grazing.[71] Allan Wilson was appointed farm manager and an extensive programme of improvements put in hand, which cost almost £4,000.[72] Wilson turned out to be a bad appointment and was described as having 'had a good many dealings, some of them of a suspicious character'.[73] He was dismissed and replaced by William Nicholson, who was to turn out little better. Part of the problem was that the Marquess encouraged the manager to think of himself responsible to him and not to the factor.[74] Factors frequently get a bad press and yet they are often the unsung heroes in the history of landed families. The autobiography of C.D. Gairdner, who was factor at Culzean before moving to the Eglinton estates, was edited by the Earl of Eglinton as an unusual tribute to a loyal servant.[75]

The other outcome of the review was a decision to build new stables and a hay shed at Culzean. The old stables behind the coach house had been gutted by fire in July 1863, but only £53 was received in com-

pensation from the insurance company, hardly sufficient to cover the cost of a replacement. In any event they were too cramped to house the large number of brood mares now kept at Culzean. The new stables of a plain functional design, which were on the castle side of the home farm, took two years to complete and cost some £1,800.[76] These investments inevitably bit into the Marquess's income, particularly in 1868 and 1869, when with little improvement in the weather arrears climbed to £1,818. By the end of the year the factor was 'left with nothing in hand to meet the current expenditure at the commencement of the year …'.[77] If a balance of £6,000 on the Marquess's own account had not been carried forward from the previous year, he would have needed to increase his borrowings and this Hunter Blair & Cowan would not allow. His personal debt still stood at a little under £127,000 with £48,000 owing on the drainage account. Interest charges and associated life assurance premiums were now £8,932, 26 per cent of the total rental but over half of his own remittances. Such a state of affairs was not unusual. On Murray of Broughton's estate in Kirkcudbright and Wigtownshire interest accounted for 29 per cent of the rental.[78] This did not of course obviate the need for strict economy.

One way out of this trap was to find some

source of income other than agriculture. On leaving Eton after a brilliant school career as a king's scholar,[79] the Marquess's eldest son, the Earl of Cassillis, lived for the first six months of 1866 in Maybole Castle, learning about the management of the estate which he would eventually inherit. Rather than going to university, his father in August purchased him a commission in the Coldstream Guards for £12,000 by extending the borrowings against the estate.[80] The advantage of a commission in the Guards was that during peacetime they were permanently stationed in London. The Earl lived in a rented house, 64 Ebury Street, kept horses, rode to hounds and went to parties. Attending old Lady Egerton's ball, she accused him of gate crashing. Denying the charge, he produced the invitation and was so incensed that he 'spread it all over the Club and by this time it is half over London'.[81] He was by now a keen sailor, acquiring his own yacht, the fifteen-ton *Snowdrop* and becoming a member of the Royal Northern Yacht Club in 1866 at the age of just nineteen.[82, 83] Taking after his father, he was interested in yacht design. He purchased ship models in 1868 as a

Officers of the 2nd Battalion Coldstream Guards with the Earl of Cassillis, third from the left at the back.

means of teaching himself about hull shapes and took classes at the Institute of Naval Architecture.[84]

When his duties allowed he was a regular visitor to Culzean. During 1869 he and his father decided to begin building and repairing boats at Culzean. The first step was to build a much larger workshop there.[85] They also planned to begin competing in forty-ton yacht races and ordered a yacht from William Fife of Fairlie, the leading yacht designer and builder in Scotland with a string of winners in different classes to his credit. His boats tended to do best in a stiff breeze, common conditions in open waters of the Firth of Clyde.[86]

Before these plans could be executed disaster struck. The Marquess was thrown from his horse while out hunting near Kilmarnock on Friday 3 March 1870. He was taken to the George Hotel in the town and by the following morning he seemed to have recovered sufficiently to be moved to Culzean. Before his journey could commence he suffered a relapse and his wife hurried to his bedside. On Saturday 19 March he insisted on being taken home, travelling by rail to his town house in

Wellington Square, Ayr, and then on by road to Culzean. By the time he reached home pneumonia had set in and he died that night.[87] His funeral took place a few days later at Maybole, with a special train laid on from Ayr. He was buried not in the collegiate church but in a new vault at Culzean on a site overlooking the sea which he had chosen long before. Once again all the staff including the dairymaids were issued with mourning clothes at a cost of £310.[88] Two years later a monument, designed by the Edinburgh architect J.M. Wardrop,[89] was erected in memory of the 2nd Marquess, which can still be seen at Culzean.[90]

His widow the Dowager Marchioness, whom he had always known as Judy, was left a jointure for the remainder of her life of £3,000 a year. Alexander Hunter, the family lawyer, made it very clear that she could expect no more and must live within her income.[91] She moved

TOP
The Eglinton hunt in the late 1860s, with the Earl of Eglinton, the Master, in the centre and the 2nd Marquess of Ailsa in the red coat on the right behind the two ladies.

BOTTOM LEFT
The imposing monument to the 2nd Marquess of Ailsa with a prominent view across Culzean bay.

BOTTOM RIGHT
Lovel Hill, the Windsor home of the widow of the 2nd Marquess for the remainder of her life.

out of Culzean almost at once and went to live in Mayfair and from April 1871 at Lovel Hill in Windsor to be near her eldest daughter, Lady Julia. The previous December Lady Julia had married one of her brother's fellow officers, Captain Robert Follett of the Coldstream Guards. The Dowager Marchioness took her two younger daughters, Lady Evelyn and Lady Constance, with her. Her barouche was sent south by rail in June and her horses and dogs followed in July. At Windsor she and her daughters rode to hounds almost daily during the winter, becoming close friends of Prince Christian, Queen Victoria's son-in-law and ranger of Windsor Great Park. In the summer they went to the races, played tennis, followed the cricket and went boating. The queen herself never invited her to Windsor Castle, even though she showed much affection to her uncle King William IV's illegitimate offspring.[92]

CHAPTER 8

Sailing into sadness:
1870–92

The Earl of Cassillis, now a captain in the Coldstream Guards, became 3rd Marquess of Ailsa and immediately resigned his commission. Ironically the death of his father at a young age cleared the estate of much of the debt at a stroke as all his personal loans of about £128,000 were either covered by life assurance policies or because of their terms died with him. He was left with the drainage advance of just under £47,000, which was in any event being repaid by the tenants, and a loan of £10,000 to cover the cost of improvements made by his father but which, under the terms of the entail, could be charged to him.[1] There was also a provision of £36,000 for his two younger brothers and three sisters. This sum remained as a loan against the estate and was to cause problems later. He, himself, took out a modest advance of £20,000 to cover the cost of various improvements and the investment in the boat building enterprise.[2] This was secured as a 'charge against the rents' of the entailed estate and had periodically to be renewed in terms of the agreement with the lender. The total debt was in the region of about £115,000. Like his great grandfather, he was a businessman with an eye for financial detail, although as time went on he became increasingly unwilling to draw the necessary conclusions from the estate accounts. It was not for nothing that he excelled at mathematics at Eton. He wanted much

> Foxhound *racing against the much larger* Vanguard *off the Longships light near Landsend in her first season in 1870.*

fuller accounts, particularly for the garden and the farms in hand than his father had ever done. These provide a fascinating insight into their management.

The farms of Morriston, Hogston and Ardlochan were run as a mixed farm, growing wheat, potatoes and oats and producing beef, pork, mutton and dairy produce. Sales totalled almost £4,000, yielding a profit of over £1,500, which was consumed in paying off the overdraft incurred as a result of the improvements. Culzean Home Farm, which was managed by James Muckart, was given over to growing potatoes and producing mutton, pork, poultry and dairy produce. Most of the output from the dairy went either to David Colledge, the butler at the castle, or to work people in the policies. The home farm, such as those on many other estates, was still losing money. The forestry department, managed by Charles France, was on the other hand very profitable, returning over £1,640 on a turnover of £3,007. Wood was sold to the Dalrymple Bobbin Mill, which made bobbins for thread manufacturers, to the acid works at Kilkerran, and to the bakery at Culzean; pit props to the Dalmellington Iron Co.; and fencing stobs and other timber to local merchants. The department ran its own sawmill and nursery for growing new stock, and maintained an active programme of new planting. The gardens now produced fruit and

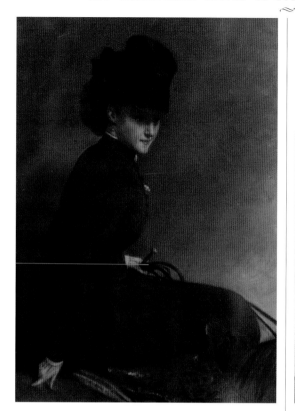

vegetables almost exclusively for the castle. When the family was in London or elsewhere hampers of provender were sent by rail. William Baxter, the head gardener, was paid £80 a year and the total wage bill was £452. The most worrying feature of the estate accounts was the mounting level of arrears which had now climbed to £2,673, almost 10 per cent of the rental.[3] As was practice at the time these arrears were written off against the estate of the 2nd Marquess.[4]

The yacht, which was under construction at the time of his father's death, was launched on 5 May and named *Foxhound*.[5] At the same time the Marquess placed an order with Fifes for a much larger schooner. Costing £1,143, the *Foxhound* was unashamedly designed for racing in the increasingly popular forty-ton class. In her first season the Marquess

LEFT
Lady Evelyn, the first wife of the 3rd Marquess, riding sidesaddle. She was a keen horsewoman in her youth.

RIGHT
The handsome dressing case, which included nautical instruments as well a conventional toiletry accessories, given by the 3rd Marquess to his first wife as a wedding present.

loyally employed a local skipper, Captain Matthew Sloan, and a crew made up of fishermen and a couple of Largs weavers. Although 'excellent her crew were no match for the Southern racing crews'. Regretfully Captain Ben Harris of the Itchen Ferry, who had successfully raced the sixty-ton *Vanguard*, was engaged for the 1871 season. The majority of the new crew came from the Solent, but some local west of Scotland sailors were kept on. In her first season under Harris, *Foxhound* won twelve of the twenty-one races in which she was entered.[6] Cheekily the Marquess entered her for the Queen's Cup at the Royal Yacht Squadron's regatta at Cowes, which for the first time was open to yachts of all classes. Previous winners were heavily handicapped. Rather grudgingly, the editor of *Hunt's Yachting Annual* commented: 'After a long, tedious and uninteresting race the little *Foxhound* without time allowance crept ahead of the whole fleet, being about the smallest vessel which ever won such a prize of such value.'[7] Following in his father's footsteps, the Marquess commissioned paintings of his boats, including a view of *Foxhound* winning the Queen's Cup and a replica of the cup from Hancock & Co., the London silversmiths.[8] He was already a member of nine yacht clubs on the south coast including the Royal Yacht Squadron, the Royal Alfred Yacht Club, the Royal Thames Yacht Club, the Royal St George's Yacht Club and the Royal Southampton Yacht Club, of which he was commodore.

Just as his father's passion for hunting kept him away from Culzean for much of winter, so his son's passion for yachting kept him away in the summer months on the south coast. Captain Harris and the Marquess raced *Foxhound* again in 1872, but 'had not such a rosy time of it this season but by sheer good management contrived to show to advantage on the winning list'.[9] Nevertheless they were beaten into second place by *Myosotis* in the Commodore's Cup at the first regatta of the newly founded Royal Cornwall Yacht Club.[10] The problem was that *Foxhound* was now too small to compete effectively in the forty-ton class.

Owning and racing yachts was to be financed by repairing and building boats at Culzean and also used to advertise the Marquess's skill both as a designer and a sailor. During 1870 new moorings were laid in Culzean Bay for the Marquess's own boats and those in for repair or modification. The first boat to be built on the shore beside the laundry was the steam launch *Growler*, for use by the boat yard and as a tender for the yachts.[11] It was transported up and down to Southampton by rail during the racing season.[12] Work on the new boat-house began in December 1871.

A year after his father's death, the 3rd Marquess married on 7 March 1871 Evelyn, the third daughter of the 12th Lord Blantyre who lived at Erskine House on the southern bank of the Clyde opposite Bowling. They had got to know

each other through her elder sister Ellen, who had married Sir David Baird, the Marquess's cousin, in 1864. The Bairds were regular visitors to Culzean accompanied sometimes by the deeply religious Blantyres and their two younger daughters.[13] The Blantyres were well connected. Lady Blantyre, who died in 1869, was 'one of the reigning beauties of her time' and the daughter of the fabulously wealthy 2nd Duke of Sutherland, who had greatly extended his grand Scottish home, Dunrobin Castle, specifically to accommodate his grandchildren during the summer holidays.[14] One of her sisters was married to the Duke of Argyll and another to the fabulously rich Marquess of Westminster. Lord Blantyre was a Scottish representative peer, sitting as a Liberal. He took little active part in politics, preferring to devote much of his energies to lawsuits against the Clyde Navigation Trustees.[15]

The family's London home was at 44 Berkeley Square and they also owned the charming Lennoxlove Castle in East Lothian, where the Dowager Lady Blantyre lived. It was an odd match politically, as the Marquess had abandoned his Liberal roots and now supported the Conservative Party. They both, however, shared a passion for sailing and on 22 January the bride-to-be launched the Marquess's new schooner, naming her *Lady Evelyn*. Their wedding took place at the very fashionable St George's Hanover Square on 7 March and the honeymoon was spent at Trentham, the magnificent Staffordshire home of her uncle, the 3rd Duke of Sutherland.[16] The newly-weds' homecoming to Culzean on 18 March was nearly as extravagant as that of his parents. Bonfires were lit in Maybole and the couple's health toasted in whisky by the one hundred and seventy tenants and their wives who sat down to dinner.[17] Triumphal arches were put up along the causeway at Culzean and a banquet given at a total cost of £515.[18] As a committed temperance campaigner, Lady Evelyn would not have approved of all the drinking.

Much of the summer of 1871 was spent cruis-

To the Bay of Biscay, oh!

ing in the newly delivered eighty-one-ton yacht *Lady Evelyn*, following the *Foxhound* around the coast from regatta to regatta. Built by Fifes, she cost over £4,000.[19] This pattern was repeated the following year until the end of July, but instead of the yacht being laid up at the end of the season the Marquess left in early November for a five-month cruise to the Mediterranean and the Black Sea. The voyage from Southampton was stormy and eventful. Off Cape Finisterre the ship was twice struck by lightning and some of her rigging carried away in a series of squalls.

Lady Ailsa joined him at the beginning of December at Villa Franca on the Côte d'Azur. They cruised slowly along the French and Italian coast, reaching Naples by 17 December, from where they visited Pompeii 'to see the wonders'. In Naples they purchased terracotta figures and vases, a fine marble bust of Seneca and commissioned some paintings of the frescoes at Pompeii from G. Mormile. These now hang in the picture room at Culzean.[20] They were in Greece by the end of January, visiting Athens. At Piraeus they were met by the steam launch *Growler*, which had been chartered out for the winter. They then made their way through the Greek Islands to Constantinople and then up the Bosphorus with assistance from HMS *Antelope* into the Black Sea. They returned by way of Corfu, Malta and Algiers, from where they took the steamer home in mid-March.[21]

Back home, the 3rd Marquess turned his attention to the management of the estate, while his wife devoted herself to good works in the neighbourhood, and making her new homes more comfortable. One of Lady Ailsa's first projects was to persuade her husband to convert two cottages in Kirkoswald into a working men's club.[22] Her family were evangelicals and closely associated with their evangelical neighbour at Erskine, Archibald Campbell of Blythswood, who had split with the

A sketch of the yacht Lady Evelyn *crossing the Bay of Biscay in a storm. This was used by the artist Barlow Moon in the painting commissioned by the 3rd Marquess on his return. He and his wife spent a belated honeymoon on the* Lady Evelyn *in the Mediterranean and the Black Sea during the winter of 1872-73.*

Episcopal Church of Scotland in 1856 over the failure of the bishops to condemn high church ritual.[23] He had supported and helped finance St Silas's church, an evangelical Church of England congregation in Glasgow. Lady Evelyn had grown up with the Blythswood children, who in London also lived in Mayfair. The eldest son, who became Lord Blythswood in 1892, was a distinguished soldier and continued the family's commitment to the evangelical cause when he inherited the estates in 1868. His brother the Reverend Sholto Douglas* was a leading evangelical clergyman in the Church of England and was associated with the visit to Britain in 1870 of the American Quaker evangelist Pearsall Smith.[24]

Every autumn evangelical clergy were made welcome at Culzean. Anthony Trollope wickedly caricatured their visits in his novel *The Eustace Diamonds* in which Portray Castle is a thinly disguised Culzean. The Reverend Joseph Emilius was described as 'among the most eloquent of London preachers', but 'he did not get on very well with any particular bishop and there was doubt in the minds of some people whether there was or was not any – Mrs. Emilius'.[25]

Since much of the arrears in rent accumulated towards the end of his father's life could be attributed to taking the Morriston farms in hand, one of Lord Ailsa's first actions was to let them, leaving only the home farm to supply the family's needs. The brass bell at Morriston used to summon the workforce was put up in the gardens at Culzean.[26] With all the ruthlessness of youth, he called in the leases of tenants who had fallen behind and advertised them at higher rents. Now that the bad weather of the 1860s was behind them, new tenants could be found who were willing to take leases. If they had had any inkling of the problems that lay ahead they would

*He changed his name to Douglas in 1868 on inheriting the estate of Douglas Support in Lanarkshire from his kinsman General Sir Thomas Monteath-Douglas.

not have been so rash.[27] In 1872 the Marquess set about improving the cottages at Dougalston near Maidens, which 'through natural decay had fallen into a dilapidated state and become quite untenantable' and the abandoned acid works were also converted into cottages. As a result of these initiatives total receipts rose from £42,500 in 1870 to £45,500 in 1874. Since the cost of servicing the debts over the estate had been much reduced, the Marquess was left with a much greater income to indulge his interests. Although he was rich, he was not as well off as other west of Scotland landowners, such as the Duke of Buccleuch, the Duke of Portland, the Earl of Eglinton and the Earl of Stair.[28] Moreover he did not have either the income or the ready access to capital of well-to-do merchants or the newly rich industrialists; but he did have expensive tastes.

By 1874 the Marquess was not happy with the way the gardens at Culzean were being run. It was discovered that William Baxter, the gardener, had

LEFT

A magnificent tureen with a painting of the Lady Evelyn *on one side. This can now be seen in the library at Culzean.*

RIGHT

One of the paintings of Cupid from the frescoes at Pompeii purchased by the 3rd Marquess and his wife on their honeymoon cruise.

misappropriated funds and he was dismissed. Unable to pay what he owed, he signed a bond promising repayment within a year. He went east to work in the gardens of Dalkeith Palace for the Duke of Buccleuch, but shortly afterwards fled to Chile.[29] The palace gardens were at that time the largest in Scotland. The kitchen garden alone contained more than thirteen Scots acres with vineries, melon frames, conservatories, pine (apple) stove and greenhouses. The Duke's gardener, who was well-known for the quality of the training he gave both apprentices and journeymen, recommended David Murray, one of his foremen, for the post of gardener at Culzean.[30] Keen to have someone who was familiar with growing grapes, the Marquess also asked the opinion of William Thomson, an expert in viticulture from Galashiels, who was to supply new vines to Culzean in the coming years.[31] Murray quickly became the Marquess's confidant and collaborator in a variety

of schemes, particularly the growing of exotic plants and breeding trout and salmon.

In the early 1870s the Marquess had become friendly with Frank Buckland, one of Her Majesty's Inspectors of Fisheries and an eccentric naturalist, who was considered the greatest authority in Britain on salmon fishing. He had pioneered techniques for breeding salmon and trout and written extensively about the subject. He recommended the installation in a greenhouse of a series of boxes about '20 inches, 4½ inches deep and six inches wide, which can be placed one above the other so that the water can fall either by means of lips over the side or over the end'. The boxes were partially filled with gravel into which a series of glass rods with the fish ova were attached. The ova were collected by netting wild fish and stripping the females. When hatched the fry were brought on in ponds before being released into the wild. By 1863 several landowners, such as the Duke of Argyll, Viscount Powerscourt, and Captain Berkeley, were already using his apparatus.[32] Apart

LEFT
The very devout Lady Evelyn, first wife of the 3rd Marquess of Ailsa.

RIGHT
The bell from Morriston hanging in the walled garden today.

from fishing, Buckland was also interested in exotic animals and was happy to advise clients on how to obtain them. He helped the Marquess of Bute establish a colony of beavers at Mount Stuart on the Island of Bute.[33] Unusual animals appealed to the Marquess of Ailsa in much the same way that birds had to his forebears. His hapless gardener was soon to find a whole variety of unusual manures at his disposal.

The Marquess began his experiments in rearing fish in December 1875, when Robert Main was paid to transport minnows from Tunnock Park to Culzean.[34] The necessary equipment and associated plumbing was installed in the greenhouses and rearing ponds formed at Swinston, which were covered with netting to keep out predators. From December to February teams were employed in collecting ova at the head of Loch Doon and in the Water of Minnoch. The Marquess was so delighted with the result of these experiments that he decided to build a new one hundred and thirty-two-foot peach

house in the gardens which would also double as a fish hatchery. Work began in 1877 and was completed the following year. A visitor from Cardiff described this new fish hatchery five years later:

> This range is utilised in an ingenious way in connection with the artificial breeding of salmon. Throughout its length are placed in direct line a series of oblong boxes covered with lids, rising in successive levels so that a stream of water entering at the upper level falls successively from level to level until it escapes at the bottom. These boxes are filled with fine gravel and many ingenious contrivances have been resorted to ensure a natural filtration and the constant movement of the water and disturbance of its surface which observation has shown to be necessary for the successful hatching of salmon.[35]

By this time the rearing of fry after hatching had been abandoned and, instead, at six weeks the 300,000 fry, which were hatched annually, were transported to the Doon at Cassillis and released.

The construction of the new peach house was just a small part of a much wider scheme for the

LEFT

The Nursery wing at Culzean added very sensitively by Wardrop and Reid in 1877, showing the replica field guns in their original position on the West Green.

RIGHT

Lady Ailsa's boudoir as it was in 1908.

improvement of the house and gardens which probably owed as much to the Marchioness as her husband. She was not used to living in uncomfortable houses and little work had been done at Culzean since the 1st Marquess completed it some sixty years earlier. The house, which had been designed in the late eighteenth century, was inconvenient and cost a fortune to heat. The Marquess and Marchioness were keen to retain the Adam feel of the house while at the same time making it less cramped and easier to service. The Marquess wanted office space for his boat building and repairing business and the Marchioness wanted rooms in which to entertain. She also wanted better accommodation for herself and her three children, Archibald (known as Baldie to distinguish him from his father), Evelyn and Charles.

Early in 1877 the Edinburgh architects, Wardrop & Reid, were invited to devise a scheme for making substantial alterations to the house, and also redesigning the layout of the surrounding grounds. Wardrop had already designed the monument to the 2nd Marquess and the practice had recently designed the grand new stable block at neighbouring Kilkerran. Since no one any longer made beer for their staff, they proposed that Adam's brewery wing, apart from the elaborate

wine cellar, should be converted into a new nursery wing connected on three floors to the existing house. The hall was to be enlarged with a new portico and, by incorporating the old buffet room, the dining room was to become a sitting room with its views over the gardens. The dressing room and library were to be knocked together to form a much larger dining room. On either side of the new portico, offices and plan and model rooms were to be fitted up for the Marquess. Wherever possible, as many of the original Adam fittings were to be reused. Two complete bookcases from the library were to be installed in the Marquess's offices and the chimneypiece was to be moved to Lady Ailsa's boudoir on the first floor. In the hall the elaborate display of armour commissioned by the 1st Marquess was to be preserved intact and added to, so as to fill the additional wall space. In June Charles Reid, one of the partners in the architectural practice, visited Culzean to complete the drawings for modernising the castle.[36] Altogether the plans supplied by Wardrop & Reid cost £900, giving some indication of the complexity of the project.[37]

By then work was already in progress in refashioning the gardens. The old walled garden beneath the terraces was finally abandoned and the wall opposite the castle knocked down. In the

LEFT
The fountain installed in 1876.

RIGHT
Charles Street where the Marquess and Marchioness of Ailsa had their London home from 1877 until the end of the century.

centre of what was to become a formal garden a large fountain was installed. This was made by Austin & Seeley of London at a cost of £134, with a granite base supplied by Smith & Co. of Dalbeattie for £33. Construction work was carried out during the autumn of 1876 by John Gilmour, a local mason.[38] Under Lady Ailsa's direction the southern half of the walled garden was turned into a flower garden for her use.[39] At the same time the long neglected deer park was refurbished to provide a home for exotic animals. The alterations in the gardens necessitated a great deal of replanting, particularly of fruit trees in and around the walled garden. By 1882 the old terraces were 'covered with a variety of choice shrubs and climbers, while the borders at the foot are filled with a riot of bedding plants'. The fountain was filled with trout. The conservatory, which was described by David Murray as 'not favourable to the growing of plants', was 'filled with large camellias, azaleas, and a general collection of greenhouse plants'.[40]

Before work could be done on the castle at Culzean, the Marquess and his wife and three children needed somewhere to live. Their first decision in the spring of 1877 was to give up the lease on Ebury Street and to purchase 12 Charles Street, where the 11th Earl had lived on his return from

America. The house was to be completely refurbished to form a grand residence at a total cost of £18,000. For the previous five years they had been buying new and antique furnishings for their town house and for Culzean from such fashionable suppliers as Harvey Nichols & Co., Holland & Sons and John Watson in London and Wylie & Lochhead of Glasgow.[41] Their new home in Charles Street was furnished initially with purchases from Christies and J. Watson and with pictures from W. Grindlay.[42] This was a prelude to the complete restoration of the house by Johnstone & Jeans of New Bond Street later in the year. Although Johnston & Jeans were principally cabinet-makers specialising in expanding tables, they also undertook house fitting. In the 1880s they began to make Regency revival pieces.[43] The Charles Street house was fitted out in the height of fashion with further furnishings from J. Watson of Oxford Street (£2,073), carpets from Vincent Robinson & Co. (£745), bedding from Heal & Son (£137), glass and china from J. Matloch (£157), and furniture from J. Raines (£378), Edwards & Roberts (£1083) and Holland & Sons (£432).

Edwards & Roberts of 21 Wardour Street were among the foremost English cabinetmakers of the Victorian era.[44] The firm dealt in 'articles of vertu' and produced furniture of modern design, as well as reproductions of eighteenth- and early nineteenth-century pieces.[45] They supplied the bulk of the furniture for all the rooms in the house, including the drawing room and boudoir, the dining room, and the morning room. The most expensive piece of furniture was an elaborately carved Chinese enclosed sideboard with a large glass back, which cost £73 10 shillings. They restored some furnishings from Culzean or Cassillis, including two 'very handsome richly gilt Chippendale chimney glasses and a richly gilt gerandole.[46] The total cost of refitting and furnishing their London home was almost £7,500.[47] The style seems to have been Adam revival.[48] While the work was going on the Ailsas rented 42 Upper Grosvenor Street as their London home. The Marquess and Marchioness were in

London from May to July and while the Marquess sailed the Marchioness supervised the work.[49]

At Culzean major work on the castle had to wait until the tenant at Cassillis, Major Fergusson, had died allowing the Ailsas to move in. Well before building work started an inventory of the pictures in both houses was prepared. The drawing room or old picture room on the first floor was crowded with an eclectic collection of paintings including a painting of the *The Return from Donnybrook Fair* and one of Nasmyth's paintings of Culzean. The portrait of Lord Mountstuart, which the 10th Earl had had reframed in 1790, had been relegated to the Steward's room. The 1st Marquess's much cherished full-length portrait of Napoleon was in the long drawing room while the boudoir contained the recently commissioned paintings of *Foxhound* and *Lady Evelyn*.[50] The two Lutyens portraits were in the Green Room and the ante-room was filled with the Landseer and Lutyens engravings, as was the dining room. The state room or saloon was dominated by the portrait of Lady Susannah Eglinton. Oddly, the family seemed to have been unaware, from the descriptions of the subjects of the paintings commissioned by the 11th Earl, of his various naval actions. Even stranger is the absence from the inventory of the Mosman and Batoni portraits of the 9th Earl and the portrait of his brother.[51] One of the reasons for compiling this inventory was that part of the refurbishment was to involve regilding and where necessary reframing the collection.[52]

Construction began at Culzean during the autumn of 1877 and in the New Year the gamekeepers were instructed to mount guard over the house at night.[53] In the spring joiners and glaziers were busy replacing window frames and fitting new glass. From January until August the family were in London, so that work could commence on the alterations to the main house.[54] They then came up to Cassillis for the shooting season, returning south from February to March 1878.[55] The work inside the house was carried out with considerable care to prevent needless damage and to ensure that the

alterations were in keeping with Adam's intentions, something that the 1st Marquess had singularly failed to do when he completed the staircase and the saloon. Greatest attention was given to conserving and creating the ceilings. The principal exponents of the use of *papier-mâché* in ceiling design, Jackson & Sons of London, were employed to form the dining room ceiling in sharp contrast to Adam who had relied on local Ayr plasterers. Jacksons worked closely with the London decorators, Wright & Mansfield, who were the principal exponents of the Adam revival style. Their craftsmanship was awesome and is an essay in blending revival with contemporary aestheticism, reflecting a similar treatment of the garden. A new chimney piece for the dining room was created by Galbraith & Winton and Holland & Sons were commissioned

The new dining room at Culzean formed out of the old library and the Earl's dressing room. The room was carefully designed to be in keeping with Adam and all the original fittings were reused.

to make a new sideboard.[56] The other ceiling work was carried out by local Ayr plasterers, John and Thomas Reddick.

The castle was redecorated from top to bottom by Bonar & Carfrae of Edinburgh, who also regilded the frames of the pictures and the mirrors and reupholstered much of the furniture. Less important furniture restoration was undertaken by J. Rewcastle and Wilson & Co. of Ayr. An elegant front door to the new wing was constructed with a charming tympanum carved by the Edinburgh sculptor, John Rhind.[57] The West Green adjoining the new wing was levelled from October 1879 to May 1880 which entailed carting great quantities of soil.[58] The total cost of the whole project including the architects' fees was just under £18,500, but excluding £2,569 paid to Bonar & Carfrae for 'gilding, frames and upholstery work'.[59] Included

TWENTY-NINTH ANNUAL CONGRESS
OF THE
INCORPORATED SANITARY ASSOCIATION OF SCOTLAND,
STRANRAER, SEPTEMBER, 1903.
PHOTOGRAPHED AT CASTLE KENNEDY, 2ND SEPTEMBER, 1903.

within the project was the reconstruction and re-equipping of the gas works, which from now on would provide the main source of heating and lighting for the castle. The courts gave permission for £16,899 of this expenditure to be charged against the estate rather than the Marquess's income. The family and servants returned from Cassillis to the newly refurbished Culzean in the spring of that year.

Moving back into the castle was a major operation, as much of the furniture had been stored in the castle in Maybole. Bonar & Carfrae continued to work at the castle for another year, during which time further upholstery work was undertaken by William Affleck of Ayr, bedroom chinaware was purchased from John Mortlock & Co. of London, and A. & J. Main, the Glasgow engineers, were commissioned to fit elaborate wine racks in the cellars.[60] One of the family's first actions on returning home was to buy new liveries for the servants.[61] John Latta, a photographer in Maybole, was

The annual meeting of the Sanitary Association of Scotland at Castle Kennedy in 1903. Both the first and second wives of the 3rd Marquess were enthusiastic supporters of this evangelical organisation.

commissioned to take a series of shots of the completed building in October and November.[62] The enlargement of the castle allowed the pictures to be hung quite differently. With filial piety the Marquess hung the Lutyens portrait of his father over the mantelpiece in the new dining room with, on either side, the equestrian portraits of his grandfather (the 13th Earl) and his great-grandfather the 1st Marquess. The portrait of the 11th Countess was hung over the sideboard. The old eating room was filled with his father's fine collection of Lutyens and Landseer prints. The saloon was now dominated by the full length Mosman portrait of Sir Thomas Kennedy, the 9th Earl, and not the Countess of Eglinton.[63]

The Marchioness was concerned that the staff at Culzean should also benefit from these improvements and they were given recreation and reading rooms, furnished with improving literature, which were fitted up in the loft of the new stables.[64] By

TO THE

WORKING MEN
OF MAYBOLE.

CASSILLIS HOUSE, AYR, JANUARY 8TH.

I HAVE received the following Letter, bearing the Maybole post-mark. I know that none of you can have written it, as you have always received me with kindness and goodwill; and while you continue to do so, I shall, God willing, visit among you.

Though you may not be able to find and expose the cowardly writer, I know that I can entirely trust myself among you.

EVELYN AILSA.

COPY OF LETTER.

"MAYBOLE

"Beware when you come to Maybole the a oz of lead or a "six blade nife is your Reward

"REVENGE

"No. 1 WARNING"

Addressed, "The Marchiness of Ailsa "Castles Maybole"

JOHN WATSON, PRINTER, MAYBOLE.

now she was deeply involved in the Ayrshire evangelical and temperance movements. When at Culzean she was a frequent speaker at meetings throughout the county. At her own expense she built a mission church and reading room for the fishermen at Maidens.[65] Such activity was very much in keeping with the work of Lord Blythswood and his brother the Reverend Sholto Douglas, who was a visitor at Culzean and probably preached at Maidens.[66] She also insisted that better houses were built for the workmen employed on the estate calling on the assistance of the Scottish Sanitary Association to help her. This had been established in the late 1860s as a public health response to the evangelical and temperance movement to improve 'cleanliness, ventilation, free space in the home'.[67] Representatives of the association were employed to inspect properties on the estate, including farms, and make recommendations. Cottages were built at Maidens and in Maybole and

LEFT

Printed notice from Lady Ailsa.

RIGHT

Reverend Sholto Douglas, 2nd Baron Blythswood, a prominent evangelical and a friend of Lady Evelyn, Marchioness of Ailsa.

on several farms.[68] During 1880 a new pier was built at Maidens for use by the fishermen.[69]

As a total abstainer, Lady Ailsa persuaded her husband in 1879 to open a coffee shop in Maybole, where customers got a free cup of coffee if they signed the pledge. As an additional incentive allotment gardens were laid out for more deserving abstainers. A coffee tent was also erected by the manager of the shop on Ayr Racecourse during training of the Ayrshire militia in the summer months and at the Western race meeting in September. The opening of the coffee shop was too much for one man in Maybole who penned a note to the 'Marchioness of Ailsa, Castles Maybole':

Beware when you come to Maybole the a oz of lead or a six blade nife is your reward
Revenge
No 1 Warning

Furious, Lady Ailsa had an address printed 'TO THE WORKING MEN OF MAYBOLE'.[70] The three total abstinence societies in Maybole – the Good Templars Lodge, the Abstainers Union and the Free Templars Lodge – immediately presented an illuminated address to the Marchioness:

to convey to your Ladyship our high appreciation of your Ladyship's efforts to counteract the prevailing habits of intemperance in the district by your having provided for the working men of the Town a thoroughly equipped Coffee room with reading and amusement rooms.[71]

This act of philanthropy was expensive. The shop and related activities had an income of £409 in 1880–81 while the expenditure was £747.[72] On the Edinburgh agent's insistence costs were soon contained, largely by putting up a shed on the racecourse to avoid the expense of hiring tents.[73]

In October 1880 the Marchioness played host at Culzean to one of the most prominent evangelicals of the day, Lord Radstock, who had gained considerable recent notoriety by his efforts to evangelise the Russian aristocracy.[74] A career army officer, he had returned to the evangelicalism of his childhood during the revival of the 1850s in which his fellow army officers, such as Lord Blythswood, played a part and which was heavily influenced by American experience. His first efforts had been to encourage prayer meetings and bible readings amongst the aristocracy and this is probably how Lady Ailsa first encountered him. Disappointed at the lack of response he cast his net more widely, particularly in the East End of London, and became a significant force behind the spiritual and philanthropic movements of the period.[75] Lady Ailsa held similar prayer meetings for the aristocracy in both Scotland and London, at one of which she is credited with converting Lieutenant Henry Sherbrooke, a Lifeguard, who went on to become the vicar of Clifton in Bristol, a fashionable evangelical parish.

After his ordination he visited Culzean. Other aristocratic evangelical and committed Protestant visitors included the former Lord Chancellor, Earl Cairns, whose daughter Henry Sherbrooke married as his second wife, Sir William Houldsworth of Coodham, Lord Brabazon, Lord Belper and Lord Rosslyn.[76] Although Lady Ailsa attended the Church of Scotland and supported inter-denominational Protestant bodies such as the Christian Union, she remained an adherent of the evangelical wing of the Church of England in the tradition of Lord Blythswood. Lady Ailsa was determined that her children should also be brought up in the evangelical tradition. They learned popular evangelical hymns at their mother's knee. Reputedly during one of their London visits, the nurse was wheeling the young Earl of Cassillis through the park when he began to sing at the top of his voice: 'A Ruler once came to Jesus by night to ask him the way of salvation and light.' The nurse fled with her young charge in embarrassment.[77] The children's governess Miss Schmitz was a German evangelical with links to America. When the Earl of Cassillis went to Eton in 1884, the Marchioness made sure he had an evangelical tutor.

While his wife devoted herself to her evangelical and philanthropic activities, the Marquess was busy with his yachts and his interest in exotic animals and salmon breeding. After the fencing of the new deer park was completed in 1878, the Marquess acquired buffaloes, wild pigs, which were kept in the kennels at Thomaston, ostriches and unusual fowl. The buffaloes, which had been expected to live outside, had to be provided with a shed early in 1879, presumably because they were not accustomed to the wet. The Abyssinian sow was obviously not a success and was put on the market in 1879.[78] During the summer a party of racoons was installed in the pagoda. The bakery in the Castle soon had to add them to their list of customers.[79] Emus and wild turkeys joined the menagerie in 1881 and in September of the following year William Kerr of Dalry supplied an Indian cow and calf.[80] These animals were not just for show. By 1883

Indian buffalo was on the menu at the castle and on board the Marquess's steam yacht.[81]

Yachting remained the Marquess's real passion. He gained his master's certificate during 1874, by which time the appearance of Major Ewing's *Norman* in the forty-ton class had made the *Foxhound* completely obsolete. The Marquess toyed with the idea of buying the half-completed sixty-ton *Neva* which was sitting on the ways at William Fife's yard because her owner had died. Instead he commissioned a forty-ton racing yacht from Fifes and the *Bulldog*, a steam yacht, from Alfred Payne of Southampton at a cost of £2,500.[82] The *Foxhound* was traded in part exchange for the new racing yacht, *Bloodhound*, which as a result only cost £436. Known as the *Dog*, she was one of the first real racing machines 'with no fittings except a seat along each side'.[83]

At the beginning of her first season in 1874 she had a 'badly standing mainsail' which spoiled her performance. After alterations she was evenly matched with the leading boats in her class, the *Norman* and the *Britannia* which was owned by the chartered accountant Cuthbert Quilter.[84] In the following season the *Bloodhound* had rather the best of it. She started twenty-four times and won sixteen, earning £500 in prize money and the prize cup of the Royal Albert Yacht Club.[85] To celebrate her achievements replicas of a number of trophies were commissioned at great expense from the London silversmiths, Stephen Smith & Sons, Hancocks & Co., Elkington & Co., R. & S. Gunard & Co., and S.J. Phillips.[86] While competing *Bloodhound* in the Royal Cornwall Yacht Club's regatta on 30 August 1875, along with the rest of the fleet the Marquess accidentally came under artillery fire from Pendennis Castle. On complaining to the commander-in-chief, HRH the Duke of Cambridge, he was informed that the 12th Duke of Cornwall's Volunteers had been over-enthusiastic and all such practices were forbidden in future.[87]

On 17 November 1875 the Marquess attended an historic meeting in London at Willis's Rooms in St James to discuss the formation of what was to become the Yacht Racing Association with the objective of codifying and standardising sailing rules and handicaps 'such as would be capable of easy modification to suit the regatta courses of each club'. Although previous attempts had failed, it was now generally agreed that the existing state of affairs with each club applying its own rules was impractical and unfair. At the meeting the Marquess was elected to the Council of the new association, which was to be chaired by the Marquess of Exeter. Another member was Warrington Baden-Powell, a newly converted enthusiast to small class racing, making the thrill of yachting accessible to those of moderate means.[88] He had designed the *Diamond* in 1873, which was built at Shoreham. She was reputedly the first small yacht to imitate the practice of bigger vessels by moving round the coast from regatta to regatta with the crew living in cramped conditions on board.[89] During the previous season, Baden-Powell had been the first winner of the Royal Canoe Club's challenge trophy. He had strong views about the method of measuring yachts, which coincided with those of Lord Ailsa and they soon became firm friends. The members of the council worked incredibly hard to have new rules in place by the beginning of the 1876 season. The new regulations were not, however, immediately accepted, particularly by the Royal Yacht Squadron.[90]

By this time the original intention of opening a commercial boatyard seems to have been put into abeyance. When the *Lady Evelyn* and the *Bloodhound* were refitted in 1876 the work was carried out elsewhere. During that year the Marquess commissioned two more boats. The *Beagle*, a racing yacht to replace the now obsolete *Bloodhound*, was designed to conform to the new YRA rules and was to be built at Culzean. A very grand steam yacht, the two hundred and sixty gross ton *Marchesa*, was ordered from the Renfrew shipbuilders Lobnitz Coulborn & Co. at the enormous expense of £16,000. She was sumptuously equipped, each 'state room is fitted with a swing cot and pneumatic bells that communicate with the pantry, and the panels

of the yacht are ornamented with cutlasses and muskets enough, if properly handled to defend her against all comers'. She was delivered in the autumn of 1877 and on 21 November, along with his friends Wade Brown, E.R. Boyle and R. Staples, the Marquess sailed her from Ayr to the West Indies by way of Lisbon, Madeira and the Cape Verde Islands.[91] The *Beagle* was run down and sunk in the Kyles of Bute by the schooner *Niaza* when she was only a few months old. The loss of the new yacht prevented the Marquess from competing in 1878. More prosaically harkening back to his childhood adventures, the Marquess had taken a half share during 1876 in the fishing boat *Nimrod*, operated by Andrew Girvan at Maidens. He also acquired an interest in the fishing smack *Retriever*, which was repaired at Culzean with advice and assistance from William Fife of Fairlie. His total outlay on yachts between 1876 and 1878 was as much as the cost of the alterations to Culzean.[92]

This scale of expenditure could not

LEFT

A trophy won by Bloodhound *in her last season during the 3rd Marquess's first period of ownership, which is now on the sideboard in the dining room at Culzean.*

RIGHT

The steam yacht Marchesa, *which was built by Lobnitz & Co. for the 3rd Marquess in 1877, newly arrived at Demerara in February of the following year. The funnel can just be made out amidships beneath the awning.*

continue if the estate was to remain solvent and could only really be afforded by men with a considerably larger income than the Marquess. His solution was to charter his fleet of boats to the Earl of Eglinton and the Earl of Verulam, which produced an income of almost £1,000 in 1878.[93] At the same time he decided to begin building and repairing boats in earnest at Culzean, converting part of the home farm into new engineering and joiners' shops. The engineering machine tools were supplied by P. & W. MacLellan and Tangye Brothers of Birmingham and the woodworking machines by John McDowall & Sons of Johnstone in Renfrewshire.[94] A mold loft was created above the new stables.[95] The only new purchase in 1880 was the fishing smack *Mastiff* at an estimated cost of some £500.[96]

Before shipbuilding began, the *Lady Evelyn* and the costly *Marchesa* were sold, leaving the Marquess £8,000 better off.[97] The successful but now outmoded

Bloodhound was also part exchanged for another new boat from William Fife of Fairlie, the *Adeona*, which consumed almost £2,000 of this windfall.[98] However she was soon sold at a handsome profit of £1,000 which was put towards the cost of yet another new yacht the *Sleuthound*.[99] The Marquess also began to build to his own designs and on his own account at Culzean a five- and a seven-ton yacht designed to appeal to the less well-heeled sailor.[100] Writing in 1894 George L. Blake commented: 'The Clyde yachtsmen were the first to appreciate the value and capabilities of the little ships for affording good all-round sport.'[101] The five-ton *Cocker* was launched in 1881 while the seven-ton

Finette was sold to G.H. Matthews of Harley Street. The Marquess raced the *Cocker* in the 1882 season in Scotland and in Ireland, winning twenty-three races and coming second in five. For every win the two man crew were paid a bonus of £1, equivalent of two week's wages. She was managed by William Fife & Sons at a total cost of £143, less £30 prize money.[102] At the end of the season she was sold to R.B. Mitchell of Glasgow. Fittingly the first boat to be delivered from the Culzean yard was a fishing punt for the Marquess's father-in-law, Lord Blantyre in August 1881. This was followed in 1882

by a small boat for the Ayrshire Christian Union of which his wife was a supporter, two yacht dinghies and two yacht cutters for A. & J. Inglis, the Glasgow shipbuilders, a steam launch for Mr Jamieson of Liverpool, a racing gig for Sir William Houldsworth of Coodham, a friend of the Marquess and his wife, a racing cutter for the London stockbroker Edward Quilter (Cuthbert's brother), a set of ship boats for Ramage & Ferguson, shipbuilders in Leith, and a fishing boat for Arthur Bignold, the shooting tenant at Craiglure.[103] In June 1882 the Marquess sent the three-ton *Snarley Yow* to London by rail. He had built this yacht in collaboration with Warrington Baden-Powell, his friend on the YRA council. The *Snarley Yow* was designed to the three-ton class specification of the Royal Portsmouth Corinthian Yacht Club by Baden-Powell and raced by him and the Marquess in the 1883 season.

Larger orders were soon secured for the yard at Culzean, including a steam launch for R.C. Munro-Ferguson of Novar (originally named *Bandog* and later rechristened more appropriately *Novar*), and a fishing smack for the Earl of Leitrim.[104] The size of some of these vessels demanded the installation of a new launching slip

at what was now called the Laundry Boat Shed.[105] Early in 1883 Lord Dunmore sent his steam yacht to Culzean to be repaired and Albert Wood of Liverpool ordered a steam launch. The legendary New York newspaper proprietor and yachtsman, J. Gordon Bennett, also placed a contract for a cedar built lifeboat and a steam launch. Sir Andrew Walker, the Liverpool brewer and philanthropist, who rented fishing on the Doon from the Marquess, ordered a cedar launch, lifeboats, two gigs, and a dinghy. Lady Brassey, the intrepid yachtswoman and wife of the distinguished yachtsman Lord Brassey, purchased a cedar built gig.[106] This custom clearly resulted from the Marquess's contacts amongst the sailing fraternity.

Although the income from these activities in 1883 was only £2,784 against expenditure of £4,396,[107, 108] there was sufficient confidence in future prospects to move the yard to Maidens. The harbour below the castle at Culzean was small and access very restricted and unsuitable for building larger boats. Work began in March 1883 and the new yard was completed in September.[109] When his sister Lady Julia was staying at Culzean during that month, she walked to Maidens to see the new yard and the mission church and reading room.[110]

LEFT
The Sleuthound *at the foot of the slipway at Fife's yard at Fairlie.*

RIGHT
The newly completed Maidens shipyard with a yacht ready to be launched.

Instead of the yard being managed through the estate, it was leased to William Fife junior, the son of William Fife of Fairlie, in October and transferred the following month to a limited company, the Culzean Shipbuilding & Engineering Co. The new company had a capital of £10,000 divided into one hundred shares. The Marquess held sixty-two shares, his father-in-law Lord Blantyre five shares, Evan Hunter who had succeeded his father as the agent for the estate and lived at Newark Castle five shares, William Fife senior four shares and William Fife junior four shares. Ayr and Maybole businessmen held the remainder of the shares including Thomas Rennie, a banker in Maybole five shares, James Bell, a shipowner in Ayr one share, Charles and William Wilson, upholsterers in Ayr two shares, William Macrorie, a solicitor in Ayr two shares and John Cameron, an ironmonger in Maybole one share.[111] It was just as well the yard had moved, as in October 1884 the port and jetty at Culzean as well as the laundry were inundated in a violent storm.[112] One of the first boats to be built at Maidens was a new steam yacht for the Marquess, named *Titania*. The yard did not remain long at Maidens, moving again in 1886 to the yard of the defunct Troon Ship-

building Co. at Troon, which belonged to the Duke of Portland. The Culzean Shipbuilding & Engineering Co. went into liquidation and the yard now traded under the name of the Ailsa Shipbuilding Co.[113] The slipway and buildings at Maidens were mothballed. The engineering workshop at Culzean moved to Troon and its premises became the home of the estate maintenance and building department.[114] Along with the shipyard the Marquess acquired Portland Villa in Troon which he used as his base when on company business.

In the meantime the Marquess had been racing his new yacht *Sleuthound* with as much success as her predecessors. In her first season in 1882 she won the Albert Cup and the Queen's Cup. She won the Queen's Cup again the following year and spectacularly took the King of Netherlands's Cup with a prize of three-hundred guineas. The morning of the race dawned with gale force winds from the south, which later veered north-west. At breakfast the club steward told the Marquess not to think of racing that day. The Marquess rejoined with a request for some cold pie to take with him, which was against the club rules.

LEFT
The mission chapel at Maidens, which was built out of her own funds by Evelyn, Marchioness of Ailsa, during the 1870s.

RIGHT
The Marquess's new steam yacht, Titania, *on the ways at the Maidens yard. The number 22 is its yard number, indicating that this was the twenty-second contract undertaken by the business.*

The steward responded: 'Of course you shall have it and I hope you will live to eat it.' Pitted against much larger boats including the Prince of Wales's *Aline*, the Duke of Rutland's *Shark* and Evelyn Baring's *Waterwitch*, the *Sleuthound* trailed at the back of the field, until the change of wind gave her an unexpected advantage. Approaching the finish her spinnaker came adrift and she crossed the line in the lead with it wrapped round her top mast, earning the accolade as 'the finest all-round boat that ever lay in Cowes Roads'.[115] She was sold at the end of the 1883 season to Lord Francis Cecil, who won the Queen's Cup for a third time in 1884. Three years later to celebrate Queen Victoria's golden jubilee, he competed her in a two thousand-mile ocean race in the North Sea.[116] With the sale of the *Sleuthound*, the Marquess was left only with his steam yacht *Titania* and no new sailing yacht was laid down. Like his father and grandfather before him he had run out of money. Never short of enthusiasm, he turned to photography and took his camera with him wherever he went.[117]

Despite his best efforts, the 3rd Marquess had not been able to sustain his increased income. This was not a good time to own a predominantly agricultural estate. With the opening up of the Russian steppes and later the mid-west of the United States by railways, cheap grain flooded Western European markets, depressing prices and heralding a long agricultural recession which was to continue in Britain until the outbreak of the First World War. At first husbandry areas in the west of Scotland with ready access themselves to the rail network were insulated from the worst effects of the recession. The turning point in the fortunes of west of Scotland landowners came in 1878 when the fraudulent collapse of the City of Glasgow Bank sent shock waves throughout the economy, paralysing the building industry and contributing to the largest number of bankruptcies in Scotland during the whole nineteenth century.

Thomas Dykes, who had been appointed the Marquess's factor thirty-six years earlier, died on 12 June 1879. It was his daughter and not the Marquess who paid for the ornamental granite fountain in his memory on the Town Green in Maybole. This must be one of the few monuments to a factor in Scotland. He was succeeded by Thomas Smith who took up his appointment on 12 August.

Although Ayrshire was not as badly hit by the agricultural depression as other counties in the south-west,[118] the Marquess's ordinary income fell by almost £3,000 in 1879 and 1880 as a result of unpaid rents.[119] As in the previous crisis in the mid-1860s, rents were reduced for the coming year. Already it had been decided to raise more cash by selling a further bond over the annual rents of the entailed estate for improvement expenditure to the North British Insurance Company of Glasgow for £22,688, and borrowing £10,000 against the unentailed lands.[120] The list of improvements, for which borrowings could be made, had been extended through the Entail Amendment Act of 1875 to include alterations and additions to the mansion house or houses and gardens, which had previously and perhaps wisely been excluded.[121] This made it possible to include in any calculation the cost of the extension and refurbishment. The total indebtedness of the estate now stood at about £145,000, which incurred annual interest and repayment from the rents of almost £8,300. These new borrowings were partly needed to discharge advances from the Edinburgh agents, Hunter Blair & Cowan, and partly to meet the cost of the work at Culzean. So as to help increase the annual income Craiglure Lodge had been refurbished and in 1877 rented out with the shootings to Henry C. Bucknall, a shipowner.[122] Perhaps because of the recession or the lack of game, he did not renew his lease in 1879 and Craiglure remained unlet until 1880 when it was taken by Basil Sparrow. He in turn was quickly followed by Arthur Bignold. There were similar difficulties in finding a tenant for the neighbouring Craigmalloch shootings.[123] At the same time the London house began to be rented out for the six months the family was not in residence.[124]

Thomas Smith's first action was to reorganise the administration of the estate, which had not been changed since the time of the 1st Marquess. The objective was to bring together cognate areas of expenditure, for example the costs of maintaining the various households and boating activities, while at the same time disentangling new ventures such as fish propagation. Repairs and maintenance were also separated from improvements. At the insistence of Hunter Blair & Cowan the new reporting procedures drew a distinction between necessary expenditure on the estate and other expenditure charged against the surplus, such as the deer park with its buffaloes, the Culzean Yacht and Steam Launch Works and the Maybole Coffee House. Although this approach was much more rational, the traditional method of 'charge and discharge' book-keeping was retained whereby all the income was listed followed by the expenditure. These necessary changes made it possible for Evan Hunter, the agent, to respond firmly to a proposal from the Marquess in December 1881 to add to the estate by purchasing more land. Estimating the balance against the Marquess to be almost £11,000, he advised against in the strongest terms, but suggested by way of an olive branch that 'perhaps at

some future period funds may be looking up' which would make the purchase possible.[125] Such salutary advice did not endear him to the family. Lord Alexander, the Marquess's brother, commented: 'My own opinion is that Hunter is a useless ruffian, and I wish I could get someone who understood money matters to take him in hand.'[126] Agents and factors often had to suffer such opprobrium from those they served.

Sleuthound running full and bye to win the Queen's Cup at Cowes in 1882 by the artist Barlow Moon.

By the summer of 1882 rental income had recovered, but there were indications that all was not well, due largely to the Marquess's continuing extravagance. He owed Hunter Blair & Cowan over £4,500 and this rose to £10,389 the following year and to almost £19,000 by 1884.[127] Urgent action to contain expenditure was essential. Although the *Sleuthound* was sold and subscriptions to some yacht clubs stopped, the debt was cancelled by once again charging £27,277 of improvements against the entailed estate and borrowing an additional

£10,750 from the City of Glasgow Life Assurance Co.[128] These manoeuvres, although perhaps expedient, were hardly prudent, particularly as by July 1886 the Marquess once again owed his agents over £11,000.[129] This time he simply negotiated an overdraft of £11,000 from the Union Bank of Scotland, which still left him almost £8,000 in debt to his agents. The annual cost of borrowings was now almost £11,000 a year compared with £6,300 when he inherited the estate.[130] In 1887 his total income from the estate was only £13,000 due to a further steep rise in abatements of rents because of the 'agricultural depression'.[131] Further reductions had to be given the following year and even more money borrowed.

The Marquess was now in as serious financial difficulties as any of his predecessors. Although the Marquess's subscriptions to no fewer than nine yacht clubs were cancelled, nothing else was done and in fact expenditure rose. Improvements con-

tinued at a remarkable rate. During the winter of 1884 new heating apparatus was installed at considerable expense in the vinery, by James Boyd & Sons of Paisley.[132] In 1885 and 1886 almost £5,000 was spent on new estate buildings, including a completely new steading at Macmanniston and labourers' cottages at Glenlui. The following year the total was £6,000, including new houses at Martnaham Mains, Glenalla and Knockjarder.[133] A legacy at Culzean of the failure to control spending is the second magnificent Nasmyth painting which was purchased for £200.[134] The only concession to economy was the abandonment of the fish hatchery and the sale of the buffalo, no doubt to the relief of the gardener. However he still had to feed the emus.[135] Such financial difficulties were common place amongst landed families and

> LEFT
> *The monument to Thomas Dykes, the factor on the Culzean and Cassillis estates, which still stands on the green at Maybole.*
>
> RIGHT
> *The sumptuous saloon and more functional chartroom on the* Titania, *the Marquess of Ailsa's steam yacht.*

in fact the Ailsa's indebtedness was much less than some of their neighbours. The Earls of Galloway, whose estate with a similar rental adjoined their property on the Wigtownshire border, had debts of £315,000 in 1873.[136]

For the Marquess, these years were overshadowed by his wife's illness and death. The Marquess and his wife were visited in September 1883 by his sister Lady Julia and her husband Colonel Bobby Follett. Her diary gives the impression of a serious household, where the Marchioness only ventured out to prayer meetings and to church. Most of the holiday was spent on a week's cruise in the *Titania* off Oban. On the Sunday while the men went walking, Lady Julia and the Marchioness attended the Salen Free Church on Mull where they 'found the service

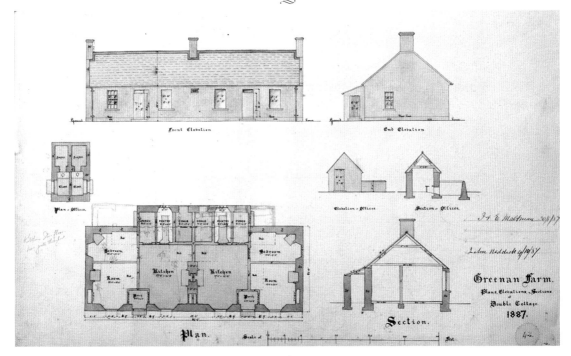

Front Elevation

End Elevation

Plan - Offices.

Elevation - Offices.

Section - Offices.

Bedroom

Kitchen   Kitchen

Room   Room

Greenan Farm.

Plans Elevations Sections
of
Double Cottage
1887.

Section.

Plan.   Scale of

conducted in Gaelic'. They returned exhausted to the yacht to a 'late lunch'. The high point was meeting the *Pembroke Castle* on her maiden voyage in the Sound of Mull with the prime minister, William Gladstone, on board as the guest of the owner Sir Donald Currie.* As 'the day was lovely, went up Loch Linnhe again to Ballachulish; here we took a waggonette & drove to Glencoe'.[137]

Early in November the Marquess and his wife sailed for Cannes in the *Titania* for the good of the Marchioness's health and did not return to London until the end of March 1884.[138] While they were away the children were left in the charge of Miss Schmitz, the German governess who shared the Marchioness's enthusiasm for abstinence. Lord and Lady Ailsa only came to Culzean in mid-August 1884 for the shooting. They spent January to mid-May of 1885 in London. The Marchioness was reported to be much better, but not well enough to

> New workmen's
> cottages for
> Greenan farm, 1885.

embark on a planned family cruise to Norway in the summer.[139] Instead her husband went alone, accompanied by his cousin Admiral Sir John Kennedy Baird. They fished and hunted at Namsos in Norway with their cousin Edward Briggs Kennedy, a noted Scandinavian sportsman,[140] before travelling on to Gunnarvattnet in central Sweden. They fell in love with the area and with the help of Ole S. Fiskum they negotiated a lease of the fishing and shooting in the area. A hunting lodge, named the Skottland Jagt-Hus was to be built seven kilometres from Gunnarvattnet towards Mount Myrklumpen, along with stables and kennels and a private road.[141]

While the Marquess was away, to keep the draughts out of Lady Ailsa's bedroom at Culzean, double glazing was installed.[142] She still had the energy to take an interest in the estate, insisting that the programme of improvements to provide better accommodation for workmen should be maintained. This included twelve tenements and three cottages at Maidens and cottages on a number of farms.[143] During December the family was struck down with diphtheria and the only daughter, Lady

*Sir Donald Currie (1825–1909) was the founder and owner of the Castle Line, which merged with the Union Line to form Union Castle in 1900.

Evie, died at Culzean on 9 January 1886. A month later, with the young Earl of Cassillis and Lord Charles still recuperating, the family went to London. They did not come back until June.[144] While they were away a 'rustic house' for Lord Charles was built under David Murray's supervision by the estate masons and joiners alongside the pine stove in the walled garden.[145] On the roof was a dovecote where he could keep his pigeons. It was surrounded with heathers, which were cultivated in a new greenhouse.

Despite her illness Lady Ailsa managed to press ahead with the refurbishment of Cassillis House and with plans for building a summer convalescent home at her own expense at Ardlochan in memory of her daughter.[146] The Marquess contributed a bowling green with a handsome pavilion for the patients' use.[147] By this time James Wardrop was dead and it is likely that these contracts were entrusted to Hew Montgomery Wardrop of Wardrop & Anderson, who was working nearby at Ballochmyle House. As at Culzean the work at Cassillis involved the construction of an entirely new wing with a library at the top.[148] The decoration and refurbishment reflects

LEFT
The charming rustic house in the walled garden at Culzean, which was built for Lord Charles, the second son of the 3rd Marquess.

RIGHT
The convalescent home at Ardlochan, which was built in memory of Lady Evelyn Kennedy, who died at the age of nine in 1886. The text above the window reads: 'Come unto me all ye who are troubled and heavy laden and I will give ye rest'. The building is now used as the office of a caravan park.

the Adam revival style employed at Culzean. All the building work was completed by the spring of 1887 as Lady Ailsa was busy in London ordering carpets for Cassillis from Harvey Nichols and a dinner service from John Mortlake & Co., and advertising for the first incumbents for the convalescent home: 'Working Men recovering from illness who require Sea-air and rest'. Admission was refused to those recovering from infections, the mentally ill and disabled and drinking alcohol on the premises was strictly forbidden.[149] The family again had been in the south since January. In the Marchioness's absence the convalescent home was looked after by the children's governess Miss Schmitz, who acted as honorary secretary.

At this time there was growing concern about the naval threat posed by Germany. The Conservatives' victory in the general election in 1886 was due partly to their stance on this issue. Lord Salisbury's new government established the Royal Naval Auxiliary Volunteers and the Marquess was amongst the first to come forward, establishing an Ayrshire brigade and placing the *Titania* at its disposal for training each summer. Mr Smith, the factor, was called on to raise funds.[150] During these

years Lady Ailsa became close to her aunt, Caroline, Countess of Seafield, daughter of the 11th Lord Blantyre, who shared her evangelical outlook.[151] She had married the Earl of Seafield in 1850 and on his succession to the title in 1853 had persuaded him to terminate the generous provisions made by his father to his four younger brothers and his sister. In a bitter family feud the estate was disentailed. On the death of their son and only child the 8th Earl of Seafield in 1884 the Countess had succeeded to the vast Grant and Seafield estates of almost five hundred square miles with great houses at Cullen and Castle Grant.[152] The Ailsas went north to stay with her for five weeks at Castle Grant and to fish the Spey in June 1887. The Marchioness gave instruction to the factor to forward all their mail: 'I shall be especially anxious for the badly written ones as they are applications to the Convalescent Home.'[153] By the time she returned in mid-July the convalescent home was

The 3rd Marquess of Ailsa landing a fish on the Countess of Seafield's water on the river Spey.

fully occupied with ten male patients and the Marquess's uncle Lord David and his wife had taken up residence at Cassillis. Lord Ailsa did not stay long at Castle Grant but joined the *Titania* for a romantic voyage to retrace the steps of his cousin Anne Disbrowe in Russia. His cousins Admiral Kennedy and Edward Briggs Kennedy accompanied him. They stayed at the British Embassy in Moscow and travelled on overland to Moscow. He was back at Castle Grant for the start of the shooting season on 12 August.[154]

The family was in London once more from January to May 1888 where Lady Ailsa's health continued to decline. She died at Culzean on 26 July, having insisted on attending the mission chapel at Maybole on the Sunday before.[155] On her instructions her funeral was to be a simple ceremony and her grave unadorned. The Church of England funeral rite was read by her friend the Reverend Sholto Douglas, now vicar of St Silas's Church in

Glasgow, which had been built by his brother.[156] Only the male servants who attended the service were bought mourning clothes.[157] Deeply distressed the Marquess could not bear to be at Culzean and set off within ten days for Craiglure to be alone.[158]

He instructed the governess Miss Schmitz to look after his four surviving children, particularly Lady Aline, who was eleven and Lord Angus who was just six. They were packed off to stay with their great-aunt Caroline, Countess of Seafield. With her only son and child dead, she became a second mother to her charges. Archibald, Earl of Cassillis was to remain more attached to Cullen and Castle Grant than to Culzean for the rest of his life. He was neglected by his father and was forced to borrow pocket money from his tutor. He had to write more than once to the factor to obtain his monthly £10 allowance.[159] At Cullen his cousin Walter Stuart, the Master of Blantyre, took the place of his father. He was twenty years his senior and until the death of the 8th Earl of Seafield had lived part of the year at Seiberscross near Rogart in Sutherland.[160]

In the first week of October 1888 Culzean was shut up. The only staff remaining in the house were the housekeeper and two maids. Joseph Catchpole, the butler, and Arthur, the first footman, were taken as stewards on the *Titania* when the Marquess sailed to the Mediterranean for a six-month's cruise in the company of his friend the Honourable Granville Waldegrave, the heir to Lord Radstock.[161] The butler was kitted out with:

> one suit of strong blue pilot cloth, the jacket being double breasted sailor's monkey or reefing jacket with plain horn buttons and a blue yachting cap with peak also a shooting jacket knickerbockers and gaiters of the brown flax sort of stuff that the keepers used to be dressed in here.[162]

Another surprise addition to the crew was the Culzean kennelman who was to assist with planned sporting excursions.[163] Lord Ailsa remained in the Mediterranean throughout the autumn and into the winter, sailing as far as Corfu by way of the North African coast, Vicenzo, Volpicelli, and Naples. He then ventured up the Adriatic to Albania where he hunted wild pigs.[164] He returned to London at the end of March but did not travel north until May 1889, bringing with him a wild pig captured in Albania.[165] While he was away the Ailsa shipyard at Troon had completed on his account the little sailing boat *Black and Tan* and a small steam yacht *Lily*.[166] The *Lily* was subsequently sold in the spring of 1890.[167]

The two younger children remained with their great-aunt at Castle Grant during the autumn of 1888. Miss Schmitz reported to the factor Thomas Smith on 1 December:

> The dear children are getting quite hardened here in the Highlands they are well and in very good spirits … We are having beautiful fine frost weather. The deer and big old stags come lowing under our windows, there are between 40 and 50. The children delight in watching them; they are so fond of animals. The number of their own pets has become enlarged by a little tortoise and a tiny green frog Lord Ailsa sent them from Ajaccio.[168]

They were joined for Christmas at Cullen by the Earl of Cassillis and Lord Charles with the Reverend William Webb Peploe, their tutor at Eton who came from a notable evangelical family and was to become vicar of St Paul's Onslow Square in London. They went back to school in January, leaving Lady Aline and Lord Angus at Cullen.[169] At Eton the Earl and his brother were constant visitors to their grandmother's house at Lovel Hill and regularly saw their three aunts. They were all at Culzean at Easter to see their father, who had sent precise instructions from the *Titania* as to where they were to sleep.[170] In September the younger chil-

Anthony Trollope's writing.

dren also went to Windsor where they stayed with their governess until the New Year of 1890, when they left for Culzean on their way to stay with another great-aunt, Lady Andrew Buchanan, at Bishopton House in Renfrewshire and then with their grandparents at Erskine.[171] They spent most of 1890 at Culzean where Miss Schmitz became effectively the housekeeper, much to the irritation of the factor. She and her charges were in London early in 1891, intending to go to Bournemouth at the end of February to stay at Holy Trinity Vicarage. She asked that the Culzean gardener send a weekly hamper with 'a few fowl, a leg of mutton, a few rabbits, some vegetables, and a few flowers snowdrops and such like, a few fern leaves …'[172] The holiday had to be postponed as Lady Aline got measles.

Their father had been at Culzean for a only couple of months during the summer of 1889 when the factor and Hugh Lennox of E.A. & F. Hunter &

Co., who had succeeded as agent after Evan Hunter's death earlier in the year, tried to get him to face up to his financial difficulties. Apart from debts secured against the estate, he owed Hunters some £20,000.[173] With the Marquess away and overcome with grief, Thomas Smith, the factor, had been left to pilot the estate through troubled waters. The rental income had continued to decline albeit with abatements and arrears contained and expenditure on improvements reduced. Nevertheless, so as to be able to retain and attract tenants, some new building work was essential, particularly as farms were consolidated in response to the depression. The factor like his predecessors was unable to control the Marquess, who had happily agreed to a request from David Murray, the gardener, for new heating apparatus for the renewal of the pine stove and the vineries by Mackenzie & Moncur, the well-known horticultural engineers of Edinburgh.[174] The pine

stove, which had been built by the 1st Marquess, was described by a visitor to the garden in 1882, who reported that it contained 'healthy stocking fruit' guaranteeing a succession of pink pineapples. Four leading varieties were grown – the Queen, Prince Albert, Count Rothschild and Smooth Cayenne.[175] It was late in the day to be still growing what had been regarded as the king of fruits, as supplies were now regularly being shipped from abroad.[176] Both the pine stove and vineries were in bad repair, as in 1887 the estate joiner requested a large supply of putty to make them watertight.[177] In 1890, apart from David Murray, there were eight other gardeners including one apprentice compared with five a decade earlier when money was less tight.[178] The Marquess's uncle, Lord David Kennedy, continued to live at Cassillis House. His rent was increased from £200 to £350 to cover the cost of maintaining the house, garden and policies, which were charged directly against the estate.[179] Craiglure Lodge and shootings were again let but a reduction in rent had to be made because of the death of grouse due to disease.[180] Anthony Trollope poked fun at the lack of birds in his novel *The Eustace Diamonds* when Lady Eustace, the fictional owner invited a guest to

> LEFT
> *The bag after a successful hunt for wild pig in Albania.*
>
> RIGHT
> *Castle Grant, which became the second home to the Earl of Cassillis and his brothers and sister after their mother's death in 1888.*

shoot her 'three annual grouse'.[181] Despite the factor's best efforts, expenditure still ran consistently ahead of income, particularly on the household and family.

The Marquess left Culzean in 1889 before any decision as to how to reduce expenditure could be reached. In July and early August he was cruising the *Titania* in Hardanger Fjord in the south of Norway. Despite good grouse shooting at the beginning of the season at Culzean and an excellent bag of partridges in September, he set sail again on the *Titania* before the end of the month, once more for Norway. He was back in November before sailing to the Canary Islands. He took with him Robert Ballantine, the keeper from Hallowshean, but this time Joseph Catchpole, the butler, declined and resigned his position. He cruised off the Spanish and north African coast in November and December, making two unsuccessful shooting expeditions into Spain and Morocco.[182] He then set off for the Gambia in search of better sport, cruising two hundred and thirty miles up river into the bush in January 1890 where he shot all day. The Marquess reported from Bathurst on 1 February just before returning up river for another three weeks shooting:

We have had a splendid time fine weather and a lovely climate … Our bag up to now is nearly 400 head consisting of 75 brace partridges, 25 ditto sand grouse, 24 ditto black breasted bustard (a lovely bird both to shoot and to eat) 34 crocodiles, 2 deer, 1 hippopotamus besides guinea fowl, duck, geeses, quail etc etc.[183]

He sailed from the Gambia for Grand Canary at the end of February, leaving behind two boxes and two barrels of crocodile skins, which arrived at Culzean in May.[184] He returned to Culzean by way of Milford Haven in April. While he was away the clock in the armoury had been sent to Frank Flower in Piccadilly to have its face white enamelled.[185] During the summer he and his cousin Admiral Sir John Kennedy Baird visited the newly completed Skottland Jagt-Hus. Spending so much time abroad, the Marquess no longer had any need for his London home, which was permanently let.[186] At the same time, as if making a break with his old life, the *Titania* was sold and the last of the emu in the deer park disposed of.[187]

Having acquired a taste for big game hunting in west Africa, the Marquess embarked for India in the autumn of 1890, leaving instructions that his 'cases of books, glassware and bedstead' should be sent out to Admiral Baird, who had taken up residence in the Skottland Jagt-Hus.[188] On his voyage out he met Captain Heat RN, the head of the Indian Marine, who had in his fleet the *Mayo*, which had been built by the Ailsa Shipbuilding Company. He was delighted when he gave 'a good account of her economy and speed'.[189] From Bombay his journey took him to Calcutta, Delhi, Lucknow and Benares. Wherever he went he bought souvenirs, particularly local handicrafts such as rugs and shawls. In Delhi he acquired a variety of Indian wares and at Cawnpore he purchased two tents from the Elgin Mills for future Scandinavian expeditions.[190] While at the shooting camp at Kutch Behar his party shot in one week

'two buffalo, three tigers, two leopards, two bears, two rhinoceroses, besides sundry stags wild boar etc.' He added regretfully: 'I have not been very lucky in getting shots myself but I got one of the leopards and was in at the death of the Rhino contributing my share of bullets.'[191] Visiting Benares he shot a tigress from a howdah on an elephant and ordered a carpet from the prison for the dining room at Culzean to replace the worn existing one. The factor was instructed to send a drawing of the floor area with the exact position of the two pillars carefully marked 'so that they make the holes exactly to fit'.[192]

Reproduction Persian carpets were made in prisons throughout India, particularly in the Punjab at Amritsar and Lahore. Occasionally new designs were introduced, such as the 'Taj' and 'Parrot' patterns of the Agra jail.[193] On his voyage home in April the Marquess met and fell in love with Isabella [Isa or Belle], the daughter of Hugh MacMaster, a market gardener from Kausani in the North West Provinces whose family came from Brooklynn near Blairgowrie. This caused considerable confusion in the Scottish press which presumed the fiancée must be from New York.

Lord Ailsa did not get back to Culzean until May 1891 and remained there until July. In August and September he was trying out his new tents up country from Skottland Jagt-Hus in Sweden with his cousin, Admiral Baird and his wife, a distinguished yachtswoman.[194] They spent their time shooting elk and ryper (grouse).[195] The Marquess was back home in October shooting with his friends. He remarried on 3 November but remained at Culzean with the house party for about another week. On 8 November he and his brother Lord Alick and three friends shot one hundred and eight-six birds and rabbits.[196] The following day he was gone. While they were away the factor was left instructions to get Wilson & Co. of Ayr to carry out essential repairs to the furniture and where necessary supply replacements.[197]

The Marquess and his new wife were back at Culzean from Christmas until May 1892 where they

were forced by the factor and Hugh Lennox of E.A. & F. Hunter & Co. to face up to the recurring financial problems of the estate. Thomas Smith, the factor, considered, quite properly, that he had a duty to the 'heirs at entail', the Earl of Cassillis and his brothers. He therefore refused to allow their father to burden the estate with any more debt unless it could be justified in terms of improvements, which by law could be charged to the heirs. Under his diligent guardianship the programme of improvements and repairs had been maintained but he was reluctant 'to see any burdens however small put on the estate'.[198] In any event an additional charge on the estate would require the permission of the Earl of Cassillis's trustees, which, given the relations between the Marquess and his sons, might not be forthcoming.[199] An obvious economy was to sell the

The Skottland Jagt-Hus near Gunnarvattnet in Sweden, which was built by the 3rd Marquess and his cousin Admiral Sir John Baird. The two ladies are unknown. The men from left to right are Lord Charles Kennedy (later the 5th Marquess of Ailsa), Ole S Fiskrum and Daniel Jonsson Bergman, a local farmer.

London house but no buyer could be found as the lease had only eighteen years to run and a further £5,000 would need to be found to extend the lease by forty-five years.[200] In any event this was not a good time to sell London property with the city still reeling from the effects of the collapse of Barings Bank in November 1889 and the economy in serious recession. Another and perhaps less palatable solution was to move out of Culzean. With this in view Lady Ailsa went to see over Newark, which had remained empty since Evan Hunter's death, but she was too taken with her new home to contemplate leaving it. Consequently no decision was taken.

With the London house on the market, the Marquess took the lease of the houseboat *Merrivale* on the Thames. This was obviously a grand affair with room for Arthur Cox,

the butler; other servants, the 2nd coachman; Thomas Warner, and the Marquess's engineer, William Sloan, the son of Captain Matthew.[201] The Marquess and his wife spent the summer cruising on the river using the Guard's Boat Club at Maidenhead as their base and attending the Henley Regatta. On leaving the Thames at the end of July he and his wife returned briefly to Culzean before setting off with the children for Skottland Jagt-Hus on a fourteen-week fishing and shooting expedition, once again accompanied by Robert Ballantine, the keeper from Hallowshean.[202]

Winter came unusually early, with heavy snow from 1 September, by which time the Marquess, Admiral Baird and their friends were camping some hours distant from the Jagt-Hus shooting.[203] These long summer Scandinavian excursions were to become an annual event until the end of the century and replaced the yachting holidays. In 1893

The Titania *at anchor in Hardanger Fjord, photographed by the 3rd Marquess.*

they did not go at first to the Skottland Jagt-Hus but stayed fishing in Bjugum farmhouse near Hegre so that Lord Ailsa could return quickly to London to help vote down Irish home rule in the House of Lords. Travelling by liner from Newcastle to Trondheim, they went well prepared, sending their own 'thunderbox' or dry earth closet in advance, along with garden seeds.[204] When the home rule vote was postponed they travelled on to Gunnarvattnet.[205] Astonishingly, even in Scandinavia they were supplied with fruit, vegetables and flowers from the Culzean gardens.[206] In 1893 the Marquess complained that tomatoes had arrived over-ripe and instructed that greener ones should be sent in future. He added:

Tell Murray [the gardener] to include next time Peas, Beans, young Carrots & turnips, French beans 4 cauliflowers, 3

or 4 cabbages, lettuce, parsley and any other small things he has ready. These can be in a hamper separate from the fruit.[207]

The catch of Lord Ailsa and his friends in just three weeks in July 1893 was five hundred and twenty pounts of fish and the largest fish was thirty-eight pounds caught by Admiral Fairfax, commander of the Channel Squadron.[208] Admiral Baird was at the Jagt-Hus for most of the winter, occasionally sending reindeer and other game for the larder at Culzean.[209]

While the family was away, the Marquess and his wife continued to be generous in allowing access to the castle and grounds on a Wednesday afternoon, both to individuals and to professional and charitable organisations. Lord Ailsa could, however, be prickly if he thought advantage was being taken of this privilege. In 1897 when a weekly tour was advertised by a Mr Cockburn, char-a-banc proprietor in Ayr, on Saturdays in addition to his normal Wednesday excursion without his consent, he replied angrily to the factor:

LEFT
A shooting party preparing to leave the Skottland Jagt-Hus.

RIGHT
The gun dogs waiting to set out for a day's sport from the Skottland Jagt-Hus. The game keeper from Culzean is the one on the right in a bowler hat.

'I have not the slightest intention of allowing the Char-a-banc to pass through Culzean grounds on Saturdays … if there is any repetition of a party being sent into the grounds on a Saturday as happened a year or two ago I shall withdraw the permission to visit the grounds on Wednesday altogether.'[210]

Throughout these years the children saw little or nothing of their father, although he wrote to Lady Aline regularly. They do not seem even to have been at his second marriage. Although their governess, Miss Schmitz had difficulty in getting paid,[211] she was generously treated to a holiday in Colorado in the summer of 1892 to visit her brother and sisters, whom she had not seen for a long time.[212] This was no doubt partly to allow Lady Ailsa to get to know her step-children over the summer holidays.

The Earl of Cassillis had left Eton during 1890 and had gone up to Trinity College, Cambridge, the first member of the family to attend university for almost a hundred and fifty years. In his last year at school he had joined the Ayrshire volunteer battal-

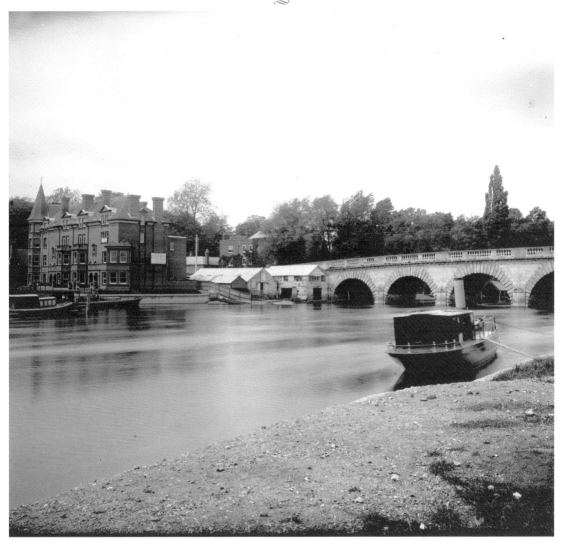

ion of the Royal Scots Fusiliers. While an under-graduate he spent most of his vacations in London staying with his aunts and uncles. He left Cambridge without graduating, but sensing that the days of the great estates were over, with no great love for Culzean and well aware of his father's debts, he was determined to become a soldier. He studied for his commission in London, writing from Highgate in May 1893 to the factor: 'I wish I had got through all my exams by now & was in the Army, so that I had no more anxiety about work.'[213] He passed with flying colours

Marlow on the Thames photographed by the 3rd Marquess where he and his second wife spent their honeymoon.

in the spring of 1894. Miss Schmitz was delighted, commenting: 'It will make such a difference to see Lord Ailsa so pleased with his eldest.'[214] For some reason he did not join the army but instead decided to practise at the Scottish bar, taking law classes in Edinburgh. He qualified as an advocate in 1897 but began his practice in London, working as a parliamentary agent and taking briefs for Scottish cases in the House of Lords. His brother Lord Charles was inter-ested in agriculture and chose to go on from Eton to the Royal Agricultural College at Cirencester.

CHAPTER 9

Economy and expenditure:
1892–1938

On Lord Ailsa's return to Culzean in October 1892, life had resumed its old capricious pace. New duck and geese houses were ordered for the pond.[1] The Marchioness was determined to continue the charitable works of her predecessor including the convalescent home, the coffee house and reading rooms. She asserted her authority by immediately cutting Miss Schmitz's salary from £130 to £100 a year and taking over all her philanthropic duties.[2] When the youngest child, Lord Angus, went to Eton in 1896, she was dismissed.[3] Although the Marchioness was given control of domestic expenditure, she showed little interest in the practicalities of managing the household or in controlling expenditure, to the factor's dismay. She revelled in the grandeur of Culzean and her new found social position. Having been brought up on a market garden in India, one of her first demands was for the installation of central heating and an overhaul of the chimneys.[4] She also insisted that the old clock in the tower at Maybole be restored and be fitted up in the stable tower at Culzean. James Weir of Glasgow duly did this in March 1893.[5] New blue livery was ordered for the servants and much of the table linen replaced.[6] For his birthday she gave her husband a model of HMS *Canopus*.[7]

In November 1893 the Marquess and his wife took up residence in Charles Street, for which a buyer had not yet been found, but were back at Culzean by early the following month. They returned to Charles Street at the end of December and in March finally found a tenant for the coming season in the Earl of Cork and Orrery, who was to serve as the Queen's Master of the Horse.[8] They moved out in early April, going to stay at Mackellar's Hotel in Dover Street. By this time urgent action was required to address their financial situation, as the Marquess's brother Lord John, who was unwell, wished to be paid £5,000, part of his legacy from his father. This, along with similar legacies to his other brother Lord Alexander and his three sisters, had been allowed to remain as loans secured over the estate. This was common practice and caused many landed families serious difficulties in the late nineteenth century, as infant and child mortality declined and more and more provision had to be made for younger children.[9] With the need eventually to discharge all these debts, the agent, Hugh Lennox, and the factor, Thomas Smith, conducted a careful review of the position. Although Lennox's firm E.A. & F. Hunter were willing to allow their debt of £23,000 to be carried over until the London house was sold, the factor considered this imprudent as in the current market a sale could not be guaranteed. Since there was no prospect of a reduction from 'the surplus of the estate', the factor favoured cancelling the debt by borrowing at lower

The devastation caused by the great storm of October 1884, similar in scale and intensity to that of a decade later.

rates of interest, otherwise 'the balance will quickly increase to a formidable amount'. He reckoned it would be necessary to raise a further £34,000:

> to put the financial position on a sound and economical basis. It will no doubt necessitate some economy and careful financing till the rent charges fall in 1902 and 1905. To meet the additional payments and keep the balance at Messrs. Hunter & Co. from increasing it will be necessary to reduce the expenditure on the estate and also a little reduction may be made about the place, without much sacrifice of efficiency. All this will however have to be gone carefully into with your Lordship.
> And if the London House is sold the proceeds will form a Fund in hand which will meet any extraordinary demands in connection with the Family establishment without incurring any new debt.'[10]

Lord Ailsa's response to this dismal assessment was encouraging: 'I am sorry to learn that the total result is so unsatisfactory but I quite agree with you that it is better to face the difficulty now than to let it go on increasing.'[11]

Having agreed on this course of action, the agent and the factor explored the best method of raising such a sum.[12] Their first inclination was to borrow from an insurance company against the security of a life policy. The Marquess rejected this inevitably expensive option in favour of selling some of the unentailed lands, which he was quite entitled to do. With land prices depressed, selling land was not considered prudent and instead the agent got agreement to raise a further loan against the value of improvements on the entailed lands.[13] Although the Earl of Cassillis as party to the loan would be left worse off when he inherited the estate, his father was reluctant to pay his life assurance premiums, which would give him security

when he had to shoulder the burden of debt:

> As to Lord Cassillis's insurance, though it would be a very good thing for him and the estate in after years, I confess that I very much grudge an expenditure of over £400 a year under present circumstances when it is almost impossible with the greatest economy and keeping down estate expenses to make both ends meet.[14]

Lying behind this retort was no doubt the fact that, as a consequence of this further financial review, the Marquess's personal expenditure would no longer be charged against the estate but met from his own resources. As part of the economy drive the fire grates throughout the castle were all replaced and reduced in size with new tile surrounds.[15] Having decided to sell Charles Street or let it again, the family still needed a London home and in May 1895 the estate brought No. 65 Lancaster Gate and some of its contents.[16] With Charles Street let furnished to the stockbroker Panmure Gordon, most of the furniture had to be sent down from Culzean or Cassillis which was empty as Lord David had left.[17] For the rest of the decade the family spent the spring in London before leaving for Sweden.

There was real social distinction in the mode of travel between Scotland and London. The family and the governess went by sleeper while the staff had to go overnight sitting up.[18] With the family away for so long the staff at Culzean was much reduced. The housekeeper was given notice and Mrs Cameron, the cook, took over her duties with just a young maid to help her clean. This proved a disaster as neither she nor the maid had any idea of how to care for the antique furniture and furnishings. The factor advised that an 'an elderly experienced housekeeper' should be recruited.[19] The family were in residence at Culzean in December 1894 when the Ayrshire coast was struck by a violent storm which did an enormous amount of damage on the estate. The laundry was inundated by the tide and the roofs ripped off many farm-houses. The bowling green on the Fountain Lawn was flooded and had to be drained. The roadway from the gasworks to Swallow Craig was swept away in places and the launching slip between the laundry and the boathouse was covered in debris.[20] The gamekeeper's house on Ailsa Craig was almost completely demolished and the lighthouse itself badly damaged.[21]

In January 1895 the Marchioness gave birth to her first son Hugh at 12 Charles Street. The arrival of this second family seems to have eased the estrangement between the Marquess and the children of his first marriage. The Earl of Cassillis and his younger brothers began to visit Culzean again. They enjoyed sailing with their father in the little six-ton yacht *Canty Queen*, built for him by Adams of Gourock in 1894. They delighted in the fishing and shooting at Craiglure which was enlarged and made more comfortable and to make up for the lack of grouse, wild duck and pheasants began to be reared in large numbers.[22, 23] The Marquess also shared in his eldest son's interest in history, becoming a friendly critic of the Galloway historical novelist, S.R. Crockett, whose books, such as *The Gray Man*, made reference to the Kennedys and their estates.[24]

After the departure of Miss Schmitz, Lady Aline became close to her stepmother. In the summer of 1897 they went together to Castle Grant and attended the Western Race Meeting at Ayr. Thereafter they were often in each other's company until Lady Aline's marriage in December 1901 to Francis Browne, later 5th Baron Kilmaine. Queen Victoria had died at Osborne House on the Isle of Wight in January of that year and the Marquess had been on board the Parliament steamer to view the procession on the Solent and later with his wife in the peers' stalls at St James's Palace.[25]

Relations between the Earl of Cassillis and his father improved markedly after the Earl was taken seriously ill with typhoid on a visit to the West Indies and North America in the summer of 1898.[26] Thomas Smith junior, the son of the Culzean factor, was sent to New York to bring him home when he was well enough.[27] On his return the Earl, who had been given the lease of a house in Kirkoswald in 1893 to enable him to vote, began to make regular use of it.[28] While in Ayrshire he took an active interest in Unionist politics and in the local masonic lodges. Early in 1900, now a major in the Royal Scots Fusiliers, he volunteered to fight in South Africa with the regiment, taking with him as his batman, David Doig, the hall porter at Culzean.[29] He fought with distinction as an intelligence officer in the campaign, winning two medals and five clasps. Seriously wounded he returned home late in 1902.

The Earl's younger brothers had likewise to fend for themselves. Lord Charles also served in South Africa, as a captain with the Prince of Wales Light Horse, but was sent home after only a few months' service because of repeated attacks of dysentery. In March 1903 he left for America to work on a ranch in Wyoming belonging to Archibald Murray.[30]

While the brothers were away on active service, their grandfather, Lord Blantyre, died and as his son the Master of Blantyre had predeceased him the estate was divided amongst the children of his three daughters, including the Earl of Cassillis and his brothers and sister. These legacies gave them a modest income and made them less dependent on their father. Because the Master had acted as a second father to the Earl, Lord Blantyre left him his desk and his claymores which hung in his dining room at Balmacara (now another National Trust for Scotland property), along with pictures from the Blantyres's home in Glen Elg.[31]

These were years of remarkable stability on the estate with the rental almost static at about £28,000 and no accumulation of arrears but at the price of increased expenditure on improvements and repairs. This was in sharp contrast to the estates of the Earl of Galloway to the south where rental income fell by 24 per cent between 1878 and 1900 and whose arrears totalled a staggering 53 per cent of his income[32] The Culzean estate was fortu-

nate in having good access to the railway network, which allowed tenants to send fresh milk to market in Glasgow and the other towns in the Clyde valley rather than make butter and cheese. Carrick's dependency on milk was neatly summoned up in the children's rhyme:

> Kyle for a man,
> Carrick for a coo
> Cunninghams for butter and cheese
> And 'Gallowa for 'oo'.*[33]

The very fertile land in the coastal part of the estate, warmed by the Gulf Stream, was ideal for growing new potatoes (usually the Epicure variety), which commanded a premium price.[34] The pioneering farms, such as Balchriston, Greenan and Morriston, were nearly all on the Culzean estate. The insulation of much of Ayrshire from the effects of the agricultural depression was

*wool.

confirmed by John Hannah, the successful tenant farmer at Girvan Mains, who when asked by the Royal Commission on Agriculture, 'Is there any depression in your part at all?' responded tersely 'Not much.'[35]

Nevertheless, expenditure at Culzean continued to be consistently greater than income. In 1895 the overrun was £3,512 and in 1899 £5,988.[36] The remittances to E.A. & F. Hunter & Co., the Edinburgh agents or commissioners as they now called themselves, were about £11,000 a year out of which the Marquess had to find a pension of £3,000 a year for his widowed mother and to meet his personal expenses such as the construction of Skottland Jagt-Hus and the costs of his pleasure boats. His partnership in the Ailsa Shipbuilding Company brought only scant relief, allowing him to withdraw between £255 and £1,474 a year.[37] The biggest headache for the factor continued to be expenditure on the household, garden and policies, which were beyond his

A letter written by the Marquess from Le Grand Hotel Guichard in Pau where he and his wife had gone for the good of their health and their bank balance telling the factor that as he had become an ethusiastic golfer he wished to become a playing member of Prestwick Golf Club.

control. After the Marquess's second marriage and the coming of age of the Earl of Cassillis in 1893, the household and family expenditure climbed to well over £5,000.[38] One remarkable economy was Lord Ailsa's enthusiasm for 'safety' bicycling instead of using horses and traps. A bicycle court was fitted up behind the castle and his lordship was often to be seen cycling to and from meetings both in Ayrshire and, more improbably, in London.[39] He was briefly a supporter of the Road & Path Cycling Association.[40] He fell off in May 1895 after skidding on a 'freshly watered' road in London and was laid up for a fortnight with a badly sprained ankle.[41]

On the whole David Murray, the gardener, managed prudently but when he wanted something he got it. For example, in 1894 the cucumber and melon houses were replaced and the Lower Conservatory put in good order and in 1902 the heating in the vineries and pine stove was renewed.[42] Alive to the financial difficulties, he became depressed and took to the bottle.[43] There was no problem with the large game establishment, which still comprised eleven keepers and three rabbit killers and cost well over £1,000 a year, as it paid for itself. The rent from the shootings and the fishing brought in more than the whole of this outlay and the sale of game to Manchester and Glasgow butchers yielded between £300 and £500 a year. However a good deal of the shooting around the castle was kept in hand and little used. In 1899 under pressure from the Edinburgh agents the Marquess agreed to let them. These and other economy measures were designed to help reduce the debt owing to the agents, which by then stood at £40,000. Some £16,000 was raised by 1902, leaving a further £24,000 to be found.[44]

A time-honoured way for the landed elite to save money was to reside abroad for at least part of the year. In this tradition the Ailsas took up residence in Le Grand Hotel Guichard in Pau, a spa town on the French side of the Pyrenees, from February to April 1898, taking their bicycles with them on the train. They had no servants. It was hoped that the mineral waters and mountain air would be good for Lady Ailsa who was expecting her second child. The intention was to save the wages of the servants in London, as, when the family were not in residence, they were paid off with what was termed 'board' wages, in other words one month's wages and the cost of the fare to travel home.[45] The Marquess was soon bored and wrote within a week of his arrival: 'I have been obliged to begin to learn golf at last as there is not much else to do except bicycling. There is a very good well managed golf club here and I am taught by a French professional.'[46] He soon became a member of the club at Plaine de Billère, which had been founded in 1856 largely to meet the needs of British winter visitors. This was the first golf club to be founded in Europe and numbered amongst its first members the improvident Duke of Hamilton.[47] By mid-March the Marquess had become an enthusiast, no doubt to the factor's complete dismay when he learned:

I have taken seriously to the game here, in fact there is not much else to do. I am instructed by a French professional, a really good teacher, and have engaged him on time charter for 3 months in summer & autumn at Culzean when these links are closed on account of the heat to continue my instruction at home when I shall further utilize his services by getting him to lay out the Turnberry links as a private course.[48]

Within a month he had changed his mind and become even more ambitious regardless of the expense:

When you are at Culzean will you take an opportunity of looking at the turf in the deer park and in the field above it and see whether it would take much trouble to establish some decent putting greens in these two fields?

As our golf is quite in its early stage, I think it would probably be better to make a course of 9 holes in one or both of these two fields which would be much more convenient for practice than a course at Turnberry.[49]

All this must have been only too familiar to the factor, ominously reminiscent of the craze for yachting. Whatever his misgivings may have been, he had no choice but to reply in the affirmative in the slender hope that the expense might deter his lordship's enthusiasm. If that was the case he was to be disappointed, as in his next letter Lord Ailsa informed him:

I propose getting a professional from Prestwick or Troon to meet me at the ground at an early date to mark out the course, so that the putting greens may be put into some sort of shape before we return from London …'[50]

On 4 May Charles Hunter, the professional at Prestwick, duly met his lordship at Culzean 'to settle about the putting greens'.[51]

Work on the new course began at once under the supervision of John Campbell from Kirkoswald, and some of the putting greens had been formed by June when Dominique, the professional from Pau, arrived to cut the first holes and 'complete the fitting up of the course'.[52] He was to stay for the summer to provide tuition in return for his board and thirteen guineas.[53] Campbell was employed throughout the autumn and into the summer of 1899 digging out tree roots, filling up hollows, reducing knolls, digging out boulders, cutting and laying turf, erecting iron pillars, standards and stays for the fences, laying water supplies to the greens and coating them with sand. An old railway guards van did duty as a club house and was soon christened by the family the 'Guard's Club'.[54] In October 1898 David Wilson was appointed the first green keeper and a number of horse drawn mowing machines were purchased. Over £800 had been invested in the new course by the end of 1899, not exactly the providence that it had been hoped would result from the holiday in Pau.[55]

Since the new baby, a daughter Marjory, was born on 4 September, the Marquess could get to Sweden for only three weeks that autumn. As much of the winter was unusually to be spent at Culzean, the Marquess's mind turned to curling. Construction of a new curling pond house at Morriston Bank had begun even before the golf course in October 1897 and was completed in the following May. During that summer the existing pond was cleaned and much enlarged and at the same time a new curling pond house was also put up at Sunnyside.[56] If there was a long period of frosty weather the estate staff and tenants could expect to be called away from their duties for days on end. This was not to be, as early in December, the Marquess was taken seriously ill with an infection from which he took some weeks to recover. In the summer of the following year he went down with what was described as rheumatic neuritis, which put an end to his autumn shooting expeditions to Sweden. In any event the owners of the sporting rights in Gunnarvattnet wished to increase the rent to a level which neither Admiral Baird nor the Marquess could afford.[57] This left Lord Ailsa more time for golf, and Dominique was re-engaged for the next summer when he advised on the possible layout of a full size course at Turnberry.[58] This had first been proposed in 1892, but rejected by the Marquess as 'spoiling the only good bare ground' left in the area. The idea had been revived in 1896 when it was proposed to lay out a golf course and build an hotel. Before any approach was made to the estate, a committee was formed to promote the project. By the time negotiations were opened with the factor in 1898, the Marquess was already smitten with the golfing

craze. His tenants, however, had refused to agree terms and the matter had been left 'to lie over meantime'.[59] In April 1898 John Herron, who worked in the estate office, was sent to inspect the Troon Golf Club course where he met William Fernie, their professional golfer and a former open champion. He agreed to become involved in the design and layout of the proposed new course.[60] This was too much for the factor with the debt to E.A. & F. Hunter escalating yet again.

The Marquess had been regularly reminded for some time of the need either to increase the income from the estate or slash expenditure. He now hit on ways of both having his golf course and raising capital and revenue. In November 1892 he had been elected a director of the Glasgow and South Western Railway in succession to the Earl of Glasgow, to represent the interests of the agricultural community.[61] With the passing of the Light Railways Act in 1896, he seized the opportunity of promoting a new branch line off the Ayr to Girvan line, which would run around the coast by way of Dunure, Culzean and Turnberry. Such a line would have the advantage of improving the access of the farms and fishing communities along the shore to markets and, perhaps more importantly, held out the possibility of holiday developments along the coast. The Glasgow & South Western engineers surveyed the course of the proposed line during the summer of 1897 and the following April the board agreed to proceed.[62] The route of the new line was finalised and the way leaves negotiated, principally with the Culzean estate. The contracts were put out to tender late in 1899, but, when in the following spring the lowest price received was £205,000, the directors decided to postpone a decision for a year.[63] During this interval the Marquess proposed to his fellow directors that the Glasgow & South Western Railway should build the first purpose-built golfers' hotel at Turnberry alongside the proposed light railway. For his part he undertook to lay out a new golf course which the railway would be able to rent.

He no doubt had in mind the links courses,

which already jostled each other alongside the line from Glasgow to Ayr directly it touched the coast at Troon. He had converted his non-playing membership of Prestwick into full membership as soon as he got the 'bug'. Glasgow Gailes, opened by the long-established Glasgow Golf Club in 1892, even had its own private station.[64] In 1897 another course was opened at Gailes to the seaward side of the Glasgow club. Known as Western Gailes, it was an immediate success with three hundred members subscribing within two months.[65] The idea was welcomed by the Glasgow & South Western board.[66] In making this suggestion the Marquess was perhaps alive to the greater possibilities for travel afforded by the motor car. He acquired his first car in the autumn of 1900 (registration number SD 1) and a shed had to be built for it at Culzean. He proudly claimed to have the first car in Ayrshire to which Sir Edward Hunter Blair of Blairquhan rejoined that he had the first car which

The Marquess of Ailsa's first motor car with his engineer, Willie Sloan at the wheel.

worked. With the coming of the car there was no longer any need for the New Stables and these were converted into a recreation hall for the staff in 1905.[67]

New tenders were invited for the railway in June 1901, and in August the Glasgow & South Western Railway came to an agreement with the Marquess to build a hotel and championship golf course at Turnberry.[68] For his part the Marquess agreed to lay out the course at his own expense on the understanding that the railway company would lease it at a favourable rent directly the hotel was completed. Work had already begun on this course and any further improvements to the Culzean course were abandoned. Lord Ailsa was, however, reluctant to let it become completely derelict and suggested that the greens might get 'an occasional cut and roll in the meantime'.[69] Andrew Dick, the tenant of Turnberry Warren, had to be compensated for disturbance to his sheep, which were to be

allowed to graze the fairways, and for the loss of the land enclosed to form the teeing and putting greens. The course was formally opened on 30 November 1903, although play had started eighteen months earlier.[70] Within a year there were almost two hundred and fifty members.[71] Lord Ailsa was annoyed to learn that there were lady members amongst the first subscribers:

> I write to say that it will never do to start a mixed club in this way. I never heard of any such arrangement in any golf club I know of. Lady's clubs and lady's courses are always kept separate, and it certainly will not do with a course like the Turnberry Links to start with a mixed club. The usual thing is that ladies wishing to play may do so with their gentlemen friends being members

LEFT
Ladies'
championship, 1921:
Cecil Leitch and
Joyce Wethered,
finalists.

RIGHT
The sumptuous
Turnberry hotel
designed by
James Miller,
which was
built to cater for
golfing visitors.

or in some cases, ladies who have a low handicap are allowed to play round a man's course by themselves on certain days, not being holidays or Saturdays.[72]

The revised tenders for the railway were received in April 1902 and that from Morrison and Mason, the Glasgow contractors, for £201,316 was accepted.[73] The line was to include a halt at Glenside for the use of the estate and the Ailsa family. It was not until March of the following year that approval was given by the board for the building of the hotel at an estimated cost of £50,000 to the sumptuous designs of the Glasgow architect James Miller.[74] As part of these plans and perhaps in response to demand from women players (including his wife), the Marquess persuaded the railway company to lay out a smaller nine hole ladies' golf

course, along with tennis courts, bowling greens and croquet lawns. The railway line and hotel were opened in May 1906. The hotel had one hundred and thirty-one bedrooms and there was every facility for luxurious living. It was so successful that in October the Glasgow & South Western board agreed to a twenty-bedroom extension with an additional two sitting rooms. The following month the railway company recompensed the Marquess for the £2,018 he had invested in the golf course and agreed to lease it from the estate. Meanwhile land had been feued by the estate for holiday homes along the line of railway, particularly at Greenan and Turnberry. Lord Ailsa took advantage of James Miller's presence on the estate to use him to design an extension to Newark Castle for the new tenant Archibald Walker, a wealthy distiller, and to the shooting lodge at Craiglure.[75] Before the arrival of the Walkers, one colourful tenant was the Earl of Lonsdale, who processed to Western Meeting in his legendary yellow coach.[76]

The decision to invest in golf courses coincided with a programme of refurbishment of the park beginning in 1900. Over the next three years the Swan Pond (then known as Culzean Pond) was

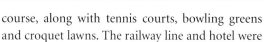

LEFT
A goods train negotiating the Maidens and Dunure Light Railway. The line brought considerable benefit to the Culzean estate but never made money for the railway company.

RIGHT
The new retaining wall and ornamental boat steps at the Swan Pond, built in 1903.

completely cleaned out and the banks repaired. In the autumn of 1900 stepping stones to the island were installed and the following year new water pipes and filters were fitted and new foundations laid for the boat house.[77] The island was enlarged in 1902 and 1903 and a new retaining wall built.[78] At the same time rockeries were built in the walled garden and beside Swinston pond and the following year a wooden bridge erected across the pond.[79] In a December gale in 1902 the boat house at the Swan Pond was blown into the water and had to be fished out by the Ailsa Shipbuilding Co.[80]

While all this work was going on, masses of bulbs, trees and new shrubs, particularly rhododendrons, were planted each year throughout the policies. A pinetum was created in 1902 between Happy Valley and Swinston Avenue, perhaps as a reminder of Scandinavian holidays.[81] Although a variety of unusual conifers was planted, great care was taken to preserve the character of the deciduous woodland by collecting seed, particularly of the planes, to grow new trees. Wire netting fences were put up to keep the rabbits off the young plants. Visiting Culzean in 1903, Sir Herbert Maxwell, who owned Monreith in Wigtownshire,

commented on the beauty of the gardens: 'The terraces are rich with those flowers and shrubs which revel in the moist warmth of the west coast and the walls are thickly clothed with myrtles, camellias, lemon verbena, fuschias, and escallonias.'[82]

The Marquess thought he could afford these improvements because with the death of his mother in January 1899, he no longer had to find £3,000 a year to support her. She was buried beside her husband in the mausoleum at Culzean, which she had visited only very occasionally during the last thirty years. Lord Ailsa's assumptions were in fact wrong as Hugh Lennox of E.F. & A. Hunter, the Edinburgh commissioners, explained to him in March 1902:

> Of course our Account has not got the benefit of the cessation of Lady Ailsa's Annuity & the Charles Street rent charge. These amounted to £3,900 yearly but during the three years since Lady Ailsa's death Mr Smith's remittances on account of the rents have *never* been less than £2,000 yearly short of what they were previously; while in addition we have had to pay £1,000 yearly for the new rent charge & £600 yearly for the

LEFT
The rockery in the walled garden as it is today.

RIGHT
Julia, Lady Ailsa, photographed at Lovel Hill towards the end of her life.

death duty on Lady Ailsa's Annuity. These practically wipe out the £3,900.

> The remittances on account of rents are I am afraid going to be still further shortened as the January remittance was only £4,000. Formerly that half years remittance was never less than £6,000.[83]

The Marquess was deeply depressed by this intelligence: 'The worst feature of the difficulty is the constant shrinking of income as fast as fresh economies are decided on.'[84] Privately Lennox let the factor, Thomas Smith, have a note of the debts over the estate which now totalled over £120,000. The factor replied that he was 'going into the expenditure on the estate and also on the establishment at Culzean with a view of leaving both reduced to a minimum'.[85]

The biggest drain on resources was the huge cost of running Culzean, particularly in the winter months. In an effort to reduce expenditure the gasworks had been converted to acetylene in the summer of 1901 with equipment supplied by the Bon Accord Acetylene Gas Company of Aberdeen.[86] During that year it had been decided to retreat to London with all provisions being sent from the home farm and garden at Culzean. Because she reg-

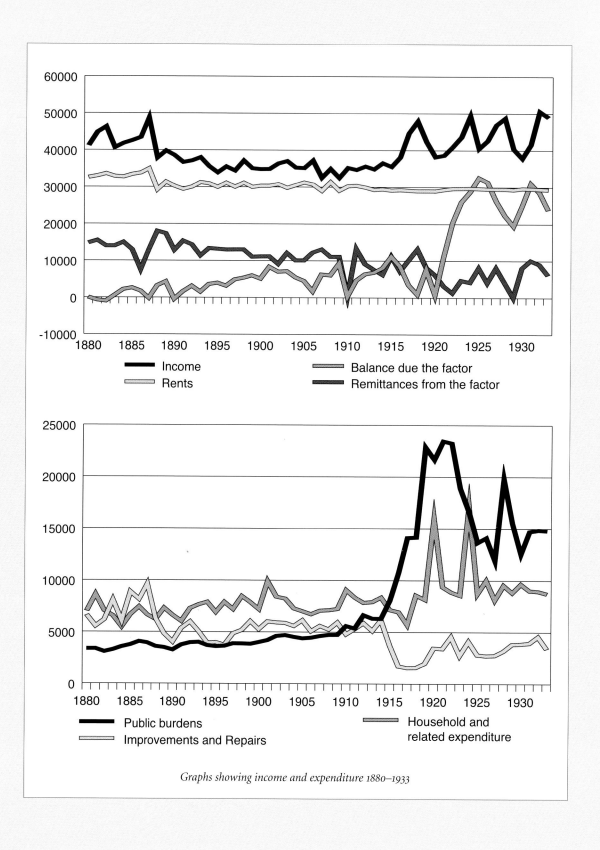

Graphs showing income and expenditure 1880–1933

ularly overspent the budget, oversight of household expenditure was transferred to the factor from the Marchioness who was required to submit regular returns of all her expenditure to the estate office.[87] The family had gone south in late November and remained in London until the beginning of August 1902, but made regular short visits to Scotland.[88] In March the Marquess noted: 'As the move has been made to London and if the railway definitely goes on it would not be so difficult to shut the place up for a bit.'[89] He confided in his wife that he could see 'no way of meeting and overcoming the difficulty'. She was quick to realise 'things must be in a bad way that they have been brought up again – Do let us face it and get honourably clear. Is it to be done? And how?'[90] Lord Ailsa made a small contribution to economy by deciding in April not to hire a second coachman as the head coachman could get along well enough with the aid of two grooms.[91] The factor had no doubt that such a reduction in expenditure would not of itself produce a sufficient surplus to reduce the debts.

By mid-April Hugh Lennox and Thomas Smith had completed their review of the financial position of the estates. They could offer no simple solution such as the reduction of interest rates. The only course of action they could propose to cut the high cost of unsecured borrowings was to dispose of the Charles Street house and even other parts of the estate. The alternative to selling agricultural land was to borrow more against the security of the entailed estate with the agreement of Lord Cassillis as heir of entail.[92] Charles Street was put on the market for £25,000 and sold to become along with the adjoining property at No. 13, the Junior United Services Club. The best furniture was sent to Culzean in March 1903. The extending dining room table was put in the dining room, a large easy chair in the library and the two large mirrors (originally from Culzean) in the Long Drawing Room.[93] When the family were in Ayrshire during that year, they spent much of the

Graphs showing the income and expenditure on the estate from 1880-1933. Since a complete set of the Marquess's private accounts with his Edinburgh agents do not survive, it is impossible to provide a graph of interest payments.

summer and autumn at Craiglure which was cheap to run. Despite the financial problems Lady Ailsa hankered after more commodious accommodation: 'If his Lordship does not see his way to building another lodge as we talked of some time ago, it would be well to make the present one more finished.' As a result further expensive additions and alterations were undertaken to make the house more comfortable. In 1909 a gas plant and central heating were installed and new stables built, ostensibly to make it easier to let to shooting tenants but also for the comfort of the family.[94] The Culzean shootings, which were let to a syndicate, were put on a more business-like footing with the tenants agreeing to put down over five thousand pheasant and two thousand duck eggs to hatch out.[95] In July and August 1903 Lord Ailsa went to Ireland with his gardener David Murray to look at property which might be rented cheaply if Culzean were to be abandoned or possibly converted into an hotel.[96]

His eldest son the Earl of Cassillis married in April of that year Frances Emily, the third daughter of Sir Mark MacTaggart-Stewart of Ardwell in Wigtownshire, a member of parliament and a barrister. She brought with her considerable means inherited from her mother, who had died the year before and had been the heiress of Sir John MacTaggart of Ardwell. A condition of the marriage was that her husband's income from the estate should be increased. The Marquess was reluctant and Hugh Lennox confirmed that it could not be done 'without incurring debt and cutting down his lordship's already diminished income'. The Earl's stepmother intervened and insisted 'sacrifices ought to be made'.[97] Thomas Smith, the factor, was only too willing to be helpful by selling some standing timber, but advised: 'It must be regarded – meantime – as a Cabinet secret, his Lordship as Prime Minister.'[98]

On the day of the wedding a twelve-gun salute was fired from the battery at Culzean. Lord Ailsa

considered it unlucky to fire the thirteen guns stationed there.[99] The Earl and his new countess were deeply in love with each other and remained close friends for the rest of his life. Much of their honeymoon was to be spent at Craiglure, and they took all their provisions with them including a house cow for milk.[100] Thomas Smith, the factor, could not understand why they should wish to go there: 'I fear it will be rather tiresome for them there all alone, notwithstanding the picturesque country and lovely views from the hilltops.'[101] They spent their time fishing and walking. On one Sunday they climbed Kirriereoch and the Merrick, but lost their way on Craig Neldricken, trying to find the Dungeon. Contrary to the factor's prediction, they were enthralled by Craiglure and returned with friends year after year.

His wife's wealth and a modest allowance from his father meant he no longer needed to prac-

ABOVE
The mirrors in the picture gallery or long drawing room which came from the London house.

OPPOSITE
'Baldie', the 4th Marquess of Ailsa, as a young man, painted by W. E. Miller. He delighted in his Scottish origins and learned Gaelic to help him understand the early history of south-west Scotland.

tise at the bar very much. He continued to devote a good deal of his time to Unionist politics and the masonic lodges, becoming provincial grand master for Ayrshire in 1905 and in 1913 first grand principal of the Supreme Grand Royal Arch Chapter of Scotland. This branch of freemasonry had its origins in France in the early eighteenth century. The Earl regarded freemasonry 'as the leading social form in which wide association among men was responsible and yet free, enabling people of goodwill and varied experience, irrespective of nation, class or faction, creed or station to meet and understand each other'.[102] Suiting his actions to his words, he was an indefatigable traveller to all corners of the world to visit lodges. The Earl acted as chairman of the Scotland's Day Celebration at the Scottish National Exhibition on 24 June 1908, the anniversary of Bannockburn. His speech had a strong nationalist

flavour.[103] Nevertheless, he and his wife lived most of the year in Mayfair and divided their time when in Scotland between Galloway visiting Lady Cassillis's father and Castle Grant where Lord Cassillis was much involved in helping Lady Seafield manage the estates, particularly the sporting activities.

He was a keen shot and an enthusiastic fisherman. He regularly played host to the king and the Prince of Wales when they were staying at Tulchan Lodge outside Grantown.[104] After their marriage Lady Cassillis quickly came to share her husband's enthusiasm for the history of Strathspey. In return he became interested in the Stewartry of Galloway and learned Gaelic so as to pursue this interest. They collaborated in researching the antecedents of the Cassillis family, particularly in the preparation of the family's entry in the new edition of Douglas's peerage of Scotland.[105] With their love of Craiglure, it was at their behest that Loch Doon Castle was put into good repair in the summer of 1911. During that year the Earl published for his aunt the Countess of Seafield, with whom he

LEFT
Fishing at Loch Bradon in the hills above Craiglure.

RIGHT
Loch Doon castle on its original island site. It was restored by the Earl of Cassillis just before the First World War. His father, the 3rd Marquess of Ailsa, provided a diver to assist with the archaeological investigation.

OPPOSITE
The bronze bust of King Charles I left to the Earl of Cassillis by his great aunt the Countess of Seafield. It can now be seen in the armoury at Culzean.

still stayed regularly, *The Rulers of Strathspey – A History of the Lairds of Grant and the Earls of Seafield*.[106] She died that October, leaving her estates to her great nephew and making substantial legacies to members of her own family. The Earl of Cassillis, who was a trustee, and his wife were left £4,000 along with contents of the Kneller dining room at Cullen and a bronze of Charles I, now in the armoury at Culzean.[107] His brothers received substantial legacies and his sister, Lady Kilmaine, a good deal of the contents of Cullen House. Lady Seafield left a beautiful bust of Proser-pine on a marble column to her cousin Emily Stuart of Eaglescairne in East Lothian. On her death it passed to the Earl of Cassillis and is now at Culzean.[108] In the winter of 1911 Lord and Lady Cassillis travelled to India to be present at the great coronation Durbar of their friend King George V. The Earl reported to the factor:

The Durbar itself was a splendid sight, so was the Review of 50,000 troops & the Garden Party at the Palace at the fort of Delhi. The King &

Queen with their crowns & robes on sat on the ramparts & were acclaimed by the multitude.[109]

The Marquess and his family had already gone south when the 'crisis', as the factor called it, struck in April 1904.[110] The exact cause of the crisis is unclear but it seems likely that it was associated with the renewal of the rent charges and concerns expressed by Lord Cassillis and Lord Charles about the financial management of the estate. In the circumstances there could be no abatement of rents as was happening on other estates. The factor explained:

> 'No doubt there will be plenty of grumbling and complaints on account of the bad season and damage to crops kept in the fields after being cut, but many of our tenants had no great cause or indeed any to complain – I consider all are moderately rented – and if the Proprietor is expected to be a partner and share the losses in a bad year or slackness of management – it is a very one-sided arrangement – heads you win – tails I lose.[111]

He made it plain to Lady Ailsa, however, that she had to bear some responsibility for the financial problems. She replied to him from London:

> It will be a great satisfaction to me if this difficult time can be tided over successfully. The difficulty is to get the servants to recognise how much they may help if they will only work intelligently.[112]

Her response was that Culzean should be 'shut up during the summer when she would take the children to some bracing place in England'.[113]

For the first time since her marriage Lady Ailsa had to take a genuine interest in the management of the household. Since she had relinquished keeping the accounts three years before, there had been problems. The butler had absconded with cash and been prosecuted. Her first reaction was

> how much keeping the establishment just going absorbs the income – one wants to get the right proportion over all. Personally I am glad to have this opportunity to try to get a better idea of how things stand for I wish to do all I can to help.[114]

She was suddenly full of practical advice. She suggested that in shutting up Culzean:

> As to putting away of china – I wonder if it would not be almost better to leave it in the rooms as there would be a great difficulty in getting it out again. The best way to mark it is to get gum labels like shops have for prices and stick on each piece.[115]

She also queried:

> whether we need have any vegetables from Culzean – certainly having them has been a help for vegetables are very expensive in London but the point is whether the carriage does not exceed the cost of what the vegetables would cost here.[116]

The family left London in late June to take up residence at Hooton Levett Hall not far from Rotherham in Yorkshire where they lived very modestly until November.[117] Provisions continued to be dispatched by rail from Culzean, occasionally giving rise to complaints:

> It is difficult about the butter from Culzean – within the last fortnight it has

tasted very strongly of turnip. It is so strong that it is not good for cooking – when it is like that it is necessary to supplement it with other butter so no saving is effected.[118]

Nevertheless Lady Ailsa and her children enjoyed their time at Hooton Levett:

> even if the move has not effected the economy one would wish it has been a time of valuable influence for the children for they have lived more simply than it is possible to do at Culzean – and the best thing for the future generation is to strengthen it, not weaken it.[119]

They returned to London in mid-November and remained there until the first week of June 1905 when Culzean was opened up once more. Despite Lady Ailsa's pessimism about the lack of improvement in the family's financial situation, costs had been contained. The management of the household was now placed under her direct supervision rather than that of the butler. She was given an allowance of £1,800 to cover all the outgoings (including provisions from the estate) for which she had to account directly to the factor rather than her husband. The staff was reduced. Culzean was to remain shut up from December to June with the family in London and if the Marquess or Marchioness was in Ayrshire they were to put up at the new hotel in Turnberry.[120] Lady Ailsa's attempts at domestic economy were not always successful and she often over-ran her budget.[121] She hired a cook who indulged in expensive recipes and she found it hard to prevent the servants from drinking and gambling.[122] With domestic arrangements on a firmer footing David Murray, the gardener, was given permission to renew and extend the peach house and build a new tomato house over the winter of 1906. The new peach house was supplied by Mackenzie & Moncur of Edinburgh. Over the same period the gateway into the walled garden

facing directly down the avenue was rebuilt and reduced in width and the pond near the gardens enlarged.[123]

Throughout these years the Ailsa Shipbuilding Company, which was converted into a limited company in 1901, traded profitably. The Marquess originally held 13,000 £1 shares but by 1906 his investment had increased as a result of rights issues to almost £20,000 paid for out of profits. In addition he was earning between £1,000 and £2,000 a year in dividends over and above his director's fees.[124] Out of these earnings he commissioned the yard in 1906 to build him a very modest motor sailing cruiser to his own designs, the *Red Riding Hood*. Rigged as a lugger, she was just eight tons and thirty-six feet in length with no cabin. He took her to Cowes in her first season and true to his youthful form came second in the motor cruiser class, even though he doubted

King George V and Queen Mary in their coronation robes at the Delhi Durbar in 1911, which was attended by the Earl and Countess of Cassillis.

she could be 'classed as a cruiser without a cabin'.[125] In the spring of the following year he bought the forty-ton steam yacht *Parole*, which was lying at Dartmouth and about to be scrapped. After patching her up, he sailed her north in late June encountering bad weather and being forced to spend 'five days at anchor in various ports'.[126] He reported his progress daily by wire to his wife in London to allay her fears. She was relieved when on 5 July the *Parole* arrived at Crinan, telling the factor: 'His Lordship wired to me today from Crinan Pier, reporting thick fog and bad weather. The thought of the Canal is soothing to my anxiety.'[127] During the summer the *Parole* was lost, but Lord Ailsa noticed in a newspaper that his old yacht *Bloodhound* was about to be scrapped by her owner Thomas Dunlop, a Glasgow shipowner, despite the fact he had won forty-five races in her in the previous five seasons.[128] Nothing could

prevent the Marquess from buying her back. With customary zeal and lack of regard for expense, the Marquess began to restore and refit his old friend, now rechristened *Bloodhound*. His first inclination was to use her for cruising as this verse from a ditty he composed with apologies to Rudyard Kipling suggests:

> But our Bloodhound's done for racing now that others take her place,
> Her name still stands on the Yacht List, may it stand a little space
> For she's now set free for cruising to watch others sail the main
> Free of all the seas can give her, save to sail her mates again.[129]

However the temptation to race was too great and her rigging was altered and hollow spars fitted to improve her speed. He sailed south with her in late June 1908, taking five days to reach Cowes.[130]

TOP LEFT
The new entrance to the walled garden at Culzean built in 1908.

TOP RIGHT
The steam yacht Parole *which the 3rd Marquess purchased in 1907.*

OPPOSITE
The summerhouse at the end of the battery built in 1908. The flagpole, which was in the centre, has long since disappeared.

The *Bloodhound* sank at her moorings early in July and was soon raised with not 'much damage beyond sails and fittings spoilt with mud and water'.[131] She was ready to begin racing by the time the family took up residence at Oaklawn, a villa in Wootton on the Isle of Wight, in mid July for the whole summer. She 'began well by winning her first race at Ostend' with Lord Angus at the helm and again the following day.[132] In strong winds she enjoyed an advantage as she could carry much more sail than more modern boats, but in light airs she did not stand a chance.[133] Unfortunately during the Royal Yacht Squadron's regatta, the *Bloodhound* was run down near the Victoria pier and sunk, much to the Marquess's disappointment: 'it was really sickening to lose her in such a stupid way after all the trouble and thought expended in bringing the old ship up-to-date.'[134] However he was touched by 'the genuine sympathy and warm feeling' from the yachting fraternity.[135] She was raised a week later and

repaired at the expense of the underwriters by Whites of Southampton. The Marquess had already decided prophetically that:

> if she is worth repairing … I shall take the opportunity of putting a more modern bow on her at the expense of the other fellow, which is all she wants to make her go a lot faster yet. If this plan comes off she will lead her competitors a dog's life of it yet.[136]

As a thank you to the Royal Yacht Squadron he presented the library with an album of photographs of the *Bloodhound* and a large framed photograph entitled 'Last of the Fighting Forties'.

The Marquess was more determined than ever to defy those who believed that such a veteran yacht could not compete even with a handicap against the latest vessels. In defiant mood, he added more verses to his ditty, beginning with her past glories:

> Oh gallant was our 'forty' from her brazen rudder head

LEFT

The motor cruiser Red Riding Hood, *the steam yacht* Parole, *and the yacht,* Bloodhound, *in the harbour at Tronn in 1908.*

RIGHT

Bloodhound *under tow after being raised following her collision with L'Esperance in 1908.*

> To her fighting flag a chevron and her keel of solid lead
> She looked every inch a lady when we sailed her for the line
> And no 'forty' on the water the *Bloodhound* could outshine.

And ending with the promise of the future:

> May be that Fate will give us luck once more to cross the line
> Win some poor race on handicap, as ne'er in days Lang Syne:
> But today we mourn the forties, their palmy days long past,
> And the tough old shells, who sailed them going to find their rest at last.[137]

Even his wife became enthusiastic, racing with him for the first time in the Clyde Regatta in June 1909. She wrote: 'There was a firm breeze and it was real sailing – I enjoyed it thoroughly.'[138] At the Royal Cornwall Yacht Club regatta, there was only one entry for the Prince of Wales Cup for fifteen-metre yachts, the *Mariska*, belonging to A.K. Stothert and sailed by Lord Angus Kennedy, the Marquess's son. Like the *Bloodhound*, she had been built by Fifes of Fairlie but was only a year old. His father entered the *Bloodhound* to make a race of it and won.[139] Despite her new bow, she still did not do well in light winds. At Cowes that year she won her first race on the Monday 'when it blew fresh', but for the rest of the week the weather was 'too fine … for our old lady to travel her best'.[140] By the middle of August the weather had become more unsettled and *Bloodhound* began a winning streak which was to last to the outbreak of war. Between 1909 and 1914 she won one hundred and forty-two prizes of which sixty-four were firsts. In her last season before the war out of thirty starts she secured nineteen firsts. To compete at this level a new set of sails was required every year. Brook Heckstall-Smith, a noted yachtsman, dubbed this achievement 'one of the most peculiar and interesting circumstances in yachting history'.[141] Just prior to the outbreak of war Lord Ailsa commissioned White Bros, the yacht builders at Southampton, to carry out a further extensive refit including new sails, mast and spars and rigging.[142] Her old mast and tiller were presented to the Royal Yacht Squadron where the mast still serves as the squadron's flag pole.[143] Despite the war the Marquess sailed her in the 1915 season but thereafter she was laid up in the Solent under the care of Captain Diaper and cleaned and varnished every year.[144]

Sailing was almost certainly a welcome distraction from the mounting problems of the estate and kept the family away from Culzean for much of the summer from 1909 until 1914. No longer did they take coach and horses with them but instead a motor landaulet and a chauffeur.[145] In common with other estates, the biggest factor contributing to a decline in income was unpaid rents as tenant farmers found it increasingly difficult to make ends meet in the face of foreign competition. By 1914 arrears in rent were averaging about £3,000 a year. The other problem over which the family had no control was a sharp rise in taxation following the

election of the Liberal government in 1905 with a mandate for social reform and improved education. 'Public and parochial burdens' had been paid from time immemorial by Scottish landowners to support the salaries of ministers of the Church of Scotland and schoolmasters and to meet the cost of poor relief. They were now confronted with new taxes imposed by the Liberal government as a deliberate attack on the great estates. The Earl of Cassillis, as a Unionist, played an active part in the formation in 1906 of the Scottish Land and Property Federation, and in 1908 joined the Ayrshire Agricultural Defence Association. The objectives of both these bodies were to defend the landowners against the attacks from the Liberal government, which became punitive with the introduction of land taxes in Lloyd George's 1909 People's Budget.[146] Cassillis commented:

> Any one at all interested in Land should use every endeavour to oppose these proposed new Land Taxes, & to show the people that the labourers, tradesmen etc. are just as much interested in the question as the landlord or large farmer.

He was critical of the Ayrshire Association for its failure to mobilise support in the county:

> It is quite time that the Peers should throw out the proposed Land Taxes, but to enable them to do this, they will require the support of strong expressions of disapproval of this measure from the community[147]

After the House of Lords rejected the budget, as he had hoped, Cassillis played an active part in the ensuing election campaign both in support of his father-in-law, Sir Mark MacTaggart-Stewart in Kirkcudbrightshire, and the candidate in South Ayrshire. Although Sir Mark won the seat he had lost in the Liberal landslide of 1906, the Unionists failed to regain South Ayrshire.[148] Despite losing

LEFT
Bloodhound *gybbing in the Royal Irish Regatta off Kingston in 1909.*

RIGHT
The grand staircase in its full Victorian glory in 1908.

one hundred seats to the Unionists, the Liberal government remained in power with the support of the Labour party and the Irish Nationalists and the budget was passed. As a result the burden of taxation on all landed property increased to an unprecedented level. On the Earl of Galloway's estates, the tax burden climbed from 15 per cent of the rental in 1900 to over 20 per cent by 1914 and the same was true at Culzean where it advanced from 13 per cent to 21 per cent.[149, 150] In these circumstances debts began once more to accumulate and there was now no alternative but to sell property. Early in 1907 Doonbank in Alloway was sold to the wealthy Colonel William Baird of Cambusdoon for £19,000.[151] Lady Ailsa also tried to save money by stopping paying a month's 'board wages' when a servant was dismissed.[152]

In the autumn of 1908 a large sale of surplus furniture from Culzean was arranged by Mrs. R.M. Melven from Glasgow through Christies's in London and Dowells in Edinburgh. The Marquess was free to sell these as they were not considered part of the entailed estate. Included in the sales was a large mirror that had previously hung over the fire place in the saloon. The furniture was auctioned at Christies on 26 February 1909 in a general sale. The lots from Culzean were 'a pair of Sheraton mahogany urns, formed as oviform vases and covers, inlaid with fluting, festoons and ribands in satin-wood, on square pedestals'. These did not reach their reserve. A Louis XV library table, with three drawers, of inlaid tulip-wood, mounted with ormolu borders, corner-mounts and handles chased with foliage and scrollwork, made £294. This was almost certainly part of the collection of French furniture from Dunottar, which had been assembled by Alexander Allardyce. A fortnight earlier Mrs Melven had brought in 'a pair of Wedgwood blue ewers, with figures of Muses in relief', which were sold in March, and it is possible that these also

came from Culzean.[153] No details survive of the items sold at Dowells. The proceeds were used to meet the costs of an extensive refurbishment, redecoration and where appropriate refurnishing of the castle. The finest pieces of furniture were repaired and cleaned under the supervision of W. Adams, an Edinburgh antique dealer, who sent the very best items to Mallett & Son's workshops in Bath to be restored. These included a side table and card table by Robert Adam, a Chippendale table, a Sheraton grandfather clock and a claw and ball settee.

The redecorated and refurnished saloon, after restoration in 1911.

When these were returned Mrs Melven made herself responsible for arranging them in the rooms at Culzean and gave advice on redecoration.[154] As a skilled needlewoman and upholsterer, she restored the fabrics and hangings herself and where appropriate commissioned new ones including blue damask curtains for Lady Ailsa's sitting room.[155] The red colour scheme on the walls of the saloon was replaced by green more in keeping with Adam's original design but the ceiling remained white and the surrounds to the doors and shutters primrose.[156]

The refurbishment of the house also included the creation of Adam style marble overmantles in the principal bedrooms and the rebuilding of the chimney pieces in the dining room and first drawing room.[157] Mrs Melven advised on purchases of eighteenth-century furnishings and furniture in a conscious attempt to recreate the Adam interior, which was never of course completed. These included wall brackets sold by the well-known dealer F.W. Phillips of Hitchin, who described himself as an antiquary, in December 1909,[158] and champagne flutes from A. MacCallum, an expert in antique furniture in Ayr, in March 1911.[159]

When the refurbishment was nearing completion the distinguished editor of *Country Life*, Edward Hudson, came to review the results with the idea of publishing an article on the house.[160] At the time he was in the process of restoring Lindisfarne Castle on Holy Island off the Northumberland coast with the help of Edwin Lutyens, Charles Lutyens's son, and Gertrude Jekyll. Although he took photographs away with him, no article appeared in his magazine until 1915.[161] The Marquess assured his son and his wife that the new furniture and furnishings were an investment for their future when they eventually came to live at Culzean.[162]

Despite the financial problems there was still room for further extravagance in the estate expenditure, such as the building of a new summer house beneath the flagstaff at the end of the battery. The Marquess particularly asked for this to be painted a stone colour while the interior was to be sea green.[163] The large old-fashioned walking beam engine which drove the shipyard sawmill at Troon was dismantled and re-erected 'as a curio' at the home farm.[164] Such expenditure contributed to an overdraft of £9,000 on the estate account by the end of 1909 and a debt to the Edinburgh agent of almost £21,000.[165] This was paid off by raising a further rent charge of £36,111 from the Scottish Widows Fund in March 1910, very necessary at a time when the shipyard had been trading at a loss for the previous two years.[166] As a dreadful warning of what might lie in store if expenditure were not controlled, the most lucrative part of the estates of the Earl of Galloway, including Galloway House itself, was sold in the summer of 1908 to a wealthy merchant.[167] Perhaps with this in mind, a very detailed inventory of the contents of Culzean was

made in 1911, which were valued at £50,293, of which the pictures accounted for almost £21,000. The most valuable painting was considered to be of Margaret Erskine of Dun, against which a later hand added 'much over-valued'. The most striking thing about the inventory is the complete absence of any of the 9th Earl's grand tour collections of pictures, statuary or books. These may have been in London, but that would seem unlikely. The library was modest with the exception of technical books about ships and shipbuilding which were mostly of recent purchase.[168]

There was, however, no cutting back on repairs and improvements on the Culzean and Cassillis estates. In 1910 the harness room and part of the stable at Maybole Castle was converted into a drawing office for this purpose.[169] Much of the work was simply routine repair but there was a determined effort to improve the water supply to farms, particularly those engaged in dairying as it was required by sanitary regulation. In addition a new pier and breakwater was built at Maidens at a cost of almost £2,500 from 1913 and 1914.[170] If the estate were to retain their best tenants there was no alternative but to continue to invest as returns made to the Scottish Land and Property Federation in 1909 illustrated. West of Scotland estates of about the same size but with large incomes from coal and other mineral workings could afford to invest much more. Between 1888 and 1905 on the Culzean and Cassillis estates some 14.8 per cent of the total rental was invested in improvements whereas on the coal rich estate of the Earl of Hume at Douglas in Lanarkshire 21.9 per cent of the rental was invested between 1879 and 1908. On the Duke of Hamilton's Hamilton estate 14.69 per cent was invested over the same period despite that family's serious financial problems. Smaller agricultural estates simply could not afford to compete. The Fergussons at Kilkerran invested less than 1 per cent of their rental between 1899 and 1908.[171] Thomas Smith, who had been factor for thirty years, died in 1910 following an accident and was succeeded by his son, Thomas Smith junior, who had been standing in for his father during his last illness. The obituary in the *Factors' Magazine* commented perceptively:

> He was a man of sound judgement, of warm heart, and a kindly nature. His work on the estates demanded energies of no common order, but Mr Smith was equal to every call. His public work alone would have taxed the resources of many men, but in all that he did Mr Smith was always found to be giving of his best.[172]

This was an understatement of Thomas Smith's commitment to the management and survival of the estate in what were very difficult times. Although relatively well off and respected in the community, if he had chosen any other career at the time with his business acumen he would have died a rich man.

The Marquess became an enthusiastic aboriculturist, planting waste ground around Culzean with conifers and also some of the unproductive ground in the Carrick hills. Many of the upland farms were no longer viable, as a letter from Maggie Barker, the wife of the tenant of Glastron on the hill road from Dalvennan Bridge to Dalrymple, graphically described:

> we have lost all our money in this farm … I said to my brother who died lately we were loosing (sic) money & should give it up he said no, he would help us, – as it would break his heart not to come back to the old homestead where he was born.[173]

A new tree nursery was formed in 1907 beside Glenside Lodge.[174] Many of the trees were unusual species grown from seed in the nursery or purchased from well-known growers such as W. & J. Samson of Kilmarnock, who had been supplying the estate for over one hundred and fifty years,

Benjamin Reid of Aberdeen, Peter Scott of Knittlesheim, J. Heins & Sons of Halstenbeck, and Conrad Appel in Darmstadt.[175] Plantations of Sitka spruce and Douglas firs were established on Mochrum Hill. There was a tax advantage in planting trees as plantations were exempt from death duties.

As a result of all these various pressures, remittances to the commissioners in Edinburgh fell to just over £6,000 in 1914 by which time the estate was in fact running at a loss before allowing for rent and interest charges. In the face of these difficulties the Marquess could call on dividends from his shipbuilding business, which had returned to profit in 1911, but these were scarcely sufficient to cover the deficit.[176] Despite the 1904 crisis, almost no progress had been made in reducing expenditure on the household or the gardens and the fact that it seems to have been difficult to retain staff suggests the family was struggling. After the dismissal of the butler in 1902 for petty theft, none stayed more than for a year or two. Similarly after the dismissal of David Murray, the long-serving gardener, for assaulting his own maid in July 1910, his successor Charles Tate, who came from the Duke of Northumberland's Alnwick gardens, stayed for only two years as the Marquess wanted someone with more knowledge of shrubs.[177] He was followed by Robert G. Hepburn, who joined the army in June 1916.[178] Nevertheless, nothing much changed. The gardener still supervised the collection of ice each winter and its storage, packed in straw, in the ice house. Orders were placed with well-known seedsmen and nurserymen for seeds, plants and bulbs even though for much of the summer the family were not at Culzean to enjoy them. Photographs taken around 1911 for the magazine *Country Life* show a well-tended garden immaculately kept with no suggestion that there were any financial constraints.[179] Flowers and vegetables continued to be dispatched by rail to the London house or other places where the family were staying. The game establishment did not experience such a turnover in staff, largely because

Thomas Smith, the factor to the 3rd Marquess of Ailsa.

it remained self-financing. There were still strange extravagances. In 1914 the distinguished architect Sir Robin Lorimer was commissioned to design a new memorial stone for the 11th Countess to be placed in Holyrood Abbey, which was carved at considerable expense by Allan & Sons of Edinburgh.[180]

It is almost impossible to know what the Marquess imagined the future held by the time war was declared in August 1914. He could have had no doubt that Culzean was much too expensive to be supported from his diminishing income. Perhaps he hoped that the agricultural depression would eventually pass and rents rise or perhaps he was already resigned to being the last of the family to own the estate in its then form. He may have wished the suffragettes had evaded the armed keepers and burned down the castle in their campaign the previous summer.[181] Already the Liberal government had massively increased death duties in the 1911 budget, making it hard for great landed estates such as his to be handed on without efficient tax planning.

Immediately on the declaration of war the Earl of Cassillis joined his battalion and sailed with the British Expeditionary Force for France where he was to serve for the next four years. Although a committed Unionist, his political attitude was moving even more in a nationalist direction, calling in 1915 for a measure of home rule. He complained that:

> we have in Scotland, unfortunately, too much reason to complain of extreme niggardliness on the part of the Exchequer with regard to Scotland, and the consequent neglect of her castles, her palaces, and her abbeys.

He pointed to the generous government funding of the Antarctic expeditions of Sir Ernest Shackleton and Captain Scott, and the failure to provide any funds for Dr Bruce (the leader of an entirely Scottish expedition to the Antarctic). He was particularly incensed at the lack of expenditure on

defence and the mean-mindedness which had resulted in James IV's chapel in Stirling Castle being converted into a storeroom. He attacked the inequitable tax burden in Scotland compared to Ireland and rounded on the Scottish radical MP who had written to the *Glasgow Herald*: 'We have a vague idea that, compared with England and Ireland we receive less than justice … The idea is not "vague"; its accuracy has been proved over and over again.'[182] In her husband's absence, Lady Cassillis devoted herself to war work, becoming a member of the executive of the National Union of Women Workers and the Professional Classes War Relief Committee, and vice-president of the Women's Emergency Corps.[183]

One consequence of hostilities was to drive up the price of agricultural produce, bringing relief to the farming community. However the government quickly took measures to control food production and fix prices. A corollary of these measures was that landowners were prevented from benefiting from the increased prosperity of their tenants even

Robert Hepburn, head gardener at Culzean, with his staff just prior to the First World War.

though wartime inflation drove up their own costs. The Corn Production Act of 1917, which guaranteed prices for wheat and oats, expressly forbade landowners from taking advantage of this subsidy by raising rents.[184] In addition the rents of houses were controlled from 1916. Belatedly economy measures were taken at Culzean in 1915, probably prompted by the national emergency rather than any sense of an impending apocalypse. Once again subscriptions were slashed and a more determined effort made to reduce household expenditure. Instead of two chauffeurs and several grooms working in the stables, there were just two chauffeurs who were expected to look after the horses as well as the cars. There were still nine gamekeepers in 1917 even though shooting had more or less stopped. It was not until the crisis on the Western Front of the following year that the number fell to six, with the head keeper George Cassidy at the front. By then arrears had fallen back but the financial position was as parlous as ever due to the enormous rise in taxation to pay for the war effort. By 1918 income tax and public burdens were consuming almost half of the rental income. The only way this could be afforded was by carrying out only limited improvements and repairs. In the first two years of the war Lord and Lady Ailsa spent about half the year in London, thereafter they were mostly at Culzean. There was a good deal to occupy the Marquess in Ayrshire with his shipyard overwhelmed with both naval and merchant contracts.

During the war the west bank of Loch Doon, which was part of the estate, was the site of one of the most publicised contract scandals. Schools of aerial gunnery proved successful in France and in 1916 the War Office decided to build one on Loch Doon largely because the area was sparsely populated and the steep hills on either side could be used to lay rails for launching targets. The only drawback was that the unevenness of the ground made it prohibitively expensive to build an airfield. Eventually it was decided to drain the peat bog beside the Bogton Loch for this purpose. Work was soon delayed. The rough unmetalled estate roads broke up under truckloads of materials. Draining the bog proved much more difficult than anticipated. In April 1917 the well-known contractor Robert McAlpine was called in to take over. By the summer there were 1,400 civilians working on the site and over 1,000 German prisoners of war along with detachments from the Royal Engineers and the Royal Defence Corps. A weir was built at the northern end of the loch to control the water level, and huge tanks constructed in the hills to hold water for general use and for fire fighting. A Blondin aerial ropeway was erected from which men could practice gunnery while being propelled along it in cages. They could fire at huge Telfer targets, a gravity target on rails laid down the hillside, or at railway mounted targets on flat land near the loch side. A seaplane station was built along with a dock for motor boats, and a small village laid out with a cinema to seat four hundred.

In 1918 officials of the newly created Air Ministry, concerned about escalating costs, visited

the site. The commander of the base confessed that the heavy rainfall, a feature of the Carrick hills, rendered the school unusable for at least half the year, and in any event there was nowhere nearby that a plane could safely make a forced landing. As a result work stopped immediately. MPs and peers soon began to ask embarrassing questions about the cost of the project and whether proper engineering advice had been sought. The matter was referred to the Select Committee on National Expenditure, which issued a report on the 'Loch Doon Scandal' in May, naming those responsible.[185] The remains of some of the construction work can still be seen on the shores of the Loch. The estate received no compensation for all the disruption until 1926 when some £1,200 was paid.[186] However the Marquess was compensated in 1922 for the commandeering of Turnberry golf course as an airfield in January 1917 to provide cover for convoys making for the Clyde or Liverpool.[187] Officers at the base rented Ardlochan, which had ceased to be a convalescent home and become a summer residence for the factor, and also the shootings at Turnberry.

Since the Corn Production Act and rent restrictions were to continue after the armistice in 1918, prospects for all estates remained uncertain, and a further round of welfare legislation made any prospect of a reduction in the wartime level of income tax unlikely. The Liberal Party, which remained in power, had long been committed to land reform, particularly though the creation of smallholdings under the Small Landowners (Scotland) Act of 1911.[188] Immediately after the war a scheme was launched for the settlement of ex-servicemen on such holdings, to which the Marquess contributed by providing land in Dalrymple at Burnton, Drumgabs, Laigh Balsarroch and Merkland for eighteen holdings.[189] Despite escalating annual deficits and dwindling remittances, life at Culzean resumed its pre-war tempo largely because the losses on the estate could be offset against healthy dividends from the shipyard. Nevertheless, the Marchioness ran up an overdraft

of £6,000 which the factor had to pay off.[190] Robert Hepburn decided not to return to the gardens and was replaced by A.T. Harrison, who, like his predecessor in the time of the 1st Marquess, was allowed to run them as a market garden taking a 10 per cent commission on all sales.[191] He was soon ordering plants, seeds, bulbs and other supplies.[192] George Cassidy was back at his post as head keeper by February 1919, and by the end of the year had an establishment of thirteen keepers. Although pheasant rearing did not resume until the following year, shooting began again and the income as in the past more than covered the costs.

The well-tended garden at Culzean photographed for Country Life in 1915.

On his discharge from the army the Earl of Cassillis had returned to his legal practice in London where his interest in the Gaelic language and culture took a new turn. He became friendly with Edward Thomas John, the Welsh Liberal MP and activist, who was the driving force behind the formation of the Celtic Congress.[193] He went with him to attend the second meeting of the congress (the first was in 1917) on the Isle of Man in 1921, which he much enjoyed. Afterwards he was pleased to receive a copy of the nationalist journal *Welsh Outlook*, which suggests his political views were moving away from Unionism.[194] The following year he left London for Edinburgh, to live in some splendour at Newhailes on the eastern outskirts of the city.* The house was well known to him, as until her divorce in 1919 it had been the

*Newhailes is now owned by the National Trust for Scotland.

home of his sister-in-law, Lady Margaret, wife of Sir David Dalrymple. After the divorce she and her only son Charles had moved to a newly enlarged house on the Culzean estate at Croy. The cost of this new house and his son's education had bankrupted Sir David and the Newhailes estate was placed in trust until Charles came of age in 1936. As a trustee the Earl of Cassillis no doubt felt his presence was required on the property. As if to confirm the return to normal after the war, the Ailsa's youngest daughter, Lady Marjory, was married to Lawrence Merriam MC on 21 April 1921 in Maybole parish church with a choir and orchestra brought in for the occasion. Additional servants were hired for the week and a pavilion erected on the lawn for a dance.[195] Only the *Bloodhound*, laid up at Southampton, now in the charge of Captain Judd, remained as a reminder of the vanished Edwardian world.[196] She was destroyed in a shipyard fire in 1922. With insurance compensation of almost £3,500, the Marquess ordered a replacement motor lugger from the Ailsa shipyard, the *Fair Maid*.[197]

By the end of 1921, with clear signs that the whole economy was in recession, all was far from well on the estate. In the following March the factor's overdraft with the Union Bank of Scotland reached £28,000, which was £3,000 in excess of the credit limit.[198] On learning that there was little prospect of any immediate improvement, the bank pressed for more stringent economies and additional security for their liability,[199] but refused agricultural land preferring instead the more certain proceeds of life assurance policies and investments. Until this was provided the bank refused to honour the payment of Lord Ailsa's supertax for the current year.[200] In these circumstances the Marquess had no alternative but to agree even if it would inevitably constrain the room for manoeuvre if the going got tougher.[201]

There was every sign that it might. To the south the Earl of Galloway's estates were in their final death struggle and to the north the Earl of Eglinton was known to be in difficulty.[202] This, for the latter, would lead in 1925 to the sale of the con-

tents of the castle and the removal of its roof. The family then went to live at their other Ayrshire home, Skelmorlie Castle, near Largs. The most telling evidence of the end of the great estates in Ayrshire was the rapid growth of owner-occupiers in the inter-war years, which has been dubbed the 'agricultural revolution of the twentieth century'. In 1901 over 87 per cent of the farms in the county were rented and by 1938 less than 50 per cent.[203] In every part of the country alarm bells were ringing. Leader after leader in the *Estates Gazette* proclaimed that England was changing hands. Even the greatest landowners, such as the Dukes of Beaufort, Northumberland and Rutland, were selling huge acreages.[204]

In June 1921, with world commodity prices falling, the government repealed the Corn Production Act along with the whole system of wartime subsidies. This was bitterly dubbed the 'Great Betrayal' by the farming community, which was now faced with unparalleled difficulties. To make matters worse the shipbuilding industry plunged into recession and dividends dried up completely.[205] There was now need for urgent action if the Culzean estate were to survive but this was a forlorn hope. By the autumn of 1923 the bank overdraft stood at over £41,000, £6,000 in excess of a new limit set when the additional security had been provided. By the turn of the year the bond-holders had got wind that something was amiss and were pressing the Edinburgh commissioners for information. On 27 December Hugh Lennox wrote to the factor:

> I noticed you spoke of sending a further £7,000 to the Bank at this time. I hope this means that you are going to send us something. It is badly wanted![206]

Lord Cassillis for the first time was made aware of the seriousness of the situation and advised by both Hugh Lennox and his partner Frank Hunter that the 'only thing is to disentail'. Mindful of the consequences of the disentailing of the Seafield estates,

Lord Cassillis was reluctant to agree despite assurances that 'the rights of myself & my brothers … could be safe-guarded so that the rules of succession are not changed'.[207] Fearful that their step-mother might be left the whole estate, he, his brothers and his sister refused. A further accommodation was reached with the Union Bank during 1924 to raise the credit limit to £45,000 on the understanding that the factor again paid off Lady Ailsa's overdraft on the household account of £8,000 and that in future she maintained a credit balance. To reduce the debt the London house was to be sold and the furniture put into store and further unentailed lands offered to tenants.[208] In common with many other businesses, staff wages were cut and numbers reduced from sixty-two to forty-nine.[209]

At the end of 1924 Norman Hird, the general manager of the Union Bank, reviewed the position and demanded to know why the results for the year showed expenditure so much in excess of budget.[210] When even after the proceeds of the sale of unentailed lands had been credited the overdraft exceeded the limit once again in October 1925, the bank put a stop on further payments.[211] Since it was impossible to refinance these debts through a new charge on the rents, the only thing to do was to cut expenditure and pray that no word of the financial difficulties became public. Lord Ailsa with his wife were to live frugally at Culzean on the produce of the garden and the home farm in much the same way as his father and mother had done in the 1860s. Like them visits to London were now to be spent in a hotel. It does not seem to have occurred to them that the state of their finances should have precluded any such expeditions.

The first garden produce book to survive is that for 1924. Throughout the winter months the castle was supplied with Jerusalem artichokes, parsnips, beetroot, endless Brussels sprouts, celery, carrots, swedes, leeks, kale, broccoli and, of course, cabbage. Water cress became available from mid-February, rhubarb and spinach in late April, the first lettuces in early May and spring cabbages,

potatoes and cucumbers later in the month. Peas were harvested from the beginning of June but broad beans were grown as an autumn crop. Gooseberries and figs were ready by the end of June, strawberries in the first week in July, tomatoes by the middle of the month and peaches at the end. Cauliflower were harvested in quantity in August along with masses of peas. French beans and runner beans were not ready until September and grapes the following month. In November the cycle began again. Interestingly, although they grow well in the west of Scotland and had certainly been grown at Culzean, asparagus and sea kale were no longer on the menu. The gardener was also still responsible for sending hampers of produce and flowers to the family, friends and to charities, particularly in the spring when great quantities of snowdrops, daffodils, early rhododendrons and violets were dispatched all over the county. During that year Lady Ailsa was a lady-in-waiting to James Brown, the high commissioner to the General Assembly who lived outside Ayr, and as a result the Culzean gardens kept Holyrood Palace supplied with flowers throughout his week's residence in mid-May.[212]

In the meantime the Edinburgh commissioners negotiated the transfer of the overdraft to the Edinburgh-based Commercial Bank of Scotland, which allowed further unentailed lands and securities to be sold. Staff in every department were reduced 'to the lowest minimum if these are to be maintained at a minimum efficiency'.[213] With another disastrous attempt at domestic economy, the Marquess and his wife went off to East Africa for the winter of 1926–7 to live with their newly married youngest son Lord Hugh on his farm at Nanyuki.[214] All that happened was that any savings in running Culzean were swallowed up by their increased personal expenditure.

Living at Newhailes, the Earl of Cassillis became a kenspeckle figure in Edinburgh dressed in his kilt, plaid and bonnet. He was a regular attender at the Mod and much involved in the affairs of the Church of Scotland. He and his wife entertained their wide circle of friends at Newhailes including numerous representatives from around the world of the many charitable and religious organisations they were involved with, such as the YMCA, the Church Army and the Masonic Order. Their visitors included Princess Louis Löwenstein-Werthenheim-Brandenberg, General Sir Percy Cox, Air Marshal Lord Trenchard, General Sir Ian Hamilton, Lord and Lady Weir, Princess Alexandrine Cantacuzene of Romania, Princess Helena Victoria, and in 1934 Queen Mary.[215] The Earl spent most of his leisure time with his wife's family in Galloway researching the history of the Gael in the Stewartry. He and his wife continued to travel, usually representing the Royal Arch Chapter. In 1924 they went to the Far East and Australia visiting lodges in Manila, Hong Kong, Shanghai and Australia and New Zealand and in 1926–7 travelled to the United States and Canada. While in North America in January 1927 they made a family visit to his father's sister Lady Constance Fawkes, who lived in a house named Culzean on Mayne Island in British Columbia.[216] Throughout the English-speaking world he 'considered this Ancient Order to be the main agent working towards the fusion of emigrant peoples'.[217]

With the Marquess in his eightieth year there was real concern in 1926 about the possible death duty liability. One way round the problem was to convert the estate into a limited company as many other families, such as the Buccleuchs, the Butes, and Devonshires, had already done.[218] The Edinburgh agent and the factor investigated this option for the very good reason that death duties when added to the debts over the estate would almost certainly result in its total disappearance. Nothing was done immediately as the Commercial Bank was itself now concerned about the level of the overdraft, and in early November 1927 imposed a moratorium on transactions until the overdraft was reduced from £42,000 to £36,000.[219] Thomas Smith, the factor, was deeply troubled, as until the rents were collected at the end of December there was no possibility of raising any income. Any

further reduction in staff would be counter-productive. Since much woodland had already been sold to make ends meet, there was

> not much mature timber left and this is
> mostly in the policies about Culzean,
> and prices are much depreciated by the
> amount of timber thrown on the market
> by recent gales, so that no large sum
> could be obtained from this source.[220]

There was no alternative but for Lord Ailsa to reduce his own personal expenditure, but even so it was necessary, as a desperate measure, to raise a further rent charge of £5,000 to pay the income tax for the year.[221] Moreover the local authority was pressing for the payment of rates and salaries of the parochial ministers were due.[222] Under the terms of the Church of Scotland (Property and Endowment) Act of 1925 which was consequent on the amalgamation of the Church of Scotland and the United Free Church, the opportunity now existed for this obligation to be discharged by making a composition with the general board of trustees.[223] Lady Cassillis was so distressed by this parlous state of affairs that she offered to return the bracelet given to her by her father-in-law on her marriage to help reduce the debt.[224]

The outlook may have been bleak, but the estate was insulated from the worst effects of the repeal of the Corn Production Act. Little grain was grown and tenants still had the advantage of good rail access to send dairy produce and new potatoes to market. Until 1930 the rental remained remarkably buoyant with arrears more or less contained. As in wartime, improvements to the estate were few and far between, but a programme of repair and maintenance was maintained, as such expenditure could be set against income tax. It proved impossible for the Marquess and his wife to keep the cost of the household within bounds, even though the London house had been sold. Like many of their contemporaries, they were bewildered by the social and economic upheaval caused by the war and could not adjust to

their new circumstances. They could not understand that the delicate paternal balance of the estate, which had existed for almost two hundred years, had come to an end. Their servants still wore livery and the butler his apron as they had done a century before. Each year a licence fee was paid to allow armorial bearings to be displayed on the motor car. There were still gatekeepers in the lodges, albeit by 1927 the number had fallen to four.[225] When A.T. Harrison resigned as head gardener the following year, he was replaced by William J. Orr, who had been gardener to the Earl of Haddington at Tyninghame in East Lothian.[226] Under him the garden continued on its well-established path, with large quantities of flowers and vegetables being grown for the house.

Newhailes on the outskirts of Edinburgh which was the home of the Earl of Cassillis and his wife from 1922 until 1936.

The impact of the world-wide slump in 1930 was immediate. Many tenants found it difficult to pay their rents. By March of the following year, the financial situation was desperate with the Inland Revenue threatening to take legal proceedings unless their demands were paid.[227] With the agreement of the Earl of Cassillis and his brothers so as to 'carry on the estate' a further £25,000 was raised as a charge on the rents and his father agreed to sell his government stock of some £9,000 to reduce the overdraft.[228] Lord Charles, the Marquess's second son, came to live at Culzean after the death in November 1931 of his wife, the widow of his cousin Admiral Sir John Baird. He busied himself about the policies cutting out and burning *ponticum*. In the midst of this fresh crisis Hugh Lennox, the Edinburgh commissioner, died suddenly in December 1932, leaving George Harvey as sole partner in E.A. & F. Hunter & Co. This had the unfortunate result of threatening the firm's own liquidity, which might have had disastrous consequences for the estate.[229] Hurriedly, in the spring of 1933 the factor, Thomas Smith, reviewed the possibility of assuming the duties previously performed by Hunters.[230] As part of this process, he conducted an exhaustive review of expenditure to find ways of covering the annual deficit of some £5,000. He identified savings of some £2,500, but considered that any further reduction would materially effect the upkeep of the grounds. With equal urgency he worked out the likely benefit of disentailing the estate and forming a limited company, calculating that there would be a saving in government duties of some £43,000.[231] It would have the additional benefit of making the Marquess a tenant of the company and therefore obliged to meet any over expenditure out of his own rather than the estate's resources. These were limited to his stake in his shipbuilding company and a small portfolio of shares, mostly in railway stock acquired when Turnberry was sold.

Meanwhile the financial situation was becoming more and more desperate. Towards the end of March the local authority applied for summary warrants for the collection of arrears of rates, which, if not paid by the end of the fiscal year, would attract a surcharge of 10 per cent.[232] The estate's predicament could now no longer be disguised and the Marquess, encouraged by his three eldest sons, agreed to disentail the estate.[233] The application to the Court of Session in May was the cause of considerable speculation in the locality, as the Marquess would be able to sell his property. Any intention of disposal was strongly denied.[234] Obtaining the permission of the court was time consuming, involving lawyers representing the Earl of Cassillis and his brothers, Lord Charles and Lord Angus, and their sister Lady Kilmaine. In the meantime the factor pressed ahead with making the nec-

essary arrangements. Since neither the Earl of Cassillis nor his next brother Lord Charles had any children, the family heirlooms were to be placed in trust for the son of their third brother Lord Angus, [Archibald] David, who would become 7th Marquess on the death of his uncles and his father. To the relief of the family and the factor, the Cassillis and Culzean Estates Company was formed in April 1934 with a capital of £250,000 and the Marquess and the Earl of Cassillis as its first directors.[235] The Marquess was issued with £90,000 worth of 8 per cent debenture bonds, which were designed to provide him with an income.

It took time for the new arrangements to settle down, as Lord and Lady Ailsa found it difficult to understand that if they overspent their private or household accounts they could no longer expect the estate to cover the deficit. Writing in November to the factor, George Harvey, the commissioner in Edinburgh, made it clear that 'further savings must be effected' in the household and personal expenses. He identified fuel, lighting and the garage as areas where substantial savings must be made. This meant that much of the castle would have to be shut up during the long winter months.[236] Moreover the carbide plant was now obsolete and in poor repair, making lighting the castle difficult if not dangerous.[237] There was no money to convert to electricity. For much of the time the Marquess and his wife were holed up in the new wing where a small kitchen was fitted up. He was now an old man, crippled with arthritis and increasingly confined to a wheelchair. His wife tried to keep the worst of the financial news from him, but the signs of decline and decay all round him cannot have escaped his notice.

He died in April 1938 in his ninety-first year and was buried beside his father in the family burying ground. His life had been as eventful as any of his ancestors and, like all but his father, he had made a distinctive contribution to the appearance of both Culzean and Cassillis. He had tried to reverse the tide of the effect of the agricultural depression by investing in his own shipbuilding

business. Although other members of the aristocracy, such as the Dukes of Devonshire and Portland, had shipbuilding and marine engineering interests only he and the Honourable Sir Charles Parsons were practising naval architects and engineers. Like his forebears, he had played an active part in local government, serving on the newly formed county council, school boards, harbour boards and many other committees. He had taken these duties seriously, often travelling up from London especially to attend meetings, but, as the factor admitted in 1906 when standing for the Barr School Board: 'Owing to changes in the tenancy on the Estates, there are not so

The portrait of the 3rd Marquess painted by Fiddes Watt and presented to him by the tenants on the estate on the occasion of his 85th birthday in 1932. Unbeknown to them the estate was in the grip of a serious financial crisis, which would lead to the sale of the greater part of the property mostly to the tenants.

many on whom I can depend for plumpers.'*[238] The old political and social structures had come to an end and the estate was now essentially a very long-established family business with all that that implied. In reflecting on his long stewardship of the estate, his obituarist in the *Glasgow Herald* commented 'perhaps the most important work carried out by the Marquess in his own domain was the development of his Maidens and Turnberry portions of his estate as summer resorts'.[239]

*Those who could be relied upon always to vote for their owner's candidate.

CHAPTER 10

Leaving the family home: 1938–58

The Earl of Cassillis, still known as Baldie to his friends, became the 4th Marquess. He and his wife had left Newhailes in May 1936 when his nephew and heir to the Newhailes estate Charles Dalrymple came of age. Although the Marquess of Ailsa had offered them Cassillis House at a rent of £500 a year,[1] the Earl and his wife had declined and gone to live at 6 Carlton Terrace in Edinburgh. On moving into town, Lady Cassillis had sent her prize-winning collection of Chinese ducks and geese to be cared for at the Swan Pond at Culzean. She was an eccentric, much interested in chemistry, with her own laboratory. She had a whimsical way of settling her accounts by always paying more than the invoice so she was in credit with her suppliers.[2]

By the time he inherited the title, her husband was far from well, suffering from the long-term effects of his wartime injuries. Knowing he probably had little time left to live he was troubled about the future of Culzean, which he and his next brother Lord Charles knew the family simply could not afford to run, let alone to maintain. Much to the distress of his stepmother who had devoted her time to refurnishing and refurbishing the castle for the future,[3] he had no intention of ever living there and made only occasional visits mostly in the summer months. As an antiquarian and with a pride in his family's history, he did not want to see the roof removed to save rates and the contents dis-

persed as had already happened to Eglinton. His first thought was to offer it to the county council as a home, but, before making a decision, he contacted the recently formed Country House Committee of the National Trust, probably through the Marquess of Salisbury, the Conservative leader in the House of Lords and a member of the committee.

Although most Tory landowners received short shrift from the radical members of the committee, the 4th Marquess had such wide interests that he was well received.[4] A member of the Royal Scottish Geographic Society since 1908, he had become vice-president in 1930. Given his antiquarian interest, he was an enthusiastic member of the place name committee from its inception.[5] A Gaelic speaker, he had been elected president of the Royal Gaelic Society in 1937. The following year he published an article entitled 'Scotland's share in Magna Carta', which in keeping with his long-cherished views had a strong flavour of nationalism about it. He concluded that it was essential to teach history 'from a Scots and not merely from an English standpoint and have chairs of Scottish History at our Scottish Universities'.[6]

Sometime in late 1938 or early 1939 Sir John Stirling Maxwell, the president of the National Trust for Scotland, which had been established in 1931, visited the Marquess and his wife at Culzean and explained that the country houses scheme did not at present extend to Scotland. The Marquess

The 4th Marquess of Ailsa towards the end of his life.

made up his mind that Culzean should be an early candidate for consideration, and made what he hoped were the necessary preparations in settling his estate. He withdrew from the Culzean Estates Company and placed his interest in trust for his nephew David Kennedy, who would become 7th Marquess. His nephew, Lord Kilmaine, and Sir John Milne Home, the factor to the Buccleuch estates and a member of the executive committee of the NTS, were appointed trustees and became directors until such time as David Kennedy inherited the estates. Negotiations with the National Trust were interrupted by the outbreak of war, when Lord Ailsa offered Culzean to the government as an emergency hospital, which was declined. In the meantime Lord and Lady Ailsa had decided to move to Culzean for the duration of hostilities, letting their Edinburgh home to Lady Ailsa's sister, the Dowager Duchess of Grafton. With almost no heating and no gas lighting, they lived in the west wing and played host to nieces and nephews evacuated from London. Their memories are of a bitter cold.[7] In 1941 the Scottish Education Department considered evacuating a school there, but on inspection the idea was abandoned.[8]

While living at Culzean for the first time since his early childhood, the 4th Marquess and his wife set about collecting together all the historical documents they could find relating to the house and family, which were to be gifted to the nation and deposited with the Scottish Record Office (now the National Archives of Scotland).[9] Despite the war, Lord Ailsa's ambition was still to hand Culzean over to the NTS. Unfortunately the Country House Scheme did not become operational in Scotland until a few weeks before his sudden death in March 1943 after a minor operation went tragically wrong. His obituarists remembered him as a modest man of simple tastes and 'quiet pervasive learning of the sort which enhances quality and balances judgement'.[10] One of the last letters he wrote was to instruct his lawyers to put in motion the donation of Culzean to the trust. Until that happened, in the event of his death his widow was to enjoy a life rent

of the castle. This was largely because his heir and ultimate owner of Culzean, his brother Lord Charles, was comfortably settled in his second wife's home, Hensol, a fine country house and estate near Castle Douglas in Dumfriesshire. She was the widow of Major Cunninghame of Lainshaw, who with no heirs had left her all his property. She was known as 'Aunt Wee' to her friends and family because of her small stature.

Frances Lady Ailsa, the widow of the 4th Marquess, was deeply upset by the loss of her husband: 'It is so – well – beyond words – without him – we were such friends.'[11] She and her sister-in-law, now the Marchioness, were very keen to see Culzean pass to the NTS:

> The only difficulty is the Endowment for though Cassillis [the 4th Marquess] made every arrangement possible for his Death duties he died 2 months before his own were of use – & these death duties following so quickly on the already impoverished Estates has forced the sale of a great part of the lands & makes the endowment of this place for the National Trust scheme impractical. On the other hand – we feel it carries its own endowment with proper development – The big garden though only used for vegetables since 1940 – is paying over £300 a year – (this without a lorry, telephone etc.) & there are wonderful possibilities in the gardens & houses in the grounds for growing & experimenting on tress, shrubs, plants & vegetables that would be profitable for the Nation.[12]

With the need to effect the sale of much of the unproductive hill ground above Straiton to the Forestry Commission, discussions were broken off. In the spring of 1941, 5,000 acres of this land around Loch Doon had been devastated by fire when heather burning by the tenant had got out of control.[13] The Forestry Commission urgently needed such ground to replace the huge amounts of timber felled during the war and was prepared to pay good prices. One consequence of the sale of much of the hill ground to the Forestry Commission was the demolition of the lodge at Craiglure in the mid-1950s. Little survives of Craiglure except a pile of stones alongside the footpath from the Stinchar Bridge to Cornish Hill. Frances, Lady Ailsa in June 1944 again approached Sir John Stirling Maxwell, who as a member of the Scottish National Committee of the Forestry Commission had been much involved in the negotiations for the purchase of the hill ground. She began her letter engagingly: 'Please forgive me troubling you – when you have more than enough to think of already – you must just cast this aside if it is too much bother.'[14]

Although Sir John certainly did not take this advice, little happened until after VE day on 8 May 1945. Later that month Lady Frances visited Sir John at Pollok House 'to get things clear about the National Trust'. By that time Lord Charles, the 5th Marquess, had concluded:

> I do not consider it practical for the family to live at Culzean under Modern Conditions. Since the Family will in my opinion NOT be able to live there, I consider that the Family would rather see Culzean Castle being used by the wounded of the War than by any one else. I am of the opinion that it would be better to build a small modern house for the use of the Family in an accessible place at a cost of about £1,500 or £2,000.[15]

His wife, 'Aunt Wee', did not share these sentiments and encouraged Lady Frances to push ahead with the negotiations with the Trust:

> but you must discuss reserving a few rooms for the use of family and yourself for life, etc. Charles is on to that ridiculous idea of a new house & I can't get

him off it but he will come off it in time when he realizes how many charming old houses could be made comfy on [at] Culzean if rooms are not kept in the house itself.[16]

On 5 June 1945 a meeting took place between representatives of the family and Major Brebner from the NTS and Arthur Russell, who was acting secretary of the NTS and its law agent. Events then moved swiftly, encouraged by the 5th Marquess, who had been won over by his wife. He expressed the strong wish that the top floor of the castle should be converted into a flat for the use of General Eisenhower, the supreme allied commander in Europe, as a thank offering. With relations strained with the United States over questions of the post-war settlement, the Foreign Office was enthusiastic. A further condition of the gift was that houses would be built around the Swan Pond for disabled ex-servicemen, who might find gainful employment in the gardens and policies. The Marquess was full of delightful ideas about how to increase the revenue: 'I think the N. Trust should be advised to get the "House Salmon Net" going again – I saw 14 salmon caught in it once before breakfast.'[17] Agreement was reached in October with the family making over to the trust the castle, the policies, the gardens and the home farm, which it was calculated would yield £1,655 against an estimated expenditure of £2,395.[18] For the remainder of her life Frances, Lady Ailsa was to have the use of the west wing in which a new staircase was to be installed. It was intended that Eisenhower would fly to Scotland in November to accept the gift, and afterwards to be entertained at a shoot. The factor was concerned that some of the beaters would be German prisoners of war. Colonel Stevenson, the secretary of the Trust, reassured him:

> I do not think that the fact that some of the beaters will be Germans will make the slightest of differences or that General Eisenhower will care, in fact it

may be a golden opportunity for him to do what I feel he must have wished to do for the last few years.[19]

In the event the German prisoners were never put at risk as Eisenhower was taken ill. The public announcement was made in his absence and an appeal launched to help maintain the castle and grounds.[20] In the circumstances the response to the appeal was encouraging with £3,500 pledged by August 1946 from such well-known figures in Scottish public life as Viscount Weir and his brother James, Lady Invernairn and Sir James Lithgow.[21] Others came forward with the offer of furniture, including Sir George Campbell, and Sir Angus Cunninghame Graham.[22]

Culzean was only the third country house which the NTS had accepted. The other two were the House of Binns, not formally handed over until 1946, and Leith Hall in Aberdeenshire, the home of the Leith Hay family, against whom Lord Kennedy had made his famous wager over a century before, which had only just been acquired.[23] Caring for a country house was a new experience and the NTS seemed strangely unwilling to learn from others, an error which was to have serious repercussions. Interestingly, James Lees-Milne, who worked assiduously for the National Trust's Country House Committee, makes no mention of Scotland or the leading figures in the Scottish Trust, in his book *People and Places – Country House Donors and the National Trust*.[24] The NTS did not seem to recognise that the grounds had been open to the public for over a hundred years and that the 3rd Marquess, in the face of mounting financial problems, had gone to enormous trouble and expense to conserve and perhaps recreate the Adam interior, and also to maintain the gardens. The whole approach to the policies was that of a municipal park. Sir Iain Colquhoun, the chairman, in his 1945 annual report summed it up:

The intention is to develop the policies, which include the home farm, the build-

ings of which were designed by Adam. There will be facilities to the public for bowling, tennis and boating. The old kitchen and billiard room [the original steward's room] of the castle will be converted into a restaurant. The existing golf course laid out by James Baird, will be restored, and it is also hoped to lay out a seaside course. The wooded policies contain a 13-acre walled garden, and the sandy foreshore affords safe bathing and should be an added attraction.

If Lord Ailsa had any qualms about this rather brutal approach to his family home, he was much too much a gentleman to say so. Over the next ten years, however, he did his best gently to remind the Trust that he and the family knew a good deal about the history of the castle and the perils of trying to care for it. In the discussions leading up to the hand over, he sagely advised Colonel Stevenson:

One is apt to upset the Balance by tampering with old Buildings, and using these for a purpose the Designer did not have in mind when he made his creation. But that is an affair for your own architect.[25]

His nephew the 7th Marquess later warned Colin McWilliam, who wrote the first guide book in 1954:

I always feel it is a great mistake to think of the Castle being finished by the time Adam died. I think the main features had been finished but not many of the accessories. In fact work continued there under the guise of another until the new wing was built in 1876.

I am well aware that a tremendous amount will always be conjecture but often by discussion and observation on the ground fairly good arguments can be found for all the conjectures.[26]

Despite this entirely correct advice, the NTS was to remain fixated by Adam at Culzean for another fifty years. The 5th Marquess also stated that Culzean was subject to periodic hurricanes which could be expected to strike every ten to fifteen years or so and to cause enormous damage to both the policies and the fabric of the castle, however much had been done to maintain the stonework.[27]

General Eisenhower made his much delayed visit to Scotland in October 1946, when he was presented with the flat and also received the freedom of the city of Edinburgh and the burgh of Maybole, played golf on the Old Course at St Andrews and was the King's guest at Balmoral. On leaving Culzean he declared: 'We have encountered only genuine hospitality and gracious welcome.'[28] In drawing up the guest lists for these events the trust inadvertently overlooked the 5th Marquess's brother and heir to the title,

The visit of General Eisenhower to Culzean in 1946 with on the left the 5th Marquess of Ailsa, who gave Culzean to the National Trust for Scotland and on the far right his wife, known as Aunt Wee. Next to her is Lady Frances, the widow of the 4th Marquess and next to her David, Earl of Wemyss, chairman of the Trust.

Lord Angus. This error was to contribute to strained relations with the family which persisted for a long time. It soon became clear that the trust had perhaps bitten off rather more than it could chew. In presenting his annual report in 1949 the Earl of Wemyss, now chairman, noted ruefully: 'In spite of careful calculations at the time the Trust took Culzean over it has been impossible to avoid running at a loss.'[29] Jamie Stormonth Darling, who became secretary in that year, realised from the outset that every effort had to be put into raising funds for Culzean otherwise the future of the whole trust would be in jeopardy. In his worst nightmares about the trust finances, his only consolation was a vision of the castle sliding gracefully into the sea and being engulfed by the waves.

On taking over the castle, the priority of the NTS was to open the house and gardens to the public. Although the grounds had been open

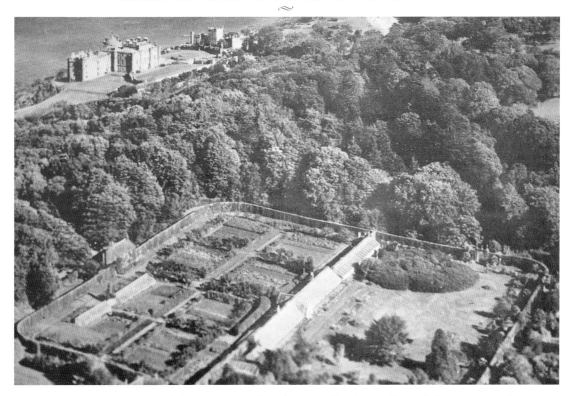

throughout the war, some of the mature timber had become dangerous because of the lack of labour to remove fallen trees and broken branches. The gardener, Willie Orr, and his staff found it hard to adjust to their new masters. They particularly resented the public park mentality and the tone adopted by Jim Russell, a partner of Graham Stewart Thomas in the Sunningdale Nurseries, who was brought in to advise. With no research and little consultation a new planting scheme was imposed on the gardens and policies.[30]

A view of the walled garden at about the time the National Trust for Scotland acquired the property.

Shortly after the war the NTS acquired the Gigha collection of rhododendrons, which had been built up by Sir James Horlick and in 1951 Crathes Castle in Aberdeenshire with an internationally renowned garden created by Lady Sybil Burnett with the help of her husband Major General Sir James Burnett of Leys. Both collections were used to propagate plants and shrubs for Culzean irrespective of whether they were appro-

priate for the garden. Glades were cut in Happy Valley to provide a sheltered home for tender azaleas and rhododendrons and large beds of shrubs created on the Fountain Green. The majority of shrubs introduced by Russell from his nursery were hydrangeas, fuschias, leptospermum, senecio and cistus.[31] Rather late in the day the NTS expressed concern that some of this planting was perhaps inappropriate when the shrubs were killed by the winter winds and Willie Orr was forced 'to fill up the vast expanses with annuals and phlox'.[32]

The house was opened for the first time in the summer of 1947 and attracted 6,000 visitors.[33] There was no lighting or heating as the acetylene plant was beyond repair and there was concern that if heating was not restored the fabric of the house and its contents would deteriorate beyond repair. A local committee, chaired by Lady Fergusson of Kilkerran, was formed to have oversight of the arrangements for opening the house and the neces-

CULZEAN CASTLE
AND GROUNDS
OPEN TO VISITORS
APRIL TILL SEPTEMBER   DAILY 10 A.M. TILL DUSK
MEALS SERVED

Nearest Station, Maybole.   Buses from Maybole, Ayr and Girvan.

Further particulars from:
THE NATIONAL TRUST FOR SCOTLAND
4 GREAT STUART STREET, EDINBURGH, 3

sary works. Influenced almost certainly by her husband, the historian Sir James Fergusson, she was determined to restore Culzean castle 'to its rightful place as conceived by Robert Adam 160 years ago'.[34] The Marchioness of Ailsa recalled in 2002 that when the family questioned Sir James's opinions he retorted 'Allow me to be right.' Lady Fergusson set to work with a will:

> We have turned out an incredible amount of junk (<u>really</u> junk – walrus teeth – red Indian suits – skulls etc.) each are like drawing teeth to poor Mr. Gray [the factor] – the pictures have also been blitzed and re-hung, an enormous improvement –

Some of this 'junk' was almost certainly significant ethnographical objects brought back from North America by the 11th Earl in the eighteenth century.

LEFT
Lord Angus, 6th Marquess of Ailsa.

RIGHT
The first poster issued by the National Trust for Scotland to advertise Culzean.

The unfashionable collection of stuffed animals was also destroyed to the fury of the family and the estate staff.[35] Many of the pictures still belonged to the family and the trustees of the 4th Marquess had gone to some trouble and expense to restore some of them. Nevertheless in 1952 the Pilgrim Trust, which was chaired by Lord Kilmaine, the Marquess's nephew and chairman of the 4th Marquess's trustees, provided funds for replacement of the obsolete acetylene gas plant by electricity. The removal of the gasoliers and other fittings from every room required restoration of the plasterwork roundels in the public rooms. With the advice of the Edinburgh house decorators and furnishers, Whytock & Reid, and a grant from the newly formed Historic Buildings Council of Scotland, all the public rooms were redecorated.[36]

Isa, Lady Ailsa, the widow of the 3rd Marquess, who had assisted her husband in the restoration of the house, had died in London in

1945 and Frances, Lady Ailsa, had died in 1949. The 5th Marquess took over the lease of the flat in the west wing for which he had little use as he was rarely at Culzean. Relations between the family and the NTS continued to be strained very largely because the trust had failed to learn from English experience. Visiting the castle in January 1954 Lord Kilmaine:

> noticed the shockingly bad arrangement of the furniture, objects of art, pictures etc. in some of the state rooms at Culzean, and have heard very adverse comments on these from English visitors to Culzean who are used to the skill and taste with which these things are looked after in great houses in England which are shown to the public.

He condemned out of hand the rehanging of the pictures.[37] This was no more more evident than when one pair of the curtains in the saloon were cleaned and repaired by the skilled fabric restorer Lady Meade Featherstonehaugh, in her workshops at Uppark. Because of the expense, it was decided to hang them somewhere else as they 'were not Adam material' and replace the curtains rather than having the others restored.[38] Lady Featherstonehaugh was incandescent with rage at what she regarded as a slight on her reputation. The irony was that they were almost certainly the original curtains commissioned by the 1st Marquess when the saloon was finally completed after 1815. The family was also upset by the superior attitude taken by the local committee about the furnishings which were regarded as 'not really up to standard'.[39] What was regarded as more suitable furniture was borrowed from other families. For example the Earl of Buckinghamshire, who had recently inherited the Earl of Camperdown's Scottish properties including Camperdown house in Dundee, loaned some 'lovely chairs', the Duke of Montrose two chairs and Lady McTaggart Stewart, Frances Lady Ailsa's sister-in-law, two large mirrors and a pink empire

suite.[40] Lady Fergusson and her committee were still not satisfied:

> If any munificent millionaire of exceptional taste (!) offered us carpets, curtains (of the richest damask), exquisite Sèvre china, or some really lovely and suitable furniture in the form of sofas (18th century) and chairs for the drawing rooms we would accept them with joy.[41]

In the circumstances it is not surprising that the family took the best pieces of their furniture to their own quarters.

Despite all the difficulties and the tensions, the castle was reopened to the public on 3 April 1954 by the Earl of Wemyss, the chairman of the NTS, after a meeting of the council. It was by now one of the most popular tourist attractions in Scotland. Almost fifty thousand people visited the grounds in 1952 and nearly six thousand the castle and within two years the number of visitors had climbed to sixty thousand.[42] The secretary of state for Scotland, Arthur Woodburn, attended along with other guests. The event was marred by the tragic death of the Earl of Wemyss's eldest son and heir, Lord Elcho.[43] At the annual meeting later in the year Jamie Stormonth Darling declared with completely misplaced optimism: 'It does now look as if this large concern will be able to run itself from now on' and anticipated creating a reserve fund out of the operating surplus.[44]

It was hoped that the appointment as assistant secretary of the NTS in April 1954 of David Kennedy, the son of Lord Angus and heir to the Marquessate, would help ease relations with the family. On leaving the army after wartime service, he had worked at Inverewe, the famous gardens in Ross-shire, to learn something of conservation forestry. Part of his duties as assistant secretary was to oversee the management and development of Culzean. His uncle, the Marquess, gave him and his young wife the use of the flat in the west wing. By the end of the season he had formed the view that the informed visitor deserved something better:

> There is no doubt that it is now becoming the fashion to visit the great houses in the country and from all that I have seen and heard it is certainly true that the standard of 'showmanship' is increasing at a pretty hot pace. I know that at a place like Culzean a large proportion of one's visitors are quite content with being put through the 'sheep fank' and a more intelligent, subtle reception and guidance would be lost on them; but frankly, I wonder whether we are yet geared to give full satisfaction to the more intelligent visitor? I cannot deny that I have heard it from those of good will but of discrimination that they were disappointed in the general reception and guiding at Culzean and I just wonder whether we have not got to lift these duties out of the hands of the people such as we have at the moment and try to get in one or two more intelligent and cultured people.[45]

Although the local committee was wound up, little was done to progress this idea as relations with the family were again difficult.

At first the new arrangement worked smoothly and there was a more measured approach to repair and maintenance. A serious quarrel between the family and the NTS developed, however, over the pictures. Sir James Fergusson took it into his head that the fine portrait, which was described as the 6th Earl of Cassillis, must in fact be the 8th Earl and had the label altered. He was right that it could not be the 6th Earl but wrong in thinking the subject the 8th Earl. The portrait is probably of the 9th Earl's uncle David Kennedy, a successful lawyer. The 5th Marquess was furious at this interference with his property

without any discussion.[46] The dispute soon spilled over into a more serious argument about the care of the whole collection of pictures, many of which were very personal to the family. The NTS remained unaware of their significance for over fifty years. The succession of Lord Angus as 6th Marquess on the death of his brother, the 5th Marquess, in 1956 did nothing to improve relations between the family and the NTS. Lord Angus had been ill for some time and was almost blind. He died the following year when the 4th Marquess's trust came to an end. The trustees handed the estate over to his son, David, now the 7th Marquess. Reflecting on the unhappy events since the premature death of Evelyn, Lady Ailsa in 1888, Lord Kilmaine penned a note to Jamie Stormonth Darling to inform him:

> I'm afraid I feel little sense of personal loss & for him one can only regard his death as a most merciful release. David now comes in for a great inheritance … Our brief 'reign is in fact over! – but one feels an immense sense of relief that the period of awkward trusteeship is safely over & the future is no longer our concern … How ill-starred the poor family has been! – nothing but tragedies & poisoned relationships for years.[47]

As part of the settlement of the estates of the 5th and 6th Marquesses, further paintings and furniture passed to the NTS or were sold. After the responsibility for the house passed to local representatives, the 7th Marquess resigned his position with the NTS and shortly afterwards moved out of Culzean and went to live close by at Cassillis, bringing to an end almost four hundred years of Kennedy occupancy. The direct link with the family was severed and the stewardship of one of Scotland's greatest houses passed irrevocably to the National Trust for Scotland.

In many ways the story of the Kennedys and Culzean follows the familiar trajectory of the for-

tunes of British agriculture from the eighteenth century, but in others it is very different. Culzean is the only castle of the three earls (Cassillis, Eglinton and Loudoun), who dominated Ayrshire politics during the eighteenth century, to survive intact and with at least some of its collections. Moreover unlike in the other estates, the family has preserved the best, some of the finest agricultural land in the west of Scotland. The almost certain reason for this achievement is the fact that neither the 9th Earl nor his brothers had children, and the estate was inherited by a wealthy American naval captain, who had made a fortune during the Seven Years War. His capital allowed his son, the 1st Marquess, to live like a prince and to withstand the shock of gambling debts which would have destroyed many other estates. With good advice and the strong management of Edinburgh lawyers, who are too easily criticised for failing their aristocratic clients, the estate was preserved despite the extravagance of the 3rd Marquess and the decline in his income during the long agricultural depression which persisted (for

The 7th Marquess of Ailsa and his wife, the last members of the family to live at Culzean.

the landowners) from the late 1870s until the 1950s. Locally in Ayrshire the estate was well served by a succession of loyal and able factors.

It is very difficult to know how typical this tale is of the Scottish aristocracy as a whole, largely because of the absence of any equivalent studies. Although that is a time honoured excuse of historians, it is nevertheless true. That does not, of course, prevent generalisation. The Kennedys do seem to be different from their pro-consular neighbours and that difference must lie in their Jacobitism and later (and oddly) their Whig principles and reputation for excess. In other words, they were not to be trusted, and by the time they were in the Victorian and Edwardian period, the 3rd Marquess was simply not interested. One cannot imagine him as a governor general, even if the income would have helped reduce his debts. In response to David Cannadine's challenge, Culzean has been peopled with three-dimensional personalities (as far as the sources will permit).[48] It is for others to judge if they represent anything more than their whimsical selves.

Notes

There are four collections of manuscripts relating to the Kennedy family and the Cassillis and Culzean estates.

In 1943 the 4th Marquess left the contents of the charter chest at Culzean to the nation and these were transmitted to the Scottish Record Office (now the National Archives of Scotland) not long after his death in March 1943. They form GD25 and contain the papers of the Earls of Cassillis and the Kennedys of Culzean until about the end of the eighteenth century. Although there is some later material it is largely inconsequential. Until the Kennedys of Culzean inherited the title in 1759, the papers of the two estates are confused.

The Cassillis and Culzean estate office in the castle at Maybole holds a complete collection of estate records from the 1830s to date. This includes a complete run of financial records, correspondence of the 3rd Marquess and his wife with the factor and runs of factor's letter books. There are some fine estate plans but many seem to have been lost.

The family still retains at Cassillis House the correspondence of the 1st and 3rd Marquess along with photograph albums and fragments of the library of the 9th Earl and of John Allardyce of Dunnottar.

The National Trust for Scotland at Culzean Castle holds the diaries of the 2nd Marquess together with a collection of photographs and other papers which have been assembled over the years.

None of these collections is adequately catalogued.

The archive of the National Trust for Scotland, which is held at the head office in Edinburgh, contains files on the acquisition and subsequent management of Culzean and its grounds.

ABBREVIATIONS

BL	British Library
CCEO	Cassillis and Culzean Estate Office
Cassillis MSS	Manuscripts held at Cassillis House
Culzean MSS	Manuscripts at Culzean Castle
GUA	Glasgow University Archives
HL	Huntington Library, San Marino, California
Kilkerran MSS	Manuscripts of the Fergusson family held at Kilkerran House in Ayrshire
NAS	National Archives of Scotland
NLS	National Library of Scotland
NTS	National Trust for Scotland
PRO	Public Record Office
RCAHMS	Royal Commission on Ancient and Historic Monuments in Scotland

THROUGH THE RUINED ARCH

1 J.T. Ward, 'Ayrshire landed estates in the nineteenth century' in *Ayrshire Collections*, pp.97–123; R.H. Campbell, *Owners and Occupiers – Changes in Rural Society in South-West Scotland before 1914*; and David Hancock, *Citizens of the World, London Merchants and the Integration of the British Atlantic Community, 1735–1785*.
2 Ian Anstruther, *The Knight and the Umbrella – An Account of the Eglinton Tournament 1839*.
3 Henry Blyth, *The Pocket Venus: A Victorian Scandal*.
4 John Davies, *Cardiff and the Marquesses of Bute*; and Karl W. Schweizer (ed.), *Lord Bute Essays in Re-interpretation*.
5 Sir David Oswald Hunter Blair, *John Patrick, 3rd Marquess of Bute, K.T. (1847–1900) a memoir*.
6 Keith Brown, *Noble Society in Scotland – Wealth, Family and Culture from Reformation to Revolution*.
7 There is a useful essay on the Hamiltons – 'The improvement of a great estate', in T.M. Devine, *The Transformation of Rural Scotland – Social Change and the Agrarian Economy 1660–1815*, pp. 93–110.
8 Eric Richards, *The Leviathan of Wealth: the Sutherland Fortune in the Industrial Revolution*.
9 David Cannadine, *The Decline and Fall of the British Aristocracy*; and *Aspects of Aristocracy – Grandeur and Decline in Modern Britain*.
10 Edward J. Cowan, *Montrose for Covenant and King*.
11 R.K. Marshall, *The Days of Duchess Anne, Life in the Household of the Duchess of Hamilton*.
12 Michael Fry, *Dundas Despotism*.
13 Henry Blyth, *Old Q – The Rake of Piccadilly – A Biography of the 4th Duke of Queensberry*.
14 Sydney Checkland, *The Elgins 1766–1917 – A Tale of Aristocrats, Proconsuls and their Wives*.
15 There are a few, such as Ramage Craufurd Tait, *Drumlanrig Castle and the Douglases with the Early History and Ancient Remains of Durisdeer, Closeburn, and Morton by Craufurd*.
16 Gordon Donaldson, *Sir William Fraser: the man and his work*.
17 See for example L. Stone and J.C.F. Stone, *An Open Elite? England 1540–1880*.
18 J.V. Beckett, *The Aristocracy in England 1660–1914*.
19 John Habakkuk, *Marriage, Debt, and the Estates System – English Landownership 1650–1950*.
20 See for example David Spring, *The English Landed Estate in the Nineteenth Century: its administration*.
21 G.E. Mingay, *English Landed Society in the Eighteenth Century*.
22 F.M.L. Thomson, *English Landed Society in the Nineteenth Century*.
23 Elizabeth Bowen, *Bowen's Court*, Cork.
24 Vita Sackville West, *Knole and the Sackvilles*.
25 Merlin Waterston, *The National Trust – The First Hundred Years*, pp. 113 and 116–17; and J. Lees Milne, *People and Places – Country House Donors and the National Trust*.
26 See for example William Addison, *Audley End*; and Mary Mauchline, *Harewood House*.
27 See for example Merlin Waterston, *The Servant's Hall: a domestic history of Erdigg*; Charles Saumarez Smith, *The Building of Castle Howard*; and Charles Spencer, *Althorp – The Story of an English House*.
28 Ian G. Lindsay and Mary Cosh, *Inveraray and the Dukes of Argyll*.
29 Charles McKean, *The Scottish Chateau: The Country House in Scotland 1500–1700*.
30 James Macaulay, *The Classical Country House in Scotland 1660–1800*.
31 See for example Ian Gow, *The Scottish Interior*; Ian Gow and Alistair Rowan, *Scottish Country Houses 1600–1914*; and Ian Gow, *Scottish Houses and Gardens from the Archives of Country Life*.
32 David Cannadine, *Aspects of Aristocracy*, p. 294.
33 *Culzean Castle & Country Park*, pp. 6–7.

CHAPTER 1

1 Romney Sedgwick, *The House of Commons, 1715–1754*, p. 382.
2 There were other spellings particularly Cullean or Cullen, both of which were used well into the nineteenth century.
3 C.J. Brown, *The Soils of Carrick and the Country round Girvan*, p. 243.
4 R.C. Reid, *Wigtownshire Charters*, pp. 79–81.
5 David Hamilton, *Golf – Scotland's Game*, p. 54.
6 Robert Pitcairn, *Historical and Genealogical Account of the Principal Families of the Name of Kennedy*, pp. 13–14.
7 This account is based on ibid., pp. 1–71.
8 Sir William Brereton, *Travels in Holland, the United Provinces*, p. 121.
9 Ibid., p. 121.
10 *Records of the University of Glasgow*, p. 86
11 In the *Statistical Account of Scotland, 1791–1799*, vol. 10, p. 485, it is claimed it had been enclosed for 200 years.
12 *Munimenta*, p. 125.
13 National Archives of Scotland (NAS) GD 25/9/29/2, fragment of account of his visit to France by Sir Archibald Kennedy, n.d.
14 Edmund S.J. Van der Straeten, *History of the Violoncello, the Viol da Gamba, their Precursors and Collateral Instruments*, London, p. 107.
15 NAS GD 25/9/45, NAS GD 25/9/45.
16 NAS GD 25/9/29, life of Sir Archibald Kennedy in his own hand.
17 NAS GD 25/9/2 Covenanters, letter of Earl of Perth to Sir Archibald Kennedy, 17 May 1685.
18 Ibid., letter of Duke of Queensberry to Sir Archibald Kennedy, 9 June 1685.
19 James T. Gray, *Maybole – Carrick's Capital*, p. 116, and Alison Mitchell (ed.), *Pre-1858 Gravestone Inscriptions Carrick Ayrshire*, p. 106.
20 *Reports of the Royal Commission on Historical Manuscripts, Downshire*, vol. 75, part 1, p. 38.
21 NAS GD 25/9/45.
22 *Historical Account of the Most Noble Family of Kennedy*, 1849, p. 36.
23 All the quotations from Sir Archibald's excursion to Ireland at this point are taken from NAS GD 25/9/29.
24 *29th Reports of the Royal Commission on Historical Manuscripts, Portland*, vol. 5, p. 203.
25 NAS GD 16/34/37, letter of Sir Archibald Kennedy to Earl of Airlie, 1708.
26 The Scottish name is derived from the Latin *sola bassana*.
27 NAS GD 25/9/40, letters of Sir Archibald Kennedy 1693–1707.
28 *Historical Account of the Most Noble Family of Kennedy*, p. 32.
29 *Statistical Account of Scotland, 1791–1799*, vol. 10, p. 485.
30 T.M. Devine, *The Transformation of Rural Scotland*, pp. 52–3.
31 *Historical Account of the Most Noble Family of Kennedy*, p. 35.
32 William Abercrummie, 'Carrick in 1696', p.9.
33 NAS GD 25/9/30/2/1, account for flower-pots, 1705.
34 NAS GD 25/8/867, lease of the saltpans, 1709.
35 William Robertson, *Old Ayrshire Days*, pp. 70–1.
36 NAS GD 25/9/27/1, list of Sir Archibald Kennedy's debts, 1710.
37 NAS GD 25/9/30/2/1, account for flower pots, 1721.

38 James Paterson, *History of the Counties of Ayr and Wigtown,* vol. 2, pp. 341–2.

39 NAS GD 135/2887, scheme of ranking of the creditors of the Earl of Cassillis.

CHAPTER 2

1 *Munimenta*, p. 186.

2 NAS GD 25/9/25, letters of Sir Archibald Kennedy 1693–1707, letter from the Earl of Balcarres, 8 June, n.d.

3 NAS GD 25/9/29/2, notebook of Sir John Kennedy.

4 NAS CS 238/SH C/2/53.

5 NAS GD 25/9/40, letters of Archibald Kennedy to Sir Thomas, 1747–54, referred to in letter to Sir Thomas, 23 June 1748.

6 NAS GD 25/8/1028, discharge of David Kennedy, 1726.

7 NAS GD 25/46/1, naval 1665–1863, account for loss of boat, n.d.

8 Frances Wilkins, *Strathclyde's Smuggling Story*, p. 41.

9 NAS GD 25/9/26, miscellaneous bundle D, document dated 1718.

10 NAS GD 25/9/40, correspondence of Sir John Kennedy, 1717–40.

11 NLS MSS 16609 fol. 157, Sir Thomas Kennedy to Lord Milton, Lord Justice Clerk, 1748.

12 NAS GD 25/9/13, financial papers 1735–40, invoice 22 September 1735.

13 Ibid., invoices 1733–42.

14 NAS GD 25/9/44, Linen.

15 His name was often spelt this way.

16 NAS GD 25/9/72.

17 F.O. Shyllon, *Black Slaves in Britain*, p. 15.

18 NAS GD 25/9/13, financial papers 1735–40, invoice 22 September 1735.

19 Ibid., invoice 1742.

20 NAS GD 25/9/46/2/2, Countess of Eglinton to Sir John Kennedy, 2 June 1734.

21 NAS GD 25/9/30/2, bundle history and politics 1483–1869, Susanna Countess of Eglinton to Sir John Kennedy, 13 April 1741.

22 NAS GD 25/9/13, horticulture 1735–40, invoice 10 January 1730.

23 NAS GD 25/9/32, accounts for seeds 1638–1742.

24 NAS GD 25/9/59, rent book p. 23 makes reference to building up the garden wall in 1751.

25 GD 25/9/14, vouchers 1736–42, and *Archaeological Works on the Terraces at Culzean Castle.*

26 *Archaeological Works.*

27 CCEO, plan of Culzean, 1755.

28 James Paterson, *History of the Counties*, vol. 1, part 1, pp. 58–9.

29 Ibid., p. 116.

30 Ibid., p. 116.

31 NAS GD 25/9/13, bundle D.

32 W. Innes Addison, *The Matriculation Albums of the University of Glasgow from 1728 to 1858*, pp. 14–15.

33 See for example NLS MSS 16609 fol. 157, letter of Sir Thomas Kennedy to Lord Melton, 1745.

34 NAS GD 27/7/328, executory papers of David, Earl of Cassillis, 1792–4.

35 NAS GD 25/9/13, funeral expenses for Sir John Kennedy.

36 NAS GD 25/9/14, financial papers, 1743–57.

37 NAS GD 25/8/1119, obligation Sir Thomas Kennedy to Lady Kennedy, 1744.

38 NAS GD 25/8/110c, list of plenishings of the House of Culzean provided by Lady Kennedy's contract of marriage, 1743.

39 Inferred from the will of Lady Jean Douglas or Kennedy, 1751, in NAS GD 25/9/79 and the list of household plenishings at Culzean belonging to Lady Kennedy at Culzean, 1743, NAS GD 25/8/1128.

40 Kilkerran MSS, box 65, bundle 24, discharge of Sir Thomas Kennedy to his curators, 1747. In the absence of class lists it is impossible to be certain if he attended the University of Glasgow but the fact that both his brothers attended make this very likely.

41 Kilkerran MSS, box 1, bundle 35, letter of Sir Thomas Kennedy, 25 May 1744.

42 PRO WO 25/20 p. 294.

43 Ibid., letter of William Blane to Lord Kilkerran, 18 June 1745.

44 See Albert Lee, *History of the 33rd Foot*, 1922.

45 Cynthia O'Connor, *The Pleasing Hours*, pp. 8 and 119.

46 James Wilson and Patrick Shaw, *Cases Decided in the House of Lords on Appeal from the Courts in Scotland*, pp. 240–1.

47 NAS GD 25/8/1131, copy confirmed testament of Sir John Kennedy of Culzean, 3 December 1744.

48 NAS GD 25/9/79, inventory of Sir John Kennedy, 1744.

CHAPTER 3

1 Kilkerran MSS, box 1, bundle 35, Lady Kennedy to Lord Kilkerran, June 1744.

2 Ibid., Lord Kilkerran to Sir Thomas Kennedy, 22 June 1744.

3 Ibid., Craufurd of Ardmillan to Kennedy of Kilhenzie, June 1744.

4 Ibid., Lady Kennedy to Lord Kilkerran, June 1744, and NLS MSS 1669 fol. 157, letter of Sir Thomas Kennedy to Lord Melton, 1745.

5 Ibid.

6 NAS GD 25/8/1173, rental 1745, p. 4.

7 CCEO, plan of Culzean estate, 1755.

8 Kilkerran MSS, box 1, bundle 35, Lord Kilkerran to Lady Fergusson, 13 November 1744.

9 Ibid., William Blane to Lord Kilkerran, 18 June 1745.

10 Ibid., same to same, 24 December 1744.

11 Ibid., letter of Lady Kennedy to Lord Kilkerran, June 1744.

12 NAS GD 25/9/40, letters of Archibald Kennedy to Sir Thomas Kennedy 1747–50, letter of Archibald Kennedy to Sir Thomas, 15 January 1751.

13 Angus Stewart, *The Minute Book of the Faculty of Advocates, 1751–85*, vol. 3, p. 21.

14 NLS MSS 166609 fol. 157, letter of Sir Thomas to Lord Melton, 1745.

15 HL Loudoun MSS, Sir Thomas Kennedy to Earl of Loudoun, 14 March 1745.

16 Ibid., Lee.

17 PRO SP 36 65, fol. 217.

18 James Holloway, *Patrons and Painters*, p. 98.

19 Sebastien Le Prestre de Vauban, *De l'attaque et de la déense des places*, p. 95.

20 *Lodge St. John No. 11 Maybole, Quarter Millennium Celebration, Saturday 11 October 1975.* Copies are available from the lodge.

21 NAS GD 25/9/58, estate rental 1747–54, p. 27.

22 Ibid., letter of January 1749.

23 NAS GD 25/9/13, financial papers 1735–40, invoice 1739–41.

24 NAS GD 25/9/1, account book of Archibald Kennedy, 1745–54.

25 Frances Wilkins, *George Moore and Friends – Letters from a Manx Merchant*, pp. 263–4.

26 NAS GD 25/9/1, account book of Archibald Kennedy, 1745–54.

27 NAS GD 25/9/43, letters miscellaneous, William Blane to Sir Thomas Kennedy, 27 August 1748.

28 NAS GD 25/9/40, letters of Archibald Kennedy to Sir Thomas Kennedy 1747–50, Archibald Kennedy to Sir Thomas, 18 September 1753.

29 *Sporting Magazine*, vol. 13, 1798–9, pp. 48–9.

30 NAS GD 25/9/40, Sir Thomas Kennedy to Archibald Kennedy, 20 August 1747.

31 A. Gallier, *L'Académie d'Equitation de Caen*, 1909.

32 L.W.B. Brockliss, *French Higher Education in the Seventeenth and Eighteenth Centuries – A Cultural History*, p. 450.

33 NAS GD 25/9/40, letter of Sir Thomas to Archibald, 1 January 1748.

34 Ibid., same to same, 11 January 1754.

35 James Wilson and Patrick Shaw, *Cases Decided in the House of Lords*, p. 242.

36 John Ingamells, *A Dictionary of British and Irish Travellers in Italy, 1701–1800*, p. 858.

37 NAS GD 25/9/38, letters of introduction, 1750–60.

38 NAS GD 25/9/40, Archibald Kennedy to Sir Thomas, 15 January 1751.

39 Ibid., Archibald Kennedy to Sir Thomas, 21 January 1752.

40 NAS GD 25/9/43, letters miscellaneous, William Blane to Sir Thomas Kennedy, 27 August 1748.

41 NAS GD 25/9/1, account book of Archibald Kennedy, 1745–54.

42 NAS GD 25/9/40, letters of Archibald Kennedy to Sir Thomas Kennedy 1747–50, Sir Thomas to Archibald, 26 October and 21 December 1749.

43 NAS GD 25/9/1, account book of Archibald Kennedy, 1745–54.

44 NAS GD 25/9/40, Sir Thomas to Archibald, June 1749.

45 William Ferguson, *Scotland 1689 to the Present*, p. 168.

46 See for example *Statistical Account of Scotland*, vol. 12, 1791–9, pp. 82 and 84.

47 NAS GD 25/9/59, estate accounts, 1745–55.

48 NAS GD 25/9/40, Archibald Kennedy to Sir Thomas, 15 January 1751.

49 Ibid., same to same, 22 August 1751.

50 Ibid., Sir Thomas to Archibald Kennedy, June 1749.

51 NAS GD 25/9/14, financial papers 1750–4, bundle of accounts for mansion house repairs includes a voucher for building the garden dyke and the outer stables, and CCEO, Culzean estate plan, 1755.

52 NAS GD 25/9/59, rent book p. 22.

53 NAS GD 25/9/40, Archibald Kennedy to Sir Thomas, 6 June 1749.

54 Inferred from NAS GD 25/9/30/2, diary of planting 1755–6.

55 NAS GD 25/9/40, Sir Thomas to Archibald, 6 June 1749.

56 Ibid., Sir Thomas to Archibald Kennedy, 6 October 1749.

57 Ibid., same to same, January 1750.

58 Ibid., same to same 26 October 1749.

59 NAS GD 25/9/40 op. cit., Archibald Kennedy to Sir Thomas, 15 January 1751.
60 NAS GD 25/9/1, commissions etc.
61 NAS GD 25/9/40, Archibald Kennedy to Sir Thomas, 15 February 1751.
62 Ibid., and GD 25/9/14 financial papers 1750–4.
63 This is preserved in the Edinburgh City Library.
64 NAS GD 25/9/59, rent book p. 23.
65 NAS GD 25/9/14, financial papers 1750–4, bundle of accounts for mansion house repairs.
66 NAS GD 25/9/40, Archibald Kennedy to Sir Thomas, 15 February 1751.
67 Ibid., same to same, 15 February 1751.
68 Ibid., NAS GD 25/9/14.
69 NAS GD 25/9/40, same to same, 22 August 1751.
70 NAS GD 25/9/59, rent book, p. 23.
71 NAS GD 25/9/40, Sir Thomas to Archibald Kennedy, January 1749.
72 NAS GD 25/9/14, financial papers 1750–4, voucher for fruit trees and plants sent from Dalquharran.
73 NAS GD 25/9/7, financial papers 1755–68 and 1760–7.
74 James Paterson, History of the Counties, vol. 1, part 1, p. 25.
75 Statistical Account of Scotland 1791–1799, vol. 21, p. 42.
76 NAS GD 25/9/40, Archibald Kennedy to Sir Thomas, 21 January 1752.
77 NAS GD 25/9/7, financial papers 1748–54, statement of account of Sir Thomas Kennedy and Thomas Dundas, 1748–53.
78 John Ingamells, A Dictionary of British and Irish Travellers, p. 420.
79 NAS GD 25/9/40, Archibald Kennedy to Sir Thomas, 21 January 1752.
80 PRO SP 93/28, Hamilton 20 March 1773.
81 NAS GD 25/0/23, letter of Abbé Grant to the Earl of Cassillis, 5 May 1768.
82 NAS GD 25/9/40, Archibald Kennedy to Sir Thomas, 22 August 1751.
83 Quoted in O'Connor, The Pleasing Hours, p. 110.
84 NAS GD 25/9/14, account 18 May 1751.
85 Quoted in O'Connor, The Pleasing Hours, pp. 110–11.
86 Ibid., pp. 114–15
87 Ibid., p. 116.
88 R.A. Houston, Social change in the Age of Enlightenment, p. 216.
89 'The Musical Society of Edinburgh and St Cecilia's Hall', The Book of the Old Edinburgh Club, vol. 19, 1933, p. 245.
90 Lord J.C. Charlemont, 12th Report of the Royal Commission on Historical Manuscripts, vol. 1, p. 184.
91 B.R.S. Megaw 'Mount Strange and the "Manx Derby" Races', pp. 9–12.
92 NAS GD 25/9/46, folder – horse racing.
93 NAS GD 25/9/7, financial papers 1748–54, statement of account of Sir Thomas Kennedy and Thomas Dundas, 1748–53.
94 NAS GD 25/9/27, invoices 1744–65, no. 4
95 Lord J.C. Charlemont, 12th Report of the Royal Commission on Historical Manuscripts, vol. 1, p. 185.
96 John Ingamells, A Dictionary of British and Irish Travellers
97 NAS GD 25/9/79 will of Lady Jean Douglas or Kennedy, 1751.
98 NAS GD 25/9/40, Archibald Kennedy to Sir Thomas, 11 January 1754.
99 Ibid., same to same, 18 September 1753.
100 Ibid., same to same 5 June 1753.
101 Ibid., same to same, 21 June 1753.
102 Ibid., same to same, 18 September 1753.
103 Ibid., same to same, 11 June 1754.
104 Ibid., same to same, 11 January 1754.
105 Ibid., same to same, 29 March 1753.
106 Ibid., same to same, 18 September 1753.
107 NAS GD 25/9/1, Archibald Kennedy's notebook.
108 NAS GD 25/9/40, Archibald Kennedy to Sir Thomas Kennedy, 5 June 1753.
109 Ibid., same to same, 29 March 1753.
110 NAS GD 25/9/40, op. cit., Archibald Kennedy to Sir Thomas, 19 March 1754.
111 Ibid., same to same, December 1754.
112 NAS GD 25/9/25, bundle 9, account with Hugh Pype, 17 May 1754.
113 NAS GD 25/9/42, factor's accounts, 1745–54.
114 NAS GD 25/9/40, Archibald Kennedy to Sir Thomas, 19 March 1754.
115 NAS GD 25/9/59, rent book p. 25.
116 NAS GD 25/9/40, Archibald Kennedy to Sir Thomas, 18 September 1753.
117 NAS GD 25/9/28, letters of introduction – Rome and Paris.
118 There are accounts for these at NAS GD 25/9/7, accounts for farmhouses 1755–68 (in fact 1769).
119 NAS GD 25/9/40, Archibald Kennedy to Sir Thomas, 18 September 1753.
120 Information for David Earl of Cassillis, defender, against Sir Adam Fergusson of Kilkerran, 26 April 1777, Cassillis Library, pp. 4–5 and 11.
121 Kilkerran MSS, Box 2, bundle 213, copy letter of Sir Archibald Kennedy to Earl of Cassillis, 20 June 1776.
122 NAS GD 25/9/1, commissions etc.
123 Frances Wilkins, Scottish Customs & Excise Records with particular reference to Strathclyde from 1707 onwards, pp. 13–14.
124 Frances Wilkins, George Moore and his Friends, pp. 218–21.
125 Manx Museum, George Moore to Archibald Kennedy, 14 April 1753, transcribed by Frances Wilkins.
126 Same to same, 2 August 1754.
127 Statistical Account of Scotland, 1791–1799, vol. 10, p. 487.
128 NAS GD25/8/1278A.
129 Statistical Account of Scotland, 1791–99, vol. 10, pp. 486–7.
130 William Aiton, p. 622.
131 Sir William Chambers, A Treatise on Civil Architecture and Eileen Harris, The Genius of Robert Adam, p. 319.
132 CCEO plan of the southern part of the barony of Straiton by James Gregg, 1765.
133 Forbes W. Robertson, Early Scottish Gardeners and their plants 1650–1750, pp. 195–6.
134 NAS GD 25/9/42, rental 1755.
135 Based on NAS GD 25/30/2, the diary of planting, 1755–6, Forbes W. Robertson, Early Scottish Gardeners and their plants 1650–1750, pp. 195–6.
136 NAS GD 25/9/7, garden accounts.
137 Ibid., financial papers 1755–68.
138 Ibid., account with Gavin Hamilton, 1761.
139 J.B. (Jean-Baptiste) Du Halde, A Description of the Empire of China and Chinese-Tartary.
140 Hon Robert Boyle, The General History of the Air.
141 The Natural History of Bees.
142 Alvaro Alonso Barba, The Art of Metals.
143 Andrea Palladio, The Architecture of A. Palladio.
144 John Gay, Fables.
145 John Gay, Wine, a Poem.
146 Samuel Clarke, A General Martyrologie.
147 NAS GD 25/9/23, letters of introduction 1750–60, introduction to the Marquis Frescobaldi, 1 January 1760.
148 NAS GD 25/9/46, file on hunting.
149 Manx Museum, George Moore to James Hutchison of Ayr, 20 February and 21 August 1758, transcribed by Frances Wilkins. The best account of smuggling in the North Channel in this later period is to be found in L.M. Cullen, Smuggling and the Ayrshire Economic Boom of the 1760s and 1770s.
150 Ayrshire Archive Centre CE 76/1/3, petition 6 January 1760.
151 PRO HCA 25/42, letter of marque for the Dorset, 13 April 1757.
152 NAS GD29/46/1, naval papers, file on the Dorset privateer.
153 Frances Wilkins, Strathclyde's Smuggling Story, pp. 27–8.
154 James Paterson, History of the Counties, vol. 1, p. 343 and NAS RT 911/28/39.
155 R.H. Campbell, Owners and Occupiers, pp. 108–9.
156 John Habakkuk, Marriage, pp. 1–49.
157 see Henry Blyth, Old Q.
158 PRO SP 54/8/21, letter of Earl of Ruglen, 5 July 1715.
159 House of Lords Journal 1760–4, p. 144.
160 NAS GD 25/9/38, private letters 1567–1909, bundle 1761–6, Isa Douglas to Countess of Cassillis, 3 February 1762.
161 Statistical Account of Scotland, 1791–1799, vol. 6, p. 104.
162 James Paterson, History of the Counties, vol. 1, part 1, p. 389, and NAS GD 25/9/30/2, folder entitled 'woods', sale of Dalrymple woods, 1762.
163 William Robertson, Ayrshire 1st History and Historic Families, Ayr, 1908, p. 32.
164 William Abercrummie, 'Carrick in 1696', p. 9.
165 NAS GD 25/9/1, commissions etc.
166 NAS GD 25/9/41, bundle of letters from John Bell.
167 John Ingamells, A Dictionary of British and Irish Travellers, p. 568, which cites NAS GD 248/99/3, letter of Abbé Grant to the Earl of Cassillis, 3 October 1764.
168 NAS GD 25/9/29. This portrait was misidentified as being of David the 10th Earl.
169 NAS GD 25/9/23, letter of Abbé Grant to the Earl of Cassillis, 5 May 1768.
170 Ibid., financial papers 1764–8, letter of Earl of Cassillis to Thomas Coutts, 4 April 1768.
171 Ibid., bundle of accounts with Thomas Coutts & Co., vouchers 1764–5.
172 These are scattered through the collection drawings of Culzean held by the RCAHMS.
173 NAS GD 25/9/14, bundle of papers concerning Arab horses.
174 NAS GD 25/9/20, bundle of accounts with Thomas Coutts & Co., letter from Sir Thomas Kennedy, May 1765. This seems to be the same Andrew Turnbull who was behind the New Smyrna settlement in Florida, see David Hancock, Citizens of the World, p. 161, and for a more positive view Jane G. Landers (ed.), Colonial Plantations and Economy in Florida.
175 NAS GD 25/9/1, Miscellaneous papers, memorandum, n.d. and information supplied by Charles Wyvill.
176 NAS GD 25/9/14, op. cit.
177 Sporting Calendar (London: 1770).
178 NAS GD 25/9/20, financial papers, 1772.
179 NAS GD 25/9/42, factor's accounts, 1743.
180 NAS GD 25/9/8, bundle Culzean buildings, 1766–7.
181 NAS GD 25/9/9, financial papers, 1766.

182 NAS GD 25/9/8, bundle Culzean buildings, 1766–7, memorandum.
183 NAS GD 25/9/9, financial papers 1766.
184 NAS GD 25/9/8, bundle Culzean buildings, 1766–7, memorandum.
185 Ibid.
186 NAS GD 25/9/8, financial papers 1772–3.
187 J. McBain, *The Merrick and the Neighbouring Hills*, pp. 204–5.
188 NAS GD 25/9/8, financial papers 1766–7.
189 *Statistical Account of Scotland, 1791–1799*, vol. 3, p. 589.
190 NAS GD25/9/44 bundle 6, repairs to Maybole Castle, 1771.
191 Ayrshire Sasines, No. 3497, 28 July 1792.
192 http://www.maybole.org/familyhistory/Archives/Maybole
193 Andrew Wight, *Present State of Husbandry in Scotland*, vol. 3 part 1, p. 167.
194 *Statistical Account of Scotland, 1791–1799*, vol. 10, p. 490.
195 Ibid., p. 174.
196 NAS GD 25/9/14, financial papers 1767–8.
197 L.M. Cullen, *Smuggling*, p. 4.
198 Ayrshire Archive Centre, CE 76, 24 January and 27 February 1765.
199 Frances Wilkins, *Manx Slave Traders*, p. 119.
200 Ibid., p. 120.
201 Ayrshire Archive Centre, CE 76 1/10, 24 February 1778 where he is described as 'late merchant in Liverpool now residing at Greenan'.
202 David Hancock, *Citizens of the World*, pp. 121 and 139.
203 Coutts' ledgers vols 45, p. 45 and 49, p. 145.
204 NAS GD25/9/27/1, Florida speculation, 1767.
205 Quoted in Jane G. Landers, *Colonial Plantations*, p. 14, Ballindalloch Castle Muniments 659.
206 Ballindalloch Castle Muniments 474.
207 NAS GD 25/9/41 letters from John Bell, letter of 22 January 1770.
208 Coutts' ledgers, vols 52, p. 158 and 56 p. 104.
209 For an account of this catastrophe see Charles W. Munn, *The Scottish Provincial Banking Companies 1747–1864*, pp. 29–36 and Frank Brady, *So Fast to Ruin*.
210 A list of prominent shareholders in given in William Robertson, *Old Ayrshire Days*, pp. 269–70.
211 NAS GD 25/9/41 letters from John Bell, letter of 3 August 1772.
212 NAS GD 25/9/20, financial papers 1676–1875, bundle of drafts on Douglas Heron & Co., 1772.
213 Sir Lewis Namier and John Brooke, *The House of Commons, 1754–1790*, vol. 1, p. 471.
214 Coutts ledgers, vol. 52, p. 158.
215 Ibid., vol. 2, p. 5.
216 *Letters of George Dempster to Sir Adam Fergusson 1756–1813*, p. 67.
217 NAS GD 25/9/8, financial papers 1768–74, account with John Bell 1773–4.
218 These events are described in Namier and Brooke, *The House of Commons*, pp. 470–3.
219 William K. Wimsatt Jr and Frederick A. Pottle, *Boswell for the Defence 1769–1774*, p. 168.
220 *20th Report of the Royal Commission on Historical Manuscripts, Dartmouth*, vol. 1, p. 370, letter from Sir James Oughton, 16 November 1774.
221 HL Loudoun MSS.
222 PRO SP 54/46/145, fols 159–61.
223 NAS GD 25/9/9, accounts with John Hunter, partner in Sir William Forbes & Co.
224 NAS GD 25/9/9, bundle funeral expenses of Thomas Earl of Cassillis.
225 James Wright, *A Recommendation of Brotherly Love*, p. 12. The only copy known to the author is in the library at Cassillis House.
226 PRO Prob 1017 q.116, p. 153.
227 HL Loudoun MSS.
228 NAS GD 25/9/9 bundle 4, election expenses.
229 *Annual Register*, 1789, pp. 298 and 304.

CHAPTER 4

1 NAS GD 25/9/9, bundle accounts with John Hunter, partner in Sir William Forbes & Co. and farm papers and accounts, 1777.
2 *Information for David Earl of Cassillis, defender, against Sir Adam Fergusson of Kilkerran, 26 April 1777*, Cassillis Library, pp. 6–7.
3 Ibid., pp. 11–13.
4 Kilkerran MSS, box 2, bundle 213, copy letter of Sir Archibald Kennedy to Earl of Cassillis, 20 June 1776.
5 West Yorkshire Archive Service, C/3/1/5/1/14.
6 *Statistical Account of Scotland, 1791–9*, vol. 10, p. 477.
7 Rob Close, *Ayrshire & Arran*, pp. 173–4.
8 NAS GD25/9/9 bundle 3, account for cutting foundations, 1777.
9 Coutts ledgers, vol. 68, p. 88.
10 Coutts ledgers, vol. 72, p. 101.
11 E.H.M. Cox, *A History of Gardening in Scotland*, p. 107.
12 NAS GD 25/9/9, Hugh Cairncross's accounts 1777–80.

13 *Tour of the Western Highlands* (1788, p. 119), cited by A.T. Bolton, *The Work of Robert Adam*, vol. 2, p. 274, and Eileen Harris, *The Genius of Robert Adam*, p. 321.
14 Coutts ledgers, vols 76, p. 103; 78, p. 106; and 80, p. 125.
15 For example Margaret H.B. Sanderson, *Robert Adam in Ayrshire*, p. 22.
16 I am grateful to Dr John Shaw of the National Archives of Scotland for this information.
17 Irma S. Lustig and Frederick A. Pottle, *Boswell: the Applause of the Jury 1782–1785*, p. 14.
18 See Michael W. McCahill, 'Scottish Peerage in the House of Lords', p. 190.
19 Cassillis MSS, letter of Sir Grey Cooper to the Earl of Cassillis, 30 April 1789.
20 Andrew Wight, *Present State of Husbandry*, p. 174.
21 *Statistical Account of Scotland, 1791–1799*, vol. 10, p. 491.
22 NAS GD 25/9/20, financial papers 1789–90.
23 Alison Mitchell, *Pre-1858 Gravestone Inscriptions*, p. 140.
24 Robert Heron, *Observations*, p. 325.
25 Eileen Harris, *The Genius of Robert Adam*, p. 321.
26 NAS GD 18/5486/16.
27 Eileen Harris, *The Genius of Robert Adam*, p. 333.
28 NAS GD 25/9/10, bundle 1–51.
29 The connection with the Whites has long been suspected (see for example Andrew Sclater, 'Picturesque privacy: landscape improvement at Culzean from c. 1750') but has now been proved from an entry in the ledgers of Drummonds Bank in the Royal Bank of Scotland Archive for 1790, which shows a payment by the Earl of Cassillis to Thomas White of £30 17 shillings and 5 pence. See also David Brown, 'Lancelot Brown and his associates', and Deborah Turnbull, 'Thomas White: 18th-century landscape designer and arboriculturalist', unpublished PhD thesis, University of Hull, 1990.
30 A.A. Tait, *The Landscape Garden in Scotland – 1735–1835*, pp. 148–73.
31 A.A. Sclater, 'Picturesque privacy', pp. 23–4.
32 Royal Bank of Scotland Archives, ledgers of Drummonds Bank, 1790.
33 A.A. Tait, *The Landscape Garden*, p. 156.
34 James Paterson, *History of the Counties*, vol. 2, p. 389.
35 John Strawhorn, *The History of Ayr*, pp. 115 and 117.
36 *Statistical Account of Scotland, 1791–1799*, vol. 21, p. 32.
37 NAS GD 25/9/20, unnamed bundle, letter to Hunter & Co., 8 December 1789.
38 NAS GD 25/9/12, abstract of trustees accounts, 1796, and rental 1795 and NAS GD 27/7/328, letter of John Hunter to Thomas Kennedy of Dunure, 16 January 1793.
39 NAS CS230/C/10/1, representations by Sir Andrew Cathcart, 1795.
40 NAS RD2/257 p. 44, will of 10th Earl of Cassillis.
41 R.H. Campbell, *Owners and Occupiers*, p. 109 and John Rankine, *A Treatise on the Rights and Burdens Incident to the Ownership of Lands and Heritage in Scotland*, pp. 1043–56.
42 NAS GD 27/7/328, letter of John Hunter to Thomas Kennedy of Dunure, 16 January 1793.
43 NAS GD 25/9/42/9, letter to James Chalmers, 26 August 1807.
44 NAS RD2/257 p. 44, will of 10th Earl of Cassillis.
45 For a biography of Archibald Kennedy (on which much of this section is based) see Milton M. Klein, 'Archibald Kennedy: imperial pamphleteer'.
46 Timothy J. Shannon, *Indians and Colonists at the Crossroads of Empire*, p. 20.
47 Lawrence Leder, *Colonial Legacy*, p. 79.
48 BL MSS Eg.Ch. 7926.
49 Lawrence Leder, *Colonial Legacy*, p. 84.
50 Ibid., p. 83.
51 *Collections of the New York Historical Society*, pp. 285–6.
52 Ibid., p. 286.
53 Montgomery Schuyler, *The Schuyler Family*.
54 Lawrence Leder, *Colonial Legacy*, pp. 76 and 86–7.
55 Ibid., pp. 73–4 and Kennedy, *The Importance of Gaining*, cited in text, pp. 6 and 15.
56 Ibid., pp. 87–8.
57 Timothy J. Shannon, *Indians and Colonists*, pp. 29–30.
58 Carl Van Doren, *Benjamin Franklin*, pp. 212–13.
59 Lawrence Leder, *Colonial Legacy*, pp. 95–6.
60 Quoted in ibid., p. 97 from Kennedy, *Observations*, cited in text, pp. 30–1.
61 Quoted in his entry in *American Dictionary of Biography*, and Archibald Kennedy, *Serious Considerations and the Present State of Affairs of the Northern Colonies*, 1754
62 Lawrence Leder, *Colonial Legacy*, p. 98.
63 Carl Van Doren, *Benjamin Franklin*, p. 218.
64 David B. Morrison, *Two Hundredth Anniversary of Saint Andrew's Society*, p. 8.
65 Quoted in Lawrence Leder, *Colonial Legacy*, p. 105, and J.L. Bullion, *A Great and Necessary Measure*, p. 212.
66 John Charnock, *Biographia Navalis*, p. 253, and Julian Gwyn, *The Enterprising Admiral*, pp. 432–3.

67 PRO ADM 51/662, captain's log book of HMS *Otter*.
68 Pitcairn Jones, *Sea Officers of the Royal Navy 1660–1815*, National Maritime Museum, entry for A. Kennedy.
69 PRO ADM 51/171, captain's log HMS *Centaur*.
70 Stanley M. Pargellis, *Lord Loudoun in North America*, pp. 68–71.
71 HL Loudoun papers include manifests of the cargoes.
72 PRO ADM 106/259 contains Captain Kennedy's letters to the Admiralty concerning this assignment.
73 HL Loudoun papers, letters of Captain Kennedy to Earl of Loudoun, 16 October and 15 November 1756.
74 *Collections of the New York Historical Society*, p. 287, and Frederick W. Ricord and William Nelson (eds), *Documents Relating to the Colonial History of the State of New Jersey*, p. 460.
75 Based on Louis P. Masur (ed.), *The Autobiography of Benjamin Franklin*, pp. 136–9. I am grateful to Commander Roger Parkes for drawing my attention to this reference.
76 *The Commissioned Officers of the Royal Navy 1660–1815*, vol. 2, p. 511. Copy in National Maritime Museum.
77 Sir J.W. (John William) Fortescue, *A History of the British Army*, vol II, pp. 342–3.
78 See PRO ADM 1/2010, captain's letters, Archibald Kennedy, 1757–60.
79 Michael Lewis, *A Social History of the Navy 1793–1815*, pp. 316–30.
80 Daniel A. Baugh, *British Naval Administration in the Age of Walpole*, pp. 110–17.
81 See for example C.R. Boxer, *The Portuguese Seaborne Empire 1415–1825*, pp. 164–7.
82 Michael Lewis, *A Social History*, pp. 333–40.
83 This action is described in PRO ADM 1/2010, captain's letters, Archibald Kennedy to the Lords of the Admiralty, 14 September 1759.
84 PRO ADM 51/3835, captain's log book of HMS *Flamborough*.
85 PRO ADM 1/2010, captain's letters, Archibald Kennedy to the Lords of the Admiralty, 26 November 1759.
86 W.L. Clowes, *The Royal Navy – A History from the Earliest Times to the Present*, vol. 3, p. 302.
87 This section is based on *Annual Register* 1760, pp. 101–2, which itself is a digest of PRO ADM 1/2011, captain's letters, Archibald Kennedy to the Lords of the Admiralty, 14 April 1760.
88 PRO ADM 51/3835.
89 *Annual Register*, 1760, p.142.
90 PRO SP 89/53, fol. 126.
91 PRO ADM 1/2011, captain's letters, Archibald Kennedy to the Lords of the Admiralty, 13 March 1761.
92 Based on John Charnock, pp. 253–5 and PRO ADM 51/79 captain's log of HMS *Blonde*.
93 His son, the 1st Marquess left £27,750 in Portuguese 5 per cent Bonds, £46,318 in 3 per cent British government consols and £29,342 in Bank of England stock, which it seems safe to assume he had inherited from his father (CCEO Vidimus of the Affairs of the late Most Honourable Archibald Marquis of Ailsa, 1 April 1847).
94 See PRO ADM 1/2012, captain's letters, Archibald Kennedy to the Lords of the Admiralty, 15 February 1765 and 15 January 1766.
95 PRO ADM 51/213, captain's log of HMS *Coventry*.
96 Ibid., and ADM33/436, accounts for HMS *Coventry*, 1763–8 final folio.
97 This account is based on Neil R. Stout, 'Captain Kennedy and the Stamp Act'. The supporting documents are to be found at PRO ADM1/2012, captain's letters, 1765–7, section letters produced by Archibald Kennedy in his defence.
98 See *Report of the Royal Commission on Historical Manuscripts, American MSS*, 59/4, p. 281.
99 Marchioness of Tullibardine, *A Military History of Perthshire 1660–1902*, pp. 396–9.
100 NAS GD 25/9/25. financial papers 1781–95, account for a week's lodging 1781.
101 Coutts ledgers, vol. 72.
102 NAS GD 25/9/79, will of Captain Archibald Kennedy, 1782.
103 Jacob M. Price, *Tobacco in Atlantic Trade*, pp. 66–70.
104 Cassillis MSS, letter Sir Grey Cooper to the Earl of Cassillis, 30 April 1789.
105 James Wilson and Patrick Shaw, *Cases*, pp. 242–3.
106 Sir Herbert Maxwell, *Memories of the Month*, p. 200.
107 NAS GD 25/9/29/1, genealogy, inferred from letter of John Hunter to Captain Kennedy junior, 16 July 1792, and *Scots Magazine*, vol. 53, 1791, p. 103.
108 Violet Jacob, *The Lairds of Dun*, p. 279.
109 PRO ADM 22/4, p. 281.
110 NAS GD 25/9/79, will of Archibald, Earl of Cassillis, 1794.
111 Coutts ledgers, vols 89, p. 604; and 92, p. 641.
112 Marchioness of Tullibardine, *A Military History*, pp. 397–8.
113 NAS GD 25/9/45, military miscellaneous, caricature of General Small.
114 Inferred from NAS GD 25/9/78, will of Archibald, Earl of Cassillis, 1794.
115 NAS GD 25/9/20, bundle A.
116 NAS GD 125/7/327.
117 See NAS GD 25/9/29/2.
118 NAS GD 25/9/20, unnamed bundle, letter of 5 October 1790.
119 Francis Grose, *The Antiquities of Scotland*, p. 209.
120 NAS GD 25/9/10, account book of Hugh Cairncross, 1787–92.
121 Ibid., bundle 2, audited account with Hugh Cairncross, 1794.
122 Ibid., bundle 1.
123 Ibid., bundle 1, item 37.
124 Ibid., bundle 1/42.
125 NAS GD25/9/1.
126 NAS GD 25/9/42/1, letter Richard Campbell to Earl of Cassillis, 12 December 1796.
127 *Statistical Account of Scotland, 1791–1799*, vol. 12, pp. 85–8.
128 NAS GD 25/9/29/2, genealogy, letter John Hunter to Captain Kennedy junior, 5 June 1792.
129 *Scots Magazine*, vol. 53, 1791, p. 103.
130 J.E. Cookson, *The British Armed Nation 1793–1815*, p. 135.
131 NAS GD 25/9/29/2 genealogy, letter John Hunter to Captain Kennedy junior, 16 July 1792.
132 NAS GD 27/7/328, petition to Lord Craig from Sir Andrew Cathcart, 28 January 1793.
133 NAS CS 230/C/10/1, case papers.
134 NAS GD 27/7/328, letter of John Hunter to Thomas Kennedy of Dunure, 16 January 1793.
135 Ibid., same to same, 23 January 1793.
136 Ibid., same to same 28 January 1793, and NAS GD 25/9/35, Cathcart case papers.
137 Col. William Fullarton, *General View of the Agriculture of the County of Ayr*, p. 91.

CHAPTER 5

1 Information supplied by the National Gallery of Art, Washington.
2 NAS GD 25/9/42/2, file of letters from the Reverend Alexander Kennedy.
3 NAS GD 27/7/328, letter of John Hunter to Thomas Kennedy, 12 December 1793.
4 NAS GD 25/9/42/3.
5 NAS GD 25/9/12, abstract of the trustees' affairs, 1796.
6 Ibid., rental 1795.
7 NAS GD 25/9/10, financial papers 1793–4.
8 NAS GD 25/9/79, will of Archibald, Earl of Cassillis, 1794.
9 *Army List*, 1793.
10 CCEO, Dun rental, 1839–42.
11 NAS GD 25/9/10, financial papers 1793–4.
12 Cassillis MSS, affidavit signed by Robert Kennedy, 15 November 1796.
13 Coutts ledgers, vols 141, pp. 1694–5, and 168, p. 1936.
14 Charlotte Anne Disbrowe, *Old Days in Diplomacy*, p. 19.
15 Cassillis MSS, letter of Thomas Scott to the Earl of Cassillis, January 1795.
16 Ibid., letter Jonathan Mallett to Earl of Cassillis, 16 February 1796.
17 NAS SC 6/72/5, Ayrshire Registers of Improvements, 181 p. 72.
18 Cassillis MSS, letter of Captain John Kennedy to the Earl of Cassillis, 11 September 1811.
19 Ibid., copy letter to Coutts & Co., 26 October 1802.
20 Ibid., letter of Captain John Kennedy to the Earl of Cassillis, 11 September, 1811.
21 *Scots Magazine*, vol. 55, 1793, p. 310.
22 Ann E. Whetstone, *Scottish County Government in the Eighteenth and Nineteenth Centuries*, p. 97.
23 J.E.T. Cookson, *The British Armed Nation*, pp. 133–4.
24 Ibid., p. 141.
25 Ibid., pp. 28–30 and 35–6.
26 Ann E. Whetstone, *Scottish County Government*, p. 104.
27 NAS GD 25/9/2, Maybole volunteers letter of Thomas Kennedy of Dunure to Earl of Cassillis, 6 February 1797.
28 Ibid., draft letter of Earl of Cassillis to Thomas Kennedy attached to above.
29 Ibid., letter of Thomas Kennedy to Earl of Cassillis, 13 February 1797.
30 Ibid., Richard Campbell to Earl of Cassillis, 16 February 1797.
31 His grandmother was the sister of Archibald Kennedy of New York, the Earl's grandfather, Kilkerran MSS, Box 2, bundle 213.
32 Cassillis MSS, John Shaw to same, 3 March 1797.
33 Ibid., printed notice of meeting of 24 February 1797.
34 Ibid., William Niven to Earl of Cassillis, 3 March 1797.
35 Ibid., John Shaw to Earl of Cassillis, 29 March 1797.
36 NAS GD25/9/15.
37 RCAHMS Culzean collection AYD43/96. These plans, which form part of the Culzean archive, were deposited by the National Trust for Scotland and are only partially catalogued.

38 Ibid.
39 Information supplied by Lady Shaw Stewart.
40 NAS GD 25/9/15, financial papers, 1797–9 and Coutts ledgers, vol. 147, p. 504.
41 NAS GD 25/9/23, financial papers, 1795–1800.
42 NAS GD 51/1/197/6, letter of Earl of Cassillis to Henry Dundas, 25 March 1795.
43 NAS GD 51/1/197/8, copy letter of Henry Dundas to the Earl of Cassillis, 25 May 1795.
44 NAS GD 25/9/42.
45 PRO 30/8/121, fol. 125.
46 Kilkerran MSS, Box 1, bundle 99, Thomas Kennedy of Dunure to Sir Adam Fergusson, 15 February 1803.
47 Ibid., copy letter Sir Adam Fergusson to Thomas Kennedy of Dunure, 21 February 1803.
48 NAS GD 51/1/198/3/19–22, 24, 26, 28.
49 Cassillis MSS, draft letter Earl of Cassillis to Robert Peel, n.d.
50 See BL Add MSS58983 fols 56–139.
51 Cassillis MSS, letter Lord Grenville to Earl of Cassillis, 29 April 1803.
52 Ibid., Lord Grenville to Earl of Cassillis, 2 November 1819.
53 See BL Add MSS58983, fol. 93, 30 Sept. 1803.
54 Cassillis MSS, memorandum by Earl of Cassillis 1804–5.
55 See Philip Ziegler, King William IV.
56 Sporting Magazine, vol. 9, 1796–7, racing calendar, pp. 6–7 and 18.
57 Ibid., vol. 14, 1799–1800, racing calendar, p. 41.
58 Ibid., vol. 15, 1801–2, racing calendar, p. and vol. 17, 1802–3, racing calendar, p. 21.
59 Ibid., vol. 25, 1804–5, racing calendar, p. 20, and vol. 27, 1805–6, Racing Calendar, p. 9.
60 Ibid., 1806–7, racing calendar, p. 8.
61 Cassillis MSS, memorandum by Earl of Cassillis 1804–5.
62 Ibid., letter William Maule to Earl of Cassillis, 20 May 1807.
63 James Paterson, History of the Counties, vol. 1, part 1, p. 332.
64 Nicholas Phillipson, The Scottish Whigs and Reform of the Court of Session 1785–1830, pp. 168–9.
65 Henry Cockburn, Memorials of his Time 1779–1830, p. 429.
66 NAS GD 25/9/42/5, letter David Cathcart to Earl of Cassillis 7 July 1800.
67 NAS GD 25/9/42 generally.
68 NAS GD 25/9/42/3, letter, 11 May 1800.
69 NAS GD 25/9/42/5, letter David Cathcart to Lord Grenville, 26 May 1805, copied to Earl of Moira.
70 Ibid., same to same 31 July 1806.
71 Cassillis MSS, copy letter Earl of Cassillis to Earl of Moira, 3 February 1806.
72 Ibid., letter Lord Grenville to Earl of Cassillis, 4 February 1806.
73 NAS GD 25/30/2, letter Earl of Cassillis to Earl of Moira, 4 February 1806.
74 Ibid., letter Earl of Moira to Earl of Cassillis, 7 February 1806.
75 Cassillis MSS, letter Earl of Cassillis to Lord Grenville, 19 October 1806.
76 Ibid., letter Lord Grenville to Earl of Cassillis, 24 October, 1806.
77 BL Add MSS58983, fol. 64, 17 November 1806.
78 Ibid.
79 30th Report of the Royal Commission on Historical Manuscripts, Vol. 8, p. 447.
80 Cassillis MSS, letter Lord Grenville to Earl Cassillis, 21 November 1806.
81 Ibid., draft letter Earl of Cassillis to Earl Spencer, n.d.
82 London Court Directory, 1808.
83 Inferred from NAS GD 26/13/878.
84 Cassillis MSS, invoice from George Fitcher, 18 May 1811.
85 Ibid., letter Earl of Cassillis to Earl of Cassillis, 24 March 1807.
86 Brook's betting book 1772–1892, London Metropolitan Archive, ACC/2371/BC/04/073/1, pp.79 and 80.
87 Cassillis MSS, copy correspondence between Spencer Perceval and Lord Grenville, September 1809, and letter Lord Grenville to Earl of Cassillis, 29 September 1809.
88 Coutts ledgers, vol. 218, p. 597.
89 BL Add Mss 58983 fol. 95.
90 Ibid.
91 Cassillis MSS, memorandum by the Earl of Cassillis, n.d., watermark 1811.
92 Ibid., letter Lord Grenville to Earl of Cassillis, Tuesday, n.d.
93 Royal Archives GEO 41586–7.
94 Cassillis MSS, letter Duke of Clarence to Earl of Cassillis, 21 June 1811.
95 Ibid., letter Lord Grenville to Earl of Cassillis, 26 May 1812.
96 Ibid., letter Lord Grenville to Earl of Cassillis, 19 May 1813.
97 NAS GD 25/9/42/5, notes for an Act to sell parts of the Estate to pay off debts contracted by David, Earl of Cassillis, 21 July 1807.
98 NAS GD 25/9/15, factor's accounts, 1806–7 and CCEO, factory accounts on the estate of Cassillis, 1805–6.
99 CCEO, factory accounts on the estate of Cassillis, 1805–6.
100 Cassillis MSS, account of John Hunter WS, 1807, and RCAHMS AYD 43/27.
101 NAS GD 25/9/36/3, rental of the estate including land claimed by Sir Andrew Cathcart, 1807, and report in the conjoint process of the Rt. Hon. Archibald Earl of Cassillis etc., 1810.
102 John Habakkuk, Marriage, p. 532.
103 Royal Archives GEO 41586–7, and BL MSS Add 58983 fol. 98.
104 J.C.B. Cooksey, Alexander Nasmyth HRSA 1758–1840, pp. 30, 55, 91 and 99.
105 Cassillis MSS, invoice from Rundell , Bridge, Rundell, March 1809.
106 John Wilson and Patrick Shaw, Cases, pp. 263–5.
107 Cassillis MSS, copy letter Earl of Cassillis to Lord Grenville, 15 November 1810.
108 Ibid., day orderly book, 1813–33, flyleaf.
109 Ibid., p. 2.
110 Ibid., p. 38
111 Ibid., p. 24.
112 Ibid., p. 29.
113 Ibid., p. 21.
114 Ibid., pp. 9 and 11.
115 BL MSS Add 58983, fols 114–6.
116 Ibid, fols 104 and 127.
117 Ibid., fol. 104.
118 Violet Jacob, The Lairds of Dun, p. 291.
119 Cassillis MSS, day orderly book, 1813–33, p. 76.
120 Violet Jacob, The Lairds of Dun, pp. 279–80.
121 Cassillis MSS, letter Alexander Hunter to Marquess of Ailsa, 30 December 1835.
122 Ibid., fol. 110.
123 Violet Jacob, The Lairds of Dun, p. 285.
124 Cassillis MSS, letter Alice Erskine to Earl of Cassillis, n.d.
125 Ibid., invoice from Rundell, Bridge & Rundell, 1810–11.
126 Ibid., letter from same, 26 March 1815.
127 Ibid., letter R.M. Crew to Earl of Cassillis, 13 August 1813.
128 Information supplied by De Witt Bailey.
129 Cassillis MSS, letter Adam Robertson to Earl of Cassillis, 6 August 1813.
130 Ibid., letter John Bellis to same, 17 July 1813.
131 Ibid., same to same, 25 July 1812.
132 Ibid., letter R.E. Pritchett to same, 22 August 1814.
133 Eileen Harris, The Genius of Robert Adam, p. 325.
134 Cassillis MSS, pp. 21–2.
135 Ibid., pp. 48 and 97–8.
136 A.A. Tait, The Landscape Garden, p. 167.
137 A.A. Slater, Picturesque Privacy, p. 27.
138 Cassillis MSS, day orderly book, 1813–33, p. 7.
139 A.A. Slater, Picturesque Privacy, p. 26, Ayrshire Archives CO3/5/13, p. 138 and CCEO estate accounts 1805–6.
140 Acts of Parliament, 49 George III cap. 32.
141 A.A. Slater, Picturesque Privacy, p. 27.
142 Cassillis MSS, day orderly book, 1813–33, p. 15.
143 Judith Roberts 'Well temper'd clay.
144 Cassillis MSS, day orderly book, 1813–33, p. 51.
145 Robert Lugar, Plans and Views of Buildings Executed in England and Scotland in the Castellated and Other Styles, plate 31.
146 Ibid., pp. 39 and 47 and Culzean MSS, account book 1814–19, p. 100.
147 RCAHMS, AYD 43 Culzean drawings no. 31 (two drawings).
148 Sir Herbert Maxwell, Memories, p. 200.
149 RCAHMS, AYD 43 Culzean drawings no. 108 and CCEO drawing of the Pennyglen gate lodge, n.d.
150 Ibid., no. 42 and others unnumbered.
151 Ibid., no. 112.
152 H.M Colvin, A biographical dictionary of British architects, 1600–1840, p. 975.
153 CCEO, factory accounts on the estate of Cassillis, 1805.
154 RCAHMS, unnumbered drawing.
155 Cassillis MSS, day orderly book, 1813–33, p. 25.
156 Kilkerran MSS, box 5, bundle 9, letter Earl of Cassillis to Sir James Fergusson, 12 March 1824.
157 Cassillis MSS, day orderly book, 1813–33, p. 14.
158 Ibid., p. 44.
159 Ibid., estate ledger 1809–15, p. 25.
160 Culzean MSS, account book 1814–19, p. 43.
161 Cassillis MSS, day orderly book, 1813–33, p. 29.
162 Ibid., p. 51.
163 Ibid., p. 51.
164 Ibid., p. 59.
165 Ibid., p. 63.
166 Ibid., p. 67.
167 Ibid., letter Lord Grenville to Lord Cassillis, 18 January 1816.
168 J.C.B. Cooksey, Alexander Nasmyth, p. 125.
169 Ibid., catalogue numbers D23, D24, O8 and 19, Q9, 10, 14A, 16, 17, 18, 36A, 37A, 38A, 39A, 40A, and R7.

170 NAS GD 25/9/42/5, letter David Cathcart to the Earl of Cassillis, 25 March 1813.
171 Cassillis MSS, letter of Earl of Cassillis, 25 November 1913.
172 Ibid., letter David Cathcart to Earl of Cassillis, 30 January 1814.

CHAPTER 6

1 Violet Jacob, *The Lairds of Dun*, p. 285.
2 NAS GD 25/30/2, receipt for Marshall Blücher's uniform at the battle of Leipzig.
3 General Sir James Shaw Kennedy, *Notes on the Battle of Waterloo*, autobiographical memoir. The general added Kennedy to his name on succeeding to his wife's Kirkmichael estate.
4 Cassillis MSS, letter of John Kennedy to the Earl of Cassillis, 11 September 1812 and SRO CS46/1841/6.
5 NAS GD 26/13/878.
6 J. Gleare, *The Triumph of Justice*, pp. 1–128.
7 Donald Simpson, *Twickenham Past*, p. 76.
8 Cassillis MSS, letter Lord Grenville to Earl of Cassillis, 18 September 1817.
9 J.A. Symon, *Scottish Farming Past and Present*, p. 329.
10 John Stevenson, *Popular Disturbances 1700–1832*, pp. 239–43.
11 Cassillis MSS, Lord Grenville to Earl of Cassillis, 21 October 1817.
12 Ibid., same to same, 2 November 1819.
13 NAS GD 25/9/42.
14 Deduced from Ayrshire Archives Centre ADT 60/8/10
15 Charles D. Gairdner, *Autobiography of C.D. Gairdner, Auchans, Written at the Suggestion of and Revised by the Earl of Eglinton, June, 1861*, p. 13.
16 Ibid.
17 Ibid.
18 H.M. Colvin, *A Biographical Dictionary*, p. 315.
19 RCAHMS, AYD43/27.
20 Cassillis MSS, day orderly book, 1813–33, pp. 114–20.
21 Ibid., p. 113.
22 Ibid., inventory of Culzean, 1846, p. 69.
23 Ibid., day orderly book, p. 120.
24 Ibid., p. 129.
25 Ibid., p. 129.
26 Ibid., p. 124.
27 Ibid., p. 127.
28 Ibid., pp. 135–6 and 148.
29 Ibid., p. 142.
30 Ibid., pp. 13–14.
31 BL MSS Add 58983, fol. 129.
32 Cassillis MSS, day orderly book, 1813–33, fol. 131.
33 Ibid., fol. 134.
34 Ibid., letter Lord Grenville to Earl of Cassillis, 10 December 1819.
35 Ibid., letter Lord Grenville to Earl Cassillis, 15 December 1819.
36 BL MSS Add 58983, fol. 137.
37 Devon Record Office, 152M/C1820/OH46
38 Ibid., 152M/C1820/OH47.
39 Cassillis MSS, letter Lord Kennedy to Earl of Cassillis, 28 January 1818.
40 Ibid., letter Earl of Cassillis to James Donaldson, 15 December 1823.
41 *The Repository of Arts, Literature, Fashions, Manufactures, etc.*, vol. III, no. XVI, 1 April 1824, pp. 186–90.
42 Cassillis MSS, letter Earl Grey to Earl of Cassillis, n.d.
43 Ibid., letter Thomas Thurlow to Marquess of Ailsa, 7 July 1846.
44 Ibid., letter Lord Stanley to Marquess of Ailsa, 1 February 1835.
45 Ibid., draft letter Marquess of Ailsa to Lord Stanley, n.d.
46 Ibid., draft letter same to same, n.d.
47 Ibid., letter Lord Stanley to Marquess of Ailsa, 8 January 1835.
48 Ibid., same to same, 1 February 1835.
49 Ibid., letter Marquess of Buckingham to Earl of Cassillis, 20 December 1819.
50 Ibid., letter Marquess of Buckingham to Earl of Cassillis, 21 November 1819.
51 Ibid., day orderly book, 1813–33, 11 April 1820, pp. 125–7.
52 Information supplied by the archivist of the Royal Society.
53 Cassillis MSS, letter Earl of Cassillis to Lord Liverpool, 31 October 1820.
54 Ibid., letter Lord Liverpool to Earl of Cassillis, 31 October 1820.
55 Ibid., letter Duke of Buckingham to Earl of Cassillis, 29 November 1820.
56 HL Buckingham MSS, Earl of Cassillis to Duke of Buckingham, 11 November 1820.
57 Ibid., same to same, 27 November 1820
58 Ibid., same to same, December 1820.
59 Ibid., letter James Campbell of Craigie to the Marquess of Ailsa, 1 July 1832.
60 BL MSS Add 40349, fol. 129.
61 BL MSS Add 40350, fol. 49.
62 Richard Onslow, *Great Racing Gambles & Frauds*, pp. 62–3.
63 BL MSS Add 40385, fol. 57.
64 BL MSS Add 40393, fol. 138.
65 Ibid., fol. 139.
66 Cassillis MSS, letter Sir Robert Peel to Earl of Cassillis, 7 April 1827.
67 Ibid., draft letter Earl of Cassillis to Duke of Buckingham, 21 July 1827. The actual letter is in the HL Buckingham MSS.
68 BL MSS Add. 40395, fol. 64.
69 Ibid., fol. 16.
70 Ibid., fol. 107.
71 Ibid., fol. 141.
72 Cassillis MSS, draft letter Earl of Cassillis to Sir Robert Peel, 23 January 1828.
73 C.A. Disbrowe, *Old Days in Diplomacy*, pp. 19 and 71.
74 BL Add Mss 58903 fol. 100.
75 Ibid., fol. 103.
76 Ibid., fol. 102.
77 Cassillis MSS, letter Lord Grenville to Earl of Cassillis, 16 December 1811.
78 R.G. Thorne, *The House of Commons 1790–1820*, p. 61.
79 Cassillis MSS, letter Lord Grenville to Earl of Cassillis, 13 December 1813.
80 Ibid., letter Hannah Allardyce to Earl of Cassillis, 10 January 1814.
81 Ibid., letter Lord Kennedy to Earl of Cassillis, 11 April 1814.
82 Ibid., letter David Cathcart to Earl of Cassillis, 31 December 1813.
83 Ibid., letter Lord Kennedy to Earl of Cassillis, 17 January 1814.
84 Ibid., same to same, 28 January 1818.
85 Ibid., letter Mrs Erskine to Earl of Cassillis, 14 April 1814.
86 Ibid., letter David Cathcart to Earl of Cassillis, 29 December 1813.
87 Violet Jacob, *The Lairds of Dun*, p. 287.
88 Cassillis MSS, *Summons of Declarator, Reduction, and Count and Reckoning, the Honourable John Kennedy against Alexander Hunter W.S. and Others*, 1843, p. 2.
89 Ibid., state of affairs of Alexander Allardyce, 30 September 1811.
90 Ibid., letter John Smith to Earl of Cassillis, 1 June 1814.
91 Eric M. Clive and John G. Wilson, *The Law of Husband and Wife in Scotland*, pp. 343–5 and David Murray, *The Law Relating to the Property of Married Persons*, p. 88.
92 Cassillis MSS, *Summons of Declarator* (see Note 88).
93 Ibid., letter David Cathcart to Earl of Cassillis, 30 January 1814.
94 Ibid., same to same, 31 December 1813.
95 Ibid., same to same, 4 February 1814.
96 Ibid., obligation of Lord Kennedy, 1814.
97 Ibid., letter John Smith to Earl of Cassillis, 8 December 1814.
98 Ibid., letter David Cathcart to Earl of Cassillis, 21 March 1814 and John Rankine, *A Treatise*, pp. 706–13.
99 Ibid., letter Lord Kennedy to Earl of Cassillis, 28 January 1818.
100 Ibid., note by Earl of Cassillis on the case, n.d.
101 Ibid., copy letter of Hunter Campbell & Co. WS to Alexander Smith WS, 7 April 1841, Eric M. Clive and John G. Wilson, *The Law of Husband and Wife*, p. 331 and David Murray, *The Law Relating to Property*, pp. 96–7. According to Murray the courts would not allow the intention of a post-nuptial contract to be overturned.
102 Ibid., letter John Smith to Earl of Cassillis, 6 October 1814.
103 Ibid., letter David Cathcart to Earl of Cassillis, 6 February 1814.
104 Ibid., same to same, 11 March 1815.
105 These events are recorded in NAS CS238/A7/24 and CS 233 L4/1 adjudication in *Low v. Austin*, 1815.
106 H. Oliver Horne, *Stonehaven Savings Bank 1838–1938*, p. 10.
107 Cassillis MSS, letter Lord Kennedy to Earl of Cassillis, 25 April 1816.
108 Ibid.
109 Ibid., letter John Smith to Earl of Cassillis, 23 April 1816.
110 *Complete Peerage*, pp. 67–8 footnote.
111 Peter Radford, *The Celebrated Captain Barclay*, pp. 53–83.
112 *Sporting Magazine*, New Series (NS) no. 5, 1820, NS no. 9, 1822, racing calendar p. 5, NS no. 12, 1823, racing calendar p. 5 and NS no. 14, racing calendar p. 77.
113 *Sporting Magazine*, NS 17, 1825 racing calendar, p. 36.
114 Ibid., NS 17, 1828, p. 298.
115 *Annals of Sporting*, February 1823, p. 141.
116 E.D. Cuming (ed.), *Squire Osbaldeston*, p. 236.
117 A.M.W. Stirling, *Coke of Norfolk and His Friends*, vol. II, pp. 164–6 and Pierce Egan, *Sporting Anecdotes, Original and Selected*, pp. 236–7.
118 Pierce Egan, *Book of Sports and Mirror of Life*, p. 379.
119 *Annals of Sporting*, July 1824, p. 127.
120 *Sporting Magazine*, NS no. 14, 1824, p. 174.
121 Ibid., 1826, pp. 42–4.
122 Ibid., p. 298.
123 C.A. Wheeler, *Sportascrapiana*, pp. 87–90.
124 *Sporting Magazine*, NS 17, 1825, p. 126.
125 *Annals of Sporting*, July 1826, p. 31
126 Ibid., July 1827, p. 47 and *Sporting Magazine*, 1831, p. 406.
127 E.D. Cuming (ed.), *Squire Osbaldeston*, p. 96.
128 Pierce Egan, *Book of Sports*, pp. 378–9.
129 C.A. Wheeler, *Sportascrapiana*, p. 72.

130 *Sporting Magazine*, 1828, p. 232.
131 Pierce Egan, *Book of Sports*, p. 379.
132 *Sporting Magazine*, 1831, p. 406.
133 Pierce Egan, *Book of Sports*, p. 370.
134 *Sporting Magazine*, NS 12, 1823, p. 220.
135 Ibid., NS 1824, p. 248.
136 C.A. Wheeler, *Sportascrapiana*, pp. 93–4.
137 E.M. Humphris, *The Life of Matthew Dawson*, p. 22.
138 E.D. Cuming (ed.), *Squire Osbaldeston*, p. 84.
139 C.A. Wheeler, *Sportascrapiana*, p. 106 and *Sporting Magazine*, 1826, p. 379.
140 Charles James Apperley, *Nimrod's Northern Tour*, p. 335.
141 *Summons of Declarator, Reduction, and Count and Reckoning, the Honourable John Kennedy against Alexander Hunter W.S. and Others*, 1843, p. 5.
142 George and Eva Swapp, *Dunnottar Woodland Park*.
143 James Paterson, *History of the Counties*, vol. 2, p. 269 and NAS 25/9/47/1, factory accounts 1828–9.
144 NAS GD25/9/47/1, rental 1828–9.
145 Amanda Foreman, *Georgiana – Duchess of Devonshire*, pp. 379–81.
146 John Habakkuk, *Marriage*, pp. 299–300.
147 John Rankine, *A Treatise*, pp. 686–718.
148 Calculated from NAS SC 6/72/5–19. Since there is not a complete set of factory accounts for this period this is the only source of information for improvements until the beginning of the ledger series in 1838.
149 CCEO, bundle of valuations, valuation of farms by Mr Jamieson, 1820.
150 Charles Gairdner, *Autobiography*, p. 13.
151 CCEO, Quintin Jamieson to Earl of Cassillis, 12 May 1821.
152 Cassillis MSS, day orderly book, 1813–33, pp. 188 and 193.
153 CCEO, factory accounts, 1839, branch V, payments on account of Knockjarder tilery.
154 Ibid., account book, 1829–32, pp. 17, 21 and 72.
155 NAS SC 6/72/5–19, Ayrshire Registers of Improvements, 1821–43.
156 *Gardener's Magazine*, vol. 9, 1833, p. 9.
157 William Robertson, *Old Ayrshire Days*, p. 266.
158 *Second Statistical Account of Scotland*, Vol. 5, 1845, p. 502.
159 CCEO, estate rentals, 1829–40.
160 NAS SC 6/72/8, p. 368.
161 NAS SC 6/7/9 p. 153, item 43.
162 There are a number of volumes corresponding to this title.
163 Cassillis MSS, day orderly book, 1813–33, p. 191.
164 NAS SC 6/7/10, p. 384.
165 NAS SC 6/7/10, p. 540 and 11, pp. 60, 73, and 198.
166 NAS SC 6/7/11, p. 25 item 71.
167 CCEO, rentals, 1834–36.
168 NAS SC 6/7/12, p. 173.
169 NAS SC 6/7/15, p. 57, CCEO factory accounts, 1837–9 and Cassillis MSS, inventory of Culzean, 1846, pp. 71–2.
170 H.M. Colvin, *A Biographical Dictionary*, p. 798.
171 Cassillis MSS, letter Alexander Hunter to Archibald Kennedy, 12 November 1840.
172 Ibid., day order book, 1813–33, p. 210.
173 *Gardener's Magazine*, vol. 9, 1833, pp. 8–9.
174 A.A. Tait, *The Landscape Garden*, pp. 146–7.
175 Cassillis MSS, draft letter Earl of Cassillis to Duke of Clarence, n.d.
176 Ibid., letter Duke of Clarence to Earl of Cassillis, 21 February 1827.
177 Violet Jacob, *The Lairds of Dun*, p. 288.
178 Cassillis MSS, letter Duke of Clarence to Earl of Cassillis, 27 July 1827.
179 Ibid., same to same 8 July 1828.
180 Ibid., same to same 30 July 1828.
181 Ibid., same to same 4 August 1828.
182 Ibid., same to same, 11 May 1829.
183 Ibid., same to same, 2 June 1829.
184 See Peter Radford, *The Celebrated Captain Barclay*, p. 254.
185 Cassillis MSS, letter Duke of Clarence to Earl of Cassillis, 1 December 1829.
186 Ibid., same to same, 25 April 1830.
187 Ibid., memorandum, 28 April 1830.
188 Ibid., draft letter Earl of Cassillis to Colonel Fitzclarence, n.d.
189 Ibid., same to same, 24 June 1830.
190 Ibid., letter Captain Hesketh to Earl of Cassillis, n.d.
191 University of Southampton, Wellington papers WP1/1121/23.
192 Cassillis MSS, letter Robert Peel to Earl of Cassillis, 9 July 1830.
193 Ibid., letter Sir Herbert Taylor to the Earl of Cassillis, 3 January 1831.
194 Ibid., same to same, 17 January 1831.
195 Christopher Hibbert (ed.), *Greville's England*, p. 134.
196 Violet Jacob, *The Lairds of Dun*, pp. 288–9.
197 Charlotte Anne Disbrowe, *Old Days*, p. 19.
198 Greville, *Memoirs*, p. 283.
199 Cassillis MSS, letter Sir Herbert Taylor to Earl of Cassillis, 3 January 1831.
200 Ibid., same to same, 2 October 1831.

201 Ibid., letters King William IV to Earl of Cassillis, 5 June and 29 August 1831, Earl of Cassillis to King William IV, 24 August 1831.
202 NAS GD 25/8/134, security of loan to Lady Augusta, 1831.
203 Violet Jacob, *The Lairds of Dun*, p. 289.
204 Cassillis MSS, letter Sir Herbert Taylor to Earl of Cassillis, 27 November 1831.
205 Countess of Munster, Wilhelmina Kennedy-Erskine FitzClarence, *My Memories and Miscellanies*, p. 28.
206 Cassillis MSS, letter Sir Thomas Wheatley to Earl of Cassillis, 8 December 1831.
207 Ibid., letter Earl Grey to Marquess of Ailsa, 1 May 1832.
208 Ibid., same to same, 9 August 1833.
209 Ibid., day orderly book, 1813–33, pp. 209–10.
210 *Summons of Declarator, Reduction, and Count and Reckoning, the Honourable John Kennedy against Alexander Hunter W.S. and Others*, 1843, pp. 6–9.
211 C.A. Wheeler, *Sportascrapiana*, p. 72.
212 Cassillis MSS, state of Dunnottar affairs, 1839.
213 Ibid., letter Alexander Hunter to Marquess of Ailsa, 29 April 1841.
214 Ibid., *Summons of Declarator*, pp. 8–9.
215 Ibid., letter Alexander Hunter to Marquess of Ailsa, 10 November 1835.
216 Ibid., same to same, 9 September 1834.
217 *Gardener's Magazine*, vol. 13, 1837, pp. 111–12.
218 Quoted in Ray Desmond, *Blessed Retreats*, p. 42.
219 Rupert Gunnis, *Dictionary of British Sculptors 1660–1851*, p. 388.
220 Donald Simpson, *Twickenham Past*, p. 78.
221 Cassillis MSS, letter Countess of Münster to Marquess of Ailsa, 10 December 1833.
222 Charlotte Anne Disbrowe, *Old Days*, p. 184.
223 Cassillis MSS, letter of Countess of Münster to Marquess of Ailsa, 21 January 1835, and of A. Lutteroth to the director of the Pall Mall Gallery, 27 July 1835.
224 Countess of Munster, *My Memories*, p. 8.
225 Cassillis MSS, Duke of Wellington to Marquess of Ailsa, 9 August 1835.
226 Ibid., Duke of Northumberland to same, 8 August 1835.
227 BL MSS Add 40421, fol. 133.
228 Cassillis MSS, letter Arthur Campbell to Marquess of Ailsa, 14 November 1834.
229 Countess of Munster, *My Memories*, p. 40.
230 Ibid., p. 41.
231 Cassillis MSS, letter Sir Herbert Taylor to Marquess of Ailsa, 25 July 1836.
232 Ibid., letter Marquess of Ailsa to Lady Augusta, 16 August 1836.
233 Ibid., letter Sir H. Wheatley to Marquess of Ailsa, 18 August 1836.
234 NLS MSS 2671, letter from Marquess of Ailsa to unknown person, 4 March 1837.
235 Cassillis MSS, letter Alexander Hunter to the Marquess of Ailsa, 14 October 1837.
236 Violet Jacob, *The Lairds of Dun*, pp. 290–1, and Countess of Munster, *My Memories*, p. 41.
237 Cassillis MSS, Spottiswood & Robertson's account with Marquess of Ailsa, 1837–8.
238 Charlotte Anne Disbrowe, *Old Days*, p. 19.
239 Cassillis MSS, letter James Campbell of Craigie to Marquess of Ailsa, 1 July 1832.
240 Ibid., letter Earl Grey to Marquess of Ailsa, 9 January 1835.
241 Ibid., draft letter Marquess of Ailsa to Lord Stanley, 2 January 1835.
242 Ibid., draft same to same, n.d., probably January 1835.
243 Ibid., draft letter Marquess of Ailsa to Lord Grey, 28 January 1835.
244 Ibid., draft letter Marquess of Ailsa to Sir Herbert Taylor, 1 January 1835.
245 BL MSS Add 45050, fol. 144.
246 Ibid., fol. 146.
247 CCEO, estate accounts, 1842, p. 33.
248 Cassillis MSS, letter Alex Smith to John Kennedy, 16 April 1841.
249 Ibid., letter Alexander Hunter to Marquess of Ailsa, 29 April 1841.
250 Ibid., same to same, 16 June, 1841.
251 Ibid., *Summons of Declarator, Reduction, and Count and Reckoning, the Honourable John Kennedy against Alexander Hunter W.S. and Others*, 1843.
252 Ibid., letter Alexander Hunter to Marquess of Ailsa, 15 February 1844.
253 Robert Bernard Martin, *Enter rumour*, p. 122.
254 This event is described in Ian Anstruther, *The Knight and the Umbrella*, 1963.
255 Ibid., Appendix II, p. 10.
256 Cassillis MSS, letter James Kennedy-Bailie to Marquess of Ailsa, 25 January 1840 and Robert Bernard Martin, *Enter rumour*, pp. 94–5.
257 BLMSS Add 40488, fol. 205.
258 J. Fairfax-Blakeborough, *Northern Turf History*, p. 202.
259 *Sportsman*, 1842, 2nd series, vol. 6, turf calendar, pp. 22–3.
260 Cassillis MSS., letter Alexander Hunter to Marquess of Ailsa, 10 May 1843.
261 Richard Onslow, *Great Racing Gambles*, pp. 42–91.
262 Cassillis MSS., letter Alexander Hunter to Marquess of Ailsa, 17 October 1842.

263 Ibid.
264 Ibid., same to same, 22 December 1842.
265 *The Times*, 11 September 1846, p. 6, col. e.
266 An Act to enable Archibald Marquess of Ailsa to borrow a certain Sum of Money upon the Security of his entailed Estates of Cassillis and Culzean, for Repayment to him of a Portion of the Monies laid out by him in the Improvement of these Estates, 1844.
267 Ayrshire sasines, 14 August 1844.
268 G.D. Beaumont, *The Law of Fire and Life Insurance*, p. 46, footnote A.
269 Cassillis MSS, letter Alexander Hunter to Marquess of Ailsa, 22 December 1842.
270 CCEO, ledger 1845–52, p. 6.
271 Cassillis MSS, letter Earl of Eglinton to Marquess of Ailsa, 27 October 1841.
272 BL MSS Add 40493, fol. 382.
273 BL MSS Add 40486, fol. 281.
274 Ibid., 40512, fol. 329.
275 Cassillis MSS, letter Alexander Hunter to Marquess of Ailsa, 10 May 1843.
276 BL MSS Add 40526, fol. 146.
277 Cassillis MSS, letter William Craig to Marquess of Ailsa, 21 July, 1842 and CCEO, factory accounts 1837.
278 Ibid., letter Alexander Hunter to Marquess of Ailsa, 25 April 1840.
279 Ibid., copy letter Alexander Hunter to William Craig, 3 June 1843.
280 Ibid., letter William Craig to Marquess of Ailsa, 11 July 1843.
281 Ibid., letter C.D. Gairdner to Marquess of Ailsa, 30 June 1845.
282 NLS MS 2671, letter of Marquess of Ailsa to unknown person, 6 January 1838.
283 Cassillis MSS, copy letter Marquess of Ailsa to Lord Frederick Gordon, 19 November 1839.
284 Ibid., letter Lord John Frederick Gordon to Marquess of Ailsa, 27 October 1840.
285 Charlotte Anne Disbrowe, *Old Days*, p. 71.
286 BL MSS Add 40591, fol. 78.
287 Ibid., fol. 84.
288 *The Times*, 11 September 1846, p. 6, col. e.
289 NAS SC70/4/, p. 90 and 68, p. 574.
290 *Ayrshire Advertiser*, 17 September 1846, p. 4, col. c.
291 CCEO, residual account of the Marquess of Ailsa, 1850.
292 NAS SC6/15, pp. 273–290 will and inventory of the 1st Marquess of Ailsa, 1846.
293 Cassillis MSS, Culzean inventory, 1846.
294 NAS GD 25/9/36/6, petition to sell entail land, 1849.
295 CCEO, printed sale notice, 1850.
296 CCEO, residual account of the Marquess of Ailsa, 1850.

CHAPTER 7

1 James Paterson, *Autobiographical Reminiscences*, Glasgow, 1871, pp. 198–201.
2 Ayrshire sasines, 14 August 1844.
3 CCEO, ledger 1845–52, pp. 492–3.
4 Culzean MSS, diary of the 2nd Marquess of Ailsa, 1851–3.
5 1851 census information kindly supplied by Surrey Historical Centre.
6 Culzean MSS, logbook of Sir Andrew Cathcart's ocean cruises, 1846–8, diary of 2nd Marquess of Ailsa, 1850–1, 10 July 1851.
7 The author is grateful to Ian Agnew of the Surrey Union Hunt for confirming these details.
8 CCEO, ledger 1845–52, p. 592.
9 Ibid., pp. 134 and 460.
10 Ibid., p. 374.
11 Ibid., p. 470.
12 Information supplied by Professor R.H. Campbell.
13 CCEO, ledger 1845–52, p. 469.
14 Ibid.
15 Ibid., p. 467.
16 Ibid., pp. 609–14.
17 Ibid., p. 595.
18 Ibid., p. 596.
19 Ibid., p. 548.
20 Ibid., p. 595.
21 Ibid., p. 597.
22 Cassillis MSS, abstract of account between Marquess of Ailsa and Messrs Hunter Blair & Cowan, 1850–1.
23 Culzean MSS, diary of the 2nd Marquess, 1851–3.
24 CCEO, ledger 1845–52, p. 786.
25 Ibid., p. 792.
26 CCEO, ledger 1852–60, p. 63.
27 Ibid., p. 241.
28 Ibid., pp. 183–4 and Culzean MSS diary of 2nd Marquess, 1851–3.
29 Culzean, MSS diary of the 2nd Marquess, 1854–5
30 Ibid., diary of 2nd Marquess, 1851–3.

31 Ibid., 1854–5.
32 John Borrodaile, *'Lady of Culzean' Mayne Island*, p. 29.
33 Culzean MSS, diary of the 2nd Marquess, 1853–4.
34 Turnbull & Co. were also tenants of the Kilkerran Acid Works. See David McLure, 'Kilkerran Pyroligneous Acid Works 1845–1945', p. 5.
35 CCEO, cellar book 1855–63.
36 Ibid., ledger 1852–60, pp. 303–4.
37 Culzean MSS, diary of the 2nd Marquess, 1855–6.
38 Ibid., diary of the 2nd Marquess, 1854–5.
39 Ibid., diary of the 2nd Marquess, 1855–56.
40 Ibid.
41 CCEO, game book 1855–93.
42 Culzean MSS, diary of the 2nd Marquess 1856–7.
43 CCEO, 1855–93, entry August 1856.
44 GD 25/9/46/1 papers on *Kittiwake*, 1856–9.
45 CCEO, ledger 1852–60, pp. 735 and 866.
46 Ibid., pp. 866 and 889.
47 Culzean MSS, diary of the 2nd Marquess diary, 1860–1.
48 CCEO, ledger 1867–71, pp. 143, 293 and 476. Because the garden accounts are aggregated in the ledger for 1861–7 it is impossible to determine when William Greenshields left.
49 *British Yachts and Yachtsmen*, vol. 2, p. 291 and Cassillis MSS, letter James D. Sloan to Lord Ailsa, 16 May 1939.
50 Culzean MSS, diary of the 2nd Marquess, 1860–1.
51 Ann E. Whetstone, *Scottish County Government*, p. 114.
52 CCEO, ledger 1861–7, p. 530.
53 Ibid., game book, 1855–93.
54 Culzean MSS, diary of the 2nd Marquess, 1862–3.
55 CCEO, cellar book, 1863–7.
56 Christopher Edward Clive Hussey, *The Life of Sir Edwin Lutyens*.
57 Culzean MSS, diary of the 2nd Marquess, 1863–4.
58 Ibid., and information supplied by Lt Commander C.B. Lutyens.
59 CCEO, ledger 1861–7, pp. 697 and 844
60 Ibid., cellar book, 1863–7.
61 NAS GD 25/9/46/1.
62 CCEO, ledger 1861–7, p. 388.
63 Ibid., p. 545.
64 Ibid., p. 389.
65 See for example R.H. Campbell, *Owners and Occupiers*, p. 168.
66 Cassillis MSS, State shewing amount of various branches of charge of factory accounts, 1847–63, dated February 1865.
67 CCEO, ledger 1861–7, pp. 680–1.
68 Glasgow University Archives, sequestration database.
69 CCEO, State shewing amount of various branches of charge of factory accounts, 1847–63, dated February 1865.
70 Cassillis MSS, State shewing amount of various branches of the discharge side of factory accounts, 1847–63, dated February 1865.
71 CCEO, ledger 1867–71, pp. 127–30, 140.
72 Ibid., pp. 137–8.
73 Ibid., p. 129.
74 Ibid., p. 425.
75 Charles D. Gairdner, *Autobiography of C.D. Gairdner*.
76 Ibid., pp. 288 and 422.
77 Ibid., p. 284.
78 R.H. Campbell, *Owners and Occupiers*, p. 158
79 Cassillis MSS, printed, *A List of Eton College taken at Christmas 1865*, p. 6.
80 CCEO, ledger 1861–7, p. 695.
81 Cassillis MSS, Lord Cassillis to Lady Ailsa, n.d.
82 NAS GD 25/9/16, accounts 1862–70.
83 *Transactions of the Institute of Engineers and Shipbuilders in Scotland*, vol. 81 1937–8, pp. 586–7.
84 NAS GD 25/9/16, accounts 1862–70.
85 CCEO, ledger 1867–71, p. 303.
86 *Hunt's Yachting Annual*, 1873, p. 47.
87 *Glasgow Herald*, 21 March 1870, p. 4, col. d.
88 CCEO, ledger 1867–71, pp. 401–2.
89 CCEO ledger 1870–5, p. 409 – the entry is for Mr Hardrop but this must be an error.
90 Ibid., p. 183.
91 John Borradaile, *Lady of Culzean*, p. 29.
92 Ibid., p. 69.

CHAPTER 8

1 CCEO, financial papers 1872–94, letter of Evan Hunter to Lord Ailsa, 7 January, 1874.
2 Ibid., ledger 1871–5, p. 184.
3 Ibid., ledger 1867–1, pp. 426–82.
4 Ibid., ledger 1870–5, p. 171.

5 Ibid., ledger 1867–71, p. 418 and Cassillis MSS, Culzean cellar book, 1867–71.
6 *British Yachts and Yachtsmen*, vol. 2, p. 372.
7 *Hunt's Yachting Annual*, 1872, p. 5.
8 CCEO, ledger 1870–5, p. 349.
9 *Hunt's Yachting Annual*, 1873, p. 48.
10 Lt Col. C.J.H. Mead, *History of the Royal Cornwall Yacht Club 1871–1949*, p. 18
11 CCEO, ledger 1867–71, pp. 581–2.
12 Ibid., ledger 1870–6, p. 444.
13 Ibid., cellar book 1863–7.
14 *Ayrshire Advertiser*, 2 August 1888, p. 4, col. d.
15 *Glasgow Herald*, 17 December 1900, obituary of Lord Blantyre.
16 *Times*, 8 March 1871, p. 5 col. c.
17 Cassillis MSS, Culzean cellar book, 1867–71.
18 CCEO, ledger 1867–71, p. 582.
19 Ibid., pp. 149–50.
20 Cassillis MSS, invoice from G. Mormile, 1872.
21 Culzean MSS, log book of the *Lady Evelyn*, 1871–2.
22 CCEO, ledger 1870–6, pp. 281–2, Lord Ailsa's correspondence with the factor, January 1901.
23 Walter John Trower, *A Remonstrance addressed to Archibald Campbell, Esq. of Blythswood*, and Marion Lochhead, *Episcopal Scotland in the Nineteenth Century*, pp. 106–38.
24 Kenneth Hylson-Smith, *Evangelicals in the Church of England 1734–1984*, p. 191.
25 Anthony Trollope, *The Eustace Diamonds*, p. 317.
26 Ibid., ledger 1867–1, p.601 and ledger 1870–6, p. 171.
27 See for example P.J. Perry, *British Farming in the Great Depression 1870–1914*.
28 John Bateman, *The Great Landowners of Great Britain and Ireland*, and R.H. Campbell, *Owners and Occupiers*, pp. 98–100.
29 CCEO, ledger 1867–71, pp. 749–50.
30 Ibid., p. 754 and Cox, *A History of Gardening in Scotland*, pp. 109 and 204.
31 Ibid., ledger 1875–80, p. 79.
32 Frank Buckland, *Fish Hatchery*, pp. 91–3 and 217.
33 Frank Buckland, *Notes and Jottings from Animal Life*, generally and p. 270.
34 CCEO, ledger 1870–6, p. 748.
35 A. Pettigrew, Cardiff, 'Culzean gardens', *Journal of Horticulture and Cottage Gardening*, p. 389.
36 CCEO, ledger 1875–80, p. 171.
37 Ibid., statement of expenditure on new wing and alterations Culzean Castle, 1877–80.
38 Ibid., ledger 1875–80, p. 203.
39 Cassillis MSS, inferred from letter Lady Seafield to Lady Ailsa, 10 August 1885.
40 A. Pettigrew, Cardiff, 'Culzean gardens', *Journal of Horticulture*, p. 389.
41 CCEO, ledger 1870–6, pp. 181 and 518.
42 Ibid., ledger 1875–80, p. 108.
43 Information supplied by the Victoria and Albert Museum.
44 CCEO, ledger 1875–80, pp. 280–1 and Cassillis MSS, invoice from Edwards & Roberts, 29 December 1877.
45 Information supplied by the Victoria and Albert Museum.
46 Cassillis MSS, invoice from Edwards & Roberts, 29 December 1877.
47 CCEO, ledger 1875–80, pp. 280–1.
48 Ibid., Lord and Lady Ailsa's correspondence with the factor, 1903, 24 February.
49 Ibid., ledger 1875–80, pp. 149 and 439.
50 Cassillis MSS, invoice for painting of *Lady Evelyn* from Arthur Fowles, 1873.
51 CCEO, catalogue of the collection of pictures at Culzean Castle, 1875.
52 Ibid., statement of expenditure on new wing and alterations Culzean Castle, 1877–80.
53 Ibid., ledger 1875–80, p. 361.
54 Ibid., p. 318.
55 Ibid., pp. 365–6 and 567.
56 Ibid., (sideboard only) p. 276.
57 Ibid., pp. 281, 463, and 645.
58 Ibid., factory accounts, 1879–80, pp. 104–5.
59 Ibid., statement of expenditure on new wing and alterations Culzean Castle, 1877–80.
60 Ibid., ledger 1875–80, pp. 183–5 and 273.
61 Ibid., pp. 74 and 270
62 Ibid., p. 184.
63 RCAHMS *Country Life* photographs, 1915.
64 CCEO, Factory accounts 1879, p. 60 and 1880, p. 66.
65 Ibid., p. 61 and 1880, p. 64.
66 Cassillis MSS, weight book, 1869–97.
67 Quoted in Olive Checkland and Margaret Lamb, *Health Care as Social History*, p. 8.
68 See for example CCEO, factory accounts, 1879, pp. 57–9.
69 Ibid., 1880, pp. 70–1 and 1881, p. 70.
70 CCEO, poster TO THE WORKING MEN OF MAYBOLE, n.d.
71 Cassillis MSS, illuminated address to Lady Ailsa, 31 December 1879.
72 CCEO, ledger 1880–4, pp. 135 and 246.
73 Ibid., ledger 1883–7, p. 107.
74 Edmund Heier, *Religious Schism in the Russian Aristocracy 1860–1900*, pp. 44–7.
75 Ibid., p. 32 and E. Trotter, *Lord Radstock*, p. 28.
76 Cassillis MSS, weight book, 1869–92.
77 John Borradaile, *Lady of Culzean*, p. 29.
78 CCEO, ledger 1875–80, p. 585.
79 Ibid., ledger 1880–84, p. 11.
80 Ibid., p. 403.
81 Ibid., p. 542.
82 Ibid., ledger 1870–6, pp. 517–18 and 686.
83 Sir Edward Sullivan et al., *The Badminton Library of Sports and Pastimes – Yachting*, vol. 1, p. 82.
84 *Hunt's Yachting Annual*, 1875, p. 338.
85 Ibid., 1876, p. 360.
86 Cassillis MSS, ledger 1870–76, p. 518 and ledger 1875–80, p. 106.
87 Cassillis MSS, N.B. Hawley to Marquess of Ailsa, 17 September 1875.
88 *British Yachts and Yachtsmen*, vol. 2, p. 420.
89 Sir Edward Sullivan et al., *The Badminton Library*, vol. 1, p. 331.
90 Gordon Fairley, *Minute by Minute – The Story of the Royal Yachting Association – 1875–1982*, pp. 1–6.
91 Cassillis MSS, press-cutting book p. 29 and log book of the voyage.
92 CCEO, ledger 1875–80, pp. 105 and 274–5.
93 Ibid., p. 458.
94 Ibid., ledger 1880–4, p. 218.
95 Ibid., p. 214.
96 Ibid., ledger 1875–80, p. 642.
97 Ibid., ledger 1880–4, p. 73 and abstract of income and expenditure 1878 to 1886.
98 Ibid., ledger 1880–4, pp. 269–70.
99 Ibid.
100 Ibid., p.73.
101 Sir Edward Sullivan et al., *The Badminton Library*, vol. 1, p. 324.
102 Cassillis MSS, account for yacht *Cocker* season 1882.
103 CCEO, ledger 1880–4, p. 321.
104 Ibid., p. 535.
105 Ibid., pp. 420–1.
106 Ibid., p. 535
107 Ibid.
108 Ibid., p. 620,
109 Ibid., pp. 635–7.
110 Culzean MSS, diary of Lady Julia Follett, 2 September 1883.
111 NAS BT2/1297, defunct company file.
112 CCEO, ledger 1884–7, p. 245, 1880–4, pp. 269–70.
113 NAS BT 1297, defunct company file.
114 CCEO, ledger 1884–7, p. 675.
115 Ian Deer, *Royal Yacht Squadron 1815–1985*, pp. 73–4; *Hunt's Yachting Annual*, 1883, p. 403 and Cassillis MSS, account of the King of Netherlands cup race by Lord Ailsa, 4 February 1928.
116 Douglas Philipp Birt, *The Cumberland Fleet*, p. 94.
117 Cassillis MSS, letter Lady Julia Follett to Colonel Follett, 14 May 1885.
118 *Royal Commission on Agriculture Report*, 1881 c 27778, pt. II, p. 514.
119 CCEO, ledger 1875–80, p. 670.
120 Ibid., pp. 270 and 274.
121 See John Rankine, *A Treatise*, p. 1129.
122 CCEO, ledger 1875–80, pp. 299 and 351–2.
123 Ibid., ledger 1880–4, p. 97.
124 Ibid., p. 66.
125 CCEO, financial papers 1874–90, letter Alexander Hunter to Marquess of Ailsa, December 1881.
126 Cassillis MSS, letter Lord Alexander Kennedy to Julia, Marchioness of Ailsa, 7 July 1885.
127 CCEO, ledger 1880–4, p. 674, and ledger 1883–8, p. 116.
128 Ibid., ledger 1883–8, pp. 309 and 508.
129 Ibid., p. 507.
130 Ibid., p. 511 and ledger 1870–6, p. 519.
131 Ibid., p. 494.
132 Ibid., p. 244.
133 Ibid., p. 696.
134 Ibid., p. 316.
135 Deduced from the estate ledgers. There is no reference after 1887–8 and ledger 1883–8, p. 571.
136 R.H. Campbell, *Owners and Occupiers*, p. 169.
137 Culzean MSS, diary of Lady Julia Follett, September 1883.
138 CCEO, ledger 1883–8, p. 27.

139 Cassillis MSS, letter Lady Julia Follett to Colonel Follett, 10 May 1885.
140 See Edward B. Kennedy, *Thirty Seasons in Scandinavia*.
141 Information supplied by Marianne Strandin, Jämtlands läns museum.
142 CCEO, ledger 1883–8, p. 396.
143 Ibid., factory accounts, 1885, pp. 60–1 and 1887, pp. 65–6.
144 Ibid., ledger 1883–8, pp. 241 and 436.
145 Ibid., p. 440 and Cassillis MSS, letter Lady Seafield to Lady Ailsa, 10 August 1885.
146 Ibid., pp. 469–70 and ledger 1887–91, p. 352
147 Ibid., p. 663.
148 Inferred from correspondence of Lord and Lady Ailsa held in CCEO. Since this work was paid for directly by them it does not appear in the estate accounts.
149 CCEO, correspondence of Miss Schmitz with the factor, 1890–4, 20 April 1891.
150 Ibid., Lord and Lady Ailsa's correspondence with the factor, 1887, Marquess of Ailsa to Mr Smith, 9 December.
151 Ibid., ledger 1883–8, p. 125 and Cassillis MSS, correspondence with Lady Seafield, 1885–6.
152 *Sunday Post*, 18 October 1925, p. 1, and Cassillis MSS, contents of the Earl of Seafield's estates, 1857.
153 CCFO, Lord and Lady Ailsa's correspondence with the factor, 1887, Marchioness of Ailsa to Mr Smith, 7 June 1887.
154 Ibid.
155 *Ayrshire Advertiser*, 2 August 1888, p. 4, col. d.
156 *Glasgow Herald*, 1 August 1888, p. 9, col. c.
157 CCEO, ledger 1883–8, p. 322.
158 Ibid., correspondence of Lord Ailsa with the factor, 1888–90, 6 August 1888.
159 Ibid., Miss Schmitz's correspondence, Earl of Cassillis to Mr Smith, 6 December 1890 and 6 January 1891.
160 *Northern Chronicle*, 14 April 1886.
161 CCEO, correspondence of Lord Ailsa with the factor, 1888–90, September 1888.
162 Ibid., letter of 21 September 1888.
163 Ibid., second letter of 21 September 1888.
164 Ibid., ledger 1883–8, p. 137 and CCEO, correspondence of Lord Ailsa with the factor, 1888–90, 3 February 1889.
165 CCEO, ledger 188388, pp. 124 and 527.
166 Ibid., p. 137.
167 Ibid., p. 452.
168 CCEO, Miss Schmitz's correspondence, Miss Schmitz to Mr Smith, 1 December 1888.
169 Ibid., ledger 1883–8, pp. 321–2.
170 Ibid., correspondence of Lord Ailsa with the factor, 1888–90, 24 February 1889.
171 Ibid., ledger 1883–8, pp. 515–16.
172 Ibid., Miss Schmitz letters to the factor, letter of 20 February 1891.
173 Ibid., financial papers 1874–94, letter Hugh Lennox to Thomas Smith, 14 July 1890.
174 Ibid., ledger 1884–7, p. 519.
175 A. Pettigrew, 'Culzean gardens'.
176 Tom Carter, *The Victorian Garden*, pp. 99–100.
177 CCEO, Lord Ailsa's correspondence with the factor 1887, 14 April 1887.
178 Census for 1881 and 1891, quoted in Debbie Jackson, *The History of the Kennedys*, p. 130.
179 CCEO, ledger 1884–7, pp. 13 and 216.
180 Ibid., ledger 1887–91, p. 692.
181 Anthony Trollope, *The Eustace Diamonds*, p. 193.
182 CCEO, correspondence of Lord Ailsa with the factor, 1888–90, letter 9 November 1889.
183 Ibid., 1 February 1890.
184 Ibid., 27 February 1890, and CCEO, ledger 1883–8, p. 529.
185 Ibid., 20 October 1889.
186 CCEO, ledger 1883–8, p. 579.
187 The last payments for biscuits for the emu were in September 1890, CCEO, factory accounts, 1889–90, p. 135.
188 CCEO, Lord Ailsa's correspondence with the factor, 19 November 1890.
189 Ibid., 1891, 19 December 1890.
190 Ibid., Lord Ailsa's correspondence with the factor, 1891, 12 January and 4 February 1891.
191 Ibid., 8 March 1891.
192 Ibid., 19 February 1891, and CCEO, ledger 1883–8, p. 693.
193 The author is grateful to Rosemary Crill of the Victoria and Albert Museum for this information. See Ian Bennett, *Jail Birds, An exhibition of 19th century Indian carpets held at the Mall, London, SW1 from 24 to 28 March 1987*, compiled by Kennedy Carpets – copy available in the V. & A. Library.
194 Cassillis MSS, Lord Cassillis to Miss Lyford, 4 January 1932.
195 CCEO, Lord Ailsa's correspondence with the factor, 1891, 9 September 1891.
196 Ibid., game book, 1855–93.
197 Ibid., factory accounts, 1892–3, p. 109.
198 Ibid., correspondence of Lord Ailsa with the factor, 1892, letter Hugh Lennox to Thomas Smith, 18 May 1892.
199 Ibid., financial papers, 1874–94.
200 Ibid., correspondence of Lord Ailsa with the factor, 1892, letter Hugh Lennox to Thomas Smith, 18 May 1892.
201 Ibid., factory accounts, 1891–2, p. 126.
202 Ibid., p. 134.
203 Ibid., correspondence of Lord Ailsa with the factor, 4 September 1892.
204 Ibid., correspondence of Lord Ailsa with the factor, Norway 1893, 22 and 29 May 1893.
205 Ibid., correspondence of Lord Cassillis with the factor, 1891–1903, 15 August 1893.
206 Ibid., Lady Ailsa's correspondence with the factor, 1892–3, 7 August 1893.
207 Ibid., correspondence of Lord Ailsa with the factor, Norway 1893, 21 June 1893.
208 Ibid., Lady Ailsa's correspondence with the factor, 1892–4, 10 July 1893, and Lord Ailsa's correspondence, Norway 1893, 29 June 1893.
209 See for example, ibid., Lord Ailsa's correspondence with the factor, 22 December 1894.
210 Ibid., Lord Ailsa's correspondence with the factor, 1897–8, 27 May 1897.
211 Ibid., Miss Schmitz's correspondence 1890, Miss Schmitz to Mr Smith, 25 November 1890.
212 Ibid., 1891–4, 14 June 1892.
213 Ibid., Lord Cassillis's correspondence with the factor, 1891-1904, 30 May 1893.
214 Ibid., Miss Schmitz's correspondence with the factor, 22 April 1894.

CHAPTER 9

1 CCEO, factory accounts, 1892–3, p. 66.
2 Ibid., factory accounts, 1891–2, p. 125.
3 Ibid., 1895–6, p. 129.
4 Ibid., 1892–3, p. 81 and 1893–4, p. 78.
5 Ibid., 1892–3, p. 80.
6 Ibid., 1893–4, p. 114.
7 Ibid., Lord Ailsa's correspondence with the factor, 6 June 1893.
8 Ibid., 30 March 1894.
9 John Habakkuk, *Marriage*, pp. 339–41.
10 CCEO, financial papers, 1872–94, and Lord Ailsa's correspondence with the factor, Thomas Smith to Lord Ailsa, 22 February 1894.
11 Ibid., Lord Ailsa's correspondence with the factor, 23 February 1894.
12 Ibid., Lord Ailsa's correspondence with the factor, 27 February 1894.
13 Ibid.
14 Ibid., Lord Ailsa's correspondence with the factor, 1 March 1895.
15 See for example ibid., 1896, 4 April which discusses the grate in the State bedroom.
16 Ibid., factory accounts, 1894–5, p. 123.
17 Ibid., correspondence of Lord Ailsa with the factor, 2 April 1896.
18 Ibid., 4 April 1896.
19 Ibid., factory accounts,15 and 31 July 1893.
20 Ibid., 1894–5, pp. 72–3.
21 Ibid., correspondence of Lord Ailsa with the factor, 1894, 24 December 1894.
22 Ibid., factory accounts, 1897–8, pp. 69–70.
23 Ibid., factor's letter book with Lord and Lady Ailsa, 1903–24, p. 109.
24 Ibid., Lord Ailsa's correspondence with the factor, S.R. Crockett's secretary to the factor, 27 March 1896.
25 Ibid., factory accounts, 1896–7, p. 132.
26 Ibid., Lord Ailsa's correspondence with the factor, 1897–8, letters of June and July 1898.
27 Ibid., factory accounts, 1897–8, p. 124.
28 Ibid., 1898–9, p. 138.
29 Ibid., factory accounts, 1899–1900, p. 161.
30 Ibid., correspondence of Lord and Lady Ailsa with the factor, 1903, 20 March 1903.
31 Cassillis MSS, paper titled 'Left by Lord B to Earl.'
32 R.H. Campbell, *Owners and Occupiers*, pp. 168–9.
33 The author is grateful to Professor R.H. Campbell for this song learned at his mother's knee. Ever questioning, subsequent research has led him to believe Kyle produced better cows than Carrick.
34 C. J. Brown, *The Soils of Carrick*, p. 193.
35 Quoted in R.H. Campbell, *Owners and Occupiers*, p. 126.
36 CCEO, factory accounts, 1894–5, p. 169 and 1898–9, p. 187.
37 Glasgow University Archives, Ailsa Shipbuilding Co. records GD 400/9/1, private ledger no. 1, p. 2 and GD 400/9/2 no. 2, pp. 4–6.
38 CCEO, factory accounts, 1888–9, p. 184.
39 Ibid., Lord Ailsa's correspondence with the factor, 1897–8, 30 October 1897.

40 Ibid., 10 January 1898.
41 Ibid., 1896, 18 May.
42 Ibid., factory accounts, 1893–4, pp. 127–8.
43 Ibid., Lady Ailsa's correspondence with the factor, 1904–8, letter
   10 October 1904.
44 Ibid., bundle of papers – finance, letter of Hugh Lennox to
   Thomas Smith, 21 March 1902.
45 Ibid., Lord Ailsa's correspondence with the factor, 1897–8,
   22 February 1898 and 1907–9, W.M. Sheriff to Lord Ailsa, 21 May 1908.
46 Ibid., Lord Ailsa's correspondence with the factor, 1897–8,
   12 February, 1898.
47 David Hamilton, Golf – Scotland's Game, pp. 190–1.
48 CCEO, Lord Ailsa's correspondence with the factor, 1897–8,
   17 March 1898.
49 Ibid., 17 April 1898.
50 Ibid., 27 April 1898.
51 Ibid., 1 May 1898.
52 Ibid., 25 June 1898.
53 Ibid., 7 October 1898.
54 Ibid., factory accounts, 1898–9, p. 144.
55 Ibid., 1897–8, p. 130–1 and 1898–9, p. 144.
56 Ibid., 1896–7, p. 136 and 1897–8, pp. 129–30.
57 Information supplied by Marianne Strandin, Jämtlands läns museum.
58 CCEO, Lord and Lady Ailsa's correspondence with the factor, 1897–9,
   16 December 1898 and 3 July 1899.
59 Ibid., factory accounts, 1900–1, p. 140; J.R. Boyd, History of Turnberry,
   forthcoming 2002, chap. 1.
60 Ian Nalder, Scotland's Golf in Days of Steam, p. 43.
61 NAS BR GSW1/17, p. 31.
62 NAS BR GSW 1/17, pp. 266–7, and CCEO, correspondence of Lord Ailsa
   with the factor, 1897–8, 30 May 1897.
63 NAS BR GSW1/17, p. 370.
64 Ian Nalder, Scotland's Golf, p. 39.
65 Ibid., p. 41.
66 Inferred from NAS BR GSW1/18, p. 24, minute 91 and p. 27, minute 104.
67 CCEO, factory accounts, 1904–5, p. 66.
68 NAS BR GSW1/18, p. 24, minute 91 and p. 27, minute 104.
69 CCEO, correspondence of Lord Ailsa with the factor, 13 June 1902.
70 Ibid., factory accounts, 1902–3, p. 144.
71 NAS BR GSW4/78.
72 CCEO, Lord Ailsa's correspondence with the factor, 5 May 1902.
73 NAS BR GSW1/18, p. 250
74 Ibid., pp. 417 and 461.
75 CCEO, correspondence of Lord Ailsa with the factor, 1907–9,
   25 January and 3 and 30 March 1907.
76 Douglas Sutherland, The Yellow Earl.
77 CCEO, factory accounts, 1899–1900, p. 143 and 1900–1, p. 136.
78 Ibid., 1902–3, p. 140.
79 Ibid.
80 Ibid., 1902–3, p. 143.
81 Ibid., 1901–2, p. 110.
82 Sir Herbert Maxwell, Memoirs, p. 202.
83 CCEO, bundle of papers – finance, letter of Hugh Lennox to Marquess
   of Ailsa, 21 March 1902.
84 Ibid., Lord Ailsa to Thomas Smith, 23 March 1902.
85 Ibid., draft letter Thomas Smith to Hugh Lennox, 12 April 1902.
86 Ibid., factory accounts, 1900–1, p. 122.
87 Ibid., p. 112.
88 Ibid., 1900–1, p. 128–9, and 1902–3, pp. 132–5.
89 Ibid., bundle of papers – finance, letter Lord Ailsa to Thomas Smith,
   23 March 1902.
90 Ibid., Lady Ailsa to Thomas Smith, 31 March 1902.
91 Ibid., Lord Ailsa to Thomas Smith, 13 April 1902.
92 Ibid.
93 Ibid., Lord and Lady Ailsa's correspondence with the factor,
   24 February 1903.
94 Ibid., factory accounts, 1908–9, pp. 70–1.
95 Ibid., factor's letter book with Lord and Lady Ailsa, 1903–4, p. 168.
96 Ibid., 1902–3, p. 137.
97 Ibid., correspondence of Lady Ailsa with the factor, 15 February 1903.
98 Ibid., factor's letter book with Lord and Lady Ailsa, 1903–4, p. 8.
99 Ibid., correspondence of the Earl of Cassillis with the factor,
   10 December 1901.
100 Ibid., letter of 12 May 1903.
101 Ibid., factor's letter book with Lord and Lady Ailsa, 1903–4, p. 29.
102 Cassillis MSS, printed obituary notice of Archibald Kennedy,
   4th Marquess of Ailsa, January 1944.
103 Ibid., printed address by the Right Hon. the Earl of Cassillis delivered
   at Scottish National Exhibition, 24 June 1908.
104 See for example CCEO, correspondence of the Earl of Cassillis
   with the factor, 15 August and 30 September 1908.
105 Ibid., 28 April 1904.
106 Inverness, 1911.
107 Aberdeen Free Press, 13 December 1911.
108 Cassillis MSS, note by Emily H Stuart, 18 April 1912.
109 CCEO, correspondence of the Earl of Cassillis with the factor,
   10 January 1912.
110 Ibid., Lady Ailsa's correspondence with the factor, 1904–8, 28 March 1904.
111 Ibid., factor's letter book with Lord and Lady Ailsa, 1903–4, p. 113.
112 Ibid., Lady Ailsa's correspondence with the factor, 1904–8, 30 May 1904.
113 Ibid., Lord Ailsa's correspondence with the factor, 1904–8, 20 April 1904.
114 Ibid., Lady Ailsa's correspondence with the factor, 1904–8, 4 June 1904.
115 Ibid., 8 June 1904.
116 Ibid., 10 June 1904.
117 Ibid., factory accounts, 1903–4, pp. 138–40.
118 Ibid., Lady Ailsa's correspondence with the factor, 1904–8,
   3 November 1904.
119 Ibid., letter 12 November 1904.
120 deduced from CCEO, factory accounts, 1906–7, pp. 128–41.
121 CCEO, Lady Ailsa's correspondence with the factor, 1904–8,
   18 April 1905 and 23 January 1906.
122 Ibid., 18 April and 22 November 1905.
123 Ibid., factory accounts, 1905–6, p. 130 and 1906–7, pp. 142–3 and 147.
124 GUA GD 400/5/1, register of shareholders and 400/1/1,
   minutes of annual meetings.
125 CCEO, Lady Ailsa's correspondence with the factor, 1904–8,
   6 August 1906.
126 Ibid., Lord Ailsa's correspondence with the factor, 1907–9, 7 July 1907.
127 Ibid., 5 July 1907.
128 Glasgow Herald, 11 April 1938, p. 15, col. c.
129 CCEO, Lord Ailsa's correspondence with the factor, 1907–9,
   23 January 1908.
130 Ibid., 30 June 1908.
131 Ibid., 15 July 1908.
132 Ibid., 16 and 17 July 1908.
133 Ibid., 23 July 1908.
134 Ibid., 10 August and Times 13 August 1908, p. 4, col. c.
135 Ibid., Lady Ailsa's correspondence with the factor, 1904–8,
   16 September 1908.
136 Ibid., Lord Ailsa's correspondence with the factor, 1907–9,
   10 and 25 August 1908.
137 Cassillis MSS, 'A Lay of the "Fighting Forties" by the Marquess of Ailsa,
   n.d.
138 CCEO, Lady Ailsa's correspondence with the factor, 1904–8, 24 June 1909.
139 Lt Col. C.J.H. Mead, History of the Royal Cornwall Yacht Club, p. 95.
140 CCEO, Lord Ailsa's correspondence with the factor, 1907–9,
   6 August 1909.
141 Ian Deer, Royal Yacht Squadron, p. 74.
142 CCEO, factory accounts, 1914, pp. 62–3 and 1915, p. 54.
143 Ian Deer, Royal Yacht Squadron, p. 74.
144 CCEO, factory accounts, 1919, p. 45.
145 Ibid., factory accounts, 1909–10, p. 134 and 1910–11, p. 135.
146 R.H. Campbell, Owners and Occupiers, p. 127 and David Cannadine,
   The Decline and Fall of the British Aristocracy, p. 48.
147 CCEO, correspondence of Earl of Cassillis with the factor, 1905–10,
   19 June, 1909.
148 Ibid., 28 January 1910.
149 R.H. Campbell, Owners and Occupiers, p. 155.
150 CCEO, factory accounts, 1899–1900, pp. 167–8 and 1913–14, pp. 74–5.
151 Ibid., abstracts of account current between Lord Ailsa and E.A. &
   F. Hunter, 31 January to 28 February 1907.
152 Ibid., Lord Ailsa's correspondence with the factor, 1907–9, 5 June 1908.
153 Information supplied by Christie's archives.
154 CCEO, Lord Ailsa's correspondence with the factor, 1907–9,
   24 November 1908, R.M. Melven to Lord Ailsa, 29 November 1908
   and Mallett & Son to Lord Ailsa, 21 January 1909.
155 Ibid., household accounts, 1910–11.
156 Ibid., Lord Ailsa's correspondence with the factor, 1907–9, 8,
   13 and 20 February 1909.
157 CCEO, factor's letter book with Lord and Lady Ailsa, 1903–4,
   pp. 461–2 and 523 and inferred from correspondence of Lord Ailsa
   with the factor, 1907–9, 23 March 1909.
158 Ibid., correspondence of Lord Ailsa with the factor, 1907–9,
   23 December 1909.
159 Ibid., household accounts, 22 March 1911.
160 Ibid., correspondence of Lord and Lady Ailsa with the factor, 1909–11,
   25 May 1911.
161 Ian Gow, Scottish Houses and Gardens, pp. 7–24.
162 Cassillis MSS, note by Lady Ailsa, n.d. c. 1937.
163 CCEO, household accounts, 28 July and 25 September 1908.
164 Ibid., correspondence of Lord Ailsa with the factor, 1907–9, 12 May 1909.

165 Ibid., abstracts of account current between Lord Ailsa and E.A. & F. Hunter & Co, December 1909 to January 1910 and factory accounts, 1909.
166 Ibid., April to May 1910 and GUA GD400/5/1.
167 R.H. Campbell, *Owners and Occupiers*, p. 175.
168 CCEO, Culzean Castle – inventory and valuation, 1911.
169 Ibid., factory accounts, 1909–10, p. 118.
170 Ibid., factory accounts, 1914–15, p. 64.
171 NAS GD325.1/266.
172 *Factors' Magazine*, 1910, p. 78.
173 CCEO, Lord and Lady Ailsa's correspondence with the factor, 1910–11, letter 9 July 1911.
174 Ibid., factory accounts, 1906–7, p. 119.
175 Ibid., factory accounts, 1907–8, p. 129, and 1909–10, pp. 109 and 113.
176 GUA GD 400/1/2, minutes of AGMs, 1911–14.
177 CCEO, letter to Mr Page from Jeannie Wilson 25 May 1910, factory accounts, 1909–10, p. 135, and 1911–12, p. 164, and factor's letter book Lord and Lady Ailsa, 1903–4, p. 535.
178 CCEO, factory accounts, 1911–12, p. 164, and 1916, p. 42, and Lord and Lady Ailsa's correspondence with the factor, 1910, letter 30 July.
179 RCAHMS, Country Life collection, Culzean box.
180 CCEO, factory accounts, 1913–14, p. 53.
181 Ibid., factor's letter book Lord and Lady Ailsa, 1903–24, p. 597.
182 Ibid., *The Neglect of Scots Interests in Parliament* by the Earl of Cassillis, n.d.
183 Cassillis MSS, note on Frances Emily, Countess of Cassillis, n.d.
184 For an account of wartime agriculture in Scotland see David T. Jones et al., *Rural Scotland During the War*.
185 This account is based on Iain F. Russell, *Sir Robert McAlpine & Sons*, pp. 147–9.
186 CCEO, abstracts of account current between Lord Ailsa and E.A. & F. Hunter, January to February, 1926.
187 Ibid., factory accounts, 1922, p. 9.
188 David T. Jones et al., *Rural Scotland*, pp. 247–64.
189 CCEO, Burnton Small Holdings file, 1914–23.
190 Ibid., factory accounts 1920, p. 34.
191 Ibid., 1919, p. 37.
192 Ibid., 1920, pp. 42–3.
193 http://www.everytype.com/celtcong/cc-hist-mellis.html.
194 National Library of Wales, E.T. John collection 2916 and 2947.
195 CCEO, factory accounts 1921, p. 43.
196 Ibid., p. 51.
197 Ibid., abstracts of account current between Lord Ailsa and E.A. & F. Hunter, July to August 1922.
198 Ibid., finance file 1917–24, letter 129.
199 Ibid., letter 130.
200 Ibid., letter 138.
201 Ibid., letter 139.
202 R.H. Campbell, *Owners and Occupiers*, p. 180.
203 R.H. Campbell, 'The Agricultural Revolution of the Twentieth Century', p. 55.
204 F.M.L. Thomson, *English Landed Society in the Nineteenth Century*, pp. 331–3.
205 CCEO Ailsa Shipbuilding Co. Ltd., comparative abstract of accounts for the six years to 31 May 1931.
206 Ibid., letter Hugh Lennox to the factor, 23 December 1923.
207 Cassillis MSS, letter Lord Cassillis to Lady Cassillis, n.d.
208 CCEO, factory accounts, 1924.
209 Ibid., finance file 1928–34, report by the factor on the income and expenditure, 3 March 1933.
210 Ibid., finance file, 1925–7, letter 5.
211 Ibid., letter 10.
212 Ibid., letter 16, garden produce book, 1924.
213 Ibid., letter 42.
214 Ibid., factory accounts, 1926, p. 44.
215 Cassillis MSS, Newhailes visitors book, 1925–35.
216 John Borrodaile, 'Lady of Culzean', p. 34.
217 Cassillis MSS, printed obituary notice of the 4th Marquess of Ailsa, January 1944.
218 David Cannadine, *The Decline and Fall*, p. 132.
219 CCEO, finance file 1925–7, letter 48 attachment.
220 Ibid., finance file 1925–7, letter 42.
221 Ibid., finance file 1928–34, letter 53.
222 Ibid., letters 54 and 58.
223 W.J.M. 'Stipends and Teinds', *Factors Magazine*, vol. 34, 1933–4, pp. 33–4.
224 Cassillis MSS, Frank Hunter to Lady Cassillis, 1 March 1928.
225 CCEO, factory accounts 1927, p. 52.
226 Ibid., 1928, pp. 84–6.
227 Ibid., finance file 1928–34, letter 156/31/8.
228 Ibid., letter 156/32/29.
229 Ibid., letter 156/33/6.
230 Ibid., report by factor on the income and expenditure of the Cassillis and Culzean estates, 3 March 1933.
231 Ibid., note showing saving in surtax estimated to result from transference to a company, 1933.
232 Ibid., letter 156/33/15.
233 NAS CS46/1935/5/5.
234 CCEO, finance file 1928–34, press cutting 156/33/20.
235 Ibid., press cutting 156/34/14.
236 Ibid., letter no. 156/34/55B.
237 Ibid., letter no. 156/34/62.
238 Ibid., letter book no. 57, p. 155.
239 *Glasgow Herald*, 11 April 1938, p. 15, col. c.

CHAPTER 10

1 Cassillis MSS, letter Marquess of Ailsa to Lord Cassillis, 4 October 1935.
2 CCEO, file Frances Lady Ailsa, 1946–52, letter 99/50/8.
3 Cassillis MSS, note by Lady Ailsa, n.d. c. 1938.
4 Merlin Waterston, *The National Trust – The First Hundred Years*, pp. 113 and 116–17.
5 Cassillis MSS, printed obituary notice of 4th Marquess of Ailsa, January 1944.
6 Archibald Kennedy, 4th Marquess of Ailsa, 'Scotland's share in Magna Carta', p. 18.
7 Information supplied by Christopher Brocklebank Fowler.
8 CCEO, Culzean file, 1940–1, letter no. 127/41/78.
9 Ibid., file Lady Ailsa, 1942–5, letters 229/43/58 and 60.
10 Cassillis MSS, printed obituary notice of the 4th Marquess of Ailsa, January 1944.
11 Ibid., letter Frances Lady Ailsa, 3 January 1945.
12 CCEO, file Lady Ailsa, 1942–5, Lady Ailsa to Sir John Stirling Maxwell, 7 June 1944.
13 Cassillis MSS, letter Marquess of Ailsa to Miss Coghill, 2 March 1941.
14 CCEO, file Lady Ailsa, 1942–5, Lady Ailsa to Sir John Stirling Maxwell, 7 June 1944.
15 Cassillis MSS, letter Marquess of Ailsa to Lady Frances, 28 May 1945.
16 Ibid., Lady Ailsa to Lady Frances, 28 May 1945.
17 CCEO, Culzean file 1942–5, Marquess of Ailsa to James Gray, 12 October 1945.
18 Ibid., James Gray to Col E.D. Stevenson, 17 October 1945.
19 NTSA, archive box JD 171, Ailsa family file, letter 14 November 1945.
20 Ibid., press-cutting file, 1945.
21 Ibid., file on Culzean finances from March 1952.
22 Ibid., file Culzean general C12, part I, letter James Gray to J. Stormonth Darling, 27 March 1954.
23 Douglas Bremner, *For the Benefit of the Nation*, pp. 27–32.
24 James Lees-Milne, London, 1992.
25 NTSA, archives box JD 171, Ailsa family file, letter 13 November 1945.
26 Ibid., Culzean file, letter 10 February 1954.
27 Ibid., file Culzean general C12, letter Lord Ailsa to J. Stormonth Darling, 18 March 1954.
28 Ibid., annual report, 1946.
29 Ibid., box JD 663, press-cutting file 1948–9.
30 Ibid., file C14 Culzean gardens, commenced 1 March 1943.
31 Ibid., report by James Russell, n.d., c. 1952.
32 Ibid., file Culzean general C12, part I, copy letter Lady Fergusson to J. Stormonth Darling, 1 March 1954.
33 Douglas Bremner, *For the Benefit of the Nation*, p. 35.
34 NTSA, file Culzean (folder)general C12, notes by secretary for re-opening on 3 April 1954.
35 Information provided to the author by Dr James Macaulay.
36 NTSA, file Culzean (folder)general C12, notes by secretary for re-opening on 3 April 1954.
37 Ibid., file C26 Culzean permanent 1958, letter Lord Kilmaine to J. Stormonth Darling, 8 January 1954.
38 Ibid., Adam Room file, minutes of AAP, 14 April 1959.
39 Ibid., file Culzean general C12, part I, copy letter Lady Fergusson to J. Stormonth Darling, 1 March 1954.
40 Ibid., letter James Gray to J. Stormonth Darling, 27 March 1954.
41 Ibid., file Culzean general C12, part I, copy letter Lady Fergusson to J. Stormonth Darling, 1 March 1954.
42 Ibid., comparative statement from admission charges, 1951–2.
43 Ibid., file Culzean general C12, 1 January to 31 May 1954 contains letters and papers relating to the re-opening.
44 Ibid., annual report, 1954.
45 Ibid., file Culzean (folder) general C12, draft letter Earl of Wemyss to Lady Fergusson, 9 October 1954.
46 Ibid., file CC26 Culzean permanent 1958, letter Lord Kilmaine to J. Stormonth Darling, 10 April 1957.
47 Ibid., Lord Kilmaine to J. Stormonth Darling, 4 June 1957.
48 David Cannadine, *Aspects of Aristocracy*, p. 294.

Bibliography

NEWSPAPERS, JOURNALS AND SERIES

Annals of Sporting
Annual Register
Army List
Ayrshire Advertiser
Ayrshire Notes
Collections of the New York Historical Society, 1897
Factors' Magazine
Hunt's Yachting Annual
Gardener's Magazine
Glasgow Herald
Hunt's Yachting Annual
Reports of the Royal Commission on Historical Manuscripts
Scots Magazine
Sporting Magazine
Transactions of the Institute of Naval Architecture

BOOKS AND ARTICLES

Abercrummie, William, 'Carrick in 1696', in Walter MacFarlane of that Ilk, *The Geographical Collections relating to Scotland* (Edinburgh: 1890).

Addison, W. Innes, *The Matriculation Albums of the University of Glasgow from 1728 to 1858* (Glasgow: 1913).

Addison, William, *Audley End* (London: 1953).

Aiton, William, *General View of the Agriculture of the County of Ayr; with Observations on the Means of its Improvement; Drawn up for the Consideration of the Board of Agriculture and Internal Improvements* (Glasgow: 1811).

Anstruther, Ian, *The Knight and the Umbrella – An Account of the Eglinton Tournament 1839* (London: 1863).

Apperley, Charles James, *Nimrod's Northern Tour* (London: 1838).

Archaeological works on the Terraces at Culzean Castle, Report No. 219 (Centre for Field Archaeology, University of Edinburgh: 1995).

Barba, Alvaro Alonso, *The Art of Metals: in which is declared the manner of their generation, and the concomitants of them. In two books written in Spanish in 1640 and translated in 1669 by the Edward Earl of Sandwich* (London: 1674).

Bateman, John, *The Great Landowners of Great Britain and Ireland*, 4th edn (London: 1883).

Baugh, Daniel A., *British Naval Administration in the Age of Walpole* (Princeton: 1965).

Beaumont, G.D., *The Law of Fire and Life Insurance* (London: 1865).

Beckett, J.V., *The Aristocracy in England 1660–1914* (Oxford: 1986).

Birt, Douglas Philipps, *The Cumberland Fleet* (London: 1978).

Blyth, Henry, *The Pocket Venus: A Victorian Scandal* (London: 1966).

——, *Old Q – The Rake of Piccadilly – A Biography of the 4th Duke of Queensberry* (London: 1967).

Bolton, A.T., *The Work of Robert Adam* (London: 1987).

Borrodaile, John, *'Lady of Culzean' Mayne Island* (privately printed Victoria BC: 1970).

Bowen, Elizabeth, *Bowen's Court* (Cork: 1998).

Boxer, C.R., *The Portuguese Seaborne Empire 1415–1825* (London: 1991).

Boyle, Hon. Robert, *The General History of the Air: designed and begun by the Honourable Robert Boyle, etc.* (London: 1692).

Brady, Frank, *So Fast to Ruin: the personal element in the collapse of Douglas, Heron and Company* (Ayr: 1973).

Bremner, Douglas, *For the Benefit of the Nation, The National Trust for Scotland: the first 70 years* (Edinburgh: 2001).

Brereton, Sir William, *Travels in Holland, the United Provinces, England, Scotland and Ireland M.DC.XXXIV.–M.DC.XXXV*, edited by Edward Hawkins (Manchester: 1844).

British Yachts and Yachtsmen: a complete history of British yachting from the middle of the sixteenth century to the present day (London: 1907).

Brockliss, L.W.B., *French Higher Education in the Seventeenth and Eighteenth Centuries – A Cultural History* (Oxford: 1987).

Brown, David, 'Lancelot Brown and his associates', *Journal of Garden History*, vol. 29, no. 1, 2001, pp. 2–11.

Brown, Keith, *Noble Society in Scotland – Wealth, Family and Culture from Reformation to Revolution* (Edinburgh: 2000).

Brown, C.J., *The Soils of Carrick and the Country round Girvan* (Edinburgh: 1973).

Buckland, Frank, *Fish Hatchery* (London: 1863).

——, *Notes and Jottings from Animal Life* (London: 1892).

Bullion, J.L., *A Great and Necessary Measure. George Granville and the Genesis of the Stamp Act 1763–1765* (London and Columbia: 1982).

Campbell, R. H., *Owners and Occupiers – Changes in Rural Society in South-West Scotland before 1914* (Aberdeen: 1991).

——, 'The Agricultural Revolution of the Twentieth Century', *Scottish Archives, The Journal of the Scottish Records Association*, vol. 1, 1995, pp. 55–62.

Cannadine, David, *The Decline and Fall of the British Aristocracy* (New Haven and London: 1990).

——, *Aspects of Aristocracy – Grandeur and Decline in Modern Britain* (New Haven: 1994).

Carter, Tom, *The Victorian Garden* (London: 1984)

Chambers, Sir William, *A Treatise on Civil Architecture, in which the Principles of that Art are Laid Down, and Illustrated by a Great Number of Plates, Accurately Designed, and Elegantly Engraved by the Best Hands* (London: 1759).

Charnock, John, *Biographia Navalis* (London: 1798).

Checkland, Olive, and Lamb, Margaret, *Health Care as Social History: the Glasgow case* (Aberdeen: 1982).

Checkland, Sydney, *The Elgins 1766–1917 – A tale of Aristocrats, Proconsuls and their Wives* (Aberdeen: 1988).

Clarke, Samuel, *A General Martyrologie: containing a collection of all the greatest persecutions which have befallen the church of Christ, from the creation, to our present times: wherein is given an exact account of the Protestants sufferings in Queen Maries reign. Whereunto is added the lives of thirty two English divines, together with the lives of Gustavus Ericson, King of Sweden; Jaspar Coligni, admiral of France. and Joan, Queen of Navarre* (London: 1677).

Clive, Eric M., and Wilson, John G., *The Law of Husband and Wife in Scotland* (Edinburgh: 1974).

Close, Rob, *Ayrshire & Arran – An Illustrated Architectural Guide* (Edinburgh: 1992).

Clowes, W. L., *The Royal Navy – A History from the Earliest Times to the Present* (London: 1897).

Cockburn, Henry, *Memorials of his Time 1779–1830* (Edinburgh: 1850).

Collections of the New York Historical Society (New York: 1897).

Colvin, H.M., *A Biographical Dictionary of British Architects, 1600–1840* (New Haven and London: 1995).

Cooksey, J.C.B., *Alexander Nasmyth HRSA 1758–1840 – A Man of the Scottish Renaissance* (Edinburgh: 1991).

Cookson, J.E., *The British Armed Nation 1793–1815* (Oxford: 1997).

Cowan, Edward J., *Montrose for Covenant and King* (London: c.1977).

Cox, E.H.M., *A History of Gardening in Scotland* (London: 1955).

Cullen, L.M., *Smuggling and the Ayrshire Economic Boom of the 1760s and 1770s, Ayrshire Monographs* No. 14 (1994).

Culzean Castle & Country Park (Edinburgh: 1995).

Cuming, E.D. (ed.), *Squire Osbaldeston: his autobiography* (London: 1927).

Davies, John, *Cardiff and the Marquesses of Bute* (Cardiff: 1981).

de Vauban, Sebastien Le Prestre, *De l'attaque et de la défense des places* (La Haye: 1737–42).

Deer, Ian, *Royal Yacht Squadron 1815–1985* (London: 1985).

Desmond, Ray, *Blessed Retreats* (Richmond: 1984).

Devine, T.M., *The Transformation of Rural Scotland – Social Change and the Agrarian Economy 1660–1815* (Edinburgh: 1999).

Disbrowe, Charlotte Anne, *Old Days in Diplomacy, Recollections of a Closed Century by the Eldest Daughter of the Late Sir Edward Cromwell Disbrowe* (London: 1903).

Donaldson, Gordon, *Sir William Fraser: the man and his work* (Edinburgh: 1985).

Du Halde, J.B. (Jean-Baptiste), *A Description of the Empire of China and Chinese-Tartary, Together with the Kingdoms of Korea, and Tibet: containing the geography and history (natural as well as civil) of those countries* (London: 1738–41).

Egan, Pierce, *Sporting Anecdotes, Original and Selected* (London: 1820).

——, *Book of Sports and Mirror of Life* (London: 1844).

Fairfax-Blakeborough, J., *Northern Turf History Vol. IV, History of Horse Racing in Scotland* (Whitby: 1973).

Fairley, Gordon, *Minute by Minute – The Story of the Royal Yachting Association – 1875–1982* (London: 1982).

Fergusson, William, *Scotland 1689 to the Present* (Edinburgh: 1987).

Foreman, Amanda, *Georgiana – Duchess of Devonshire* (London: 1998).

Fortescue, J.W. (John William), Sir, *A History of the British Army* (London: 1899–1930).

Fry, Michael, *Dundas Despotism* (Edinburgh: 1992).

Fullarton, Col. William, *General View of the Agriculture of the County of Ayr: with observations on the means of improvement* (Edinburgh: 1793).

Gairdner, Charles D., *Autobiography of C.D. Gairdner, Auchans, Written at the Suggestion of and Revised by the Earl of Eglinton, June, 1861* (Kilmarnock: 1902).

Gallier, A., *L'Académie d'Equitation de Caen* (Caen: 1909).

Gay, John, *Wine, a Poem: to which is added Old England's new triumph: or, The battle of Audenard a song* (London: 1709).

——, *Fables* (London: 1751).

Gleare, J., *The Triumph of Justice: or, British valour displayed in the cause of humanity. Being an interesting narrative of the recent expedition to Algiers … Illustrated with a geographical description of the kingdom of Algiers …*

Embellished with two ... engravings (Manchester: 1816).

Gow, Ian, *The Scottish Interior* (Edinburgh: 1992).

Gow, Ian, and Rowan, Alistair, *Scottish Country Houses 1600–1914* (Edinburgh: 1995).

Gow, Ian, *Scottish Houses and Gardens from the Archives of Country Life* (London: 1997).

Gray, James T., *Maybole – Carrick's Capital* (Ayr: 1982).

Greville, Henry, *Memoirs* (London: 1938).

Grose, Francis, *The Antiquities of Scotland* (London: 1797).

Gunnis, Rupert, *Dictionary of British Sculptors 1660–1851* (London: 1951).

Gwyn, Julian, *The Enterprising Admiral: the personal fortune of Admiral Sir Peter Warren* (Montreal: 1974).

Habakkuk, John, *Marriage, Debt, and the Estates System – English Landownership 1650–1950* (Oxford: 1994).

Hamilton, David, *Golf – Scotland's Game* (Kilmacolm: 1999).

Hancock, David, *Citizens of the World, London Merchants and the Integration of the British Atlantic Community, 1735–1785* (Cambridge: 1995).

Harris, Eileen, *The Genius of Robert Adam – His Interiors* (New Haven and London: 2001).

Heier, Edmund, *Religious Schism in the Russian Aristocracy 1860–1900, Radstockism and Pashkovism* (The Hague: 1970).

Heron, Robert, *Observations Made in a Journey through the Western Counties of Scotland in the Autumn of 1792* (Perth: 1799).

Hibbert, Christopher (ed.), *Greville's England. Selections from the Diaries of Charles Greville 1818–1860* (London: 1981).

Historical Account of the Most Noble Family of Kennedy, Marquesses of Ailsa and Earls of Cassillis (Edinburgh: 1849).

Holloway, James, *Patrons and Painters: art in Scotland 1650–1780* (Edinburgh: 1989).

Horne, H. Oliver, *Stonehaven Savings Bank 1838–1938* (Aberdeen: 1939).

Houston, R.A., *Social Change in the Age of Enlightenment: Edinburgh, 1660–1760* (Oxford: 1994).

Humphris, E.M., *The Life of Matthew Dawson* (London: 1928).

Hunter Blair, Sir David Oswald, *John Patrick, 3rd Marquess of Bute, K.T. (1847–1900) a memoir* (London: 1921).

Hussey, Christopher Edward Clive, *The Life of Sir Edwin Lutyens* (London: 1950).

Hylson-Smith, Kenneth, *Evangelicals in the Church of England 1734–1984* (Edinburgh: 1988).

Ingamells, John, *A Dictionary of British and Irish Travellers in Italy, 1701–1800: compiled from the Brinsley Ford Archive* (New Haven and London: 1997).

Jackson, Debbie, *The History of the Kennedys of Cassillis and Culzean*, (unpublished) (copy available in the Carnegie Library Ayr: 1988–9).

——, 'Robert Adam': the building of Culzean Castle', St Andrews University graduate diploma (2000).

Jackson, J. T., *A Short History of Blairquhan* (Blairquhan: 2001).

Jacob, Violet, *The Lairds of Dun* (London: 1931).

Jones, David T. et al., *Rural Scotland During the War* (London: 1926).

Kennedy, Archibald, 'Observations on the Importance of the Northern Colonies under Proper Regulation' (New York: 1750).

——, 'The Importance of Gaining and Preserving the Friendship of the Indians to the British Interest, Considered' (New York: 1751).

——, 'An Essay on the Government of the Colonies' (New York: 1752).

——, 'Serious Considerations on the Present State of the Affairs of the Northern Colonies' (New York: 1754).

——, 'A Speech Said to Have Been Delivered Some Time before the Close of the Last Session, By a Member Dissenting from the Church' (New York: 1755).

——, 'Serious Advice to the Inhabitants of the Northern-Colonies on the Present Situation of Affairs' (New York: 1755).

Kennedy, Archibald, Earl of Cassillis, 4th Marquess of Ailsa, *The Rulers of Strathspey – A History of the Lairds of Grant and the Earls of Seafield* (Inverness: 1911).

——, 'Scotland's share in Magna Carta', *Transactions of the Dumfriesshire and Galloway Natural History and Archaeology Society*, 1938–40, III series, vol. 22, p. 18.

Kennedy, Edward B., *Thirty Seasons in Scandinavia* (London: 1903).

Klein, M., 'Archibald Kennedy: imperial pamphleteer', in Lawrence H. Leder (ed.), *Colonial Legacy*, vol. 2, *Some Eighteenth-Century Commentators* (New York: 1971), pp. 75–105.

Landers, Jane G. (ed.), *Colonial Plantations and Economy in Florida* (Gainsville: 2000).

Lee, Albert, *History of the 33rd Foot* (Norwich: 1922).

Letters of George Dempster to Sir Adam Fergusson 1756–1813 (London: 1934).

Lewis, Michael, *A Social History of the Navy 1793–1815* (London: 1960).

Lindsay, Ian G., and Cosh, Mary, *Inveraray and the Dukes of Argyll* (Edinburgh: 1973).

Lochhead, Marion, *Episcopal Scotland in the Nineteenth Century* (London: 1966).

Lodge St John No. 11 Maybole, Quarter Millennium Celebration, 1975.

Lugar, Robert, *Plans and Views of Buildings Executed in England and Scotland in the Castellated and Other Styles* (London: 1811).

Lustig, Irma S., and Pottle, Frederick A., *Boswell: the Applause of the Jury 1782–1785* (London: 1982).

Macaulay, James, *The Classical Country House in Scotland 1660–1800* (London: 1987).

Marshall, R.K., *The Days of Duchess Anne, Life in the Household of the Duchess of Hamilton* (London: 1973).

Martin, Robert Bernard, *Enter Rumour. Four Early Victorian Scandals* (London: 1962).

Masur, Louis P. (ed.), *The Autobiography of Benjamin Franklin* (Boston: 1993).

Mauchline, Mary, *Harewood House* (Newton Abbot: 1974).

Maxwell, Sir Herbert, *Memories of the Month*, 3rd series (Edinburgh: 1903).

McBain, J., *The Merrick and the Neighbouring Hills: tramps by hill stream and loch* (Ayr: 1929).

McCahill, Michael W., 'Scottish Peerage in the House of Lords', *Scottish Historical Review*, 1972, pp. 172–96.

McKean, Charles, *The Scottish Chateau: the country house in Scotland 1500–1700* (Edinburgh: 2001).

McLure, David, 'Kilkerran Pyroligneous Acid Works 1845–1945', *Ayrshire Notes* No. 19, 2000, pp. 4–11.

Mead, Lt Col. C.J.H., *History of the Royal Cornwall Yacht Club 1871–1949* (Plymouth: 1951).

Megaw, B.R.S. 'Mount Strange and the "Manx Derby" Races', *Journal of the Manx Museum*, vol. 6, 1956–7.

Milne, J. Lees, *People and Places – Country House Donors and the National Trust* (London: 1992).

Mingay G.E., *English Landed Society in the Eighteenth Century* (London: 1963).

Mitchell, Alison (ed.), *Pre-1858 Gravestone inscriptions Carrick Ayrshire* (Edinburgh: 1988).

Morrison, David B., *Two Hundredth Anniversary of Saint Andrew's Society of the State of New York* (New York: 1956).

Munimenta Alme Universitatis Glasguensis – Records of the University of Glasgow: from its foundation till 1727, vol. 3 (Glasgow: 1854).

Munn, Charles W., *The Scottish Provincial Banking Companies 1747–1864* (Edinburgh: 1981).

Munster, Wilhelmina Kennedy-Erskine FitzClarence, Countess of, *My Memories and Miscellanies* (London: 1904).

Murray, David, *The Law Relating to the Property of Married Persons: with an appendix of statutes and notes* (Glasgow: 1891).

Nalder, Ian, *Scotland's Golf in Days of Steam – A Selective History of the Impact of the Railways on Golf* (Edinburgh: 2000).

Namier, Sir Lewis, and Brooke, John, *The House of Commons, 1754–1790* (London: 1964).

O'Connor, Cynthia, *The Pleasing Hours* (Cork: 1999).

Onslow, Richard, *Great Racing Gambles & Frauds* (Marlborough: 1995).

Palladio, Andrea, *The Architecture of A. Palladio: in four books containing a short treatise of the five orders, and the most necessary observations concerning all sorts of building with their plans, sections, and uprights* (London: 1721).

Pargellis, Stanley M., *Lord Loudoun in North America* (New Haven: 1933).

Paterson, James, *History of the Counties of Ayr and Wigtown* (5 volumes) (Edinburgh: 1864) – vol. 1 Kyle, vol. 2 Carrick, and vol. 3 Cunninghame. Wigtown was not published.

——, *Autobiographical Reminiscences* (Glasgow: 1871).

Perry, P.J., *British Farming in the Great Depression 1870–1914* (Newton Abbot: 1974).

Pettigrew, A., 'Culzean gardens', *Journal of Horticulture and Cottage Gardening*, vol. 5, 3rd series (Cardiff: 1882), p. 389.

Phillipson, Nicholas, *The Scottish Whigs and Reform of the Court of Session 1785–1830* (Edinburgh: 1990).

Pitcairn, Robert, *Historical and Genealogical Account of the Principal Families of the Name of Kennedy from an Original MS. with Notes and Illustrations &c.* (Edinburgh: 1830).

Price, Jacob M., *Tobacco in Atlantic Trade* (Aldershot and Brookfield: 1995).

Radford, Peter, *The Celebrated Captain Barclay – Sport, Money and Fame in Regency Britain* (London: 2001).

Rankine, John, *A Treatise on the Rights and Burdens Incident to the Ownership of Lands and Heritage in Scotland*, 4th edn (Edinburgh: 1909).

Reid, R.C., *Wigtownshire Charters* (Edinburgh: 1960)

Richards, Eric, *The Leviathan of Wealth: the Sutherland Fortune in the Industrial Revolution* (London: 1973).

Ricord, Frederick W., and William Nelson (eds), *Documents Relating to the Colonial History of the State of New Jersey*, vol. IX, 1757–67 (Newark: 1885).

Roberts, Judith, '"Well temper'd clay": constructing water features in the landscape park', *Journal of Garden History*, vol. 29, no. 1, 2001, pp. 12–28.

Robertson, Forbes W., *Early Scottish Gardeners and their Plants 1650–1750*, (Edinburgh: 2000).

Robertson, William, *Old Ayrshire Days* (Glasgow and Edinburgh: 1905).

Robertson, William, *Ayrshire 1st History and Historic Families* (Ayr: 1908).

Russell, Iain E., *Sir Robert McAlpine & Sons – The Early Years* (London: 1983)

Sackville West, Vita, *Knole and the Sackvilles* (London: 1923).
Sanderson, Margaret H.B., *Robert Adam in Ayrshire* (Ayr: 1993).
Saumarez Smith, Charles, *The Building of Castle Howard* (London: 1990).
Sclater, A.A., 'Picturesque privacy: landscape improvement at Culzean from c. 1750', *Scottish Archives, The Journal of the Scottish Records Association*, vol. 1, 1995, pp. 17–30.
Schuyler, Montgomery, *The Schuyler Family* (New York: 1926).
Schweizer, Karl W. (ed.), *Lord Bute Essays in Re-interpretation* (Leicester: 1988).
Sedgwick, Romney, *The House of Commons, 1715–1754* (London: 1970).
Shannon, Timothy J., *Indians and Colonists at the Crossroads of Empire – The Albany Congress of 1754* (Ithaca and London: 2000).
Shaw Kennedy, General Sir James, *Notes on the Battle of Waterloo* (London: 1865).
Shyllon, F.O., *Black Slaves in Britain* (Oxford: 1974).
Simpson, Donald, *Twickenham Past* (Twickenham: 1993).
Spencer, Charles, *Althorp – The Story of an English House* (London: 1998).
Spring, David, *The English Landed Estate in the Nineteenth Century: its administration* (Baltimore: 1963).
Stevenson, John, *Popular Disturbances 1700–1832* (London: 1992).
Stewart, Angus, *The Minute Book of the Faculty of Advocates, 1751–85* (Edinburgh: 1999).
Stirling, A.M.W., *Coke of Norfolk and his friends* (London: 1898).
Stone, L., and Stone, J.C.F., *An Open Elite? England 1540–1880* (Oxford: 1984).
Stout, Neil R., 'Captain Kennedy and the Stamp Act', *New York History*, vol. 45 (1964), pp. 44–58.
Strawhorn, John, *The History of Ayr – Royal Burgh and County Town* (Ayr: 1989).
Sullivan, Sir Edward, et al., *The Badminton Library of Sports and Pastimes – Yachting* (London: 1894).
Sutherland, Douglas, *The Yellow Earl* (1965).
Swapp, George and Eva, *Dunnottar Woodland Park* (Stonehaven: 1996).
Symon, J.A., *Scottish Farming Past and Present* (Edinburgh and London: 1959).
Tait, A.A., *The Landscape Garden in Scotland – 1735–1835* (Edinburgh: 1980).
Tait, Ramage Craufurd, *Drumlanrig Castle and the Douglases with the Early History and Ancient Remains of Durisdeer, Closeburn, and Morton by Craufurd* (Dumfries: 1876).
The Natural History of Bees: containing an account of their production, their oeconomy, the manner of their making wax and honey, and the best methods for the improvement and preservation of them (translated from the French) (London: M.DCC.XLIV).

Thomson, F.M.L, *English Landed Society in the Nineteenth Century* (London: 1963).
Thorne, R.G., *The House of Commons 1790–1820* (London: 1986).
Trotter, E., *Lord Radstock. An Interpretation and a Record* (London: 1914).
Trower, Walter John, *A Remonstrance Addressed to Archibald Campbell, Esq. of Blythswood, on Certain Resolutions to which his Name is Appended, Published in the Glasgow Herald, of November 21, 1856* (Glasgow: 1856).
Tullibardine, Marchioness of, *A Military History of Perthshire 1660–1902* (Perth: 1908).
Turnbull, Deborah ,'Thomas White: 18th-century landscape designer and arboriculturalist', unpublished PhD thesis, University of Hull, 1990.
Van der Straeten, Edmund S.J., *History of the Violoncello, the Viol da Gamba, their Precursors and Collateral Instruments* (London: 1914).
Van Doren, Carl, *Benjamin Franklin* (London: 1939).
Ward, J.T., 'Ayrshire landed estates in the nineteenth century', in *Ayrshire Collections*, vol. VIII (1967–9).
Waterston, Merlin, *The Servant's Hall: a domestic history of Erdigg* (London: 1980).
——, *The National Trust – The First Hundred Years* (London: 1994).
Wheeler, C.A., *Sportascrapiana* (London: 1868).
Whetstone, Ann E., *Scottish County Government in the Eighteenth and Nineteenth Centuries* (Edinburgh: 1981).
Wight, Andrew, *Present State of Husbandry in Scotland: extracted from reports made to the Commissioners of the annexed estates, and published by their authority* (Edinburgh: 1778).
Wilkins, Frances, *Scottish Customs & Excise Records with Particular Reference to Strathclyde from 1707 Onwards* (Kidderminster: 1992).
——, *Strathclyde's Smuggling Story* (Kidderminster: 1992).
——, *George Moore and Friends – Letters from a Manx Merchant (1750–1760)* (Kidderminster: 1994).
——, *Manx Slave Traders – A Social History of the Isle of Man's involvement in the Atlantic Slave Trade* (Kidderminster: 1999).
Wilson, James, and Shaw, Patrick, *Cases Decided in the House of Lords on Appeal from the Courts in Scotland* (Edinburgh: 1825).
Wimsatt Jr, William K., and Pottle, Frederick A., *Boswell for the Defence 1769–1774* (London: 1960).
Wright, James, *A Recommendation of Brotherly Love upon the Principles of Christianity to which is Suborned an Inquiry into the True Design of the Institute of Masonry in Four Books* (Edinburgh: 1786).
Ziegler, Philip, *King William IV* (Newton Abbot: 1973).

Index

All arrangement is alphabetical except for the detail under Kennedy. Here arrangement is firstly by forename. Thereafter the members of the Culzean family are listed first, in chronological order, followed by any other Kennedys with the same first name.

Picture credits

The majority of the illustrations came from The National Trust for Scotland's own collection, and the publishers and the author are extremely grateful for their kind permission to use them in this book. Numerous pictures also came from the Cassillis and Culzean Estate Trustees for which we are equally grateful.

We are also grateful to the following copyright holders for, in many cases, supplying copies and in all cases for granting permission for their reproduction here.

Maps. Reproduced from Ordnance Survey mapping on behalf of The Controller of Her Majesty's Stationery Office © Crown Copyright ED100018578.

Cassillis and Culzean Estate Trustees 6(r), 8, 10, 14, 19, 28(l), 29(l), 39, 48, 52(l), 58, 59(l), 64, 68, 71, 88–9, 142(r), 143(l), 154(r), 164, 166,168, 175(r), 179(r), 180, 186, 187(bottom r), 188, 190(l), 192, 196(l), 201(l), 204(r), 205, 211, 227(r), 233(r), 261, 270

John R. Hume 11, 26, 231(r)

James Hunter Blair 13, 49, 52(r)

David Killicote 20, 54

Gordon Riddle 25, 72(l), 75, 116(bottom r), 117(l), 118(l and r), 146(r), 175(l), 231(l), 232(l), 242(l), 266

James Simpson of Simpson Brown, architects 28

The British Library Picture Library 139(r), 163

Sir Charles Fergusson (photograph courtesy of the Scottish National Portrait Gallery) 41

Carnegie Library, Ayr 44

Reproduction by courtesy of the National Gallery of Ireland 46

The Yale Center for British Art and The Bridgeman Art Library 47

The Trustees of the National Library of Scotland 37, 53, 117(r), 128

Reproduced by permission of the Trustees of the Wallace Collection, London 57

Copyright: Royal Commission on the Ancient and Historical Monuments of Scotland 60, 61, 104(l), 119, 120(top l and r and bottom l)

By courtesy of the Trustees of Sir John Soane's Museum 70, 76, 95

New York Public Library (The Phelps Stokes Collection) 84

University of Glasgow Library 94

By courtesy of the National Portrait Gallery, London 105, 138

Western Meeting, Ayr 106(l)

Marchioness of Ailsa 106(r)

Sotheby's Picture Library 111

Country Life Picture Library 113(r), 199, 247, 253

George Swapp 136, 142(l)

Sir Ludovic Kennedy 159(l)

Reproduced by permission of Surrey History Service (Copyright of Surrey History Service) 172

James Knox 173(l)

By courtesy of the Mitchell Library, Glasgow City Libraries and Archives 185(l), 196(r), 201(r), 246(r)

Col. Sir Bryce Knox 187(top)

Museum of London 197(r)

Sten-Ake Jonsson 218, 220(l and r)

Royal Commonwealth Library, University of Cambridge 241

Kenneth Gray 250